A whole new world, just a few hours away from yours.

COSTA RICA
No Artificial Ingredients
www.visitcostarica.com
1-866-COSTARICA

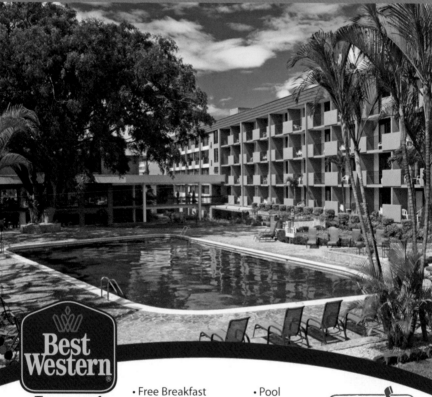

CONTENTS

Personal

Chosen from up-close and personal visits (all updated) by our staff and freelancers over the last two years and featured in Weekend in The Tico Times.

Practical

Written by our writers, who live and work here and know the score. Your own mini-directory of everything you need to know.

Welcome

General Information

Living Culture

Medical

Real Estate

Count on Change

*Change is certain, so for the very latest on new tourist destinations during the 2010 period, check The Tico Times' print edition every Friday. The newspaper's Weekend section explores Costa Rica's ever-growing tourist attractions. Also, you can explore Costa Rica via The Tico Times' Web site: **www.ticotimes.net***

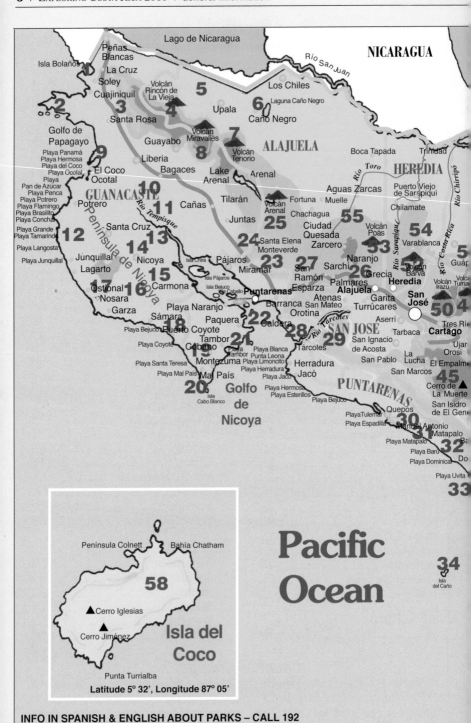

INFO IN SPANISH & ENGLISH ABOUT PARKS – CALL 192

Caribbean Sea

Barra del Colorado

Isla aleo
Ioraco

56
57   Tortuguero

Parismina

LIMON

Guácimo

Matina

Siquirrres

48   Moìn   Isla Uvita
Turrialba   **Limón**   Playa Bonita
46   Playa Puerto Vargas

CARTAGO   **47**
Chirripó Abajo

Cachí   **42**
44   Cahuita
erro Vueltas   Chirripó Arriba   **41**   Puerto Viejo   Playa Cocles
Bribrí
División   **43**   Río Sixaola   Manzanillo
▲Cerro Chirripó Grande   Sixaola   **40**

Rivas
39

San Pedro

Ujarrás
Río General   Buenos Aires   **PANAMA**

Ojochal
Cortés   Palmar Norte
Río Grande de   Coto Brus
Río Sierpe   Río Coto
Sierpe   San Vito

Rincón   **37**
Drake   **38**   Ciudad Neily
35   Golfo Dulce   Golfito
sula de   Río Coto Colorado
36   Puerto   Zancudo   Canoas
Jiménez
Carate   Playa
Zancudo

National Parks & Reserves

28 national parks, 2 nature reserves, 8 biological reserves, 73 wildlife refuges, 31 protected zones, 13 wetlands, 9 forest reserves. More than 186 private refuges are biological corridors.

Alberto Mi. Brenes Biological Reserve	**27**
Arenal Volcano National Park	**25**
Ballena National Marine Park	**33**
Barbilla National Park	**47**
Barra Del Colorado Volcano National Park	**56**
Barra Honda National Park	**14**
Barú Del Pacífico National Wildlife Reserve	**32**
Barva Volcano National Park	**52**
Bolaños Island National Wildlife Refuge	**1**
Bosque Alegre National Wildlife Reserve	**26**
Bosque Diría National Park	**16**
Braulio Carrillo National Park	**54**
Cabo Blanco Wildlife Reserve	**20**
Cahuita National Park	**42**
Camaronal National Wildlife Reserve	**15**
Caño Island Biological Reserve	**34**
Caño Negro Wildlife Reserve	**6**
Carara National Park	**29**
Cerro Las Vueltas Biological Reserve	**45**
Chirripó National Park	**43**
Cocos Island National Park	**58**
Corcovado National Park	**36**
Curú National Wildlife Reserve	**21**
Dr. Archie Carr National Wildlife Reserve	**51**
Fernando Castro Cervantes National Wildlife Reserve	**28**
Gandoca-Manzanillo National Park	**40**
Golfito National Wildlife Reserve	**38**
Guanacaste National Park	**3**
Guayabo National Monument	**48**
Guayabo, Negritos & Los Pájaros Islands	**22**
Hitoy-Cerere Biological Reserve	**41**
Iguanita National Wildlife Reserve	**9**
Irazú Volcano National Park	**50**
Juan Castro Blanco Volcano National Park	**55**
La Amistad International Park	**39**
Laguna Las Camelias National Wildlife Reserve	**5**
Las Baulas National Marine Park	**12**
Limoncito National Wildlife Reserve	**46**
Lomas Barbudal Biological Reserve	**10**
Macizo De La Muerte-Tapanti National Park	**44**
Manuel Antonio National Park	**30**
Mata Redonda Wildlife Reserve	**13**
Miravalles Volcano National Park	**8**
Monteverde Cloudforest Reserve	**24**
Nicolás Wesberg Nature Reserve	**19**
Ostional National Wildlife Reserve	**17**
Palo Verde National Park	**11**
Peñas Blancas Wildlife Refuge	**23**
Piedras Blancas National Park	**37**
Poás Volcano National Park	**53**
Portalón Wildlife Reserve	**31**
Punta Río Claro National Wildlife Reserve	**35**
Rincón De La Vieja Volcano & National Park	**4**
Santa Rosa National Park	**2**
Tenorio Volcano National Park	**7**
Tortuguero National Park	**57**
Turrialba Volcano National Park	**49**
Werner Sauter National Wildlife Reserve	**18**

Welcome to Exploring Costa Rica 2010

WELCOME to the 2010 edition of Exploring Costa Rica. As you can see, for our 17th guidebook, we have a whole new format. We think you're going to like the up-close and personal section and the completely updated practical section too.

For the Personal part, we chose some 50 unique hostelries in every corner of the country that have been highlighted in the "Weekend" section of The Tico Times over the past two years.

Our writers uncover the special offering of each place by schmoozing with the owners, staying overnight, eating, relaxing and touring, to bring you the most complete picture of the hotel, lodge or B&B, plus the fascinating area of Costa Rica it allows you to explore. Many of these establishments are "eco-conscious" (one has even earned the coveted five-green-leaf award), and some are much more than just places to stay. The fact that more and more are taking the plight of the earth seriously and showing that you can offer both luxury and ecological soundness is heartening.

With more than a million and half tourists a year, Costa Rica offers several thousand places to stay. Our choices range from one where the writer had to get into the river and help push the craft upstream, to a luxury resort with 17 hot pools, a small zoo, four restaurants and a price tag starting at the modest sum of more than $400 a night.

For the many other options available in Costa Rica, check out our pages on the Internet and Costa Rica on the Web. The Practical section also offers info on just about everything you need to know. It's also true with us, "If it's out there, it's in here."

Want to rough it? Or loll in luxury? Or do both? The choice is yours. Just read on.

Bienvenidos a Costa Rica!

Publisher:
Dery Dyer

Associate Publisher:
Abby Daniell

Editor:
Susan Hall Liang

Contributors:
Ann Antkiw, Rob Bartlett, Janiva Cifuentes-Hiss, Sonia Cordero, David Garrett, Elizabeth Goodwin, Patrick Fitzgerald, Beverly Gallagher, Ellen Zoe Golden, Maggie Jamieson, Sophia Kelley, Keely Kernon, Harry Liang, Susan Hall Liang, Chrissie Long, Vicky Longland, Dorothy MacKinnon, Mike McDonald, Sean O'Hare, Meagan Robertson, Nicolas Ruggia, Blake Schmidt, Daniel Shea, Holly K. Sonneland, Hannah Thompson, Adam Williams, Meg Yamamoto

Photography:
Jeffrey Arguedas, Michelle Bezanson, Janiva Cifuentes-Hiss, Nick Coté, Lindy Drew, Patrick Fitzgerald, Beverly Gallagher, Robert Goodier, Maggie Jamieson, Avalon Johnson, Vicky Longland, Tom O'Reilly, Dorothy MacKinnon, Whitney Martin, Nicolas Ruggia, Patrick Fitzgerald, Susan Hall Liang, Chrissie Long, Mónica Quesada, Ronald Reyes, Hannah Rexroth, Mayra Sojo, Holly K. Sonneland, Blake Schmidt, Hannah Thompson, Matthew Wyczalkowski, Meg Yamamoto

Cover Photo: Ronald Reyes

Advertising:
Martha Gamboa (Coordinator), Nicole Foote, Edwin Ramírez, Mauricio Vanegas, Cindy Vargas

Marketing: George Soriano

Systems: Edwin Cárdenas

Production Director and Design:
Mayra Sojo

Production:
Roy Arguedas, Verny Quesada

Circulation:
Diego Herrera (Manager), Damián Amén, Johnny Marchena, Clara León

Finance:
Olman Chacón, Ana Arguedas, Rigoberto León

Customer Service:
Ana Lucía Espinosa, Mauren Bonilla, Laura Borge, Bernadino Madrigal, Luis Morales

Published by:
THE TICO TIMES, S.A.
Apdo. 4632, San José,
Costa Rica 01000
Office: Av. 8, Ca. 15/17
Tel: (506) 2258-1558,
Fax: (506) 2233-6378
E-mail: **info@ticotimes.net**
Internet: **www.ticotimes.net**
U.S. residents, send mail to
SJO 717 P.O. Box 025331,
Miami FL 33102-5331
Printed in Costa Rica by La Nación

917.286
T557e The Tico Times
Exploring Costa Rica 2010 /
The Tico Times.–
17 ed. – San José, C.R.:
The Tico Times, 2009.
304 p.: il. ; 14 x 22 cm.

ISBN: 978-9968-746-13-7

1. Turismo – Costa Rica. 2. Turismo – Guías. 3. Costa Rica - Descripciones y Viajes - Guías. I. Título.

Central Valley

Photo by Ronald Reyes

*Redefining
the Three
Rs: Relax,
Renew,
Rejuvenate*

*The new two-level
pavilion holds therapy
and massage rooms
below and a yoga
studio above.*

By Vicky Longland

The full moon rises as dusk falls and a group of yoga aficionados gently stretch in the open-air exercise studio against a vista that drops away toward the forested valley floor and hills beyond.

At AmaTierra Hotel and Wellness Center, this monthly celebration is only one of the many ways to relax and renew.

Until the tragic collapse in October of the suspension bridge past the hotel across the Río Grande de Turrubares, this was increasingly the route of choice for savvy drivers looking to avoid the truck-clogged Highway 1 to the Pacific port of Puntarenas; at press time a temporary Bailey bridge was being installed and a new bridge is planned. Note: you can still reach the hotel from San José without crossing the river.

The hotel's intention is for guests to find a peaceful oasis and indulge in the wide choice of massage therapies, wellness programs and herbal consultations.

AmaTierra owner Jill Ruttenberg is a qualified American Herbalists Guild clinical herbalist, yoga instructor and massage therapist. Originally from Colorado, Ruttenberg and husband Bob decided to escape the rat race and set up a residential center catering to people who want to chill out in beautiful surroundings.

"People arrive with their 'New York baggage,' stressed and depressed, but within days they've started to relax," Ruttenberg says. With a mission that guests "feel cared for and carefree," the hotel conveys the message that a stay here means unwinding and letting oneself be pampered.

Five cottages are split into two suites each, while above, the open social area and dining balcony share views of the infinity-edge pool, deck and panoramic scenes over dense forest toward Orotina. WiFi is available.

The steep setting in the mountainside means plenty of steps to climb from one's room to the restaurant and lounge. Each cottage is tucked into the slope surrounded by mature mango or pochote trees and garden shrubs that fill the three-hectare grounds.

All rooms have a queen bed, fridge, coffeemaker, ceiling fans, Jacuzzi and TV for viewing DVDs from the hotel's free selection of nearly 350 movies. A dividing wall separates the bed from a lounge area that can be converted into an extra sleeping space if necessary. The small terrace holds a couple of chairs and seat hammock.

Decor is minimal, but the interiors are made colorful with warm sand-tone walls and soft furnishings that reflect the name of each room.

I stayed in Sangria, with its bright red bedspread, pillows and cushions. Menta, Rosa, Café and Dorado, to name a few more, pretty much go through the color chart.

An honor system operates for juice and sodas from a well-stocked fridge by the pool. Although no hard liquor is sold, Bob enjoys recommending the wines he stocks.

Photo by Simón Bolívar

In his former life, Bob was in the music promotion and marketing industry with a special interest in jazz, so music rates high at AmaTierra. Evenings often become jam sessions around the piano, accompanied by whatever instruments guests might have brought along.

Breakfast features typical *gallo pinto*, juice, fruit plate, home-baked whole-wheat breads, a wide choice of teas and fresh coffee. Lunch and dinner must be preordered, and you can choose among vegan, gluten-free, lactose-intolerant, vegetarian and fish or chicken (no red meat) dishes imaginatively prepared under Jill's supervision. There's a pleasant informality at mealtimes as guests often join up tables to share the day's adventures.

Certainly the pièce de résistance is the two-level pavilion. Built along feng shui lines, the octagonal building holds therapy and massage rooms below while above is the spacious, open-air yoga studio with synthetic thatch roof looking just like dense palm fronds.

"We are so pleased with how it's turned out," Jill says. "The whole place is very peaceful, and the upper floor can also be used for seminars and retreats of all kinds."

Jill spent many years studying under such holistic luminaries as Joel Penner, from whom she learned about traditional Chinese medicines, and Michael Tierra of the East West School of Herbology in California. She took her master herbalist certification with Andrew Weil's program in integrative medicine at the University of Arizona.

Massage sessions ($75 for one hour) range from aromatherapy de-stress, deep tissue and lymphatic massage to Jill's specialty, abdominal chi mover. This entails 45 minutes of gentle strokes to move the life force energy throughout the belly and unblock "stuck" energy that causes emotional stress and indigestion, with a 10-minute final head and foot rub.

She also gives sound therapy to rebalance chakras using the hauntingly penetrating tones of Tibetan singing bowls and

Herbalist, yoga instructor and massage therapist Jill Rutten-berg makes many of the tinctures and lotions used at Ama-Tierra with herbs from the hotel's organic gardens.

Photo by Vicky Longland

other sound tools.

Other specialists come in to offer shiatsu, Reiki, ear candling, detoxification treatments and acupuncture.

Visitors are encouraged to have a personalized nutritional herbal consultation ($95 for 75 minutes) to improve health and lifestyle. Jill makes an assessment using Chinese medicine tongue and pulse methods and recommends dietary changes and custom-made herbal formulas for each person's particular constitution.

Packages are available, from a Relax & Renew Wellness Weekend to five- and seven-day packages. Because of its proximity to San José, AmaTierra makes a convenient getaway for some alternative three Rs: relax, renew, rejuvenate.

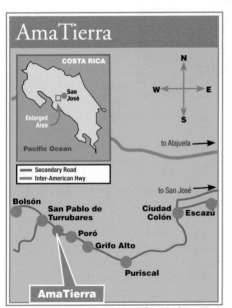

Roy Arguedas Arias | Tico Times

Getting There, Rates, Info

Take Highway 27 from Ciudad Colón to Puriscal, then follow signs for Turubari Tropical Park and Orotina. Go 19 km. past Puriscal, look for AmaTierra signs; the hotel is on right. Airport or San José pickup is offered for $60 one way. Rates for overnight for two, inc. full fabulous breakfast are $69, residents; nonresident rates for bed and breakfast are $127 single and $149 double. Lunch costs $7, dinner $15/$20, per person. Visit Web site or call for packages, such as the three-day Wellness and Adventure Package, inc. meals and lodging, two yoga classes, wellness treatment of choice, Turubari Park tour, $595 per person. The hotel is nonsmoking. No children under 4. For information: 2419-0110, **amatierra@gmail. com, www.amatierra.com**

Modern Luxury and Fine Dining

The Beacon Escazú exterior, seen from the garden.

By Ann Antkiw

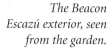

In the heart of the western San José suburb of old Escazú, known as Escazú Centro, is the Beacon Escazú, a luxury boutique hotel promising five-star services. Built on the property of an old home, the Beacon Escazú is part of Palmer Hospitality Group's Beacon Collection.

On a recent visit, the hotel's charming general manager, Susana Guevara, gave us a tour.

"I think I know the luxury-hotel scene, guests' likes and dislikes, and I'm very aware of cultural differences," Guevara said.

The folkloric witches of Escazú, for whom the area is famous, must have cast a loving spell on the lush tropical garden with its century-old trees and natural stream. Newly planted trees and flowering shrubs, specially chosen to attract butterflies, have flourished in this peaceful, secret garden away from the hustle and bustle of town.

The small pool and sundeck set among verdant greenery offer a delightful place to relax. Guests can also enjoy a meal or a drink on the patio overlooking the garden.

Costa Rican architect Gustavo Blanco melded contemporary and colonial styles to create irregular shapes, curves, nooks, high ceilings, expansive windows and French doors that integrate the spacious, airy interior of the hotel with the exterior, which is enhanced by trickling fountains, cream-colored walls, black wrought-iron trim and a red-tile roof.

Accommodations (27) include three master suites with Jacuzzis and balconies. These spacious rooms with king-size bed, living and dining area, two and a half bathrooms and a sleeping loft are an ideal choice for families. They can also be divided into two connecting rooms, allowing for total privacy.

The 14 junior suites come with a king or two double beds and sitting area, while the 10 smaller deluxe rooms have king beds. All are elegantly decorated in cream, beige and white tones, and are furnished with dark mahogany-colored, custom-designed pieces. They offer the utmost in air-conditioned comfort with down comforters and white Mascioni linens on beds piled with fluffy pillows. Other amenities include a 32-inch flat-screen TV, iPod docking station, multiline cordless phone, WiFi, data ports, work desk, safe, iron, minibar and coffeemaker.

In the large, tiled bathrooms are an array of bath products, a hair dryer, bathrobes and slippers. Room service is available, so guests can dine in their rooms or on the balcony. An on-site exercise room features top-quality machines, while the

Master suites at the Beacon Escazú come with Jacuzzis, balconies, living area and king-size bed.

Photos Courtesy The Beacon Escazú

Lather Spa offers massages, rejuvenating health treatments and a sauna. In the evenings, guests can sample international wines and nibble on tapas in La Cava wine bar, or adjourn to the Cigar Bar after dinner in The Muse Restaurant. The Rooftop Terrace, with its panoramic view of the Central Valley and Escazú mountains, has a meeting room and movie theater with catering services. It can also be used as an alternative to the ground-floor courtyard or restaurant for receptions and weddings. State-of-the-art business center and meeting facilities provide VIP service, while the concierge can arrange everything from car rental to suggesting and booking tours. Secure underground parking is available, and the hotel is wheelchair-accessible and children-friendly.

Twenty minutes from Juan Santamaría International Airport and 15 minutes from the center of San José, the hotel offers one- or two-night getaway packages for those who want to enjoy the spa, dinner and a quiet, romantic stay.

Roy Arguedas Arias | Tico Times

Getting There, Rates, Info

The Beacon Escazú is 150 m. west of the church and park in Escazú Centro. Rates, inc. tax, are $123 for a deluxe room, $186 for a junior suite, $338 for a master suite and $236, executive suite, inc. continental breakfast for two, telephone calls, Jacuzzi, pool, gym. For info: 2228-3110, **mybeaconescazu.com.**

The Muse: Inspired Cuisine

The Muse Restaurant is a perfect setting for a romantic dinner, formal or informal lunch, or traditional English afternoon tea. Near the lovely garden, its elegant simplicity is a charming change from the often pretentious surroundings that can accompany fine dining.

The decor combines creamy yellow and beige tones and comfortable, straight-back, padded chairs covered in a light sage-green fabric. Snowy white tablecloths and fresh orchid centerpieces add to the ambience. Executive chef Jean-Pierre Peiny can be observed in the glassed-in kitchen, concocting his masterpieces. The Frenchborn chef studied at the hotel school in Lyon, France, and boasts a career that spans the gastronomic world from France to the United States.

The Muse's ideally sized menu offers tempting selections, including beef tenderloin with a black pepper sauce, grilled tuna and *paella valenciana* for two.

When we dined there, Peiny offered to give us a mixed sampler, but we decided to opt for the à la carte menu and were delighted we did. For starters, I chose the scallops, which were superb, served in a light, honey truffle sauce. The salmon, lightly crusted with pistachios and served with leeks and a pinot noir sauce, was also delectable. My companion ordered the arugula salad with beets, crispy wontons and creamy goat cheese, a colorful combination and a fusion of flavors that proved an enjoyable way to start a meal. Her main course, jumbo shrimp in a light curry sauce, was also excellent. The presentation of the dishes is sparing but elegant.

The restaurant offers an excellent selection of wines, and the house wine, a reasonably priced Chilean Terra Andina carménère, was pleasantly palatable.

Caveats? Our dessert choices, pear and almond tart and crème brûlée, were average. The coffee was tepid and tasted stewed.

The lunch menu offers salads, red snapper ceviche, tuna tartare, chicken, fish, pasta dishes and the famous J.P. Burger, made with beef, chicken or veggies and served with French fries.

The Muse Restaurant is not for the budget-minded, but you most certainly get what you pay for. Prices, inc. taxes, range from ¢4,305 to ¢7,380 ($7.50 to $13) for appetizers, ¢10,000 to ¢15,000 ($17 to $26) for main courses and ¢4,000 to ¢5,000 ($7 to $9) for desserts. Lunch choices are about ¢5,000 to ¢8,000 ($9 to $14), except for the grilled corvina at ¢10,455 ($18) and marinated beef strips at ¢12,300 ($22).

The restaurant is open 6 a.m. to 10 p.m., daily.

Photo by Vicky Longland

A plant and flower-lined path curves up to the verandah in front.

Photo by Susan Liang

Country Charm Right in Town

By Susan Hall Liang

Casa de las Tías is billed as "a country bed and breakfast in town." That may be a paradox in words, but it's paradise in reality. Congenial hosts Pilar Saavedra and Xavier Vela opened the bed and breakfast in Escazú in 1993 deciding in Saavedra's words to "pursue a dream I've long had."

Vela, a U.S. citizen from New Mexico and Saavedra from Colombia have succeeded in creating one of the loveliest bed and breakfast establishments in the Central Valley.

The inn is finished in yellow clapboard siding and turquoise trim and adorned with flower boxes. With an airy front verandah furnished with comfortable, brightly painted wicker furniture, the heritage home has become a holiday-makers cozy haven.

"We named the Casa de Las Tías after my aunts," explained Saavedra." They ran an inn in Colombia that was the center of peace and laughter.

"Here we have the tranquility of a garden estate complete with great birdwatching, yet we are only a block from the shops and restaurants of town."

Four spacious and gracious wood-paneled rooms with hard-wood floors and one junior suite (with microwave and wet bar) offer guests private baths, wooden bureaus, table and chairs, reading lamps, ceiling fans and each has a distinct theme.

"Instead of run-of-the-mill décor, I wanted to promote Latin America and give each room a unique regional flavor," says Saavedra.

The Chilean room features tapestry with Inca motifs, for example, while indig-

Corner room offers a view of the flower-filled garden.

Photo by Ronald Reyes

enous Kuna embroidery decorates the room with Panamanian flavor.

Cable TV is in the upstairs lounge in addition to many reference materials and maps of Costa Rica.

The bed and breakfast also offers WiFi, hot water, security box, telephone, and laundry service.

Indoors at Casa de las Tías is intriguing, while outdoors is exhilarating. The ample backyard is a veritable arboretum of fruit trees including grapefruit, figs, avocado, lemon and mango.

Ornamentals include epiphytes, orchids, ginger, heliconias and gladiolas, and a garden grows fresh vegetables and herbs for the kitchen.

Fresh ingredients are one reason why breakfast, usually al fresco at Casa de las Tías, is worth waking up for.

A gourmet chef, Saavedra ensures that delicious options include cereals and yogurt, eggs of all kinds, Peruvian-style sausage and raspberry waffles, among other choices.

Getting There, Rates, Info

From San José, go west on Highway 27. Take the Escazú exit, and head straight down the road, After the traffic light at the "cruce" (a Scotiabank is on the far right corner) continue (south) 100 meters and turn left immediately after the Cerutti Restaurant. Follow narrow street 100 meters to end. Rates, inc. tax and breakfast, are $81 for single, $93-104 for double and $110-121, triple. For information: 2289-5517, **www.hotels.co.cr/casatias.html, casatias@kitcom.net**

Roy Arguedas Arias | Tico Times

The oval dining table expands for more guests, but more often than not, breakast is al fresco in the back garden.

Photos by
Susan Hall Liang

The verandah is a perfect place to enjoy a glass of wine in the early evening after a long day of touring.

Both Saavedra and Vela are wonderful raconteurs and many of their B&B guests are repeat visitors, who come not only to see different parts of the country but also to see their hosts.

A graduate of the University of California at Berkeley with an MA in International Relations, between 1963 and 1992, Vela served in Brazil, Perú, Chile, Bolivia, and Panama before coming to Costa Rica to work with the U.S. Government's foreign assistance program.

Costa Rica's friendly people and the abundance and beauty of its irresistible natural wonders, made it the ideal place for him to retire.

Saavedra graduated from the University of Maryland at College Park with a major in Latin American literature. She is a world traveler and very active in the Little Theatre Group and the Birding Club. The Saavedra-Velas have been in Costa Rica since 1986.

The bed and breakfast offers airport pickup with advance notice in addition to arranging tours, car rentals, lodging outside of San José and translation and interpretation services.

Eco-Smart Design, Fine Food Are the Buzz

The green cabins blend in with the scenery.

By Sophia Kelley

For travelers who want to experience the cloud forest of Costa Rica, but don't want to rough it, a luxurious eco-resort is pampering the way.

Built by the owners of Hotel Punta Islita, an award-winning resort on the Nicoya Peninsula, El Silencio Lodge brings the same high level of service and comfort inland to the mountains of the Central Valley. About 30 minutes north of Sarchí, the lodge is nestled between Poás Volcano and Juan Castro Blanco National Park on a 500-acre reserve. The property has several km. of hiking trails, a river and three waterfalls.

Sixteen individual suites perch on a clearing of converted farmland surrounded by lush and verdant cloud forest. At check-in guests are offered fruit smoothies while being introduced to their "eco-concierge," one of the unique services here. An eco-concierge is appointed to every group and functions as a cross between a personal assistant and a naturalist guide.

Our concierge was Edgardo Camacho, a smiling 29-year-old, who gave us an overview of the property, the philosophy behind El Silencio and hiking options. After our orientation, Camacho delivered us to our hillside room in a golf cart.

The luxury aspects of the lodge are apparent. Suites are fully appointed with sublimely comfortable beds and 400-count linens, a lounge area and gas fireplace to ward off the evening chill.

Enormous bathrooms are supplied with fluffy towels and robes, and an outdoor Jacuzzi, a delightful way to appreciate cool evenings.

Designed by Costa Rican architect Ronald Zurcher (whose brother is one of the owners), the suites are built with an eye to the environment. Floor to ceiling windows allow full views of the mountain or the quietly murmuring river. Building materials including bamboo and almond wood, certified by the Forest Stewardship Council, were selected for their environmentally friendly and sustainable qualities.

The goal was to create a place in which visitors could genuinely feel nature around them. Therefore, while the hotel is luxurious, TV and Internet have been intentionally left out. Entertainment here is sitting in the wooden rockers on your private porch and watching clouds and mist roll over the mountain to blanket the peaceful valley below.

We decided to delay enjoying the view since Camacho had agreed to take us on a short hike before dinner, so we changed into our hiking boots and headed out. As we climbed the hill with the clouds settling around us, Camacho cheerfully said, "Coming here and not getting wet is not really being here."

It is a cloud forest after all, and what better way to appreciate the surrounding environment than to walk through the trees in the early evening mist?

Camacho pointed out plants and birds and explained the preservation and reforestation efforts being made. The property's location between two national parks makes preservation extremely important as the area is a biological corridor for many species of animals.

Toward the end of the hike we paused at the Magical Knot, a labyrinth created out of flowering bushes. The plants are all butterfly and hummingbird attractors. We headed back as fireflies began to flicker and light the way. It was time for dinner and a sampling of chef Marco González's creations.

The dining room is surrounded by floor-to-ceiling windows and kept warm by a gas fireplace. At outdoor seating sounds from the river provide background music for al fresco meals.

At dinner González introduces himself at each table and explains the philosophy behind the food. His goal is a Costa Rican fusion cuisine that focuses on fresh, healthy and organic-when-possible ingredients.

The restaurant is primarily vegetarian, though fish and free-range chicken are offered. Red meat is not served; however, for committed carnivores, vouchers for a steak restaurant in town are provided.

The cuisine's main strength is González's creative use of Costa Rican ingredients in novel combinations.

"This country is known for bland, boring cuisine. We have a lot of vegetables, but we just put them on the side," González lamented. However in his kitchen, vegetables get main play.

Soups such as yellow pepper and broccoli are made with little to no cream and yet taste rich and satisfying. Salads are celebrations of the half-acre organic garden that González oversees. Lovely beet leaves mix with more traditional lettuces and other fresh vegetables to create a salad as delectable visually as it is to the palate.

The peach-palm fruit, pejibaye, typically eaten with mayonnaise, gets special treatment as an appetizer called pejibaye ceviche. González's rendition will convert anyone who has never liked the rich, nutty flavor of pejibaye.

Main dishes sampled were a tasty tilapia and pasta with fresh, macadamia-nut pesto. For dessert, we selected the *tres leches* cake that proved to be another unique twist on the traditional. González uses coconut milk to give a Caribbean flavor. We agreed it was the best tres leches we'd ever had.

His sincerity was evident when González said, "If you don't cook with passion, it's not going to taste good."

Another way to pamper yourself is to partake of the spa services. The spa sits on a bend in the river and the adjoining yoga platform is wrapped in the sounds of the flowing water.

Services include facials, body treatments and massages, featuring natural products made from coffee, banana, papaya and honey. An unusual aspect of the spa is a specially designed conical room. The high, pointy-ceiling room is said to be indigenous-inspired, purported to channel positive energies while aiding the detoxification of the body.

Camacho described the experience, "I don't really believe in 'energy.' That's the truth, but once you lie down there, you feel different… it's really interesting."

During lunch the next day, Andrei Gómez, the manager, talked about their commitment to responsible tourism. El Silencio's model includes local hiring and purchasing policies, community-development programs and environmental stewardship.

The hotel buys fish from local fish farms, candles from an area candle-maker and has hired 85 percent of its employees from the region. The spa is also working to produce a line of natural beauty products. There is room for improvement here, as the bathrooms are currently stocked with L'Occitane products, which are far from local.

Gómez rattled off the many other environmental projects focusing on reducing the hotel's carbon output. Plastic bottles are not used and natural spring water is filtered and treated. Gray water goes to an onsite treatment plant. Leftovers are composted or sent to a pig farmer. Recyclables are sent into town. Cleaning supplies are natural and eco-friendly and artificial lighting is limited so as not to disturb wildlife. "Nature is so rich, we must make sure we don't cause any pollution," said Gómez.

One more part of the lodge's environmental initiative is a reforestation project inviting guests to participate. On our way out we're given a baby oak to plant anywhere on the property. The tiny tree is a sweet memory as we drive back to congested San José.

Above: a nearby creek. Opposite: rooms are outiftted with sublimely comfortable beds.

Photos courtesy of El Silencio

Getting There, Rates, Info

From San José, take the inter-American highway north. Take exit to Sarchí, turn at Pali Supermarket following signs to Jardín Botánico. Pass the garden and follow winding, steep mountainous road 20-25 km. until you see the entrance for El Silencio Lodge on right. Just outside the town of Bajos del Toro.

Rates for a double, inc. tax, three daily meals a la carte and nonalcoholic beverages, are $240 per person (residents: $150), two-night minimum stay required. Included in the room rate are the services of an "eco-concierge" and guided tour.

No children under 8 years old. For info: 2291-3044, **www.elsilenciolodge.com, manager@ elsilenciolodge.com.**

Roy Arguedas Arias | Tico Times

Top Score in Sustainable Tourism

Solar panels heat water for most of the guest rooms at Finca Rosa Blanca.

By Meg Yamamoto

Nearly 20 years since building their pioneering boutique hotel on a bare motocross field in the middle of coffee country in Santa Bárbara de Heredia, north of San José, Glenn and Teri Jampol of Finca Rosa Blanca Country Inn have received the country's highest sustainable tourism award, five "green leaves," with an unprecedented 100 percent score.

The green leaves are awarded by the Costa Rican Tourism Institute's Certification for Sustainable Tourism program. Only four hotels in the country boast five and Finca Rosa Blanca is the first to have earned a 100 percent score, meaning it fully complies with every aspect of the program (see sidebar). That's not all that's new here. Not long ago, the inn added a spa and restaurant and a tour of its certified organic coffee plantation.

The Jampols came to Costa Rica from New York in 1985 and, with Glenn's late mother, Sylvia, described by her son as the "spark plug and motor" of the project,

opened Finca Rosa Blanca in 1989, despite naysayers' warnings that "you can't open a hotel in the middle of the coffee fields."

The Jampols claim they never had a master plan. "We were very naive, but our hearts were in a good place," Glenn says. That naïveté gave birth to the first boutique-style hotel in the country, a pioneer and model for the country's now established sustainable-tourism industry.

Surrounded by forest and coffee fields, the inn with its unique architecture – a blend of Spanish Gaudí and U.S. Santa Fe styles – gives a somewhat incongruous yet appealing first impression. Locally crafted wood and iron work and murals feature prominently throughout the rooms, restaurant and common areas, accented by an eclectic assortment of art that speaks to the hand and soul of an artist: Glenn, 58, studied art at Berkeley in California, and some of his pieces adorn parts of the inn.

The two master suites and 11 junior suites are works of art in themselves, all unique and mostly named for their predominant motifs. The El Cafetal junior suite, with its coffee-plantation views and mural above the king-size bed, has a Jacuzzi with a view of the valley, while the two-level Rosa Blanca master suite features a natural-wood spiral staircase leading up to a canopied four-poster bed with a 360-degree view of the lush countryside.

All rooms come with king or queen beds with down comforters and heavenly-soft bamboo-fiber sheets – the product of Teri's search for alternative, sustainable materials – in addition to a minibar, safe, robes, slippers and hair drier.

Built in the Jampols' former home, El Tigre Vestido Restaurant and Bar Buho allow the hotel's culinary tradition to be enjoyed by guests and the public alike. The restaurant features one long table for family-style meals, smaller indoor tables and a large outdoor dining area with a view of the valley. Adjoining the restaurant is a conference room that can accommodate meetings of up to 12 people, with lunch and coffee breaks provided.

Teri, 56, a talented chef, uses fresh seafood, organic meats and poultry, and seasonal fruits and vegetables to create innovative menus.

A dinner menu might include pumpkin, corn and coconut soup, cucumber, tomato and pineapple salad with mint, lime and cilantro vinaigrette, and grilled filet mignon in tamarind sauce or roasted red peppers stuffed with goat cheese. Highlights from the lunch menu include gourmet sandwiches, jerk-seasoned pork loin or chicken salad, or a *casado* of the day. Breakfast starts with coffee, followed by options, from granola to *gallo pinto* (rice and beans) or *chorreados* (corn pancakes) to *huevos a caballo*: eggs, tomatoes, onions and cheese in tortillas and served with refried beans, chorizo and salsa.

And guests can eat with a good conscience: In keeping with the hotel's sustainability efforts, 5 percent of the profits from the restaurant and bar go to support area schools and the nearby Barva Volcano sector of the Braulio Carrillo National Park. In addition, the El Targua Spa offers

massages, body wraps and treatments, manicures, pedicures and facials. The warm coconut cream massage is a hot, slippery affair combining heated coconut milk with a relaxing massage, while the deep tissue, full-body massage is reported to leave subjects in a contented Jell-O-like

Measuring Sustainability

The **Certification for Sustainable Tourism** program certifies tourism companies according to the degree to which their operations comply with a model of sustainability. Four fundamental aspects are evaluated:

1. Physical-biological parameters: interaction between the company and its surrounding natural habitat.

2. Infrastructure and services: management policies and operational systems within the company and its infrastructure.

3. External clients: interaction of the company with its clients in terms of how much it allows and invites the client to be an active contributor to its sustainability policies.

4. Socioeconomic environment: interaction of the company with the community and population in general. Companies may score up to five levels in each category.

The final rating of "green leaves" corresponds to the lowest level achieved in any of the above evaluation areas. This is to encourage companies to advance toward a model of sustainability by giving the same degree of consideration and importance to each of the four areas evaluated.

Visit **turismosostenible.com**

Long table serves for family-style meals at El Tigre Vestido Restaurant.

Photo by Meg Yamamoto

state. But the most interesting part are the tours that explain some of the inn's sustainable practices. The tour, led by a naturalist guide, takes guests around the inn's eight acres, landscaped with native and tropical plants, including 300 fruit trees.

The tour includes stops at the laundry, which uses biodegradable soap; the solar panels that heat water; the spring-fed, solar-heated pool, featuring chemical-free water cleaned through an ionization system; the recycling center, and the compost shed, where waste and manure make compost for the coffee plantations and for the produce in the greenhouse.

The informative coffee tour is well worth the tramp through the fields. Here, guests learn how an organic-coffee plantation yields 35 percent less than a conventional one, but will be productive for 100 years, compared to a conventional plantation's 25, and how sacrificial companion plants are used instead of chemicals to deter pests. At the roasting facility guests can roast their own coffee, and the tour ends with a "coffee-cupping" session. With two decades of experience and five green leaves under their belts, the Jampols can speak with authority when they say, "Sustainability is good business."

Finca Rosa Blanca

Finca Rosa Blanca
El Roble
to Carrizal
Santa Bárbara
Alajuela
Mercedes
Barva
to San José
Heredia
Juan Santamaría
International Airport

COSTA RICA
San José
Enlarged Area
Pacific Ocean

N
W ← → E
S

Secondary Road
Inter-American Hwy

Roy Arguedas Arias | Tico Times

Getting There, Rates, Info

Finca Rosa Blanca is one km. east and 800 meters north of Santa Bárbara de Heredia. At the light in Santa Bárbara, turn east and go one km., then turn left at the Finca Rosa Blanca sign (in front of Café Britt distribution center) and head north 800 meters. The hotel is on right after passing the parking lot. Double-occupancy rates, inc. tax, breakfast, for junior suites, $328, two master suites, $384; 20-percent low-season discount for residents. At El Tigre Vestido Restaurant, a four-course gourmet dinner costs $43, inc. tax. Lunch items average about $12. Breakfast a la carte menu $3.50 to $10, not including tax. Spa treatments: $40 to $130; residents, 20 percent off. Sustainability tour, free for guests, coffee tour, $25. Also tours, activities and horseback rides. For info: 2269-9392, **info@fincarosablanca.com, sales@fincarosablanca.com**

The pool at Hotel Casa Alegre in Santa Ana offers a quiet place to hang out.

Photo by Lindy Drew

'Happy House' Offers Peace and Quiet

By Elizabeth Goodwin

Hotel Casa Alegre is an unpretentious affair nestled in the backstreets of Santa Ana, about a 20-minute drive southwest of San José. The quiet, New Mexican-style hotel transports its guests to a no-frills colonial atmosphere where they can conduct business or rest up before moving on to other tourist attractions.

Lounging in the pool in the center of Casa Alegre's courtyard, you can hear the sounds of children playing at the school across the street – but not much else. This "Happy House" is serene and quiet, offer-

ing a marked contrast to the crowded streets of San José.

Owners Alejandra and Gregory Chávez opened the hotel after stumbling upon the perfect house for it in Santa Ana. Gregory, a native of New Mexico, also owns the diver-oriented Jinetes de Osa Hotel in Drake Bay, on southwestern Costa Rica's Osa Península.

Alejandra says she and her husband always wanted to open a hotel together, and were delighted when they finally got the chance. The couple's personal touch can be seen throughout the hotel. Gregory designed several mosaics on the outside walls of the courtyard, including one of a

Superior room has two beds, covered in Guatemalan fabric bedspreads.

lizard, to add to the old-Spanish atmosphere. They personally remodeled the house from top to bottom, expanding it from three rooms to eight guest rooms, two of which are larger, "superior" rooms slightly apart from the main hotel, on the other side of the pool.

Casa Alegre manager Paola Lafuente

Getting There, Rates, Info

Casa Alegre is 100 meters north and 150 meters east of the Palí in Santa Ana, opposite the Victory School. The hotel offers transportation from the airport for $20. Double-occupancy rates are $74 for a standard room with one bed and $91 for a superior room with two beds, inc. tax and breakfast. Each additional person costs $10 extra; children under 12, free. Rooms come with TV, WiFi, full breakfast and access to local calls. For info: 2235-5485, 2203-7467, **reservations@hotelcasa alegre.com, www.hotelcasaalegre.com.**

says these rooms are perfect for couple seeking privacy. Since the hotel opened, i has built up a faithful client base of travel ing businessmen who want to stay some where peaceful but close enough to Sa José to be convenient, Lafuente says.

"Most of the people, who have com here before, come again because the know it's safe and calm, and that we try t take care of them very well," Lafuente says The hotel has attracted many of its cus tomers by marketing to businesses, and i offers a corporate discount. At first, Lafu ente says, it was difficult to get the word out about the hotel. "We kept the price very low so people could get to know us, she says. Lafuente estimates that mor than half of the hotel's guests are from th United States, and about 15 percent o them are on business. She thinks almos all hear about the hotel through word o mouth. Service is very important to the ethos of the hotel.

An outdoor terrace serves as an airy breakfast area.

Photos by Lindy Drew

"We look for fun and friendly staff," Alejandra says. The setup of Casa Alegre allows soothing breezes to make their way through the stucco-like interiors, and some rooms are equipped with air-conditioning. All come with modern TV, elegant bedspreads and simple bathrooms. Though the hotel is small, the way the house opens up onto the courtyard and gardens makes the space seem larger.

A hearty breakfast – your choice of *gallo pinto* and eggs, pancakes or cereal – is served on a sunlight-dappled outdoor terrace overlooking the pool.

Alejandra says they expect to add a few more rooms and remodel the pool and garden area sometime in the future.

"I'm living the dream of owning my own hotel," she says.

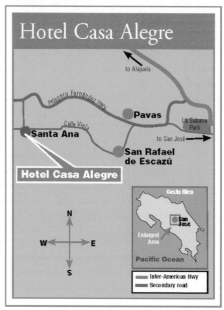

Roy Arguedas Arias | Tico Times

View of pedestrian boulevard on Calle 3.

Good Service, Affordability Downtown

By Nicolas Ruggia

Downtown San José's Hotel Casa Alfi may not be plush, but this affordable boutique lodging offers strong service, a comfortable bed and a quality Costa Rican breakfast prepared by the owner or receptionist, as well as a connection to the arts.

"They call a boutique hotel either luxurious or quirky," said Alfred Richardson, owner of the hotel. "I'm definitely on the quirky side. I guess the theme is art. Having original art, and being willing to display the art of other people that would be available for sale if they wanted."

Richardson was a painter in the United States and Africa before he entered the hotel business in Costa Rica. Born of British ancestry in Nairobi, Kenya, he spent much of his childhood living in tents in the bush. He longed to be the warden at game park.

"I was really close to nature," Richardson said. "I used to go to the game park o the natural history museum when I wasn' in boarding school. (Here) I saw the kin of trees and fruits we had back home fo the first time."

The animal motif is noticeabl throughout the building, from the paint ings on the walls in the guestrooms t Richardson's depictions of African ani mals hanging in the lobby to the mural o Costa Rican wildlife painted on the fron of the building.

The hotel attracts middle-class travel ers from Europe, Latin America, the Unit ed States and Canada.

Richardson has started to develop sev eral regular clients. Return visitors are th bread and butter of his 10-room hote

The soft comfortable chair in the sitting area invites guests to rest and read after a day's touring.

Photos by Ronald Reyes

nd he isn't trying to change that.

"I always sort of wanted to have a guesthouse hotel," Richardson said. Where I come from, when you get old nd retired, you move into a hotel. I like meeting new people every day. We don't vant to be a (bar or) restaurant. That vould ruin the whole element here." That lement is the aforementioned service and taff relationship with clients.

"Our biggest thing is personal service," Richardson said. "We help with tours and enting cars. One of the things I insist on s that my staff get part of the commisions. If we're full, they can make good noney. What I want is to have a nice place vhere friends of mine who are well-to-do vould feel comfortable." The idea resoates with the guests, many of whom rave bout their experience at Casa Alfi. "It's a very personal experience," said Shelly Threlkeld from Indiana. "It's like you're

being taken care of. We haven't seen anything like it in Costa Rica.

"Alfi is just a really great guy, and the prices are reasonable. I would highly recommend coming and staying here."

The hotel is still going through some growing pains. It doesn't have a liquor license, but if you bring your own bottle,

Getting There, Rates, Info

The hotel is at Calle 3, between Avenidas 4 and 6, in front of the main entrance to the Colegio Señoritas in downtown San José.

Rates, inc. tax, are: Single rooms are $34 a night, doubles run $45 and the large junior suites cost $57. A 20-percent discount is offered for residents. This discount applies to all guests during low season, and Richardson is willing to to talk about price when there is space. For info: 2221-2102, **casaalfihotel.com.**

The master bedroom of the junior suite offers a comfortable reading chair, bedside tables an lamps.

Photos by Ronald Reye

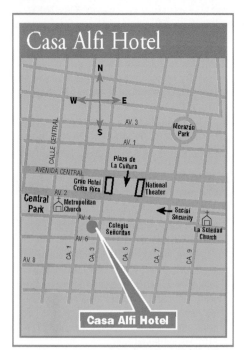

Roy Arguedas Arias | Tico Times

they will chill it for you and keep it at th bar. A Jacuzzi is in the works upstairs bu is still several months away from bein functional.

Richardson also hopes to add som top-of-the-line gym equipment soon. Th rooms come with cable television, wire less Internet and a telephone with inter national calling at a paltry $0.10 per min ute to the United States and most o Europe.

While it isn't the Ritz, Casa Alfi is a excellent option for its price range an offers tourists a comfortable alternative t the capital's seedier low-end hotels an hostels.

But don't forget that you are staying i San José. Richardson urges his guests t use caution outside of his gated doors a night.

"I tell everyone that this is San José and you've got to be careful," Richardso said. "I recommend that they take a tax after about 9 p.m."

The scenic Orosi Valley is just an hour's drive southeast of the capital.

Doing the Loop:
Varied Attractions Ring Scenic Orosi Valley

By Hannah Thompson

Feel a need to banish those city blues, but short on time? The perfect escape lies less than an hour's drive outheast of the city, in the rural charm nd spectacular beauty of the Orosi Valley. n the shadow of two volcanoes, the dranatic, undulating landscape in soothing hades of green, magnificent mountain ristas and fresh, clear air of this lush, cofee-producing region will rejuvenate even he most jaded city dweller.

A 60-km. loop through the river valley s popular not only for the scenery, but lso for the attractions along the way, ncluding colonial churches, hot springs, a ugged national park and picturesque Cachí Lake. It can all be seen in a whistletop day trip; however, with the great lodgng and restaurant options, it's worth pending a night, if only to experience

waking up to the sights and sounds of the valley as you savor the irresistible aroma of fresh local coffee.

From Paraíso, a town emerging out of Cartago, and taking the loop counterclockwise toward the town of Orosi, the landscape soon opens up to reveal the valley, cloaked in coffee fields and dotted with villages, descending steeply to the meandering river below.

Just two km. along this winding road, the Orosi lookout is the first must-stop for the magnificent panorama – look for a small, easily missed blue sign for the entrance. The grassy hillside is a perfect picnic spot.

From here, the road drops steeply into the colonial town of Orosi, a good base if you're spending time in the area. In the town center stands the beautiful 1743 Iglesia San José de Orosi, the oldest church still in use in Costa Rica. The adjoining former Franciscan monastery is a museum displaying religious art and artifacts.

The town is famed for its hot springs, one of the attractions that drew the Spanish colonists here. The public spa Los Balnearios is in town, and Los Patios is two km. along the road. But for the adventure-minded, the hot waters to be found right

---

Got More Time?

On the road back to San José, between Paraíso and Cartago, the remarkable **Lankester Botanical Garden** is a must. British botanist and orchid enthusiast Charles Lankester established the garden in 1917. Now owned by the University of Costa Rica (UCR), the garden is a world-renowned orchid research center housing more than 1,000 species, at their blooming best between February and April. Besides the orchid houses, trails go through forest and gardens home to 3,000 species of bamboo, cacti, bromeliads, heliconias, ferns, palms and other tropical plants. Open 8:30 a.m.-4:30 p.m. $5, foreigners, ₡2,000 ($3.30), residents, discounts for students. For info: **jardinbotanicolankester.org**. Prebook guided tour at 2552-3247.

---

along the Orosi River offer a closer-to-nature alternative. Unsurprisingly, it's a popular spot, so avoid weekends if you're after seclusion. Stop by the Orosi Tourist Information and Arts Café (OTIAC) to fill in the gaps about activities, tours and other lesser-known gems of the area.

Leaving Orosi, you have two options: continue along the loop, or detour to Tapantí National Park. A 5,000-hectare birders' paradise, Tapantí is one of Costa Rica's wilder and wetter cloud forests, with an annual rainfall of more than seven meters. A damp day, with the fine mist shrouding the trees, the rush and spray of waterfalls and the sparkling river water, makes for an atmospheric hike.

Back on the loop, the road crosses the river at the village of Palomo and swings around to follow it back north. This stretch is flanked by coffee plantations, glimpses of the river and Cachí Lake, and views of Irazú and Turrialba volcanoes. On a clear day you can see steam rising from the latter.

The truly stunning lake can best be seen nine km. farther on at La Casona del

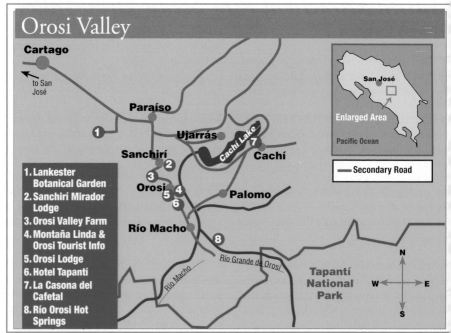

Orosi Valley

Cartago

to San José

Paraíso

Ujarrás

Sanchirí

Cachí Lake

Cachí

7

Orosi

Palomo

Río Macho

8

Río Grande de Orosi

Río Macho

San José

Enlarged Area

Pacific Ocean

— Secondary Road

Tapantí National Park

N
W · E
S

1. Lankester Botanical Garden
2. Sanchirí Mirador Lodge
3. Orosi Valley Farm
4. Montaña Linda & Orosi Tourist Info
5. Orosi Lodge
6. Hotel Tapantí
7. La Casona del Cafetal
8. Río Orosi Hot Springs

Roy Arguedas Arias | Tico Time

Ruins of Our Lady of Ujarrás, the earliest colonial church in Costa Rica.

Cafetal Restaurant, itself a highlight of the route (see "Where to Stay & Eat"). Shortly before the town of Cachí, two wood-carving workshops stand by the side of the road. Best known is Casa del Soñador (House of the Dreamer), built from coffee wood and bamboo by famous Tico sculptor Macedonio Quesada. Since his death, sons Miguel and Hermes have continued their father's tradition in coffee wood, carving masks and rustic figures that make original souvenirs.

A few meters on, talented 22-year-old Denis Sojo is also following in his father's footsteps, producing sculptures from palm-sized to life-sized pieces of fallen wood. Prices vary from $5 to $10,000, depending on size and intricacy.

The vast Cachí Hydroelectric Dam is close by on the northeastern side of the lake. About three km. farther, look for the sign indicating a left turn to the village of Ujarrás, home to the ruins of Nuestra Señora de Ujarrás (Our Lady of Ujarrás), the earliest colonial church in Costa Rica, and the stuff of legend.

The story varies, but a typical version is that an indigenous fisherman carried a box containing a painting of the Virgin Mary to this site, whereupon it suddenly became immovable. Considered a sign from God, a shrine was built, and the church itself was completed in 1693. Besieged by floods and earthquakes, the church has been left to deteriorate since 1833.

From here, a short drive completes the

Travel Info

Getting There: By car, take Inter-American Highway from San José to Cartago, then follow main road southeast out of Cartago toward Paraíso and follow signs to Orosi. Buses leave every half hour from the main terminal in Cartago to the town of Orosi (30 minutes). Buses in valley are limited. **Río Orosi Hot Springs**: Park at Río Macho bar, two km. along road to Tapantí. Cross steel bridge and cut through first opening in fence on left. Keep to main path, following the river through coffee farm for 15 minutes until you reach a small opening to a narrow path that leads down to the riverbank. **Tapantí National Park:** 7:30 a.m.-4:30 p.m., $10, foreigners and ₡800 ($1.40), residents. 2200-0090.

loop for the return to Paraíso. In an area boasting many more attractions, this introduction can only scratch the surface, but we hope enough to inspire explorations of the delights to be found a short drive from the capital.

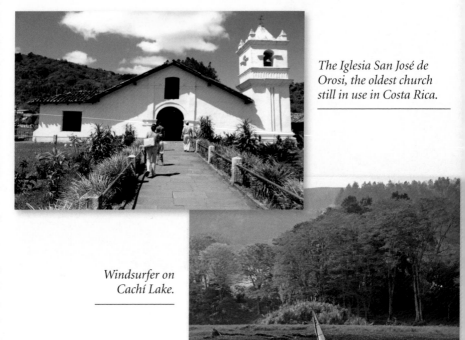

The Iglesia San José de Orosi, the oldest church still in use in Costa Rica.

Windsurfer on Cachí Lake.

Photos by Hannah Thompson

Where to Stay & Eat

Listed in order of appearance on the route.

Sanchirí Mirador Lodge: On main road two km. south of Paraíso, good food, friendly welcome, incredible valley view. Double rooms with private baths, cable TV, breakfast. $72, inc. tax. The nine Mata brothers are working hard on environmental credentials with recycling programs, a produce-farm for the restaurant, and bio-gas from their own pigs. 2574-3870, **sanchiri.com.**

Montaña Linda & Orosi Tourist Information and Arts Café: In town of Orosi, 200 m. south of park, Sara and Toine Verkuijlen have it all covered. Guesthouse rooms, $25, hostel has dorm beds, $7.50 and private doubles for $10 per person. The duo also runs a Spanish school, info center and café, open for comforting breakfasts such as pancakes and French toast and lunches such as burgers and burritos. 2533-3640, **montanalinda.com.**

Orosi Lodge: In town, tasteful doubles, $60, inc. tax, private baths, wet bar and shared patio or balcony, volcano views. Café and art shop, 7 a.m.-7 p.m., Mon.-Sat., serving hearty breakfasts, pastries and coffee. 2533-3578 , **orosilodge.com.**

Hotel Tapantí Media de Orosi: On road out of Orosi (800 m. southeast of the church) toward Tapantí, offers double rooms starting at $62, inc. tax, breakfast. The restaurant serves Italian specialties and great views. 2533-9090, **hoteltapanti. com, info@hoteltapanti.com.**

La Casona del Cafetal: Idyllic spot on lakeside, three km. south of the dam, is a favorite. Main courses start at $7, but if all that fresh air has given you a healthy appetite you'll want the huge buffet at $19, with fruit drink, dessert and good coffee. Walk off all that indulgence with a stroll through the garden. 2577-1414, **lacasonadelcafetal.com.**

View from the balcony at Pico Blanco Inn.

Simpler Times in Escazú Hills

By Nicolas Ruggia

Surrounded by green, overlooking the industrial, urban sprawl of San José, is a place that has been lost in time. The pre-Columbian masks and wildlife paintings on the walls in the main lobby recall a lost age of Costa Rican accommodations that has been crushed under the oppression of shiny floors and trendier art.

It feels like the last stand in a futile war when you stare out over the balcony of the hotel, and see the end of the tree line and the beginning of central Escazú and the capital.

You know, instinctively, that it will continue to spread, but as long as those last lines hold, the Costa Rica of old is not lost. And the view of the city lights is breathtaking at night.

"I'm developing it slowly," says owner John Botterill, a Brit with longtime roots in the country. "I'm trying to keep it as green as possible. I'm just sorry that Escazú's losing all of its green spots.

"This was my house. I realized how scenic it was and I turned it into a hotel and bar."

A hotel with sweeping views, WiFi, satellite television and a swimming pool that could double as blue-whale habitat certainly has a place in the market, and for those seeking the familiar caress of Costa Rican hospitality, Mirador Pico Blanco Inn in the western suburb of San Antonio de Escazú may reinvigorate the psyche.

"It's not a modern hotel; it's Costa Rica," Botterill says. "I started this place 25 years ago. This was the second hotel in Escazú …It's not one of the cement-type hotels you see all over the place now."

The first hotel in the mountains of

The colorful bar is an inviting place to relax in.

A wood-burning fireplace is a welcoming touch in the lobby.

Escazú, Hotel Fonda del Sol, has since gone under, leaving Pico Blanco the oldest relic of its era. And by no means do years entail wrinkles at this gorgeous hilltop hideaway.

Sometimes, upon entering a place, one can tangibly feel the essence of the people who have poured their life's work into it. Pico Blanco is one of these places.

Botterill's wife, Flor, and his sister-in-law, sons and nephews, all Ticos, make up the staff, and they take the time to establish relationships with the guests. Staying here is akin to immersion in the family for a little while. As a result, guests occasionally end up staying for a long time.

"I ended up here in the hands of John and Flor," says Mike Beyrle, a hotelier from Manuel Antonio on the Central Pacific Coast, who had been at Pico Blanco several months. "They've been with me 100 percent of the way no matter what ... better than family, better than my church ... They're the best people I've met in Costa Rica."

The friendly service appeals to both vacationers and locals, who frequent the hotel for a getaway.

"Our market is about 50-50 Ticos and Gringos," Botterill says. "We're a Tico business ... The service is laid-back, and the Ticos like that."

"On the weekend it's full of Ticos and our Gringos have been coming back for years," Botterill adds.

The 24 rooms, mostly set up with twin beds, a TV and a comfortable table and chair, at low prices of $80 per night, add quality for value to the list of the hotel's pluses.

Additionally, the hotel is away from the crime and predatory mentality that tourists may encounter elsewhere. "It's like a one-to-one ratio of clients to help and security (personnel)," Beyrle says. "I feel safe. I want security, and they have it. You don't have to worry."

If you find yourself with a fever and the only cure is the Costa Rica you used to know, this family-driven dose of the lost world might be the medicine you need. It may not be flashy, but the beauty and tradition do the trick.

Mini-suites have two beds, a small sitting area and cable TV.

"We're a hotel with a lot of heart," Botterill says. "People who come here get a good deal. We've not made a killing out of it, but we've never intended to."

Photos by Hannah Rexroth

Getting There, Rates, Info

Pico Blanco Inn is in San Antonio de Escazú, up the hill from San Rafael and Escazú Centro. From the Scotiabank at the main intersection in San Rafael de Escazú, head south up the hill and proceed to Escazú Centro. From here, continue south (uphill, behind the church) and then curving left and into San Antonio de Escazú. Turn right at the last bus stop in San Antonio, at the large Pico Blanco sign instructing you to turn right and go uphill one km.

Double-occupancy, high-season rates, inc. tax, are $80 for all rooms or cottage. For info: 2228-1908, **www.hotelpicoblanco.com.**

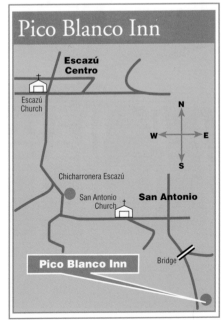

Roy Arguedas Arias | Tico Times

Many pilgrims come to Cartago annually, to visit the enormous Basílica de Nuestra Señora de Los Ángeles, on the feast day of the Virgin of the Angels, August 2.

Photo by Tammy Zibners

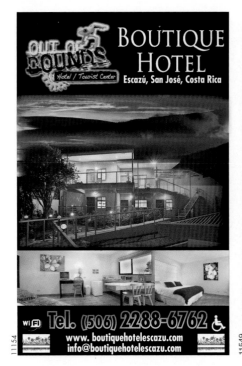
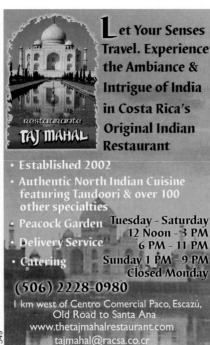

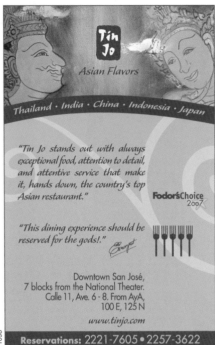

In Heredia, the townhouse of former President Alfredo Gonzáles serves as an office and community center with exhibitions and cultural performances in the evening.

Photo by Mónica Quesada

Northern Zone

Photo by Ronald Reyes

Sustainable Tourism in Bijagua

Celeste Mountain Lodge enjoys a modern, open-air design.

ıy Sophia Kelley

The lights at the end of the bone-rat-tling road beckoned encouragingly through the mist. It was dark and ınusually windy, but the first glimpse of Celeste Mountain Lodge's inviting com-nunal dining area dispelled the chill.

Though the 18-room lodge in the north entral Costa Rica town of Bijagua is his irst hotel, Joel Marchal is not a novice when t comes to tourism. From France, Marchal elocated to Canada, where he worked in ourism, specializing in Central America. The entrepreneur and his family moved to Costa Rica seven years ago to bring to frui-ion his dream of building a hotel.

"I was a tour operator for 20 years, so I know what tourists like, what they want ınd how they want it," he said.

A walk around the lodge confirmed that Marchal has developed an instinct ıbout what travelers like. From the invit-ıng dining room and open kitchen to the ounge facing a fireplace and hot tub, pub-ıc space in the hotel is designed for relax-ıtion and enjoyment.

The following day, the clouds lifted,

revealing a panoramic view of Miravalles Volcano and its foothills. A section of Teno-rio Volcano looms over the property. The lodge sits on four acres in a protected forest housing abundant wildlife, including mon-keys, toucans and even the endangered tapir.

The sunlight also brought into focus the contemporary architecture of the lodge. Marchal hired Jacqueline Gillet, a Belgian architect in Costa Rica, to design the building. Though Marchal explained that he wasn't initially interested in con-temporary design, he went with all of Gil-let's suggestions.

The design takes into account the damp climate and includes solutions such as putting the building on pillars a few inches off the ground and using ventila-tion techniques. But the interior decor is all Marchal's doing.

"I took care of the decoration," he said. "I always wanted to be an artist, but my father never let me study fine-arts. So I was able to use my creativity right here."

The rooms are decorated simply but thoughtfully, with reading lamps, shelf and counter space, and teak louvered windows that allow fresh air in, while screens keep out unwanted visitors. Marchal built the lamps and much decoration out of salvaged scrap metal. The counters are from salvaged wood, because beyond making guests feel comfortable, he has made it his goal to establish responsible and innovative tourism.

The Unreal Blue of the Río Celeste

The park ranger told us to hike the trail, visit the "Blue Lagoon" and natural hot springs, and on the way back, stop to see the waterfall, but we couldn't delay our curiosity. The Río Celeste Waterfall is unique among rain-forest cataracts for its remarkable turquoise water, the result of chemical reactions of volcanic minerals such as sulfur and calcium carbonates. As soon as we saw the signs, we headed down the slippery steps toward the pool at the bottom of 20 meters of crashing water. Once we reached bottom, with the mist and spray making rocks treacherous, we inched our way closer to the thunderous torrent. It looked like an image from a travel brochure, framed by vibrant green foliage, the falls crashing into the aquamarine pool.

Legend says that after painting the sky, God washed his paintbrushes in the Río Celeste.

The waters are definitely celestial, the blue seeming not of the earth but rather the sky, with the white torrents forming what might be tempestuous clouds.

After the moderately strenuous climb back up, we continued on to visit other areas of the park, stopping to admire a view of the towering volcano and the verdant forest. There is also the placid Blue Lagoon, a calm section of the turquoise river's course. One of the most interesting sections of the trail is called Teñideros, where two smaller rivers join together and their clear waters react to form the unique color of the Río Celeste.

The only allowed swimming is in the hot springs. Park rangers have marked with rock borders the warmer spots where natural vents heat the water. Other than the section to and from the waterfall and a couple of sketchy footbridges, the trail is an easy seven-km. hike round-trip. The El Pilón Ranger Station has bathrooms, water and maps for visitors.

From belowground to the roof, Marchal has implemented creative methods of environmentally sensitive development that should make other "eco-lodges" green with envy.

It is evident from the enthusiasm with which he discusses these projects that Marchal has not jumped on the ecotourism bandwagon just to use the trendy prefix. His vision is sustainable, both inside his lodge and in relationship to the environment and the community.

Not only was he careful to reduce waste, but also Marchal used recycled material as much as possible. He used 1,000 discarded truck tires, some to build a wall on the property and the rest to try a new system of underground water drainage that he adapted from research on the Internet.

Hot water for the hotel is produced by solar panels. Rainwater is collected for the hot tub and then heated in a chimney made from scrap metal.

For the lodge, only one tree was cut down, Marchal said. The wooden tables and counters were built from felled trees salvaged from the forest. "Bottom line, we have not used any forest wood in this building," Marchal said. In addition, he planted 200 trees on the hill above the lodge.

Some of the counters in the common area were made from post-consumer recycled plastic. Dining table benches are padded with coconut-fiber cushions and a separate bioclimatic cabin is used for air drying hotel laundry.

Marchal got excited describing some of

The fabulous Río Celeste.

Photo by Tom O'Reilly

he innovative techniques he is experiment-
ng with, including creating biogas to fuel
urners in the kitchen. Marchal plans to use
he biogas for slow-cooking items.

Although "meals included" can feel
oring at some hotels, here it is a delight.
Chef Andrés Pichardo has worked at high-
nd resorts and he combines traditional
Costa Rican ingredients with gourmet
nd creative touches. Chicken is served
ith regional vegetables and flavored with
ome-grown herbs. Another meal fea-
ures homemade fettuccini and a gor-
eous green salad with avocado. Breakfast
a substantial and tasty vegetable omelet
ccompanied by homemade bread and
ms.

We sampled two desserts, a delicious
rroz con leche (rice pudding) with *mora*
blackberry) sauce and a cheesecake with
st the right level of sweetness.

Special dietary needs can be accom-
nodated with advance notice. Most of the
ishes are served on banana leaves atop
ooden trays, creating a pleasing garnish
nd more fuel for the biogas containers.

Though it may be hard to drag yourself
om the open-air dining room with its
olcano views, the main activity in the area
hiking in Tenorio Volcano National Park
nd visiting the brilliant blue waters of the
ío Celeste. Other options are horseback
iding and white-water rafting.

Marchal is also working with a com-
unity group that wants to organize tours.

Guest room with lamps made of scrap metal.

Photo by Tom O'Reilly

"Tourism has to benefit this village, too. If
not, it's not going to work," he said.

From San José

From San José, take the Inter-American Highway north toward Liberia. Six km. after Cañas, turn
right toward Upala. Drive 35 km. to Bijagua. Pass
through the town center and look for the signs for
Celeste Mountain Lodge; turn right and go 3.5 km.
on the unpaved road. Four-wheel drive recommended. Rates, inc. tax, three meals: $130 single,
$160 double. Wheelchair-accessible rooms are
available, with one room for drivers and guides, no
additional charge. For info: **celestemountain
lodge.com** or call 2278-6628.

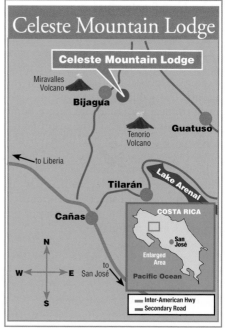

Roy Arguedas Arias | Tico Times

The main lodge overlooks a spring-fed swimming pool.

Photo by Janiva Cifuentes-His

Healing Potential of Foods, Herbs

By Janiva Cifuentes-Hiss

A "new moon" is shining over San Isidro de Peñas Blancas in north-central Costa Rica, where a long-standing expression of sustainable living recently opened its doors to visitors seeking to connect with food and nature. Some 20 km. southeast of La Fortuna and Arenal Volcano, Finca Luna Nueva Lodge provides a relaxing excursion into a certified organic, biodynamic estate in the rain forest.
The 74-acre enterprise could play an important role in cancer and inflammation research and the preservation of the planet's genetic material.

Finca Luna Nueva has long been a destination for ethnobotanists, researchers and students for its Sacred Seed Sanctuary, innovative biodynamic agriculture and organic medicinal-herb production.

The friendly staff offers an intimate introduction to agro-ecology, biodynamic farming and permaculture concepts.

Finca Luna Nueva President Steve Farrell is a fountain of information an enthusiasm. Drawing on more than 30 year as an organic and biodynamic farmer, Fa rell is cofounder of the National Organi Agriculture Association. His sincerity an passion are reflected in his interactions wit animals, plants, farm workers and soi working together to produce organic herb tropical fruits and vegetables.

Farrell has steered the farm since its pu chase in 1994 by New Chapter, a natura medicine company. He sold his own organi farm and founded Finca Luna Nueva dedi cated to ginger and turmeric production fo New Chapter's natural supplements.

The farm has become a site for interna tional conferences on natural medicin and educational tours, and is also a mode of sustainable living. The potential benefi of the plants and herbs grown on the estat are vast. New Chapter researchers believ hat herbs grown there may hold a key to esearch into cancer and inflammation.

Finca Luna Nueva specializes in herbs vith purported anti-inflammatory prop- rties. Through a process called "critical xtraction," the beneficial properties of the lerbs are processed into capsules and sold vorldwide.

Finca Luna Nueva is based on biody- lamics, a holistic form of agriculture that ;oes hand in hand with permaculture, or >ermanent agriculture based on living sys- ems. The approach is based on diversity, iving soil and ecological systems, rather han chemical inputs found in convention- l agriculture.

"The biodynamic farm is a living organ- sm," Farrell says. "Ninety percent of our ood is grown right here (on the farm)."

Finca Luna Nueva's myriad plant spe- ies are sown not in identical rows, but nterspersed and interwoven in mutually >eneficial ways. "Juan's Garden," in a circu- ır mandala, is a bright patchwork of plants ncluding Brazilian spinach, mint, toma- oes and holy basil.

In permaculture, every element has at east five uses. For example, a single plant night simultaneously provide shade for •ther crops, give fruit, provide a home for vild birds, fix nitrogen in the soil and repel ertain pests. Even the farm's animals serve nultiple roles. For example, by running heir snouts through the soil in search of ood, pigs simultaneously turn the soil and eat grubs that cause problems for ginger and turmeric, all the while dispersing their nutrient-rich manure throughout the land. The same animal provides the benefits of a tractor, pesticide and fertilizer without the chemical inputs, fossil-fuel consumption or human labor of conventional methods.

The Sacred Seeds Sanctuary is a medic- inal-plant garden preserving the cultural, medicinal and botanical heritage of the

Getting There, Rates, Info

By bus from San José: two choices: Take bus to Ciudad Quesada (Autotransportes San Jose-San Carlos, 2255-4318, Ca. 12, Av. 7/9) and transfer to the bus to La Fortuna via Los Angeles; get off in San Isidro de Peñas Blancas. Or take the bus to San Ramón (Empresarios Unidos, Ca. 16, Av.10/12, 2222-0064), then the bus to La Fortuna via Chicha- gua, and get off in San Isidro.

By bus from La Fortuna: Take bus to Ciudad Quesada (Transpisa, 2379-3153) via Chichagua or bus to San Ramón (via Chichagua and get off in San Isidro de Peñas Blancas.

By car from San José: head north on Inter- American Highway to San Ramón; exit (right) and go straight until the last stop sign, turn left, then immediately right at the traffic light. Continue three km., staying to the left. Go uphill over speed bump with small school on right, then over another speed bump and make a left at the Y intersection. This is the road to La Fortuna. Follow this road north for about an hour, after which you will come to a single- lane suspension bridge over the Peñas Blancas River. About two km. after bridge, watch for a church and cemetery on left. About 150 meters past the ceme- tery, turn left onto a rock road. Go 2.3 km. west into the jungle. Keep bearing right at intersections. When you see a large tin building, go 100 m and turn right into the driveway through the gates.

Rates, inc. tax, guided tour, breakfast buffet. $68-$90. Individual or family bungalows, $68-$124.

Rainforest Mysteries Day Tour $50 per non- guest, inc. transportation from La Fortuna, guide, lunch, snacks; $45 not inc. transportation. For info: 2468-4006 or 2468-0352,or **info@fincalunan- uevalodge.com**

Photo Courtesy of Finca Luna Nueva

region, including some endangered plant species. The project's mission is to protect the world's disappearing genetic diversity and cultural knowledge in the face of deforestation.

Guests can spend from an afternoon to a week at the lodge. Visitors can opt for tours and classes, including connecting with food through the culinary arts, sustainable living, and organic and biodynamic farming.

The Rainforest Mysteries Day Tour focuses on food, medicine and habitat, including snacks and lunch.

Finca Luna Nueva's proximity to the 50,000-acre Children's Eternal Rain Forest

Photo Courtesy of Finca Luna Nueva

Preserve provides many opportunities to enjoy wildlife.

The lodge also offers the first wheelchair-accessible trails in Costa Rica's rain forests. The 700-meter path weaves through primary forest, providing close encounters with walking palms, vines and wildlife. The wooden observation tower, soaring 50 feet into the sky overlooking the canopy, offers a view of Arenal Volcano.

Amenities include a spring-fed swimming pool, solar-heated hot tub, onsite massages, WiFi, games area, horseback riding, and fresh pizza and bread from an outdoor, wood-fired clay oven. Arrangements can also be made to join local families in making cheese or yogurt.

Meals at Finca Luna Nueva are delicious. The all-organic buffet lunch included a heart-of-palm salad flavored with cilantro, red peppers and onions, a second salad boasted bok choy, mustard greens, katuk (a tropical plant with edible leaves high in vitamin C) and basil, and a dish of golden pasture chicken with a touch of ginger, followed by homemade flan sprinkled with dark chocolate shavings.

After the meal, I lingered in the open-air foyer for coffee and homemade ginger, coconut and chocolate cookies.

Then, after a tour, I participated in the final treat: making homemade ginger ale with a simple recipe of one cup fresh sugarcane juice, half a cup of sparkling water, and one to two teaspoons of fresh, organic ginger extract to taste.

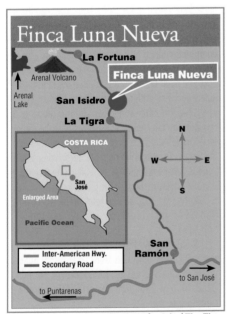

Roy Arguedas Arias | Tico Times

The island is formed by a split in the Puerto Viejo River.

Photos by Vicky Longland

Heliconias and Birds Abound on River-Isle

By Ann Antkiw

A tiny, five-acre isle created by a split in the Puerto Viejo River is home to a virtually undiscovered Garden of Eden. A naturalist's dream and birder's paradise, Heliconia Island is the site of an enchanting botanical garden, 10 minutes' drive from Puerto Viejo de Sarapiquí in north-central Costa Rica.

Previous owner Tim Ryan purchased the property in 1992 and began developing the botanical garden, where more than 70 different species of heliconias now flower throughout the year. Henk and Carolien Peters from Groesbeek, Holland, bought the property while on vacation in Costa Rica. They have been living there for two years with their two German shepherds, Ringo and Costa, brought from Holland, and Doggie, a recent Tico addition to the family.

The couple was totally unprepared for what was in store for them when they fell in love with the property.

"We had visited Costa Rica a few times before we decided on this undertaking and complete change of lifestyle," said the friendly, energetic Carolien, who owned a dog-grooming business back in Holland.

Henk, who worked for Philips for 22 years, also had to adapt, supervising the construction of their home and the lodging, in addition to struggling to learn Spanish. Featured on a Dutch reality TV show, the Peterses faced many challenges during the process of moving and settling in. For example, last April the opening of the floodgates upriver cut the island off completely, stranding the couple.

"It was a very scary experience," Henk said. "We watched the water rising and covering the first three steps of the six that lead up to the porch. "Since then we have been marooned quite often during the rainy season, but unlike the first time, it only lasts about three hours."

Accessible only by footbridge, the manicured garden with its verdant green lawn, borders, beds and shrubberies is enhanced by a purple ground cover known as *cucaracha*, Spanish for cockroach. Most of the property's 70 different varieties of heliconias are native to Costa Rica, but some come from other tropical zones around the world and are rarely seen in this country.

The garden and non-cultivated areas also feature botanical relatives of the heliconias, colorful gingers,

A footbridge provides the only access to Heliconia Island.

bromeliads, philodendrons, orchids, ferns and ornamental banana trees. Bamboo, native trees and the distinctive, fan-shaped Madagascar traveler's palm all grow together in natural harmony. Two trails lead from the garden to the meandering river, a gentle tributary of the Isla Grande River that flows past the property.

Birdwatchers will have no problem spotting their feathered friends in the early morning, throughout the day and in the evening. Birding expert and naturalist Dan Keller has reported 227 species seen on and around the island. These include colorful trogons, toucans, Baltimore orioles, tanagers and flycatchers. By the river, herons, kingfishers and sunbitterns can be spotted. Animals also roam the property; fortunate visitors might catch a glimpse of a howler monkey, sloth, armadillo, porcupine or possum.

You can visit Heliconia Island on a day trip, but if you want to stay a while, the Peterses offer accommodation in a new hexagonal construction built on stilts and comprising four attractive rooms with comfortably furnished balconies.

The small rooms have windows on three sides and a large mirror that gives them a spacious, airy feeling. Featuring bamboo furniture made by talented bamboo artist and designer Brian Erickson, they offer simple comfort, air conditioning or ceiling fans, and a choice of king, queen or two twins. The tiled bathrooms have ample hot water, but getting to the shelves placed behind the door requires some ingenuity.

Though not experienced restaurateurs,

Heliconia Island

to Puerto Viejo de Sarapiquí

Heliconia Island

Braulio Carrillo National Park

Horquetas

COSTA RICA

San José

Enlarged Area

Pacific Ocean

N
W E
S

Secondary Road

Santa Clara

to San José   to Guápiles

Roy Arguedas Arias | Tico Times

the Peterses offer a friendly, homey atmosphere in the open-air balcony restaurant and bar, where breakfast, light lunches and, on request, dinner, are served. This is an ideal, cool place to sit, relax with a cold drink and watch the nonstop activity at the bird table.

Day tours include the Tortuguero canals, rafting on the Sarapiquí River, zipping through the canopy and a visit to the nearby La Selva Biological Station. Admittance to the gardens with a self-guided tour is $10 per person; a two-hour guided tour is $15 per person. Night tours are also available.

For guests staying at Heliconia Island, the guided tour is included. This is highly recommended, as Carolien, who speaks Dutch, English, German and some Spanish, is extremely knowledgeable about what grows in her garden.

"I have been studying nonstop for the past year," she said, displaying a detailed

Carolien Peters leads a tour of her garden.

map of the garden with every plant and tree labeled.

Heliconia Island also caters to groups for $12 per person. Recent visitors have included birders, horticulturists and photographers.

More than 70 heliconia species grow in the garden.

Getting There, Rates, Info

From San José, take the highway to Limón through Braulio Carrillo National Park. After the park, turn left at the intersection for Puerto Viejo de Sarapiquí, by Rancho Roberto Restaurant. At Km. 22 there's a small, easy-to-miss wooden sign on the right side of the road; turn left down a dirt road and follow the signs for Heliconia Island. Leave your vehicle in the parking lot at the entrance and walk over the footbridge.

Rates, including breakfast, guided tour and taxes, are $62, single with fan, $72 for a double with fan, or $85 for a double room with air conditioning (payment in cash only, colones, euros or U.S. dollars). Dinner costs $12.50.

For info: 2764-5220, **info@heliconiaisland.com, heliconiaisland.com.**

A green view in the game room at Lands in Love, between San Ramón and La Fortuna.

Photo by Whitney Martin

Haven for Friends and Animals

By Daniel Shea

Resting quietly at the base of a pristine valley in the mountains of north-central Costa Rica is a tiny, secluded annex of society, a place almost hidden from the world, offering the escapism of a utopian novel combined with all the modern conveniences of a Holiday Inn.

The hotel – though it should really be classified as more of an open commune that offers daily cleaning service and a minibar in each room – is set up to provide visitors with different vacation options, many of which can be realized on-site.

The massive, impeccably maintained Lands in Love property that surrounds the buildings looks like a snaking golf course set amid primary forest, where a wild slice might send a howler monkey crashing to the jungle floor.

But as the staff is made up of animal lovers, golf is not an option. About 45 minutes south of La Fortuna and one and a half hours from the capital, Lands in Love/Tierras Enamoradas Hotel & Resort was founded three years ago by 18 Israeli friends united by the concept of animal-friendly living and a desire to lead better lives.

Though they're all vegetarians and delight in sharing their ideals with interested guests, the air isn't thick with the frustrated angst you might find if PETA opened a hotel.

"We didn't do it for the business," says Yanis Ephod, the head of reception. "We did it to come to Costa Rica and build a home with our friends."

And while they don't force their beliefs upon guests, they do take pleasure in their deftness at deceiving taste buds into believing soy is beef. (My own existence as a car-

Guest rooms are comfortably simple.

Photo by Whitney Martin

nivorous animal was called into question when I mistook their soy meatballs for delicious, butchered chop.)

The 260-acre property consists of three main structures and a small pet hotel. The reception center – a long, one-story building containing a game room, a lounge area that resembles a sofa emporium, a bar and the main restaurant – sits at the lowest point in the valley, flanked on one side by a pool and hot tub. At a higher elevation are 33 rooms, all with patios overlooking the dense valley full of strange sounds and beautiful examples of Costa Rica's biodiversity.

Along the main road are the adventure center and the roadside café. The sprawling property allows for a very private experience.

"When it's fully booked, people say it doesn't feel like there are a lot of people here, because it's pretty big and spread out," says Naama Ariel, the head chef.

At the same time, if people want to interact, the main building has common areas, the pool and a small space set up for

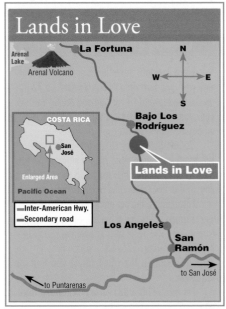

Roy Arguedas Arias | Tico Times

A zipline canopy tour is among various activities on offer here.

Canines have a hotel of their own on-site.

Getting There, Rates, Info

From San José, take the Inter-American Highway west and turn right at San Ramón. Go 32 km. on the road toward La Fortuna and Arenal Volcano. Look for the Lands in Love signs. The hotel offers an airport shuttle service.

Double-occupancy rates, are $119, inc. tax, full breakfast and guided tour, additional person, $22. (For residents, inc. tax, with three meals a day, $90 in low season and $102 in high season.)

For animals, the pet hotel costs $20 a night.

Sample prices for activities: canopy tour, $45 foreigners, $30 residents; canyoning, $65/$45; horseback riding, $35/$25. Other trips include rafting, hiking in the cloud forest and tours to attractions.

For info: 2447-9331 or **www.landsinlove. com**.

musical performances.

Even in its seemingly extreme seclusion, the hotel offers many adventure opportunities, biodiversity tours and day trips to places such as the ever-active Arenal Volcano, about 45 minutes north of Lands in Love.

The tours provide adventure lovers with the adrenaline they're looking for, accompanied by fun, comic relief from the lively staff.

The close-knit community that runs Lands in Love makes a concerted effort to welcome each guest into a warm atmosphere filled with new options.

The uniqueness of the place has drawn many repeat guests, the staff says. And with the beauty and diversity offered here, it's not a surprise.

A tile mosaic created by Alexandra Krauskopf adorns Lucky Bug's gate.

Photo by Avalon Johnson

Hospitality Is Family Business

By Patrick Fitzgerald

Getting to Nuevo Arenal without a car is no easy task. It must be obvious upon our arrival at Lucky Bug Bed and Breakfast that it has been five hours, a taxi and two bus rides since San José. So when my girlfriend and I attempt to check in and tour the spacious grounds, Monika Krauskopf, Lucky Bug's delightful owner and operator, will have none of it. "Oh no, you must be starving," she says. "Sit down and have a bite to eat first."

Hospitality has been a Krauskopf trademark since before the family built the bed-and-breakfast in the shadow of north-central Costa Rica's highly active Arenal Volcano in 2006. A native of Germany, Krauskopf, her husband, Willy, and their triplet daughters moved to Costa Rica 13 years ago.

Setting up shop a few minutes east of Nuevo Arenal, they founded the Caballo Negro Restaurant in the Tilarán Mountains. Soon, however, the family's enterprises expanded when a sealed plastic bag showed up on the side of the road. Inside was a dog, which the family adopted and named Bella. After noticing more and more animals without homes, the Krauskopf triplets, Alexandra, Katheryn and Sabrina, all 20, began selling their art to finance further rescue and shelter efforts, and the Lucky Bug Gallery was born.

Bella, now one of more than a dozen dogs and cats at Lucky Bug, follows us as Krauskopf shows us to our rooms, nestled in the hills behind the restaurant and gallery.

As we make our way through the lush gardens, past the waterfall and dock on the private lake, we encounter three extraordinarily tame chickens, also residing on the premises.

"We have everything here," Krauskopf boasts, adding that the less tame wildlife includes ducks, toucans, frogs, butterflies, monkeys, an anteater, an otter, an iguana, a turtle and a sloth.

The bed-and-breakfast consists of five rooms, each with its own wildlife theme. Upstairs are the Frog, Turtle and Butterfly rooms, with king beds featuring a wrought-iron headboard fashioned by Alexandra, reflecting the room's namesake animal, Also on the second level is the Flower Room, smaller, with twin beds.

Downstairs is the Sun Room, big enough for four, with two twins and a king bed. The bathrooms are spacious, with hot showers and ornate tile

Lucky Bug has its own private lake.

work that fits each room's respective theme. The rooms also have tile tables (for sale), alongside a bountiful collection of handicrafts and the Krauskopf daughters' art, in the gallery.

We select the Butterfly Room, one of two rooms upstairs with a balcony. While it boasts no view of the volcano, Lucky Bug more than makes up for it with gorgeous vistas overlooking the lake and verdant gardens.

In the morning, awakening to the sound of toucans in the nearby trees, we go to retrieve the eggs from the chicken coop for breakfast. We see only one, but when we walk up to Caballo Negro, Krauskopf goes to get more.

"Sometimes you have to shoo them off," she says, returning minutes later with three more eggs in hand. "Still warm," she points out.

She fries them and soon we begin breakfast. The eggs, served with toast, boast vibrant orange yolks. Next come pancakes, garnished with banana, mango and pineapple. All are delicious. Though we heard

Lucky Bug B&B

Lucky Bug B&B

Nuevo Arenal

Lake Arenal

Tronadora

Tilarán

Arenal Volcano

La Fortuna

COSTA RICA

Cañas

San José

Enlarged Area

Pacific Ocean

N / W / E / S

— Inter-American Hwy.
— Secondary Road

Roy Arguedas Arias | Tico Times

Getting There, Rates, Info

From San José, take the Inter-American Highway to San Ramón. Exit onto Highway 141 to La Fortuna. Head west out of La Fortuna for Nuevo Arenal. Lucky Bug Bed and Breakfast is 3 km. west of Nuevo Arenal. Rates, inc. tax and breakfast: four double rooms, with king bed or twins, are $78. For the larger room, with both king bed and twins, $136. All five rooms may be rented out together for a group.

For info: 2694-4515, **luckybuggallery@ ice.co.cr or luckybugcr.net**

their calls at daybreak, the toucans are gone by the time we finish breakfast. Discouraged, we head over to Lucky Bug's trail for a short jaunt into the adjacent rain forest.

Our hopes to catch a glimpse of poison dart frogs, howler monkeys or the resident sloth – rescued by the family from the middle of the road – are let down, and we emerge with nothing but muddied shoes.

Aracaris visit the feeder.

Next, I decide to take the family's kayak for a spin around the small private lake. It's stocked with rainbow bass, Krauskopf says, and guests are welcome to fish. The record so far is one guest's four-kilo bass, which the family cooked up at Caballo Negro that night. "They love that, when they can eat their own fish," Krauskopf says with a grin.

My aims, however, are more modest; I'm hoping only to see the large turtle

Dining is al fresco.

Krauskopf says inhabits the lake. But a downpour begins the minute my oars hit the water. I begin to wonder if today just isn't my lucky day.

Arenal Volcano National Park is only a few minutes away, but with the cloudy skies, we elect to spend the afternoon perusing the gallery and drinking coffee on a tiled table overlooking a small pond out front, before heading home. Several cars come and go this Sunday afternoon, many filled with tourists or residents whom Krauskopf greets by name. "I love my job," says the gregarious German. "It's something when you wake up in the morning happy, because you enjoy what you're doing."

Her passion shows, whether in the gallery, restaurant or bed-and-breakfast. She personally selects all the art sold in the gallery, knows the artists by name and can commission nearly any item you want. She supports the community by selling works crafted by street kids, and benefits the children's hospital with a massive piggy bank filled with coins from a fee imposed on non-customer bathroom use.

While we wait for a taxi, Krauskopf beckons us back one last time. "Toucans!" she alerts us. Sure enough, a fiery-billed aracari sits on the tree outside the restaurant. Suddenly, it comes even closer to perch on the small feeder right outside the doorway. Then, two more join in, munching on leftover pineapples and bananas, completely oblivious to us as we stand agape, mere feet away.

Luck, it would seem, was ours after all.

Photos by Patrick Fitzgerald

Photos by Ronald Reyes

Tourists in the Mist: Monteverde a Visitor Mecca

By Rob Bartlett

Monteverde features on the itinerary of just about every visitor to Costa Rica, but there is one thing most travel brochures and guidebooks will not tell you: It is a rough journey to get there.

Coming from San José, it is at least a five-hour bus ride, leaving at the ungodly hour of 6:30 a.m. or, more palatably, 2:30 p.m. A popular route, it is worth getting to the bus terminal earlier to avoid the risk of being left without a seat.

This is a particularly important point on this journey, as a good part of it is on bumpy, unpaved roads. Even those with their own transport should be wary: When choosing a rental car, decent suspension is a must.

The road can also become a dustbowl in dry season, meaning that no matter how hot the sun, you will want to keep those windows firmly shut, whereas in the rainy season conditions can get really treacherous.

So why do people come? The answer is that the cloud forest preserve and town in north central Costa Rica has something for everyone. Nature and wildlife, adventure, culture and entertainment – Monteverde has it all.

Nature and Wildlife

The crown jewel is, of course, the **Monteverde Cloud Forest Biological Preserve** (**cct.or.cr**, 2645- 5122, 2645-5564). Stretching up and over the Continental Divide, the preserve covers more than 4,000 hectares, and, with 13 km. of hiking trails, it is possible to find yourself alone in the forest even on the busiest day.

To catch a glimpse of the wildlife, it's worth paying extra to join a guided tour. Open daily, 7 a.m.-4 p.m. $15 for foreigners, with a guided tour an additional $15. Discounts residents, students and children. Accommodation at the park entrance and shelters within the reserve. Night tours are available.

However, the Monteverde preserve is not the only protected area. Other private and state-owned reserves abound, of which the two best known are the **Santa Elena Reserve** (**reservasanta/elena.org**, 2645-5390) and the **Children's Eternal Rain Forest** (**acmcr.org**, 2645-5003, 2645-5200). Both receive fewer visitors than the preserve, but also lack some of its infrastructure.

Naturally, when visiting these forests, the birds and animals are wild and the misty cloud cover often thick, so you may not see all you hoped to see. If you want to be sure of spotting some wildlife, other attractions in the area guarantee just that.

Outside the main entrance to the preserve, the **Hummingbird Gallery** (2645-5030) guarantees a view of many varieties of fast-flitting *colibrí*. Along the road toward the town of Monteverde, the **Paseo de Stella** building houses **The Bat Jungle** (2645-6566). This attraction is highly informative, with the chance to see live bats alongside interactive activities and displays that demonstrate just how important and unique these much-maligned creatures are. A 45-minute guided tour: $10.

A more long-standing attraction in the area is the **Monteverde Butterfly Garden** (**monteverdebutterflygarden.com**, 2645-5512). Many other *mariposarios* exist, but the this garden is still one of the area's best-known attractions. Admission: $10 for foreigners, including a one-hour, 15-minute tour.

Another butterfly garden can be found closer to the town of Santa Elena at the **Ranario** (**ranario.com**, 2645-6320). However, as the name suggests (*rana* is Spanish for "frog"), the attraction is best known as

Gaudy leaf frog.

the Frog Pond. The center has more than 28 species of amphibians.

Tour is included. Entrance to the both the Ranario and Mariposario:s $10 each for foreigners, or $16 if you choose to visit both attractions. The ticket is valid for two entries to allow visitors to see both diurnal and nocturnal species.

Back on the main road, the **Serpentario** (2645-6002) is a collection of 26 species of snakes, of which 10 are poisonous, alongside other reptiles. Admission: $8 for foreigners, with tour. A further treat for those who love creepy-crawlies is the **World of Insects** (2645-6859). The center houses a collection of 250 preserved species along with some 25 live varieties, including tarantulas and praying mantises. Admission: $9 for adults includes tour. A fantastic viewing platform is above the center.

Adventure

The main draw for adventurous travelers in Monteverde is the myriad opportunities for hiking and nature-watching. Among

Getting There

Driving from San José, take the Inter-American Highway north and turn right just before the Lagarto River Bridge at Km. 134. The last 35 km. to Santa Elena is up a steep, unpaved, scenic road. Think four hours total.

By bus, Transmonteverde (2222-3854) departs San José from Ca. 12, Av. 9/11, at 6:30 a.m. and 2:30 p.m. ¢2,350 ($4). (about four and half hours).

Where to Stay

A sampling: More than 70 hotels in the area range from backpacker havens, to super luxury suites.

Arco Iris Lodge: cabins ($70-$80, inc. tax), also secluded Honeymoon Cabin ($171-$193, inc. tax), four-poster bed, Jacuzzi, DVDs, kitchen, private garden, solar lighting, views. Breakfast, $7. 2645-5067, **arcoirislodge.com**

Cabinas Vista al Golfo: 300 m. before Santa Elena, wooden rooms, dbl beds, some shared baths, ($18-$29), apts.,($40), cable TV, WiFi, equipped kitchen, security box, inc. breakfast, tourism info, good value. 2645-6321, **cabinasvistaalgolfo.com**

De Lucia Inn: modern two-story wood house, spacious rooms. ($81, inc tax , fabulous breakfast buffet, home-made bread, jams, granola, more), Internet, balcony, excellent restaurant across road. Meals cooked to perfection, very popular, reserve. Try Peruvian ceviche, 2645-5976, **costa-rica-monteverde.com**

Hotel Montaña Monteverde: old favorite, on right en route to preserve, reserve Jacuzzi atop hotel for 5 p.m., slip into the bubbling water, watch the sun set over Nicoya Peninsula, gardens, balconies, deluxe rooms($73-$131, inc. breakfast) mini-bar, sauna, conf. rooms, trails, restaurant, wheelchair access. 2645-5046, **monterverdmountainhotel.com**

Monteverde Lodge: Renovated oldie, attractive lobby and restaurant, 1 km. along road to Monteverde Reserve. Rooms inc. tax, breakfast, $70 for single standard to $142 for a triple superior room. 2645-5046 or 2645-5338, **info@monteverdemountain-hotel.com, monteverdemountainhotel.com**.

Poco a Poco: 32 cozy rooms, family-style, nature-friendly, TV, DVD coffee-maker. From paved road in Monteverde, take a right at first intersection and drive three blocks past Frog Pond. Follow signs to Poco a Poco, first hotel on right. Rates, inc. tax: $79 to $93, single, $92 to $104, double and $101 to $115, triple. 2645-6000 or hotelpocoapoco.com, **info@pocoapoco.com**

The UGA (University of Georgia) Costa Rica campus: on a working farm in San Luis, some 20-minutes from Santa Elena. Lodging: $91 per person, inc. meals, activities and hikes. 2645-8049, **uga. edu/costarica.**

Trapp Family Lodge: closest to reserve, mountain chalet, phones, forest/volcano views, dining room, large lounge, comfy couches spacious rooms, $96, inc. breakfast, jr. suites $113, inc. breakfast. 2645-5858, **www.trappfam.com**

A pleasant but vigorous hike takes you to the San Luis Waterfall.

many private trails and reserves, are the **Ecological Sanctuary** (ecologicalsanctuary. com, 2645-5869, $10 during the day, or $15 for a night tour for foreigners (2645-5869) and **Bajo del Tigre** (acmcr.org, 2645-5003).

A little way out of town, a highly recommended hike is to the **San Luis Waterfall** ($8), particularly as it is quite possible to have the trail to yourself. The waterfall is the second highest in Costa Rica and tumbles dramatically between sheer walls of rock into an enclosed and atmospheric pool at the foot of a ravine. The hike is a bit strenuous and seems longer than the signposted one kilometer, but it's well worth it.

It seems everyone, adventurous or not, comes away from Monteverde having done a canopy tour. The basic idea is to zip through and above the forest canopy harnessed to a steel wire, and it is great fun. Several operators offer packages: The **Original Canopy Tour** (canopytour.com, 2645-5243, $45 for adults) is, as the name suggests, the oldest in town, whereas **Aventura** (2645-6959 or 2645-6388, $40 for adults) is the newest and also offers suspension bridges, ATV tours and horseback riding.

The two biggest players on the scene, however, are **Selvatura**, which also features a "Tarzan swing" as part of its canopy tour, and **SkyTrek**, known for being the fastest of all canopy tours, reaching speeds of up to 60 kph.

Both offer other activities. Selvatura (**selvatura.com**, 2645-5929, $40 for foreigners) has suspension bridges, a reptile and amphibian exhibition, butterfly and hummingbird gardens and the "Jewels of the Rainforest" display of insects. All cost extra, packages available.

SkyTrek (**skytrek.com**, 2645-5238, $60 for foreigners) includes a ride on the SkyTram cable car along with the canopy tour, and has suspension bridges, known as SkyWalk, for a close-up look at the treetops. Again, extra activities cost more, packages available.

Those looking for a more natural adventure can pop into the Monteverde branch of adventure company **Desafío** (**desafio/costarica.com**, 2645-5874) to check out activities, such as horseback riding, on offer there.

For equestrian enthusiasts, who prefer to go to the stables directly, **Meg's Riding Stables** (2645-5560, $30 per person, two hours), **Caballeriza El Rodeo** (2645-5764 or 2645-6306, $30 for foreigners, two hours) and **Sabine's Smiling Horses** (**horseback-riding-tour.com**, 2645-6894) are all reputable operators.

Culture, Food, Entertainment

If you are not yet tired out, there is still much left to do in Monteverde.

Back at the Paseo de Stella, a small exhibit (¢1,000/$2) outlines area history, including the founding of Monteverde by Quakers who left the United States in protest of the draft for the Korean War. Alternatively, if it is a Wednesday, head down to the center's auditorium at 6 p.m. to catch a

A young visitor braves the canopy tour high above the cloud forest at Selvatura.

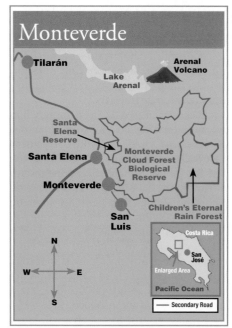

Roy Arguedas Arias | Tico Times

At left: a butterfly is born. Below, roads are bumpy but beautiful in the Monteverde area.

film screening.

If shopping is your thing, craft stores and art galleries abound in addition to the **Santa Elena and Monteverde Artisans' Cooperative**, known as **CASEM** (**www. casemcoop.org**, 2645-5190). Finally, after an action-filled day, it is time for food. But where to go? The area is certainly not short of welcoming eateries, but four restaurants will excite foodie travelers.

Back at the Paseo de Stella, hungry hikers could certainly do a lot worse than one of the savory wraps at **Caburé Argentine Café & Chocolate Shop** (2645-5020) , above The Bat Jungle. Amiable Argentine restaurateur Susana Salas has traveled the world gathering recipes, and her eclectic menu shows it, ranging from Mexican mole to Argentine *canelones*. Sala's chocolate truffles – straight dark or flavored with rum, cognac, orange or ginger – are a knockout. Wraps, sandwiches and salad and soup combos are all about ¢4,000 ($8); main course dishes run about ¢6,000 ($12).

Regular visitors to the area will know **Sofia** (2645-7017), a Latin fusion restau-

rant renowned as one of the country's top spots for dining out. Owner Karen Nielsen has opened a second restaurant nearby, **Chimera** (2645-6081), and a third one in Santa Elena, **Trio**. All offer excellent dining. At Chimera the ambience is warm and welcoming, with bright walls, plenty of flowers and the beautiful aroma of food coming from the open-plan kitchen. The tapas-only menu is enticing, ranging from *lomito* with a parsley, sweet pepper and caramelized onion sauce to a cold stack of roasted aubergine and smoked provolone with a sun-dried tomato sauce. For dessert, the chocolate mousse is a real treat. Prices range from $8 for the lomito down to $2.50 for coconut rice, with cocktails coming in about $4.50 to $5.

With so much going on, it is easy to see why Monteverde is worth the bumpy journey.

'Green' Experience to New Lengths

Rancho Margot guests practice early-morning yoga lulled by the rippling Caño Negro River.

Photos by Beverly Gallagher

By Beverly Gallagher

Lulled by calm waters reflecting an imposing active volcano, Juan Larry Sostheim decided to end his days of wanderlust and build a home in a valley connecting the Monteverde cloud forest and Lake Arenal, in north-central Costa Rica. What began as a modest plan to build a home and bed-and-breakfast and to live off of the land has mushroomed into a colossal sustainability project.

Some 35 km. from the tourist hub of La Fortuna, in Pueblo Nuevo near the small town of El Castillo, the 152-hectare Rancho Margot is off the grid. Hydroelectric power provides electricity for the communal area, 17 bungalows and a bunkhouse, with 20 two-bed rooms.

A reforestation project with 15 different kinds of trees aims to protect the natural springs on the property, while a compost system gives organic gardens the fuel to produce enough fruits and vegetables for guests and livestock. An animal rescue and reintegration center receives injured and previously captive wildlife. The rancho produces cheese and yogurt for consumption and for sale. An on-site slaughterhouse supplies meat and poultry and eggs.

The list goes on. An added step in the composting process feeds a biodigestor with 110 cubic meters of liquid storage capacity, used to heat stoves and volcanic water pools, complete with a wet bar.

Before or after soaking in the methane-heated tubs, visitors can loosen their limbs at one of the twice-daily yoga classes, or peruse the library sitting above the terraced pools.

At the ranch's La Fortuna offices, a wooden sign stretching across the building's façade reads: "Rancho Margot, a Self-Sufficient Dude Ranch." Since breaking ground, Sostheim's vision of green development and self-sufficiency has evolved.

"A dude ranch is a place where city slickers go to have a cowboy experience, and there's nothing wrong with that," Sostheim says. "A dude ranch also has a well-defined business model, and this isn't well defined. This is a work in progress."

Turning left at the ranch's entrance, you pull up to a small cluster of one-story, white buildings with wood trim and clay tile roofs. The Caño Negro River – the largest river feeding Lake Arenal – roars through the property. The temperature is mild, benefiting from a unique microclimate influenced by the cool Monteverde cloud forest, the warmer Lake Arenal and the protection offered by Arenal Volcano to the east. Almost swaying above the ranch is a mountain so lush with primary forest that you swear it is shape shifting.

Lodge rooms are nestled into the hillside.

A walkway through landscaped gardens leads to a large patio with tables. Opposite this, a sunken lounge area is surrounded by booths and a well-stocked bar.

A main attraction for is the two-hour ranch tour. Visitors can also go rappelling at nearby waterfalls, kayaking on Lake Arenal, or hiking and horseback riding to a secluded 15-meter waterfall while crisscrossing the river.

If the river is too high to cross, or if you yearn for more than one activity, don't miss the horseback ride or two-hour hike to "*El Mirador.*" From this viewpoint, you can see Arenal Volcano, Lake Arenal and the entire the Caño Negro River Valley . On a clear day, you might spot Miravalles and Tenorio volcanoes. Covered tables offer spots to enjoy lunch or a late afternoon snack.

During your visit, you are bound to meet Sostheim. Charming, gregarious and fluent in four languages, Sostheim makes the rounds chatting with visitors while responding to calls on his walkie-talkie.

Sostheim is a citizen of Chile and Germany and a resident of Costa Rica. In his "past life," as he describes it, he helped spread fast-food culture across Berlin in the 1970s as a general manager for Burger King. He later owned a chemical company that exported detergents and pool cleaners.

After suffering a small heart attack, Sostheim, 57, sold his chemical company and made Rancho Margot his new home.

Sostheim's vision is spreading beyond his property lines. The hydroelectric turbine that keeps Rancho Margot off the grid has piqued the interest of nearby hoteliers seeking solutions to their high energy bills.

"To make a sustainable business, the best thing that can happen is if a lot of people copy it," Sostheim says.

Rancho Margot's conservation efforts

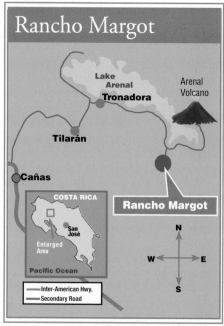

Rancho Margot

Lake Arenal

Arenal Volcano

Tronadora

Tilarán

Cañas

COSTA RICA

San José

Enlarged Area

Pacific Ocean

Rancho Margot

N

W — E

S

Inter-American Hwy.
Secondary Road

Roy Arguedas Arias | Tico Times

are as much about human beings as they are about forestry and alternative energy. After finding out that local children didn't have the option to study past the sixth grade without taking public transportation to La Fortuna, Sostheim hired a van to take them.

Six years ago, he bought school buses for free public transportation from the ranch to Rancho Margot's offices in La Fortuna. Rancho Margot also began sponsoring a program with the National Community Development Office to teach environmental education in the El Castillo Elementary School.

Guests rest on hammocks off their rooms.

With so much going on, there is still plenty of time for relaxation. Yoga classes are offered at 7:30 a.m. and 4 p.m., either in a covered studio perched above the river or on a wide deck spreading out over a lily-covered fishpond.

Spacious bungalows tucked into the hillside offer plenty of downtime. The indoor and outdoor areas are perfect for reading and socializing. Adding to the self-sufficient feeling, the armoires, bed frames and even the reading lamps are made in the ranch's woodshop from plantation teak and laurel.

On the more economical side, bunkhouse rooms with spotless, shared, hot-water showers offer a comfy night's sleep and are joined by a large deck with tables.

You will also be able to indulge in the simple yet delicious culinary delights at Rancho Margot. Those who scoff at buffet food are in for a nice surprise. Freshly picked organic vegetables prepared al dente, grilled free-range chicken, savory potato dishes and homemade brownies will draw you back for more. For dinner, à la carte orders are also an option.

So, where is this green center of innovation leading? Wherever it is going, Rancho Margot is certainly in the realm of dreamers and true believers. People drawn here rely on their ability to create through responsible tourism what so many other developments don't: education, protection for fragile ecologies and hope.

Getting There, Rates, Info

From San José, take the Inter-American Highway north and turn off at San Ramón. Follow volcano image signs to Arenal Volcano National Park (89 km.). Rancho Margot is 12 km. past the park entrance heading toward El Castillo. Signs for Rancho Margot are on an information board as you drive on the dirt road, and as you turn left toward the national park.

Free transportation is available to and from La Fortuna, departing Rancho Margot's offices at the corner of the park. (Good idea to reserve). In low season, the bus leaves La Fortuna at 7 a.m., noon and 5:45 p.m., and departs from the ranch at 5:45 a.m., 9 a.m. and 4:30 p.m., daily. In high season, a fourth bus is added. Per-person rates, are $100 in the bungalows, plus $30 for extra person, and $30 per person for a shared room in the bunkhouse ($40 without a bunkmate). Rates, inc. tax, breakfast, yoga classes, Internet access, ranch tour. For info: 2479-7259, **www.ranchomargot.org,** **info@ranchomargot.org**

Rara Avis grounds with open-air dining area in background.

Photo Courtesy of Rara Avis

Rainforest Lodge: a Rare Bird

By Beverly Gallagher

The city lights trail behind as we travel down paved roads. Passing through lands cleared for cattle, bananas and pineapples, the last remnants of modern life fade into the background. A few hours later, we jump off the back of a wagon. The only sound we hear is our rubber boots penetrating the muddy ground as we begin our trek into the unspoiled rain forest.

The journey to Rara Avis Rainforest Lodge and Reserve begins the small town of Horquetas, in the northern lowlands. Reaching the lodge is not easy. Following the wisdom that getting there is half the fun, this is one adventure that will have you laughing your knee-high rubber boots off.

Intrepid travelers climb into a covered wagon pulled by a farm tractor to begin a 15-km. ascent. Danilo Villegas, the lodge's operations manager, sits relaxed at the helm. He skillfully maneuvers the tractor

across suspension bridges, through muddy ravines and over steep, boulder-strewn sections of the path while stopping to point out oropendola nests and endangered *jícaro* (calabash) trees.

"It is important for us that staff be from the Horquetas area, and that our business be part of the local community," says Amos Bien, a U.S.-Costa Rican biologist and founding member of Rara Avis. "Another of the concepts that gave rise to Rara Avis was to allow visitors to experience the rain forest as I did when I first came 30 years ago – complete with mud, rain, rubber boots, kerosene lamps and extraordinary beauty.

"Once immersed in it, the idea is for guides to explain some of the intricacies of the forest, so that beyond beauty, there is understanding."

Many choose to walk the last three km.; whether you continue the tractor ride or walk, the journey takes about an hour. The tractor, which also delivers food and supplies to the lodge, resumes with any baggage you don't want to carry. At 700 meters (2,300 feet) above sea level, the climate is cool year-round, averaging 25 degrees Celsius – perfect hiking weather.

Though it rains a lot – 8.3 meters annually – mosquitoes are not a problem. At the 12-km. mark, we are guided into the forest, and within moments we move from secondary to primary forest. Blue morpho butterflies flit along the trail, offering a surreal contrast to the predominantly green and brown backdrop. Rubber boots with good tread, for loan at the Horquetas office, come in handy as you find your balance walking on beds of slippery clay and the wooden pavers that sporadically mark the trail.

The verdant tunnel leads to a final suspension bridge before opening out onto the manicured lodge grounds. Upon arrival, a hearty Costa Rican meal awaits the hungry traveler. Everyone sits on the wooden benches under the open-air dining area. Large plates of rice, beans, vegetables, stewed meat and a spicy, homemade salsa make the rounds in the family-style setting.

Rara Avis offers three types of accommodation: the Waterfall Lodge, the River-Edge Cabin and the Casitas.

The Waterfall Lodge is the most central and gets its name from the two-tiered cataract 200 meters away. The two-story building's eight rooms all have hot-water showers and wraparound balconies. A large patio with a small library on the second floor offers spectacular views of the treetops.

The River-Edge Cabin is a wobbly, 10-minute walk into the forest. A large balcony facing the river joins two rooms, with hot-water showers. Thick foliage reaches the balcony's edge and practically pours into the main entrance. Standing on the balcony makes you feel like Dorothy waking up in the Land of Oz.

A short walk from the dining area, the Casitas are the most economical accommodations. The four two-cabin rooms have cold-water showers.

All accommodations are comfortable and come complete with welcoming details, such as a personal towel folded into a blossom on each bed, topped with a small soap. Before you head to your rooms, Jarquín instructs you how to light and care for the kerosene lamp in your room.

The lodge has no electricity; however, the River-Edge Cabins have a few hours of solar-generated light and the dining area is lit with a generator. It's a good idea to bring a flashlight for night hikes and trips from the dining area to your room.

Rara Avis, which opened in 1983 as one of the first eco-lodges and private nature reserves in Costa Rica, sits in the middle of the 484-hectare reserve bordering Braulio Carrillo National Park. The conservation project expanded in 1987 after Rara Avis members found environmentally conscious buyers to purchase an additional 1,000 hectares of neighboring land.

Over the years, Rara Avis has brought environmental awareness to the local community, the scientific community and to

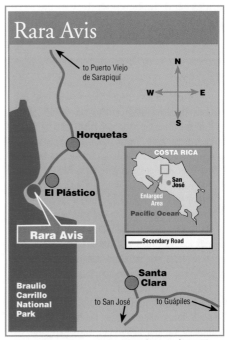

Roy Arguedas Arias | Tico Times

tourists. It has introduced economically viable, nondestructive agricultural practices, such as conserving forest on farmland, butterfly farming and planting native tree seedlings.

The private reserve has supported pivotal research, including U.S. biologist Donald Perry's steel platform vehicle, constructed in the late 1980s to promote exploration of the rain forest canopy. Researchers and tourists used to scan the treetops riding the metal contraption until it went out of operation about 10 years ago. The pioneering mechanism set the stage for the more than 200 canopy-exploring businesses – ziplines, walkways, bridges and trams – operating in the country today.

"We trained many of the first natural-

Visitors bound for Rara Avis find a spot on the padded benches of the tractor-pulled transport.

Photo by Beverly Gallager

ist guides, who went on to train new generations of guides throughout the country," Bien says.

Staff naturalists are at Rara Avis for guided hikes and for answering questions. Familiar with the area and enthusiastic about sharing their knowledge, the guides not only spot things most people easily fail to notice, but also explain them beyond just their names.

Most hikes begin after breakfast and range in difficulty from moderate to difficult. Maps are available for those who wish to venture off alone.

Rara Avis is home to more than 362 species of birds, 500 species of trees, poisonous snakes, including the fer-delance and the coral snake, and mammals such as white-faced, spider and howler monkeys, coatis, banded anteaters and tapirs. If you are in the right place at the right time, you may even spot a jungle cat. The lodge keeps an exciting book of sightings filled in by guests.

Socially responsible tourists who still want to have fun will find the adventure of a lifetime at Rara Avis. Forgoing a few creature comforts offers a new perspective on how we lead our daily lives.

"In the past 20 years, there has been a tendency in ecolodges toward increasing luxury and movement away from being immersed in the forest and isolated from civilization," Bien says. "While we want people to be comfortable and well fed, we also want to maintain the sensation of being in a place that, while constantly changing, has remained unchanged for millions of years."

Getting There, Rates, Info

From San José, take highway to Guápiles and Limón through Braulio Carrillo National Park. Shortly after leaving the park, turn left at signs for Puerto Viejo de Sarapiquí. Travel 16 km. to second entrance sign for Horquetas. Turn left at the sign for Rara Avis. Secured parking is at Rara Avis offices in Horquetas. From here, a tractor-pulled charabanc cart or jeep leaves at 9:30 a.m. for the lodge. For those who want to travel to and from lodge at different times, horses can be rented for $25. You must walk the last three km. if you go on horseback. Per-person rates, are $65 triple/quadruple, $75 double and $85 single for the Waterfall Lodge, $80 double and $90 single for the River-Edge Cabin, and $50 per person for the Casitas. Rates, inc. tax, three meals, tours, transportation. Residents: 30-percent discount. For info: 2764-1111, **rara-avis.com**.

The Springs lights up at night.

Soak in Style at Arenal's The Springs

By Meg Yamamoto

It doesn't get much better than soaking the stiffness out of your old bones in hot mineral springs while taking in the majestic sight of Central America's most active volcano. And at The Springs Resort and Spa, the new kid on the hot-springs-resort block around north-central Costa Rica's Arenal Volcano, you do it in the lap of luxury.

Owners Lee and Cindy Banks have built on the success of their wildly popular La Paz Waterfall Gardens and Peace lodge near Vara Blanca, northwest of the capital, to create a remarkable resort in the shadow of rumbling, spitting Arenal Volcano.

After nearly four years of construction, they opened the first phase of The Springs on a 59-hectare property, set 3.5 km. off the highway between La Fortuna and the volcano. Much of the wood, metal and even marble work was done on site by

some of the same craftsmen who helped build La Paz, with the design by Banks himself, says the resort's energetic general manager, Joey Duncan.

The impressive main lodge consists of five floors, starting with the reception area on the top level and proceeding down to the restaurant level, fitness and spa level, games and future casino level, and finally the pools, with guest rooms situated in a separate area beyond. Looming over it all is the ever-present Arenal Volcano, which, when not maddeningly cloud-shrouded, can be seen from just about everywhere at the resort – certainly from each of its 32 luxurious guest rooms and villas.

In addition to volcano views, all accommodations feature a private balcony with hammocks and rocking chairs, king bed, air conditioning, huge Peruvian-marble bathroom with Jacuzzi, minibar, safe and coffeemaker. Each room also has a large flatscreen TV, surround-sound stereo with

Arenal Volcano looms large at the resort.

Photo Courtesy of The Springs

CD and DVD player and iPod connectivity, telephone and WiFi.

But it's really all about the pools here, and there are no fewer than 18 to choose from, with temperatures varying from 24 to 39 C and settings ranging from cascading waterfalls to a swim-up bar to jungle seclusion with a 25-meter waterslide. The hot mineral water is captured from natural springs near the Arenal River and pumped up 130 meters to the pools in a constantly replenishing flow. Hotel literature states that The Springs' mineral water has the highest level of bicarbonates in the Arenal area, and explains that bicarbonates "assist in opening peripheral blood vessels and improving circulation, which aids against cardiovascular disease."

The pools are drained and cleaned nightly, Duncan says, and the water is also

Pito the ocelot gets his ear scratched.

Photo by Meg Yamamoto

circulated through a filtration system to eliminate foreign contaminants.

Sliding into a deliciously warm pool cloudy with minerals, a slightly rusty smell attesting to the presence of iron, it's easy to imagine the benefits to your health – and all you have to do is sit there and soak. For a break from the torpor, the resort's fitness level features a body-boggling array of cardio and exercise equipment, from volcano-view treadmill, elliptical and stair machines to a full circuit of contraptions with which to crunch, pump and pull your way to fitness.

If you happen to overdo it here, never fear: You can stagger next door for a rub-down at the spa, with treatments, from massages and body wraps to facials, manicures and pedicures. You can even enjoy a floating water massage in one of the mineral spring pools. With separate areas for men and women, the spa also features a steam room and sauna to help you return to a state of languor.

All this back-and-forth between activity and indolence works up an appetite, for which The Springs offers a several restaurants, including the all-day Tres Cascadas, poolside Treetops Grill, Ginger Sushi bar and fine dining at Las Ventanas. The Treetops Grill's mahimahi burger, served with a mound of grilled onions, wedge fries and red cabbage slaw, is a particularly tasty lunch option, while Las Ventanas' tender roasted scallops and papaya noodles salad, followed by the succulent grilled rib eye with jalapeño and cilantro butter, make for fine dining indeed.

The resort also has several bars, including the Heliconia on the restaurant level and La Laguna, a swim-up bar in the center of the largest pool.

There's a lot more to do at The Springs

than soaking, spa-ing and eating. The games level offers a pool table, dartboard, cards, backgammon and a hand-carved chess-board, with a small casino to be installed in the future, Duncan says. Horseback and ATV tours are offered, or you can hop in a requisite resort golf cart and head down to the wildlife preserve, operated by the resort in conjunction with the Environment, Energy and Telecommunications Ministry.

The preserve is home to 33 cats, including ocelots, margays, a couple of jaguarondi and a large puma that definitely lives up to its name, Guapo (Handsome), all either confiscated from poachers or donated by private preserves. Some of the cats look none too happy to be caged and hiss at visitors; others, such as Pito, the friendly ocelot, appear to enjoy human company and being petted. The resort employs a full-time veterinarian to care for the animals, which cannot survive in the wild, Duncan says.

The Springs is by no means finished; 10 additional guest rooms are under construction, with more to come. Future plans are grandiose, and include day tours, an aviary, ranarium, climbing wall and zipline, Duncan says, with the next phase of construction involving an outdoor center on the banks of the picturesque Arenal River, with kayaks, fishing and terraced pools.

Will such a wealth of attractions make it difficult to remain for long in the hot springs, fruity beverage in hand, immersed and immobile?

Not likely.

Getting There, Rates, Info

From the town of La Fortuna, head west about 9 km. on the highway toward Arenal Volcano. Just after the Hotel Arenal Paraíso, a sign directs you to turn right to The Springs Resort and Spa; the resort is a bumpy 3.5 km. from the turnoff.

Double-occupancy rates, inc. tax, are $412-$525 for a first-level guest room, $458-$571 for second-level guest room, $486-$599 for a family suite with additional king or two twins. Villas with full kitchens range from $904-$1,356. Rates, include access to the hot springs, but not breakfast. A two-day pass to the hot springs and wildlife preserve, $40.

Restaurant prices range from $6-$18 at Tres Cascadas (buffet breakfast $12.25); $8-$14 at the Treetops Grill; $12-14 for rolls at Ginger Sushi; and $6-$11 for appetizers and $20-28 for main courses at Las Ventanas.

Spa treatments cost $75-$195 for massages, $140 for body wraps, $70-$140 for facials, $45 for manicures and $55 for pedicures. Packages from $195-$395.

For info: **thespringscostarica.com,** 2401-3313, (954) 727-8333 in the United States.

Photo Courtesy of The Springs

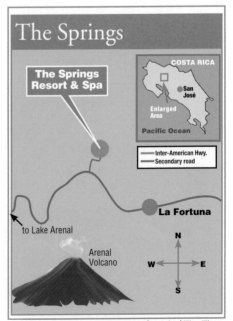

Roy Arguedas Arias | Tico Times

Caribbean

Photo by Ronald Reyes

Sit Down and Stay a While

Great Potoo Cottage sleeps up to six guests.

Photos by Ronald Reyes

By Holly K. Sonneland

Goldilocks would probably stay at Cashew Hill Jungle Lodge. Set back on a hill overlooking the Puerto Viejo area, on the southern Caribbean coast, the hotel is close enough to be able to get anywhere in the town in a few minutes' walk, but secluded enough to be able to settle into the rest and relaxation bit.

Just right.

The lodge is made up of seven themed cottages. A far cry from the spare hostel bed, Cashew Hill's cottages are well suited for couples, families and groups wanting to unpack a little as they explore the region. Each cottage has a fully stocked kitchen for those who aren't keen on eating out for every single meal or maybe just want to whip up a snack.

Some guests have almost taken too much to the self-contained cottages. Owner and Tico Times contributor Wendy Strebe says she was worried at first when one German family didn't leave the property for the first two days, with the two children running happily around the grounds. "But they went to the beach on the third day," she says with relief.

One Dutch bird-watcher originally booked for four nights but ended up staying for 10, because "he saw more birds sitting on his veranda than on all his other trips," Strebe says.

As for land animals, a five-foot-long iguana takes early morning dips in the pool sometimes, and armadillo families often snack from the compost pile. The kinkajous, known sometimes as night monkeys, though they are actually related to raccoons, make regular appearances to eat from the star-fruit trees, and sloths drop by from time to time, too. Wendy attributes the presence of wildlife to the fact that the hotel uses environmentally friendly cleaners, among a slew of other eco-conscious measures.

The wildlife aren't the only animals at Cashew Hill. Two massive English mastiffs, Elvis and Ozzie, perform lumbering patrols around the grounds. Marley, a miniature pinscher, completes the alarm system, alerting his owners of each guest's arrival with a yelp. Stevie, the one-eyed cat, roams the grounds with an eye out for rodents or a good place to nap.

While guests shouldn't miss Puerto Viejo's top-notch restaurants, they can also request vegan catering at Cashew Hill, with advance notice. The lodge always has a few cold beers ($1.50 each) and organic wine ($12 a bottle) on hand, should the mood strike.

Puerto Viejo is easy to get around on foot or bike, a good option for those who want to avoid driving. An array of gorgeous lights and beaches is a scenic – though sometimes dusty – and easy ride away.

Cashew Hill's guests come from places as far-flung as Russia and New Zealand, and a good number have come back to the hotel over the years. They go out with adventure groups, on rafting trips, dolphin tours, canopy and waterfall tours or off to explore the Bribrí indigenous reserve, Cahuita National Park or Gandoca-Manzanillo National Wildlife Refuge.

At the end of the day, they can kick off their shoes and unwind in their cottage deck hammock – the unofficial posture of the *pura vida* lifestyle.

Wendy and her husband, Erich, have effectively turned the "there's no place like home" mantra into a living. The couple bought the property in 2003, a week after arriving in Costa Rica. They went back to their U.S. home in northern New Mexico just long enough to pack up a couple of suitcases and sell everything else, and completed the permanent move three months later.

While many business owners might shun the idea of not being able to separate

Cashew Hill Lodge

Caribbean Sea

Cashew Hill Jungle Lodge

COSTA RICA

San José

Enlarged Area

Pacific Ocean

to Limón

Secondary Road

Cahuita

N
W — E
S

Puerto Viejo

Manzanillo

PANAMA

Roy Arguedas Arias | Tico Times

he office and home, the Strebes seem most comfortable with the arrangement – or rather, just doing away with the "office" bit.

"We live our work," Wendy says. "We'd rather have you in our home than in an office."

"If guests want to sit down with us every morning and plan their days, that's great," she adds. And if they've got their own plans, that works, too. Often, though, guests are eager to solicit the Strebes' help and know-how. One woman, who recently sent her young adult daughter and friend to Costa Rica, enlisted Wendy to stock the girls' room with little gifts, such as sarongs and after-sun lotion.

That the Strebes thrive on hosting is evident in their interactions with guests. Sometimes dinners are held on the deck of the Strebes' house overlooking the property, and sometimes guests just come to join the family at the end of the day and "all jive together," Wendy says.

Pool is inviting to guests and sloths alike. While lolling in a hammock on your private balcony comes highly recommended.

Getting There, Rates, Info

From San José, take the Braulio Carrillo Highway to Limón. Follow signs to Cahuita. Pass Cahuita. Coming into Puerto Viejo, take the first right after Supermercado Old Harbour and follow road to the edge of town, past soccer field on left, over wooden bridge and up dirt road to Cashew Hill Jungle Lodge.

The lodge has three smaller cottages for one to three people and four larger ones for up to six and eight. Nightly ($102 to $170), weekly ($509 to $848, or about 30 percent off nightly rate) and monthly ($1,576 to $2,543, or 50 percent off nightly rate) include taxes, cleaning services and WiFi. On-site massages and laundry are offered for a fee. For info: 2750-0256 or 2750-0001, **reservations@cashewhilllodge.co.cr** or **cashewhilllodge.co.cr**.

The exterior of spacious Casa Bromelia.

Photos by Nick Cot

'Barefoot Luxury' on the Coast

By Meagan Robertson

Geckoes Lodge on the southern Caribbean coast offers a place to sit back, relax and leave your watch behind. About a km. inland from the beach on Cocles' Margarita Road, a gorgeous expanse of unspoiled jungle holds four houses: two for guests, one for the fulltime staff and one belonging to owners Zoë Courtier and Tom Keller.

Courtier, from England, and Keller, from the Netherlands, came to Costa Rica three years ago looking for the perfect place to open a lodge. They had worked in tourism for years and, after considering numerous other countries, they decided on Costa Rica for its good economy, steady tourism and political stability.

The lodge's slogan is "barefoot luxury," evoking a place where guests can experience comfort in an unspoiled atmosphere.

The grounds are by no means perfectly manicured, but the beautiful disarray of natural plants, trees and wildlife makes the setting enchanting.

Here, the peace is broken only by bird calls, the sounds of chirping insects and a running stream and the soft padding of three dogs trotting to greet their owners. A path leads down to the stream, where fortunate visitors may catch glimpses of poison dart frogs, hummingbirds or even a sloth hanging from the branches.

In contrast to the somewhat wild outdoor area, the houses are impeccable. The covered but open-air living and kitchen areas offer guests the experience of walking in and still feeling as though they're outside. Though the bedrooms are nclosed, once the wooden shutters of the numerous large windows are thrown open, he rooms seem to become part of the nature surrounding hem.

Both spacious guesthouses are constructed of unfinished wood and have fully equipped kitchens, private plunge pools, large bathrooms with hot showers and gorgeously painted porcelain sinks, and unique wood furniture, mostly made by local craftsmen.

The larger guesthouse, Casa Bromelia, has one master bedroom

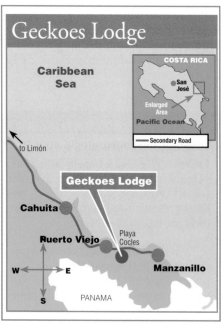

Casa del Bosque's fully equipped kitchen.

with queen-size bed and a second room with two single beds. The slightly smaller Casa del Bosque is geared more toward honeymooners, with one large master bedroom with queen bed. Unpredictable weather is a part of life on the Caribbean, and, when it rains, the size of the guest-houses at Geckoes Lodge makes a huge difference.

"It does rain here, and if you're stuck in a small hotel room, you might feel trapped," Keller says. "Here, you have your own space."

Though just four km. from the town of Puerto Viejo, Geckoes Lodge seems farther.

"You imagine in this environment that you're miles from anywhere," Courtier says. "But in truth, you're not."

They do recommend that guests have rental cars for the convenience of being able to drive to town, the beaches

Getting There, Rates, Info

From San José, take the Braulio Carrillo Highway to Limón. Follow signs to Cahuita. Pass Cahuita. From Puerto Viejo, go south three km., pass Río Negro and turn right onto Margarita Road. Head inland just over a km. until you see on your right a large purple wall with a wooden gate and two geckoes carved into it. The one-bedroom Casa del Bosque rents for $220 a night, while the two-bedroom Casa Bromelia goes for $275 a night, inc. taxes. If you stay a week, you get seven nights for the price of five.

For info: 8335-5849 or 8997-0563, **info@geckoeslodge.com** or **geckoeslodge.com**

Geckoes Lodge

Caribbean Sea

COSTA RICA
San José
Enlarged Area
Pacific Ocean
— Secondary Road

to Limón

Geckoes Lodge

Cahuita

Puerto Viejo

Playa Cocles

W E

S

PANAMA

Manzanillo

Roy Arguedas Arias | Tico Times

They seem to have achieved their goal of creating a lodge where guests can kick off their sandals and relax to the sound of nature at the end of a day's adventures.

"So many people live on a time schedule where they could never forget their watch," Courtier says.

"This is a place where we want you to leave your watch behind."

At left, the plunge pool is lit up at night, and is inviting by day.

and other area attractions. Puerto Viejo has a rental car agency for those who would prefer not to drive from San José, in addition to bicycles and scooters for rent — ideal for cruising along the beach-studded road south to Manzanillo. Courtier and Keller are more than willing to organize tours, such as a chocolate tour, zipline through the jungle, guided waterfall hike or dolphin-watching trip, for their guests.

Nearby Options just north and just south

In Puerto Viejo, an option is **Hotel Escape Caribeño** (2750-0103, **escapecaribeno.com**), 14 beachfront bungalows $79-$90, inc. taxes. Continental breakfast costs $4. Porches, fans, air conditioning, minibar, fridge, wheelchair access, hammocks, parking, bird observatory.

Next beach down at Playa Chiquita is **Aguas Claras** (2750-0131, **aguasclaras-cr.com**), five quaint equipped one-, two-, three-bedroom cottages, $70 double, $130 quadruple, fans, bed netting available, house sleeps eight, $220.

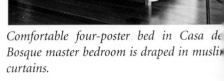

Comfortable four-poster bed in Casa de Bosque master bedroom is draped in muslin curtains.

e Caméléon Hotel near Puerto Viejo.

Luxury Hotel Shows Its Colors

y Chrissie Long

Stepping onto the grounds of the boutique hotel Le Caméléon on the southern Caribbean coast, I felt the tress of traveling immediately fall away.

Taking a seat on a half-egg-shaped hair in the stylish, whitewashed, open-air eception area, I could hear the soft background music of crickets and watch the lants sway as the breeze rippled through he gardens.

The hotel is being pitched as the first uxury hotel on the southern Caribbean oast, so I knew this visit would be different from the typical *cabina* or bungalow ccommodations of the region.

Opened just weeks before my visit, the outique resort had already made it onto he select list of Small Luxury Hotels of he World, received media attention from slew of publications and travel sites here and abroad, and hosted the Costa Rican president.

An untapped clientele never makes it to this side of country, explained Ligia Vargas, the resort's marketing director. "It's a shame," she said, "because beautiful beaches, a different culture and a relaxing environment are present here."

The idea of Le Caméléon is to give upscale travelers a sumptuous option in the Puerto Viejo area. It's not just the personal service and fine furniture that make this 23-room hotel a find. It's the chameleon theme – the images laced through the wall hangings and restaurant decor and the daily color-changing rituals – that make staying here a truly unique experience.

The rooms are dressed in white, from the marble countertops to the bare floors to the fluffy comforters. But a handful of colored display pillows and wall paintings change daily, in chameleon-like fashion, with a new color theme.

"We wanted a theme to attract guests," said Ben Abdelkader, president of Le Caméléon and a 30-year veteran of the hotel business. "And we thought the chameleon works because it represents change, not only in the natural environment, but in life, too.

"Swapping out color themes every morning represents that every day is a new day," he added.

Le Caméléon and its sister hotel, The Ocean Boutique Resort & Spa in Manuel Antonio, on the central Pacific coast, were both launched under the umbrella group Fashion Hotels. Ocean, a $20-million investment constructed in the Spanish-

colonial style, is scheduled to open soon. Le Caméléon, its Caribbean counterpart required a $5 million investment and opened quietly in 2009.

For those who worry that a new luxury hotel on this rustic coastline might threaten the character of the area, the hotel lives up to its name: Not pretentious or overly extravagant, it simply blends in with its environment.

The jungle seems to grow out of the heart of the hotel, with lush plant life lining the wooden walkways and shielding the structures from the street. Palm trees bow over the pool and Jacuzzi, creating a tangible fusion between the luxurious decor and the natural environment.

According to Vargas, the buildings were created to leave as many trees standing as possible, and the hotel uses a water treatment system that cuts down on water usage.

In the evenings, the atmosphere transforms as hotel guests are joined by nonguests for dinner or drinks on cushy patio chairs laid out in front of the bar. The gar

Getting There, Rates, Info

Le Caméléon is in Cocles, a few km. south of Puerto Viejo. From San José, take the Braulio Carrillo Highway to Limón. Just before Limón, follow signs to Cahuita, then head south through Puerto Viejo and on to Cocles. A sign announces the hotel on the right after a large white bamboo construction.

The hotel offers four room types, all with air conditioning, cable TV, WiFi, safe box, telephone and hair drier. The second-floor superior rooms, with one queen or two full beds and a private balcony, are $226, inc. taxes, year-round.

Deluxe rooms, on first floor, feature same amenities with private terrace instead of balcony for $254 to $283, depending on season. Junior suites include a living area with a full-size sofa bed, along with a king-size bed and private terrace, for $283 to $339.

And the Le Caméléon Suite includes a living space with adjacent half-bathroom, private balcony, king-size bed and larger bathroom with bathtub for $509 to $565. Rates are for dbl. occupancy, include à la carte breakfast, and taxes. Children under 12, free, sharing with two adults, Extra person: $40. Minimum stay for holiday season: four nights between Dec. 25 and Jan 3. For info: 2750-0501 or **lecameleonhotel.com.**

Daily-changing color themes offset simple white at the new luxury hotel in Cocles.

dens are lit by candlelight, and a sound system strung around the grounds plays a soothing soundtrack.

Though the chef was still shaping the menu when I visited, I was impressed with the variety of dishes – both local and international – and with the sensitivity that went into crafting each one. Every plate the waiter placed before us was carefully designed with a conscious effort in the balance of flavors.

But, like the character and decor of the hotel, the chef took a minimalist approach to the food, and I did contemplate ordering another plate to satisfy my appetite.

The bar scene was very much alive when I retreated to my room that night. Not a rowdy crowd, but somewhat mellow, matching the mood set by the music and the dimmed lights.

While Le Caméléon had offered a unique stay up to that point, waking up the next morning to the sound of waves crashing against the Caribbean shore was a whole new experience. The purity and simplicity of awaking surrounded by whiteness was a wonderful final touch to my Le Caméléon experience.

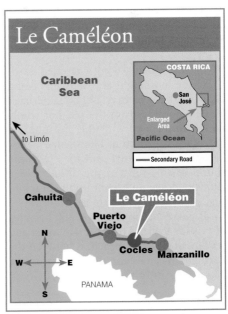

Roy Arguedas Arias | Tico Times

A long verandah fronts the lodge, sitting high on stilts.

Photo by Maggie Jamieson

Pacuare Nature Reserve: All About Turtles

By Maggie Jamieson

Imagine walking along a deserted beach in the moonlight and suddenly being witness to the magic of a leatherback turtle emerging from the sea, her whole body shimmering with the phosphorescence of sea plankton. The silence is broken only by the surf and the rhythmic sound of this relic of the dinosaur age clumsily dragging herself up the beach to find a safe nesting place to lay her eggs.

Pacuare Nature Reserve, 800 hectares of pristine lowland tropical rain forest and six km. of deserted beach, is between the Tortuguero canals and the Caribbean Sea, 25 km.. north of the Atlantic port city of Limón.

The reserve was purchased by the British-based Endangered Wildlife Trust in 1989 and was only afterward found to be an important sea-turtle nesting site, primarily for leatherbacks, but also for green and hawksbill turtles.

For many generations, the area's residents would collect leatherback turtle eggs either to supplement their diet or to sell to buyers eager to benefit from the eggs' reputed aphrodisiacal effects. The green turtle would be killed for its meat (as in green turtle soup) and eggs, and the hawksbill for its beautiful shell to make jewelry.

Turtle populations have declined drastically in recent years as a result of these activities and land development along the coastlines, and all three of these species are on the critically endangered list.

Though prohibited by law, residents still steal the eggs and kill turtles for their meat and shells. Some restaurants in

Limón offer turtle on their menus, especially during the active turtle season.

In 1994, a volunteer turtle-protection program was established on the reserve, which is now recognized as one of the most important turtle-nesting sites in Central America. In the 2008 turtle season, 543 nests were counted, of which approximately 6 percent were lost to poachers, according to the Endangered Wildlife Trust.

Photo by Maggie Jamieson

The turtle-protection program has always encouraged local participation, including visits from high-school students and employment of reformed poachers as guards.

What makes a visit to the reserve so special is the unique hands-on experience that makes visitors feel they really are contributing to the protection of the turtles.

Upon arrival, guests and volunteers receive an orientation talk in preparation for the evening turtle-protection activities.

Small groups of volunteers, guests, biologists and research assistants, on rotation throughout the night, leave to patrol the beach, primarily as a deterrent to prevent poachers from stealing the eggs, but also to collect important statistical data about the turtles.

These data are correlated at the reserve and made available to guests and volunteers.

A daily nest count during the season is posted in the community lecture room.

March through June is leatherback nesting season on the Caribbean side of Central America, while July through September is the green turtle season, with some overlap in June when both species are nesting.

Getting There, Rates, Info

From San José, take the Braulio Carrillo Highway to Limón. Access to the reserve is via Matina, a village two hours along the highway.

From there, a 30-minute drive through banana plantations leads to La Trocha, a landing stage on the Tortuguero canals, where a boat collects visitors for the 20-minute trip to the reserve.

The visitors' price, including accommodation in the lodge, meals, boat transportation to and from La Trocha, trips along the canal, guided night patrol on the beach and access to all parts of the reserve, is $80 per person, per night, minimum stay two nights. The volunteer price is $175 all-inclusive, minimum one week, staying in the cabins.

Volunteers must be 16 or older. For info: Carlos Fernández, 2234-5890, **c.fernandez@turtleprotection.org** or **carlos57fer@yahoo.com**, or **turtleprotection.org**.

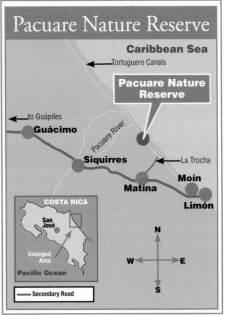

Roy Arguedas Arias | Tico Times

Photos courtesy of Pacuare Nature Reserve

Just Want to 'See' Turtles?

For rest and relaxation before or after taking care of turtles, head over to the nearby **La Laguna Lodge** (2272-4943, **lagunatortuguero.com**), between the Tortuguero canal and ocean, 80 rooms, rates per person for three-day, two-night package, inc. tax, meals, $238-$252,single, $210-$222 dbl. and $198-$214 triple, overhead fans, open-air canal-side restaurant, hammock and bar areas, butterfly garden, Frog House, two pools, Gaudi-inspired conference room.

In addition to participating in the turtle program, guests and volunteers can walk along a main trail running parallel to the beach, which offers an excellent opportunity to see the varied wildlife and birds. The reserve is home to more than 27 species of mammals, including monkeys, peccaries and deer, in addition to many reptiles. In 2008, two large cats – a puma and an ocelot – were spotted by Scott Hardy, an administrator of last year's turtle program. Additionally, some 230 bird species have been recorded over the past several years in the reserve, which is a known nesting site for the rare agami heron.

Shorter trails lead to the lagoons and other areas of special interest, such as an orchard with 42 species of fruits and vegetables, including noni and cacao trees. A boat ride can be arranged along the Tortuguero canals, where sloths, monkeys, wading birds, caimans and freshwater turtles may be observed.

Accommodation is available either as a guest staying a minimum of two nights in the lodge or as a volunteer staying a minimum of one week in the cabins.

The main lodge offers three double bedrooms with en suite half-bathroom, kitchen and sitting area. The shower area is below the house, supplied by rainwater, hot water is available, if required. The wraparound veranda overlooks the beach in front and the forest in back, where howler monkeys gather to enjoy the fruit of the mango trees.

Generally used by volunteers and staff members, the cabins are basic but quite adequate, with communal bathrooms, kitchen and dining area and lecture rooms. Guests staying at the lodge may take their meals there or join the volunteers, research assistants and biologists for some animated conversation in the communal kitchen and dining area.

There is no electricity; bright lights can disorient the turtles and affect their nesting abilities, so candlelight or kerosene lamps are used to ensure these Jurassic giants are not disturbed.

Organically grown cacao fruit: good for you, good for the earth.

Photos by Nick Coté

Center Sweetens Eco-Education with Chocolate

By Meagan Robertson

People often say that monkeys imitate humans, but in the history of chocolate production, it may be more apt to say that humans imitate monkeys; humans first noticed cacao beans because monkeys would suck on them and then spit them on the ground. This is only a fraction of the education and information available at Tirimbina Rainforest Center near La Virgen de Sarapiquí, in northern Costa Rica.

Protecting 345 hectares of mid-elevation forest with nine km. of trails, the internationally recognized, nonprofit center is situated within rain forest and river environments.

Several interesting educational tours are offered for tourists visiting for the day or staying overnight at the center's Tirimbina Lodge.

Eco-tours include bird, frog, bat and nightlife tours, in addition to the popular chocolate tour, in which employees demonstrate the entire process of making chocolate and allow visitors to taste different kinds of the sweet treat.

The path to the chocolate station crosses over two suspension bridges, one swaying high above a wide river and the other winding through the treetops, bringing tourists even closer to the monkeys scurrying among the branches, where bats cling to the dark undersides of trees and lethargic sloths can be spotted by fortunate visitors.

The chocolate-making station demonstrates all the steps involved in producing chocolate, starting with a tour of the cacao tree plantation and including a lesson on the history and evolution of the cacao bean and how it became as popular as it is today.

While offering guests a taste, chocolate expert Wendy Morera explains why Christopher Columbus disliked chocolate upon his arrival in the New World.

"Because there was no sugar, the taste was very bitter, and Columbus felt it had no value," Morera says, as her audience purses their lips upon tasting the liquid chocolate. "(The Spaniards) also didn't like the look or the name of cacao, because it made them think of human waste." (*Caca* is Spanish for "poop.")

Spend the night at Tirimbina Lodge.

Morera goes on to explain that with the arrival of sugar years later, the perception of chocolate changed. Eventually, it became such a prestigious beverage that some European kings had cups made of solid gold only for drinking chocolate, and would consume as many as 12 cups per day, she says.

This explanation is accompanied by the tasting of various delicious chocolates, and Morera also distributes some cacao beans for the visitors to take home.

Tirimbina provides educational tourism on several levels through single- or multi-day eco-education programs serving students, teachers and professors, researchers, tourists or special-interest groups. According to tour guide Willy Aguilar, the number of national and international school groups Tirimbina receives is growing steadily.

Aguilar has worked at Tirimbina for four years and says he still loves seeing the reactions of the different tour groups. As polite and friendly as he is knowledgeable, Aguilar could easily write a book with the wealth of information he provides visitors. His ability to spot and name the animals in the forest comes in handy when a visitor might not differentiate the tail of a monkey from a hanging branch.

Tirimbina's educational programs cater to the needs of different groups, ranging from elementary-school children to scientists. Researchers and higher-education students can pursue extensive research projects on the property, either under self direction or with the guidance of Tirimbina's naturalists.

Tirimbina

Puerto Viejo de Sarapiquí

La Virgen

N

W E

S

Tirimbina Rainforest Center

San Miguel

COSTA RICA

San José

Enlarged Area

Pacific Ocean

to Guápiles

to Heredia, San José

Secondary Road

Roy Arguedas Arias | Tico Times

The center also runs a free program for children, offering transportation, lunch, educational materials and educators for a whole day. In 2007, more than 2 schools participated in environmental education programs at Tirimbina, and enrollment continues to climb each year. During these visits, children learn about conservation, management of natural resources and the fragile ecosystem.

For guests staying overnight, Tirimbina Lodge offers 15 comfortable rooms near the Sarapiquí River, with one double or two single beds, air-conditioning, private bathrooms with hot water, phone and WiFi.

The center also has a souvenir store offering assorted gifts and organic chocolate bars made by the *Asociación de Mujeres Amazilia del Caribe*, a group of women from the Caribbean-slope community of Pueblo Nuevo de Guácimo.

Getting There, Rates, Info

Tirimbina Rainforest Center's main entrance is 1.6 km. north of the town of La Virgen de Sarapiquí.

Take "Guápiles Highway" that goes to Limón. Some 15 km. before Guápiles, is a crossroad, with bus station and eateries. Turn left here. Signs point to Puerto Viejo. Go 40 km. At the T-section, turn left. Follow signs. If you reach the center of La Virgen de Sarapiquí, you have gone too far.

Tour costs are $19 for the Rainforest Nightwalk, Bat Program and Frog Tour, $22 for Night Chocolate Tour and $20 for day Chocolate Tour, $24 for the Bird-Watching Tour and $22 for the Natural History Walk. Special rates are offered for children, students and groups.

Tirimbina Lodge: Surrounded by beautiful gardens, the lodge offers rooms with A/C, private baths, hot water, Wi-Fi, phone. Also restaurant, souvenir store, parking area 24/7. Rates are $67.20, single or double, inc. tax and breakfast, add $15 for additional guest. For groups, who wish to stay longer, the Tirimbina Field Station costs $20 per person, per night, or $45 inc. breakfast, lunch, dinner and tours. For info: 2761-1579, 2761-0055, **tirimbina.org**

The turtle-shaped pool invite guests to relax.

No Turtles Needed
to Enjoy Turtle Beach Lodge

By Patrick Fitzgerald

In Tortuguero, you expect tourism to revolve around turtles. The turtle-shaped pool at Turtle Beach Lodge, a few miles north of the town on the northern Caribbean coast, does little to dispel this expectation.

But a recent stay at Turtle Beach that was well outside the traditional turtle high season proved there is more to the lodge than just turtles. On 175 acres, the lodge embodies jungle seclusion. You can explore its garden and trail, take a canal tour or kayak on your own to a nearby lagoon – and if you don't see a turtle, well, it's not the end of the world.

Since 1999, the Lachenman family has owned and operated Turtle Beach Lodge, living it something along the lines of an extreme makeover. Construction has been "basically constant" from the start, says Jesse Lachenman, 27, who runs the hotel while his parents are in the United States.

The pool was built in 1999, the bar and restaurant renovated s few years ago, and new blocks of rooms have been added each year.

The lodge features 55 rooms, which Lachenman says "are all basically the same." The few original rooms are smaller singles while most others are doubles with at least two beds. The rooms are simple yet comfortable, and the bathroom showers are hot and powerful, a welcome surprise considering the lodge's relative isolation.

On our visit, my companion and I shared a corner room that had two queen-size beds as well as a couch that could double as a third bed. Towels folded in the shape of turtles awaited us on the beds. The rooms come with ceiling fans and are essentially half open-air with expansive, screened windows.

Our corner room received a pleasant

breeze to offset the jungle heat. While Lachenman says Turtle Beach receives almost all its business straight from tour companies, packages can be booked on the lodge's Web site for itineraries of two, three and four days. Custom packages are also available.

"We can set up any kind of stay you want," he says.

For most visitors to Turtle Beach, the journey begins in San José. The hotel picks visitors up early in the morning and transports them over to the Caribbean, with stops for breakfast and tours of Braulio Carrillo National Park and a banana plantation. Then, the voyage hits the water for the two-hour boat ride up the canals to Turtle Beach.

For our quick stay, my companion and I flew to Tortuguero, but I rode along with one of the tour groups to get the full canal experience. For many, it is a first impression of Tortuguero that is difficult to forget – especially when passing a crocodile taking in the midday sun on a sandbar. To get the full canal experience, however, Turtle Beach's canal tours are a must. At dinner the night before, our guide Eloy had warned us not to show up the next morning with high expectations. But we had barely left the dock at 5:30 a.m. before we encountered spider monkeys in the trees over the canal, breakfasting on hearts of palm. Soon, Eloy and our boat driver John – who proved to be an astute animal spotter as well – had guided us past basilisk lizards, a juvenile caiman, white-faced monkeys, two species of heron and a group of bats sleeping under a log.

Depending on the time of year, Turtle Beach also offers tours of its garden, day and night jungle tours, tours of Tortuguero National Park and, of course, turtle-watching tours during the Atlantic green turtle season, June through August.

If all the touring wears you out, Turtle Beach offers simple yet satisfying options for relaxation. While the surf is too rough for swimming at the beach, there are plenty of benches and hammocks where you can nap and enjoy the pristine view of the Caribbean. The aforementioned turtle-shaped pool is perfect for an afternoon dip, and ideally next to the lodge's bar and restaurant.

Simply wandering the gardens and the grounds can be a learning experience, as every tree and plant is labeled in both English and Spanish to help inform budding botanists.

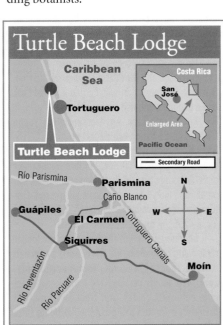

Roy Arguedas Arias | Tico Times

Getting There, Rates, Info

Turtle Beach Lodge is five miles north of the town of Tortuguero. Boats can be arranged to pick up visitors either at the Tortuguero Airport or from the Caño Blanco Marina. Fly in with SANSA (8 a.m. no flights Fri.-Sat., $98, residents, $75, **flysansa.com**, 2290-4100) or Nature Air (2299-6000, $107, discounts available, **natureair.com**) or by bus Empresarios Guapileños (2710-7780, Caribbean Bus Terminal, Ca. Ctrl, Av. 11/13), to Cariari, transfer to La Guess, transfer to boat to the Caño Blanco Marina.

The lodge also provides a minibus shuttle from San José, inc. tours of Braulio Carrillo National Park and a banana plantation along the way.

Rates per person, inc. transportation, range from $180-$245 for two days, one night; $215-$329 for three days, two nights; and $415 for four days, three nights. $250-$415 for three nights, four days. Rates go down for each additional person, inc. meals, tax, tours (depending on length of stay). Custom packages available. For info: 2248-0707 or 2258-4756, or **turtlebeachlodge.com**.

Another way to get there, is to go the longer river route from Moín, via **Riverboat Francesa Nature Tours** (2226-0986, **tortuguerocanals.com**), top-quality personalized tours, knowledgeable naturalist guides, van from San José, full breakfast at rancho alongside the Rio Danta (also offer deep-sea and river fishing).

Three meals a day are included in the room rate, served up buffet-style at the airy restaurant. (Soft drinks and alcohol are available but not included; bottles of wine start at $20.) Offerings vary, but one day's fare included: *gallo pinto*, eggs, sausage, pancakes, fruit and muffins for breakfast; *casados*, pork, pasta with meatballs, salad and vegetables for lunch; and pork, fish, mashed potatoes and vegetables for dinner, with cake and ice cream for dessert. The food was surprisingly solid for a buffet in the middle of the jungle – we often enjoyed second and third helpings – and with the array of options, even picky eaters could find something they liked. Be sure to arrive shortly after the meal gong sounds, however, as the fare tends to get cold quickly.

Turtle Beach employs about 40 workers, most from the community, and keeps strong ties to the area. The lodge helped build a two-room schoolhouse in the nearby village of San Francisco, and children from the village perform a traditional dance for visitors at the lodge once or twice a month.

There was no traditional dance during my recent visit, and no turtles, either. But we did enjoy two days alternating between breathtaking wildlife watching and placid, pool- and beachside relaxation.

Indigenous Yorkín Welcomes Travelers

Solar panels provide electricity for community building in indigenous village of Yorkín.

Photos by Ronald Reyes

By Rob Bartlett

The jungle crowds the river on both sides. The sun burns down on the back of my neck. Birds shriek and circle overhead. I swear I have seen this place before in the movies. Suddenly, the reassuring hum of the small outboard motor cuts out, replaced by the anxious splash of an improvised punting pole. The water rushes over the rocks, and the dug-out canoe struggles to move up the rapids against the current.

The young boy at the back drops the cut-off plastic bottle with which he has been bailing water and jumps overboard to push the boat upstream. It is not enough. We are slowing to a stop. Someone else needs to push. I put down my notebook, roll up my jeans and jump in.

Undoubtedly, wading upstream is not a mode of transport that will appeal to everyone. However, if you are looking for the truly authentic rather than "Pirates of the Caribbean," you'll find it here. And new experiences are what traveling is all about.

Our destination is Yorkín, an indigenous Bribrí community on the Panamanian border, inland from the beaten-path beach town of Puerto Viejo on the southern Caribbean coast.

After about an hour and a half on the river, we pull into the bank and meet Guillermo Torres, 61, who leads us to our "*albergue.*" The thatched-roof, open-air wood construction has three bedrooms downstairs and a sleeping platform with mosquito-net tents and sleeping mats upstairs.

Though each bedroom has its own bathroom, this is still very basic accommodation, with bare concrete floors and no connection to the solar panels that provide the primary source of electricity. The center of the project is next door, where hearty *típico* meals are served each day.

In the evening it is a gathering point where people can get to know each other, usually over a steaming mug of chocolate, and play the guitar as the darkness settles

Only way to get to Yorkin is to head up river.

here can be "very hard," as the community receives almost no help from the government. Residents still grow traditional crops such as cacao and bananas, but in 1996 they set up a tourism cooperative called Aventuras Naturales Yorkín, hoping that travelers looking for a truly authentic experience might offer a new source of income.

"We were looking for alternatives," says Torres, who is the leader of the cooperative. "The banana trade doesn't bring in too much. We don't have enough visitors yet, but we hope that it will eventually benefit everyone in the community."

over the jungle.

However, this is not an idyllic rural paradise. Torres acknowledges that life

Visitors to Yorkín are welcome to stay for any length of time, and many activities are on offer. Those who like adventure can go hiking and horseback riding to see the forest and its wildlife firsthand. Guests can also learn traditional hunting techniques, such as archery, and swim in the inviting waters of the Yorkín River.

Alternatively, the more culturally minded can watch artisans as they produce handmade jewelry, woven baskets and engraved gourds.

You can learn about the community's traditional agricultural industries, including the chance to see how chocolate is produced from the raw cacao pods grown there, and then try the finished product. All visitors, however, will be able to experience true cultural exchange.

A stay at Yorkín will certainly help those trying to improve their Spanish, and those staying longer will be able to help people to learn English. There is also the opportunity to learn some of the Bribrí language, which Torres acknowledges "has been lost a lot," and even contribute to the

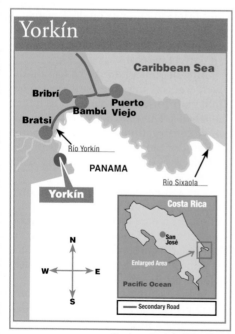

Roy Arguedas Arias | Tico Times

culture's long-term survival by documenting it. The community genuinely seems to enjoy receiving visitors. The curiosity and friendliness of the children are truly touching, and the adults are no less welcoming.

"I really like it," says Elisa Vega, 25. "[Visitors] always like the place, the people and the culture, and they go away happy. It's great. Also, we get volunteers who really get used to life here. They stay for a month or more, and you get to know them and they remember their time here. A lot call back regularly."

The community is very remote, accommodation is basic and communication is difficult for those who don't speak Spanish. However, the sense of doing something completely different is a major attraction: you simply cannot have this sort of cultural interaction at a traditional hotel.

If you are looking to get out of the comfort zone of the country's popular tourist destinations, Yorkín and rural tourism are definitely worth a look.

Getting There, Rates, Info

Tour operator Simbiosis Tours can organize transport to Bambú for groups.

For those making their own way, Bambú is approximately half an hour from the town of Bribrí, inland from the beach town of Puerto Viejo. Bribrí is served by regular bus connections from San José, Transportes Mepe, Caribbean Bus Terminal, Ca. Ctrl, Ave. 11/13, 2257-8129. 6 a.m., 10 a.m, 1:30 p.m., 3:30 p.m., 5 hrs 30 mins, and a taxi or local bus can take you between Bribrí and Bambú.

A day trip to Yorkín costs $60, including boat transport from Bambú, demonstrations of chocolate production and archery, a short hike and food. A two-day, one-night stay at Yorkín costs $70 per person, including boat transport from Bambú, a tour of the cacao and banana plantations, demonstrations of chocolate production and archery, a short hike and all food.

For info about longer stays and volunteer work, contact Aventuras Naturales Yorkín at 2200-5211, or Simbiosis Tours at 2290-8646, 2290-8651 or **info@turismoruralcr.com**. Simbiosis Tours also offers trips to other rural destinations, including national parks, wildlife reserves and ecolodges. For info: **turismoruralcr.com**.

The crystalline waters of the Caribbean invite snorkelers to take a look inside.

Photo by Ronald Reyes

Guanacaste

Photo by Ronald Reyes

Dipping pool for cooling off.

Photos by Nick Coté

Tennis and Breakfast, Anyone?

By Mike McDonald

Waking up at 15 Love Bed & Breakfast in Tamarindo is like waking up at Wimbledon with an oceanfront view. The small bed-and-breakfast, named by its owners for their passion for tennis, is quietly nestled into the side of a hill, about a 15-minute walk from downtown Tamarindo, on the northern Pacific coast.

The hotel is the vision of former Belgian tennis star Oliver Vanhoute and his wife, Emilie Cieslik. The quaint size of the bed-and-breakfast allows the couple to pay close, congenial attention to their guests.

Because the hotel has only three rooms and one suite, guests are more like neighbors and friends to the Belgian pair than one-week visitors from distant cities.

"I really like the small size of the place," Cieslik says. "We get to know our guests well, and I've met people from all over the world."

Vanhoute first gained interest in moving to Tamarindo after a 10-day visit to Costa Rica in 1999. One year later, he bought the property where the bed-and-breakfast now sits and built two tennis courts.

In 2002, the couple opened the courts and ran a tennis club. They opened the bed-and-breakfast in 2006.

The hotel entrance opens onto a small dipping pool backed with palm trees and red mats for relaxing, with a blue, wave-shaped bar off to the right. Just beyond the pool are the hotel's tennis courts, open to guests and others who wish to use them.

The view past the tennis courts continues over palm leaves and branches full of coconuts, out to the Pacific Ocean. On clear nights, the stars light the courts, and the sound of crashing waves drowns out the buzz of the bars in Tamarindo.

During the day, guests can take advan-

tage of the tennis courts and Vanhoute's skills. A surf and tennis package is also available combining lodging, tennis lessons from Vanhoute and surf lessons through the Tamarindo Surf School.

Rooms are decorated in simple, modern, IKEA-like style. Red and white make up the recurring color theme.

"We thought the red and white with the green surroundings would make a good contrast," Vanhoute says.

Each room is equipped with its own balcony overlooking the tennis courts and bordered by tropical plants.

Over a delicious breakfast, guests can share a friendly chat in the morning while

15 Love B&B

Pacific Ocean

Liberia

Playa Flamingo

15 Love B&B

Huacas

Tamarindo

Santa Cruz

Costa Rica

Nicoya

Enlarged Area

San José

N

W E

S

Pacific Ocean

Secondary Road
Inter-American Hwy

Roy Arguedas Arias | Tico Times

Getting There, Rates, Info

From San José, take the Inter-American Highway northwest to Ostional, follow signs to Taiwan Puente de Amistad (Tempisque). Head to Guaitil, then Santa Cruz. Follow signs to Tamarindo. 15 Love is 200 meters before Hotel El Jardín del Edén on the way into Tamarindo (five hrs.) or fly into Tamarindo Airport with SANSA (2290-4100, flysansa.com,) or Nature Air (2299-6000, natureair.com).

Rates, inc. taxes, are $130 for a room and $175 for a suite, including à-la-carte breakfast and access to tennis courts. A three-day Surf and Tennis package is available for $621-$733, inc. taxes, two private surfing lessons and three tennis sessions. For info: 2653-0898 or **15lovebedandbreakfast.com.** Honeymoon and other packages too.

watching Vanhoute patiently teach students how to swing a racket. After a full day of surfing and swimming on the nearby beaches of Playa Grande or Playa Langosta, guests can return to 15 Love and relax with a cold, Costa Rican brew or a freshly blended natural fruit smoothie – pineapple, banana, strawberry, blackberry and others.

Both Cieslik and Vanhoute, now seasoned veterans in a beach town that is developing and expanding almost daily, can offer knowledgeable advice about the area and its attractions.

"We're always here for the guests," Cieslik says, dressed in a white tennis skirt as she prepares to square off against her husband on the courts. "Any questions they have or any recommendations they need, they can ask us any time."

Suite at 15 Love Bed-and-Breakfast in Tamarindo. Above, co-owner Emilie Cieslik.

Owner Oliver Vanhoute shows off his back hand on the tennis court.

The open-air dining room overlooks the infinity pool at Casa Caletas.

Photos by
Vicky Longland

Boutique Hotel Offers Family-Friendly Beach Experience

By Ann Antkiw

With development running amok on the northern Pacific coast, deserted, pristine beaches are getting harder to find. But on the southern Nicoya Peninsula, a magnificent coastline harbors remote, sandy havens such as Playa Caletas and Playa Coyote.

Perched on a promontory, Casa Caletas Boutique Hotel overlooks the estuary of the Río Coyote and Playa Coyote's wide expanse of sand, with the breaking surf beyond. This stunning view can be seen from everywhere at Casa Caletas, and will captivate you from sunrise to sunset as the tide rises and ebbs.

On a 1,100-hectare working cattle farm this small hotel is built on the site where Austrian owner Sylvester Feichtinger's ranch house once stood. Though he resides in California, he makes frequent visits to Casa Caletas, which opened in 2004.

The hotel is surrounded by well-kept gardens. A mango tree and flourishing palms line the shady entranceway to the reception area and comfortable lounge with dark rattan and bamboo furnishings

A rather imposing TV is particularly popular with the small fry.

Casa Caletas is a kid-friendly place; families are welcome and their needs are catered to. Beautiful, locally grown teak used throughout the hotel embodies the essence of simple elegance and comfort. This is complemented by the limestone faux-coral floors and the hotel's signature color, a Mediterranean pea green.

The centerpiece at Casa Caletas is the infinity pool with its breathtaking view. You can soak away the hours in the lovely warm water, or relax on the deck in a comfy lounge chair with a good book.

Overlooking the pool area, the open-sided dining room with a ceramic island bar in the middle offers Costa Rican and international cuisine. Breakfasts are substantial, with three different types to choose from: continental, traditional Tico or North American. The large fruit plate is particularly appealing, and an abundance of fresh coffee is always on hand. Lunch includes sandwiches, hamburgers and salads in addition to main dishes. Kiddies have a special menu: delicious breaded fresh fish fingers or cheese sticks and French fries. Dinner choices include steak, chicken, fish and pasta. Freshly cooked, nicely presented, tasty meals are the order of the day, ranging from $7 to $16.

The hotel offers three room options. Rates, as in many boutique hotels, are pricey. The eight accommodations have French doors opening onto a small terrace or balcony with an ocean or river view. All rooms have air conditioning, ceiling fans, cable TV, tiled bathrooms with hot showers and roomy closets. The decor is simple: teak furniture, a cream and white color scheme and bedside tables with reading lamps.

The three double rooms have comfortable queen beds, but, though called deluxe, they are on the small side. Ideal for families, four rooms have a queen bed and a second-level mezzanine with two twins. The Junior Suite has a king-size bed, estuary view and balcony with its own Jacuzzi.

The Master Suite, a separate ocean-

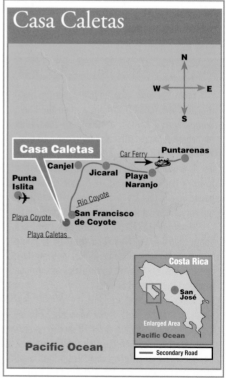

Roy Arguedas Arias | Tico Times

The exterior of the Master Suite, which has a private Jacuzzi with a view.

view villa, has two bedrooms, king-size beds, a comfortable living room and a fully equipped kitchen, plus a Jacuzzi and private terrace with a small pool.

Hotel manager Luis Alfaro also manages the cattle ranch. He is from the area, as are the friendly hotel employees, who give excellent service and will make your stay a memorable experience.

"Mr. Feichtinger is totally committed to using only local staff and is dedicated to the betterment of the community," Alfaro said.

A good source of information about the area, Alfaro recommends various tours. You can go horseback riding through cattle pastures, Jet Ski, fish, kayak or take a leisurely boat ride through the mangroves, where the trees, known for their copious development of interlacing, aboveground roots, make for an amazing sight. The river and estuary are frequented by many waterbirds, including herons, kingfishers and sandpipers.

An absolute must-do is to rent one of the hotel's golf carts – there isn't a golf course in sight – and take the jungle trail to Playa Coyote, the nearest beach and a surfer's paradise.

You can hike along the vast expanse of sand or take a dip in the shallow ocean at low tide. Beware of stingrays! They hang out in shallow water, so shuffle your feet and watch your step.

The totally deserted Playa Caletas, with its strange formation of sandstone running along the shore, is a wonderful place to watch the sunset, as is the hotel's *mirador*.

Casa Caletas also offers wedding packages.

Getting There, Rates, Info

From San José, take the Inter-American Highway to Puntarenas (two hours), then the Playa Naranjo Ferry (one-hour crossing). Call 2661-1069 for departure times, scheduled for 8 a.m., 10 a.m., 2:30 p.m. and 7:30 p.m. From Playa Naranjo, follow signs to Jicaral (one hour) and then the dirt road to San Francisco de Coyote, (1.5 hours). The signposted hotel is four km. south of town. Driving times can vary according to road and weather conditions.

Nature Air (2299-6000, **natureair.com**) and Sansa (2290-4100, **flysansa.com**) fly to Punta Islita from the Tobías Bolaños Airport in the western San José district of Pavas. Casa Caletas will arrange transport from airport to hotel.

Rates, inc. tax and breakfast, are $206 for double deluxe rooms; $249 Junior Suite and $746 for the Master Suite. Children under 10 sharing parent's room, free. For low-season, deduct $20. For info: 2655-1271, **casacaletas.com**. From the United States and Canada, call 1-800-850-4592 toll-free.

The Hideaway Hotel Lives Up to Its Name on Nicoya Peninsula

Sámara's Hideaway Hotel surrounds a gracious pool.

Photos by
Holly K. Soneland

By Holly K. Sonneland

Rosy Ríos and her husband, Doug Ancel, took the type of care naming their hotel that other people would take naming their children. They knew they wanted to create a retreat boutique hotel, but took a year to find a name that embodied that idea, until a friend finally suggested The Hideaway Hotel. The fit was "perfect," Ríos says.

The U.S. couple from Reno, Nevada, opened the Hideaway amid a quiet jungle between the Pacific beaches of Sámara and Carrillo, on the Nicoya Peninsula. They selected the area for its seclusion and relative ease of accessibility. While other, more remote places in Costa Rica are surely worth a more involved journey to get there,

Ríos says, "Not everybody's up for that type of adventure."

Moreover, Ríos appreciates Sámara's balance of offering services to tourists while not being overcome by the tourism industry.

"It's a good balance, without too many franchises," Ríos says. "It's more peaceful here."

And if there were a one-word mission statement for The Hideaway Hotel, it would be "peace."

The hotel's 12 suites are arranged in two pinwheel-shape buildings with rooms that open to the outside, the only shared walls between rooms being the bathrooms. Couples, Ríos says, usually elect the more secluded upper rooms that face the overhanging jungle trees, while families opt for the rooms that open onto the pool to provide kids with the most direct trajectory for their aquatic cannonballs.

Each room also has its own patio that often looks out on the surrounding jungle. To be able to enjoy the verdant foliage, Ríos says, is key to the hotel's concept.

"Greenery, palm trees – it's what you come to the tropics for."

The area's fauna is not to be outdone by the flora. Roaring howler monkeys serve as an arboreal version of roosters, though this reviewer slept blissfully oblivious to such a chorus until hotel staff informed her of it the next day.

Iguanas, geckos, raccoon-like coatis and hummingbirds roam uninhibited. And be sure to note the curious oversize, tree dwelling red, purple and black crabs along the road toward Playa Carrillo.

Overall, Ríos says guests appreciate the hotel's "style and privacy, and proximity to the beach."

And not just one beach, but two. The Hideaway is perhaps a 100-meter walk to Playa Sámara, dotted with small restaurants with a tucked-away cove at its southern most end. A rocky island just offshore breaks most of the waves, making calm waters for swimmers. Snorkeling and kayaks are available right on the beach, and surfing is only a 15-minute walk away, though companies will come pick you up.

Canopy, sportfishing, bird-watching, horseback riding and turtle tours are all nearby, in addition to a language school. And if the idea of performing any activity on a beach vacation strikes you as antithetical, the hotel is a five-minute walk from tranquil Playa Carrillo farther south.

Everything about Hideaway's style is deliberate and often custom. Ríos says they specifically sought out a more modern style and had many things – from the bed spread patterns to the wrought-iron deck chairs with rounded backs – custom-made for the hotel. The spacious rooms also have granite countertops, extra large pillows and reading areas complete with arguably the most comfy oversize reading chairs (two per room) in the country.

The Hideaway is designed with clear environmental consciousness in mind. Besides small conservation moves such as biodegradable soaps and numerous hooks

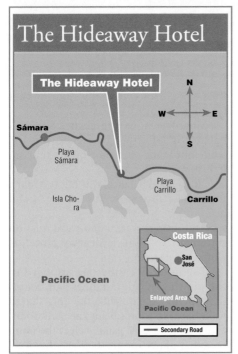

Roy Arguedas Arias | Tico Times

Rooms are light and spacious at the Hideaway Hotel.

to let clean towels dry on their own, the hotel runs on its own wastewater treatment system. While developers seemed confused when Ríos and Ancel didn't want to just route the property's waste straight into the ocean, the couple insisted on a system that was sustainable, Ríos says. The retained water, 98.5 percent pure, is used for irrigation and is key during the dry season.

Long-term, Ríos would like to convert to solar power and a carbon-neutral operation status in a move "for something responsible," because, she says, there are "not infinite resources in any place."

The hotel also boasts free WiFi and cable TV.

The hotel has a small English-language lending library and a slew of board and card games, and a line of signature cock-tails – especially ones inspired by the mangos in the hotel's backyard .

"My concepts always center around desserts," Ríos says. "And desserts will always include chocolate."

Maybe "chocolate" could be incorporated along with "peace" into The Hideaway's mission statement.

Getting There, Rates, Info

The Hideaway Hotel is at the south end of Playa Sámara on the road between Sámara and Carrillo. From San José, take the Inter-American Highway to the Puente de Amistad (Tempisque). Follow signs to Nicoya. From Nicoya follow signs south to Sámara, then south to Carrillo. The hotel is 750 meters after Villas Playa Samara. Look for hotel sign. Buses: Tracopa- Alfaro, 150 meters northwest of the Coca-Cola terminal, Ca. 14, Av.3/5 (2222-2666, five to six hours). SANSA offers flights between San José and the Sámara/Carrillo airstrip (flysansa.com, 2290-4100, 50 minutes).

Rates, inc. tax and breakfast, are $96-164. All are for single or double occupancy with $20 per extra person. Kids under 5, free. Group/corporate discounts available. All rooms sleep up to four in either two queen or one king and one full pullout bed, and are equipped with air conditioning, minifridges, irons and ironing boards. Two rooms are wheelchair-accessible. For info: 2656-1145, **info@thehideawayplayasa mara.com** or **thehideawayplayasamara.com**

The JW Marriott Guanacaste Resort & Spa on the northern Pacific coast boasts Central America's largest swimming pool.

Photos Courtesy of JW Marriott

Luxury to New Heights

By Ellen Zoe Golden

Offering world-class luxury from top to bottom, the JW Marriott Resort boasts the distinction of being the only one in Central America, and only the 40th in the world.

From the minute you drive into the colonial-style entrance within Hacienda Pinilla, just south of Tamarindo in the northwestern Guanacaste province, you feel well served by the highly trained staff of 300. Check-in takes place at one-on-one desks. We had to laugh after our bellman told us we wouldn't have much of an ocean view, only to discover a full-on seaside perch, albeit set back in the resort.

Our room, like the entire hotel, featured high-quality lavish comfort, with polished woodwork, down comforters on the king-size bed, computerized temperature controls, minibar, WiFi and CD player. In the bathroom, fine bath products accompanied the deep tub with spray jets in view of the flat-screen TV (with attachments for computer and video games).

However, given the resort's onsite attractions, there's not much call to spend time in your room, what with the beach, five food and beverage outlets, an opulent spa, fitness facility, 2,300-square-meter pool – the largest in Central America – and Hacienda Pinilla's golf facilities, in addition to tours.

During the day, guests can partake of the immense pool. Non-guests may obtain a pool day pass for $40, which can be used toward food and beverage. Just off the pool

Guest rooms, some oceanfront, offer lavish comfort, views.

is Playa Mansita, home to Wahoo Water Sports, which rents kayaks, boogie boards, surfboards, snorkeling equipment and bicycles, in addition to arranging surf lessons: $15 a day for a boogie board, $20 for a bicycle and $50 per person for groups of up to four people for surf lessons.

The spa – also the largest in Central America – offers lavish pampering. Massages cost $110 to $150, facials run from $125 to $165 and body treatments range from $60 to $165. Open-air treatment rooms are available for wraps, scrubs and massages with gorgeous views. (Indoor treatment rooms also exist for the less nature-inclined.)

Among options is the spa's signature massage, the Aromatherapy Raindrop Treatment, in which eight drops of essential oils are placed along the spine and Tibetan reflexology is then applied.

Guests are afforded a private outdoor bathing, shower, sauna, steam and rest area. The spa also has hair salon and waxing services, and a daily Sunset Ritual, 5-6 p.m., featuring music, two-for-one champagne, mojitos and fruit.

For those who can't leave work behind, the resort offers a wonderful way to mix business and pleasure with its five meeting rooms. Event managers ensure meetings go smoothly from beginning to end, and services include the computer, printer and Internet facilities in addition to secretarial, translation, audiovisual, and labor services.

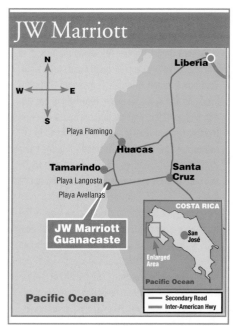

Roy Arguedas Arias | Tico Times

The spa offers both open-air and indoor rooms for an array of treatments.

According to Carlos Diago, resort manager, it's clear the region is well served by this world-class resort.

"From the guest satisfaction survey, we are already No. 10 out of all the JW Marriotts in the world," Diago said. "That is pretty great."

Getting There, Rates, Info

From Daniel Oduber International Airport in Liberia, drive two km. to main road, turn right. Continue through Guardia, Comunidad, Palmira, Filadelfia and Belén. At Belén, turn right at gas station and continue, passing through Santa Ana and Huacas. Once in Huacas, turn left and head to Villarreal. Follow signs for Hacienda Pinilla. Enter Hacienda Pinilla and guard will direct you to JW Marriott. Drive is approximately 50 km. (an hour). Rates, inc. tax: $270 for deluxe room with garden view, $327 for deluxe room with ocean view, $384 for deluxe oceanfront room, $496 for one-bedroom suite with garden view, $609 for suite with ocean view, $722 for a oceanfront suite and $1,852 for presidential suite. For info: 2681-2000 or 1-888-236-2427 toll-free from the United States, or **marriott.com/hotels/travel/sjojwjw-marriott-guanacaste-resort-and-spa.**

Culinary Adventure Awaits Resort Guests

By Vanessa I. Garnica

"A kitchen is not a democracy," says JW Marriott Guanacaste Resort & Spa Executive Chef Eric Sala, who describes himself as a boss with a "super cool" attitude.

The French-born chef's stamp is present on every mouthwatering dish. Four different restaurants range from the Asian-fusion Tamarine and the elegant Sabanero Steakhouse to the light, fresh cuisine of the Mediterranean-style Azul Pool Grill and Mansita Restaurant's gourmet breakfast extravaganzas.

The grill is always firing at Sabanero steakhouse.

The Azul Pool Grill (11 a.m. to 9:30 p.m.), overlooks Playa Mansita and the giant infinity pool, where guests can enjoy six different types of ceviche. The executive chef 's version of corvina ceviche ($14) is particularly refreshing. The fish is marinated in fresh lemon juice and coconut milk, along with jalapeño, sweet pepper, red onion and cilantro, for at least four hours and is served on a coconut shell with a mango slice on top. Enjoying this

Mansita Restaurant serves breakfast extravaganzas, both buffet and à la carte.

dish on the terrace while looking at the ocean and listening to live bossa nova is simply priceless.

If you're craving a good steak, head for Sabanero (5:30-10 p.m.), where a 14-ounce New York strip costs less than $20. This steakhouse also offers treats such as crème brûlée a la tica ($7), a Costa Rican take on the popular French dessert with coffee as its secret ingredient.

Mansita Restaurant serves breakfast (6-11 a.m. and lunch, noon-3 p.m.), from omelets custom-made by an onsite chef to homemade breads, croissants and bagels, in addition to meats, including prosciutto, salami and chorizo. Cereals, fruits and fresh juices are also on offer. A la carte prices range from $4.50 for fried eggs to $14.50 for a full North American breakfast. (Breakfast is included in some rate packages.) During high season, also open from 6:30-10:30 p.m.

Perhaps the most alluring restaurant is Tamarine (5:30-10 p.m), which combines Thai and Japanese cuisine with an immensely appealing setting. While listening to traditional Indian or Japanese music, guests can enjoy appetizers such as the Thai chicken salad, made with snow peas, shredded carrots, chopped napa cabbage and bean sprouts and topped with a peanut-ginger dressing and tasty wonton crisps ($10.50), or the popular tempura shrimp, served with an orange salsa and a coconut reduction ($18). Main dishes include chicken and peanut panang curry ($16) and spicy pork loin and zucchini, combining zesty red curry with coconut cream and soy sauce ($16).

Nonguests are encouraged to reserve (2681-2000) for any of the restaurants. All prices are subject to change, depending on market prices.

View of L'acqua Viva's suites from the reception area.

Photos by Lindy Drew

Impressive Architecture, Relaxed Ambience

By Elizabeth Goodwin

Arriving at L'acqua Viva Resort in the Pacific beach community of Nosara, on the Nicoya Peninsula, is a little like stumbling into the world of "The Swiss Family Robinson," in which a shipwrecked family dwells in an elaborate tree house in the East Indies – except there's nothing rustic about the luxurious facilities here.

The hotel is divided into many tree house-like units, each surrounded by dense jungle vegetation that blends into the thatched roofs and dark red exteriors. Large, natural saltwater pools glimmer in front of the grand reception and restaurant area, which is almost intimidating with its vaulted ceilings and austere dark wood.

The architecture of the complex will not fail to impress, with the rooms and outdoor area contributing to the overall feeling of abounding space drifting into nature.

The hotel's manager, Randall Cortés, says the architecture is inspired by the Balinese style and also represents a blend of textures. "The idea is a combination of textures, soft and hard," he says. "We also strive for harmony with nature. The hotel is located in respect to the trees, not the other way around."

L'acqua Viva's eco-friendly efforts include cutting down as few trees as possible, treating its own wastewater, using biodegradable cleaning agents, and recycling. The hotel has planted fruit trees to attract wildlife and recently completed a community reforestation project with the local Santa Marta School and the National University (UNA).

The suites are decorated with dark and light wood. The stairs are covered in bamboo, but the beds and other furniture tend to be made of richer, darker wood. Mixed discreetly in the hotel's decor are a few expensive older pieces, such as the computer table in the reception area dating back to 17th-century Italy.

Deck chairs overlook the hotel's natural saltwater pools.

Bottom floor of one of the suites is equipped with flat-screen TV and two comfortable daybeds.

Each two-story unit has balconies on both floors that look out onto the expansive courtyard. Though the units are relatively close to each other, the trees add a feeling of privacy, insulating the suites from each other.

At night, each suite lights up with glowing outdoor lanterns. The resort opened in 2008 and the staff is continually carrying out maintenance on the facilities, as well as making small additions to the hotel's gardens, lighting and decks.

Because the hotel is surrounded by the dirt road leading to Playa Guiones, a popular surf beach about two km. away, hotel employees wage a constant battle against the dust kicked up by car wheels. During afternoon hours, when guests are at the area's beautiful beaches, hotel employees fiercely wield brooms and hoses, ridding the balconies, rooms and sidewalks of dust.

Cortés says the hotel strives to provide friendly service that makes guests feel comfortable, not intruded upon. The employees generally stay out of guests'

way, and seem to go about their work almost silently.

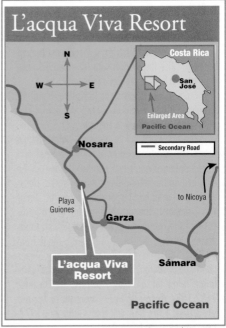

L'acqua Viva Resort

Costa Rica

San José

Enlarged Area

Pacific Ocean

N

W — E

S

Secondary Road

Nosara

to Nicoya

Playa Guiones

Garza

L'acqua Viva Resort

Sámara

Pacific Ocean

Roy Arguedas Arias | Tico Times

The open-air central reception area contains a restaurant and a bar within its vast space. The main restaurant, where a complimentary breakfast of fruit, toast and yogurt is offered every morning, is minimally decorated. Soft music, sometimes oldies, plays as diners enjoy reasonably priced meals. The bar, on the opposite side of the building, plays trendier, louder music. Alcoholic beverages are also offered in the suites' minibars, but at a

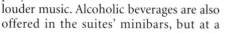

markup; a Corona beer costs $5, not including tax.

For sportfishing enthusiasts, the hotel has its own boat, which guests can rent with a guide for a day out on the waters surrounding the Nicoya Peninsula. A fully equipped spa offers massages ($80 and up) and other treatments for guests wanting a break from the beach.

The resort is a good place for weddings, as individual families can stay in their own units, with larger gatherings taking place in the restaurant or spacious deck and pool area.

Note: It's important for guests to have a car or at least a bicycle. Playa Guiones is far enough away to be a bit of an inconvenient walk. That said, L'acqua Viva's relaxed and elegant ambience makes for an ideal place from which to launch an exploration of the Nicoya Peninsula.

Getting There, Rates, Info

It's best to take a car to manage the unpaved roads and long distances between beaches around Nosara.

From San José, take the Inter-American Highway west to Puntarenas. The road turns north close to Puntarenas.

Follow the signs to Liberia and take the turn for the Puente de la Amistad (Tempisque). Once you reach the town of Nicoya, head west toward Sámara. Take the turnoff onto an unpaved road right after a big gas station on the left.

From there, follow signs to Nosara, about 45 minutes. L'acqua Viva is about two km. before Playa Guiones on the road to Sámara.

The hotel offers five types of rooms: deluxe rooms with one king bed or two queens; suites with a ground-floor living room with two daybeds and a king bed on the second floor; master suites, closer to the pool area and larger than the suites; junior villas, similar to the master suites but with a kitchen; and the commodious presidential villa. Rates during high season, Dec. 1 to April 30, range from $232 to $831, inc. tax. Rates are slightly higher during peak season, Dec. 20 to Jan. 3, and slightly lower in low season, May 1 to Nov. 30. For info: 2682-1087, **info@lacquaviva.com** or **lacquaviva.com**. From USA, toll-free 1-888-273-1977; from Canada,1-877-216-0181.

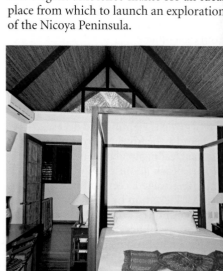

The pool area offers ocean and sunset views.

Photos Courtesy of Nature Lodge Finca Los Caballos

Horsing Around at Los Caballos

By Vicky Longland

The erstwhile fishing community of Montezuma, on the southern tip of the Nicoya Peninsula, is reached by a steep, coiled snake of a road from Cóbano. It, in turn, sits rather smugly, if dustily, at the upland crossroads linking several beach communities and the Cabo Blanco Absolute Nature Reserve at the peninsula's tip. From Cóbano, the airstrip at Tambor and ferry service at Paquera are an easy drive.

Ah, Montezuma! This beachside town positively hums with cool, bohemian vibes and youth. Dreads are the coiffure du jour, and the street boutiques proffer batiks, beads, reggae and organic ice cream.

On a recent visit, I was part of a Birding Club of Costa Rica's outing. Apart from the young set doing its thing, and some awesome waterfalls, the area is famed for its birds and fabulous beaches backed by dense forest. But as our group's bus ground

its gears down the drop into the cramped main street, where the beach sand sweeps into the shore-side stores, it seemed we upped the average age of the population by a decade at least.

Don't be put off, though. It's a friendly, vibrant place, and a cone of organic ginger and coconut ice cream is almost worth a visit in itself. The community boasts commendable eateries, especially for seafood lovers, and many places to stay, from cold-water cabins to high-end luxury.

Our choice was Nature Lodge Finca Los Caballos, four km. south of Cóbano, where the tarmac road turns to gravel, but stops short of the nail-biting drop into Montezuma. Its clever placing means guests are near the bustle of town, yet cocooned in lush, quiet serenity.

The ocean glistens invitingly over the trees to remind you it's not so far away, and at about 200 meters elevation, breezes keep temperatures comfortable. The arrival of 16 binocular-toting birders with a tenden-

enjoying a huge private deck and additional outside shower.

All rooms are tastefully decorated with warm coral-stone floors in the grotto-like bathrooms, wood finishes, fridge and stone-based, snake-neck bedside lights that invite lots of twisting to achieve the best light mood. And – thank you – the connecting walls are thick enough to avoid eavesdropping on neighbors' conversations.

cy to wander off did not faze lodge owner Christian Klein, who, along with hotel mutts Yassko and Roxie, greeted us warmly and had us quickly installed in the 12 jungle- or garden-view units.

These are split into three standard garden-view rooms near reception, five jungle-view rooms with private terrace, and four superior Pacific suites, the lower two

With so much surrounding vegetation, it would be easy to feel closed in. The open restaurant and social area solve that, however, along with a spacious teak deck overlooking the valley, perfect for alfresco dining and armchair birding, while the view from the small, free-form pool stretches down toward the Pacific and resplendent sunsets.

The wellness spa, in a nearby wooden house, offers manicures, pedicures, massages etc., ranging from $20-$70.

The original raison d'être of Finca Los Caballos (Horse Ranch) lies in its name. The priority here used to be the stables, a venture started by champion horsewoman Barbara McGregor of Canada, who built a reputation for quality mounts and tours to suit all levels. Her death left Finca Los Caballos up for sale, and it was taken on by German-born Christian Klein.

Finca Los Caballos

Paquera

Pochote

Curú

Tambor

Gulf of Nicoya

Cóbano

Montezuma

Finca Los Caballos

Costa Rica

San José

Enlarged Area

Pacific Ocean

Pacific Ocean

N

W ← → E

S

— Secondary Road

Roy Arguedas Arias | Tico Times

Klein, 47, left Munich and a career in social work with an idea to open a quality boutique hotel. Finca Los Caballos had the potential he sought, though he freely admits he knew little then about horses or equestrian tours.

With a keen eye for detail and quality, Klein completely refurbished the rooms and kitchen, added a spa, and in three years has become quite an expert in things equine.

"I rely on my stable hand," Klein acknowledges, "and the vet comes in regularly, and we have some of the best horses in the area. My tours are not the cheapest, but our mounts are well cared for and we can cater to all levels of experience."

Klein's commitment can be seen in the new stable block – which, by the way, enjoys even better views than the hotel – for eight horses. The tack is immaculate, and both horse and rider benefit from the lightweight, synthetic Western trail saddles.

Klein is also quietly creating environmentally friendly and sustainable infrastructure. The newly completed black-water treatment plant is a three-chamber filter system that produces water clean enough to irrigate the gardens or return to the river.

No air conditioning in the rooms. "It's not what I'm trying to promote here," Klein says. "It's unnatural, and most of the time, you don't need it here."

Fresh air and exercise make appetites keen, and the kitchen at Finca Los Caballos does not disappoint. Buffet breakfasts are served on an antique Indian door-turned-table with fruit, juice, fruit, cheese and home-baked bread, along with a special that might be typical *gallo pinto* or sinful chocolate sauce-draped pancakes. Because most guests are out during the day, the lunch menu is small, but, as with dinner choices, the emphasis is on what's fresh.

Being a sizeable group, we were asked the previous day to choose from options for lunch and dinner. The consensus was a definite thumbs up for the seafood rice, marlin *en papillote* with olives and spices, and the chicken in orange sauce.

Non-guests should reserve for meals. The service and atmosphere here are relaxed and relaxing. You can hike, bird and ride all you want; many don't venture farther than the poolside deck or a ramble through the grounds. It may be warm here, but it's a great place to chill out.

Getting There, Rates, Info

Montezuma can be reached via car/bus and ferry from the Pacific port city of Puntarenas to Paquera (Naviera Tambor, 2661-2084, or Ferry Peninsular, 2641-0515, foot passenger $1, car $11, one-way). Buses meet the ferry in Paquera for Cóbano and Montezuma ($2), or daily direct bus service from San José (Transportes Rodríguez, 2642-0219, $10 inc. ferry). By air, fly into Tambor with Nature Air (2299-6000) or Sansa (2223-4179); the 30-minute flight costs about $75 one-way. The lodge can arrange a taxi for about $30 one-way for the 20-km. drive. Access to Montezuma from Finca Los Caballos is a 40-minute walk, a flexibly timetabled local bus, or taxi arranged through the lodge.

Rates for double occupancy range from $100 for a standard room to $160 for a superior Pacific suite, inc. tax and breakfast. Horseback tours: $20 per hour. For info: 2642-0124, **naturelc@racsa.co.cr**, or **naturelodge.net**.

Star Mountain's pool area, with rooms tucked into the forest behind.

Photos by Vicky Longland

Star Mountain Lodge: A Stellar Place on the Southern Nicoya Peninsula

By Vicky Longland

Not quite everything is sand, surf and sun in the southern Nicoya Peninsula town of Malpaís. The main attractions inevitably focus on the area's enticing waves and wild beaches, but a couple of km. up a winding dirt road that struggles up and over to the peninsula's lee-side coast, Star Mountain Lodge quietly awaits, ready to share its pervasive serenity and woodland calm.

The lodge lies in a 90-hectare former farm, but little evidence remains of the pastures as secondary forest has flourished since it was turned into a small hotel several years ago. In fact, the property is something of a wildlife haven; bordered by two rivers, it stays green throughout dry season and is an oasis for the howler and white-faced monkeys, coatis and sloths that forage in the lush foliage. The mammal and bird list posted on the lodge's Web site should be inducement enough for wildlife observers.

Andrew Rhee, 43, took over Star Mountain four years ago. His quiet, equable hospitality seems in plain contrast to a frenetic "former life" in the United States. The former lawyer, financier and real estate broker decided to quit the rat race and bought Star Mountain Lodge on first sight while in Costa Rica on a scouting trip.

The peaceful location well suits Rhee's low-key approach to the hotel business. He has little interest in the flamboyance of some resorts popping up around Malpaís and neighboring Santa Teresa, but wants visitors to feel they can settle right in and leave day-job worries far behind.

"Star Mountain is best viewed as a retreat from the irritations of the real world," Rhee says. Without being intrusive, he shares the breakfast buffet with guests so as to offer suggestions on what to do and places to explore.

"My greatest satisfaction is seeing their big smiles as they joyfully recount their day's experiences," he says. "It seems to me that modern culture and its efficiencies have left people out of touch with nature and the more basic and real rhythms of the earth. We hope to re-expose our guests to those grounding and harmonic forces."

The laid-back focus does not imply lack of attention, however, and requests or queries are handled by staff with friendly efficiency and a genuine desire to help.

A row of four spacious rooms with attractive, ranch-style double doors and windows with wood-slat shutters leads to an ample front terrace overlooking the forest and freeform pool and Jacuzzi below. All rooms have queen beds – two have extra singles – and come with ceiling fans, refrigerator stocked with water and beer, and a roomy bathroom with plenty of hanging space and shelves for clothes.

Attractive murals brighten the walls, and I rather liked the nifty bamboo-ladder towel rack that can be moved around to be close at hand to either shower or sink. A six-person bungalow is also available, again with fridge and a sitting room that converts to sleeping quarters. In addition are fans or air conditioning, though the high ceilings keep the interior pleasantly cool. Because of its small size, Star Mountain is ideal for group bookings or several families wanting to reserve the entire place. The social area has a long, solid-wood, refectory-style dining table next to a large kitchen, and an enormous built-in barbecue dominates one wall, just calling for fish and steaks to be thrown onto the grill.

The built-in grill by the common area calls out for fish or steaks to be thrown onto it.

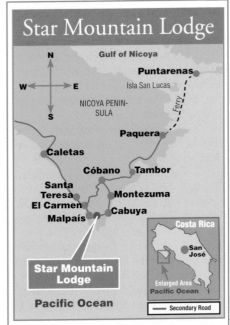

Star Mountain Lodge

Gulf of Nicoya

Puntarenas
Isla San Lucas

NICOYA PENIN-
SULA

Paquera

Caletas

Cóbano   Tambor

Santa
Teresa
El Carmen   Montezuma
Malpaís   Cabuya

Star Mountain
Lodge

Pacific Ocean

Costa Rica

San
José

Enlarged Area
Pacific Ocean

— Secondary Road

Roy Arguedas Arias | Tico Times

At left, owner Andrew Rhee. Above, one of the hotel's four spacious guest rooms.

Getting There, Rates, Info

By car, take the Inter-American Highway west from San José to Puntarenas. Then take a ferry across the Gulf of Nicoya to Paquera. Naviera Tambor (2661-2084) makes the trip at 5, 8 and 11 a.m. and 1, 4 and 8 p.m., returning to Puntarenas from Paquera at the same times. From Paquera, travel through Tambor and Cóbano toward Malpaís. Turn left at the Malpaís/Santa Teresa intersection at El Carmen. Go three km. and turn left at Mary's Restaurant onto the jungle road to Cabuya. Two km. and two river crossings later, Star Mountain Lodge is on the left.

By plane, both Nature Air and Sansa fly into Tambor, from where you can arrange a taxi or hotel pickup.

A direct bus from San José (Transportes Rodríguez, 2642-0740) leaves the Coca-Cola terminal at 7:30 a.m. or 2:30 p.m. Rates are $50 double, $65 triple or $150 for a six-person bungalow. Rental of the entire hotel is $600 (16 guests max.), inc. maid service. Prices for Christmas and New Year's are double, but otherwise no rate variation between high and low season. Freelance chefs: Demian Geneau, 8821-7546; Torsten Radtke, 8338-7099; or James Kelly, 8346-9774. For info: 2640-0101, **armountaineco.com.**

For now, only breakfast is offered and it's a feast of home-baked breads, fruits, juice and cooked dishes to order. Rhee stresses, however, that his *cocina* (kitchen) is your cocina, and guests are welcome to bring in supplies and use the lodge as a self-catering facility.

If that seems a bit too much when seeking time out from the domestic routine, the inspiring Restaurant Mary's, two km. down the road at the turnoff, offers dinner, or one of the area's excellent freelance chefs can come in to cater with a menu of your choice.

The jungle trails traversing Star Mountain's property make for good hiking, birding and horseback riding. Rhee keeps a stable of six amiable mounts, and guided riding tours are $30 per person.

Other popular excursions popular are to the new Rainsong Wildlife Sanctuary (**rainsongsanctuary.com**) and the Cabo Blanco National Park in Cabuya. The hotel will help set up trips and provide transport.

But often it's enough to soak in the pool or Jacuzzi, watch the monkeys, or play one of the many board games found in the lounge area. And if you need a fix of shore time, the sand and the waves are just a stone's throw away.

All of which add up to a pretty star sort of place.

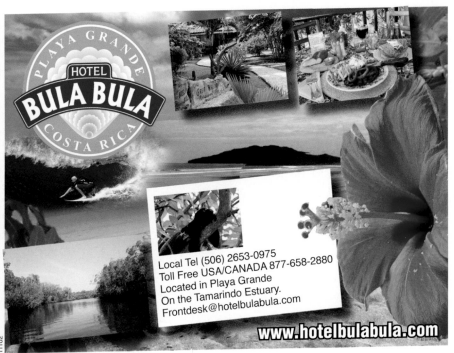

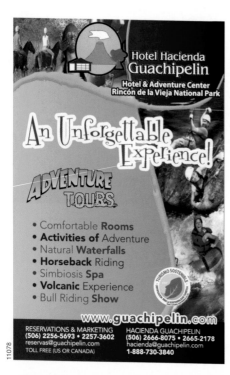

In safe coves, there's nothing more delicious than the warm water of the Pacific.

Photo by Ronald Reyes

Central Pacific

Photo by Ronald Reyes

An ATV Fun Park.

Photos by Chrissie Long

Adventure Is the Draw at Miramar Resort

By Chrissie Long

Rain splashed on our faces, almost blinding us as we crossed over waterfalls and cleared trees at 50 feet in the air. The feeling was akin to sticking one's head out of a car window in the middle of a rainstorm. Except, here, our whole bodies were immersed. Our clothes clung to our bodies, every last thread soaked. But all of us were still smiling.

We had just passed over 10 waterfalls, gliding on a wire from one platform to the next. Some of the falls we could reach down and touch with our fingers, and others we paused over, suspended in the air, as the water crashed and swirled below our feet. The rain waited until we were at the 23rd of 25 platforms. But, when it came, it added a whole new element.

"This has been incredible, rain and all," said a man harnessed to a tree next to me, who was touring the country with a singles group. "By far, the coolest thing we have

done," said a woman on the same tour.

The canopy experience is just one facet of the adventure hotel Barbara and Dietmar Maier began stitching together – almost by accident – 15 years ago. The couple came from Germany with plans to retire in the hills above Miramar, near the Central Pacific port city of Puntarenas. As they were putting up the frame of their new home on an undeveloped lot about 15 minutes from town, people stopped by and asked for a room. The Maiers looked at each other and thought, why not? So they added a handful of guest rooms to their new home.

As horse lovers, they began accumulating a stable of Andalusians and Arabians and offering tours to their guests. They added canopy lines over their property, and a climbing wall. And, step by step, Adventure Park & Hotel Vista Golfo took shape.

"This was not what I had in mind when I came here," said Barbara, who had envisioned a relaxing retirement, surrounded by the patchwork of farms and pockets of trees that cover the enveloping valley. "But I couldn't be happier."

Watching the guests come in, drenched from the rain with smiles on their faces, she added, "It gives me a sense of satisfaction." Like the hotel, the 11-waterfall canopy tour came about at the suggestion of someone else.

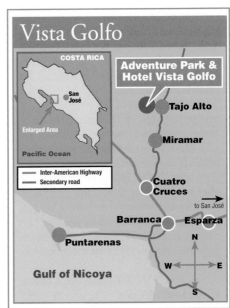

Close to eight years ago, Dietmar took a few friends on a hike to a series of waterfalls that cascaded down the mountainside less than a mile from the Maiers' home. His friend turned to him and said, "Dietmar, you should really take advantage of this. It's beautiful."

That was the beginning of the 25-platform canopy tour that now draws large groups from cruise ships, and claims to be the only canopy experience in the country that passes over waterfalls.

The hotel also has a 33-element ropes course, in the highest branches of a nearby grove. A relatively new concept in Costa Rica, the course combines rope swings, knotted ladders and suspended beams, which are intended to encourage teamwork, risk-taking and trust. The Maiers hope to attract businesses looking for day-long, team-building retreats.

Other activities include a night canopy tour, an ATV Fun Park, horseback riding and cloud forest tours. The hotel itself overlooks the valley, with distant views of the Gulf of Nicoya. The rooms are simple but clean and comfortable.

Barbara acknowledges it's not the hotel amenities that draw people here.

"We are a mountain hotel. We aren't a luxury hotel," she said, adding that the rooms and the restaurant simply provide guests an accessible way to take advantage of the tours. Offering a slew of package deals, the Maiers encourage guests to try as many of the activities as possible in a two- to three-day stay.

"We live on the edge of the world," Barbara said. "Two weeks doesn't make sense here, but three days? Yes."

Depending on which activities a guest selects from the menu of options, those three days could be exhausting. Guests may not leave Adventure Park & Hotel Vista Golfo feeling refreshed or rested, but they can carry away the satisfaction of having done something thrilling, in addition to some pretty special memories.

A canopy tour over waterfalls and horseback riding are among the options at Adventure Park & Hotel Vista Golfo.

Remember the hotel's advice to incoming guests: "Make sure you bring bug repellent, comfortable clothes, closed-toe shoes and an eagerness to experience activities unique to the country."

Getting There, Rates, Info

From San José, take the Inter-American Highway west toward Puntarenas. At the Barranca intersection, before Puntarenas, turn right toward Miramar. Drive 12 km. up into the mountains; Adventure Park & Hotel Vista Golfo will be on the left. The trip takes about two hours.

Rooms cost between $74 and $179 with an average 10 percent off for students, and can be combined with any of the tours for a discounted price. Depending on room category, amenities may include TV, minibar, WiFi, coffeemaker, fridge and ocean views. The Gold Package (one of three available) includes a room, three-course dinner, continental breakfast and any of the tours for $122 per person, double occupancy, and up. Individual tours range in price from $45 for a horseback tour or high-ropes course to $89 for the canopy tour over 11 waterfalls.

For info: 2639-8303 or 8382-3312, **adventureparkcostarica.com**

Sand, Sea, Sustainability

Arenas del Mar's buildings disappear into forested hillside.

Photos by
Dorothy MacKinnon

By Dorothy McKinnon

What you don't see is what you get at Arenas del Mar Beach and Nature Resort, a new eco-luxury hotel in Manuel Antonio, on the central Pacific coast. No cars. No crowds. No clutter. In fact, you can barely see the hotel's seven sage-and-beige buildings, melded into a forested hillside that slopes down to two glorious beaches.

How can a 38-room luxury hotel almost disappear into 12 acres of beach and forest? It took a lot of planning by masterminds Teri and Glenn Jampol, owners of award-winning Finca Rosa Blanca in Heredia.

As president of the National Ecotourism Chamber (CANAECO), Glenn has some pretty strong eco ideals. Designing this hotel was a chance to prove that luxurious can also be sustainable.

"Our goal was to create a five-star luxury resort that is also a five-leaf sustainable hotel," Teri says.

Many of the resort's eco-friendly features are invisible, but from the moment you arrive, you can feel a natural difference. The open-air welcome pavilion, at the bottom of a precipitous concrete road, is as far as any motorized vehicle goes. You then hop aboard an electric cart and wend your way up through a forest bustling with birdsong and backlit by slanting rays of sunshine.

You arrive at an elegant, open-air lobby with a soaring thatched roof punctuated by orange parasols. But your eye is immediately drawn to the large outdoor deck and small pool, and beyond that to the panorama of sparkling ocean and the sandy stretch of Playa Espadilla, ending at

Manuel Antonio's landmark Cathedral Point. From here you travel on foot or by electric cart along labyrinthine paths, edged with greenery, stone walls and split-rail fencing, to your room or suite.

At first it's hard to see the buildings for the trees, and the initial effect of the architecture is a little underwhelming. But soon you realize that's the whole point here: The buildings are camouflaged to blend in. The landscaping is natural, with the focus on native plants. The real beauty of this conserved, secondary-forest habitat is that so much wildlife feels at home here.

Because the hotel is on a slope, you are often actually at bird's-eye level, looking straight into upper branches. You can get close-up views of such middle-canopy denizens as yellow-crowned euphonias and red-legged honeycreepers, among many others.

In the surrounding forest, you'll also get your fill of the ubiquitous white-faced capuchin monkeys scrambling among branches. There are less common sightings as well.

Relaxing by the upper swimming pool, I watched a coati emerge from the forest, dive in and dog-paddle diagonally across the pool, climb out and make a beeline into the forest on the other side. I didn't even know coatis could swim.

The hotel's other precious natural resource is direct beach access, rare in Manuel Antonio. The constant sound of the sea is a reminder that you are just steps – albeit steep ones – from two glorious Blue Flag beaches.

A winding concrete path descends to Playa Espadilla, a long stretch of flat beach, perfect for walking, running, people-watching and swimming. A 15-minute walk along the beach delivers you to the entrance of Manuel Antonio National Park.

Even more secluded, separated from Playa Espadilla by a rocky headland, is Playa Playitas, also known as Playa Dulce Vida. Life is sweet here, indeed: This is the castaway-island beach of your dreams, fringed with beach almond trees, at the doorstep of the hotel's lower-level guest rooms.

Arenas del Mar tops the charts on the ecofriendly scale, with solar-heated water, recycling bins stationed at every room entrance, biodegradable toiletries and other environmentally responsible features. But how does it score as a luxury hotel with accompanying five-star prices?

The accommodations are certainly luxurious. Spacious, ocean-view suites have

Arenas del Mar

Quepos

Arenas del Mar

Manuel Antonio

Manuel Antonio National Park

Pacific Ocean

COSTA RICA

San José

Enlarged Area

Pacific Ocean

N
W — E
S

Secondary Road

two bathrooms, elegantly furnished living rooms, deluxe bedrooms and mosaic-tiled whirlpool baths on huge, private terraces. The master bathrooms are impressive, with round, rain-forest showers with glass-brick illumination. All the latest technological toys are here too: wall-mounted, flat-screen TVs, high-efficiency air-conditioning in the bedrooms and Ethernet data ports, with Wi-Fi throughout the hotel.

The interior design is understated and elegant, in earth tones with lots of natural materials and textures. The most luxurious touches are the fabulous fabrics: white-cotton linens and duvets on king-size beds piled high with burgundy and gold silk cushions; sliding-glass doors layered with woven-cotton sheers and earth-toned drapes detailed with leaf appliqués and filigree embroidery.

The modern decor is saved from cultural anonymity by gorgeous, large-scale, silk prints of heliconias. Drama is also provided by oversize entrance doors, embellished with bas-relief swirls of tropical leaves. These impressive recycled plastic-and-resin doors are proof that eco can be deco, too.

El Mirador, the hotel's restaurant, presents a surprising view – of trees with six living, pillar-like trees growing through the floor and disappearing through the ceiling.

Breakfast is excellent and sensibly served from 7 to 10 a.m. From your first sip of coffee – Finca Rosa Blanca's own – to the basket of baked cinnamon buns, macadamia muffins and moist banana bread, this breakfast is faultless. Fresh juice and fruits are included, along with many other yummy choices.

A thatched-roof snack bar and restaurant beside the hotel's second swimming pool, on Playa Playitas, offers light lunches and snacks with a view of the beach. Or help yourself every afternoon to juice and unusual root vegetable chips with salsa and dip, set out for guests. Complimentary coffee is laid out in the air-conditioned room behind reception that doubles as a gift shop and Internet café, where guests have free use of two computers.

Whether you come here to roam the property in search of wildlife, wander the beaches or simply relax by the pool or in your deluxe room, you'll find the indisputable luxuries here are the superb natural resources and the priceless serenity and seclusion.

Getting There, Rates, Info

From San José, take the Inter-American Highway west and take the La Garita exit toward the central Pacific beaches, through Atenas and Orotina. Once heading south, head on to Quepos. In Quepos, cross a little bridge and at the third corner, turn left and head uphill to Manuel Antonio. Watch for Café Milagro, facing a street with various hotel signs (the "El Parador Road"). Turn right here. Go 800 meters. On left, look for a concrete entrance wih sign: Arenas del Mar Beach and Nature Resort. Rates, inc. tax and breakfast are $509 for ocean-breeze suites, $622 for ocean-view suites, both with two bathrooms, whirlpool bath, king-size bed and sofa bed; and $328 for superior rooms with ocean view or for rainforest suites with private whirlpool bath. Add $50 for additional guests; kids under 6, free.

For info, 2777-2777, **info@arenasdelmar. com** or **arenasdelmar.com.**

Water tumbles over natural stone into the inviting swimming pool.   Photos by Vicky Longland

Close Yet Worlds Away

By Ann Antkiw

Robinson Crusoe, in Daniel Defoe's novel, made his home in a banyan tree. North Americans Jim and Barbara Thompson have built their inn around two of these amazing trees, known in Costa Rica as strangler figs. However, if you visit Blue Banyan Inn, you will not be spending the night in one of these giant botanical boa constrictors.

The inn stands on five acres of a 65-acre property known as Finca Azul. This sprawling abandoned farmland is just 13 km. (8 miles) from Quepos, a busy port town on the central Pacific coast and the gateway to Manuel Antonio National Park, with its beautiful beaches and forest. Nevertheless, Blue Banyan Inn is worlds away from what has become one of the country's busiest tourist destinations.

You drive there along a dirt road through palm plantations. This can be slightly intimidating, but when you approach the inn you realize you have reached a secluded haven surrounded by nature. The views of the rolling hills, rain forest and mountain range beyond are just one of the joys Blue Banyan Inn offers.

The hospitable Thompsons are dedicated to making their property and accommodations a relaxing hideaway. Before making the move here, Jim, a retired Canadian Air Force and helicopter pilot, and Barbara, a flight attendant from Miami, often visited Barbara's brother, Chip Braman, and Jennifer Rice, partners at the Hotel Mono Azul in Manuel Antonio. Encouraged by Braman and Rice, they purchased the property two and a half years ago and began developing the land where the inn now stands.

The beautifully landscaped gardens, manicured lawns and lighted pathways make a perfect setting for the large, inviting swimming pool with a bubbling 60-foot waterfall that tumbles over sculptured rocks. The three luxury garden cottages offer romantic seclusion and total privacy.

The cottages and the main building with its large open-air restaurant and comfortable lounge were designed by talented and environmentally aware Tico architect Carlos Rojas. His concept of mixing sight, sound and smell can be seen everywhere. The spacious cottages overlook the garden and panoramic view. The scent of flowering plants, the sight of brilliant blue morpho butterflies and the sound of birdcalls and croaking frogs are all enhanced by the products of Barbara's talents as a self-taught interior decorator.

She has made the cottages an elegant delight with her choices of natural wood furnishings, fabrics and artwork depicting the wildlife, sights and colors of Costa Rica.

Cottages 1 and 2 have two queen-size beds, while the third cottage with a living room and sink has a double and a trundle bed and is handicapped-accessible.

The large bathrooms with river-stone shower stalls have abundant hot water, and the fully screened rooms offer all the comforts of home: large closets, a small desk, sofa, bedside lamps, ceiling fans, air-condi-

Getting There, Rates, Info

From San José, take the Inter-American Highway west and take the La Garita exit toward the central Pacific beaches, through Atenas and Orotina. Once heading south, just before Quepos, turn left at the fork in the road leading to Dominical. Continue for 300 meters and turn left just past the Quepos Cemetery at the Blue Banyan Inn sign. Follow the road through the palm plantation. You'll see a colorful sign painted on a large rock; turn right and follow further signs. It's five km. to the inn from the main dirt road leading to Dominical.

Rates are $90 to $136, inc. tax and breakfast. Add $10 per additional guest. Children under 10, free.

For info: 2777-2572, 8308-6071, **info@ bluebanyaninn.com**

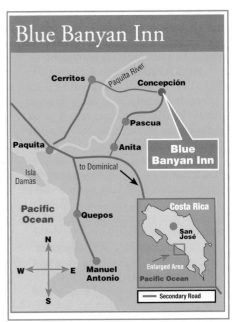

Roy Arguedas Arias | Tico Times

tioning, refrigerator, coffeemaker with complimentary coffee and DVD player. A free DVD library, Internet access and an honor-system bar can be found in the reception area. The porch of each cottage, with its comfortable furnishings, is a delightful place to sit, relax with a book or contemplate nature.

If you can drag yourself away from the pool, you can play a game of horseshoes, table tennis or darts, or walk the trails around the property. The Thompsons are happy to suggest activities in the area or book one of many available tours.

A short walk from the inn is the Animal Sanctuary, where guests can visit the

Options in Quepos

Lodging in Quepos includes: The **Best Western Hotel Kamuk**, 2777-0811, **kamuk.co.cr**), for beach and gambling aficionados, casino, $79-$158, inc. tax, breakfast, air conditioning, phones, cable TV, pool, two restaurants, conf. room.

And other options in Manuel Antonio:

Hotel California (2777-1234, 1-866-360-3105, toll free from USA, Canada **hotel-california.com**) $153-$203, inc. tax, air conditioning, cable TV, hairdryer, coffee maker, phone, safes, mini-bar, restaurant, bar, pool with waterfall, views, Jacuzzi, far from traffic, quiet, live music Fri.

Hotel El Byblos Resort & Casino (2777-0411, toll free from USA, Canada 1-888-929-2567, **bybloshotelcostarica.com**), deluxe bungalows, suites $190-$250, air, balconies, cable TV, phone, fridge, poolside pizzeria, casino, bar. House (Casa Sarita, $2000-$6000 week).

Hotel Karahe (2777-0170, toll free from USA, Canada 877-623-3198, **karahe.com**) eight beachfront rooms, $102-$169, standard rooms on hillside above, $68-90, villas, $68-$113, inc. tax, breakfast, fans, air conditioning, cable TV in lounge, pool, Internet, beachside restaurant, sportfishing.

Villas Nicolas (2777-0481 **villanicolas. com**) on hillside, six types of lovely rooms some with kitchenettes, full kitchen, range from $96-$388, inc. tax (four guests), jungle or ocean view, air, phone, balcony, hammocks, kitchen. option, pool, garden.

family of marmosets being looked after by the Thompsons. Future plans for the sanctuary, in conjunction with Kids Saving the Rainforest (**kidssavingtherainforest.org**), include creating an animal rescue and rehabilitation center, in a addition to a butterfly and medicinal herb garden.

Blue Banyan Inn is definitely for nature lovers, so don't expect any nightlife, unless you take a trip to town. The Bird and Butterfly Restaurant, decorated with a fascinating collection of wood, metal and colorful crafts by area artists, is open for only breakfast during low season. Jim is an excellent cook, and his hearty breakfasts include fruit, bacon and eggs, wonderful pancakes, and *gallo pinto*. Bottomless coffee and juice are on offer.

After that, you are on your own, but the kitchen is available if you want to cook or heat up an evening meal.

Pool area is surrounded by lush foliage.

Photos by Nicolas Ruggia and Courtesy of La Posada

Nature Is Next-Door Neighbor Here

By Nicolas Ruggia

About midday, an obviously pregnant deer cruises out of the jungle, past the pool and toward the restaurant and television area of La Posada Private Jungle Bungalows in Manuel Antonio, on the central Pacific coast.

In some places, this might be viewed as an intrusion, but at this hotel, Bambi, as she is called, is as much a part of the hotel as the pizza kitchen, comfortable, clean rooms and Thursday-night movies.

Petting the deer, which is fond of licking friendly humans, is one of the benefits of staying on a property that borders Manuel Antonio National Park. Monkeys, sloths, basilisks and iguanas also stumble onto the grounds frequently, and amazingly the rooms are insect-free.

While up-close time with animals is

certainly a draw, it is the spirit of the hotel that leaves a lasting impression. Mike Auvil, 50, from Tampa, Florida, is no life-long hotelier, and that may be the most refreshing part of the equation.

"I'm alone," Auvil said. "I'm not a corporation. I don't need to make an extra $5,000 a year by serving a continental breakfast."

That is the type of thinking that characterizes Auvil's approach. And this reporter will vouch for the breakfast choices and quality product the kitchen team puts together. Guests choose from eggs, breakfast meats, yogurt, cereal, *gallo pinto* and more.

And don't forget the aforementioned pizza. "The pizza is 90 percent for the guests. But the locals know we have good pizza," Auvil said.

It was a strange journey for Auvil, who

Bjorn Johnson, 8, from Campbell, California, gets friendly with Bambi the deer.

came to Costa Rica as a tourist following health problems and decided to stay.

"It was strictly a vacation with high school buddies," Auvil said. "I thought,

La Posada

La Posada Private Jungle Bungalows

Quepos

Manuel Antonio

N
W — E
S

Manuel Antonio National Park

Pacific Ocean

Costa Rica

San José

Enlarged Area
Pacific Ocean

Roy Arguedas Arias | Tico Times

'This is just like middle America in the 1950s' ... the wholesomeness and the high school uniforms."

A combination of common sense, listening and past experience are Auvil's guides through his venture.

"I've traveled for 20 years," Auvil said. "I know you need a comfortable bed and an air conditioner. I've just listened to people as they came. That's how I got everything." Auvil does his best to show his guests the most flattering sides of his adopted home. For guests searching for a good night of live music, Auvil, an aficionado, definitely knows which club is hopping that night.

"How would (the guests) know that (jazz and soul artist) Fuzzy Rojas sings every Monday at El Gato Negro?" Auvil pondered. "They'll be like, 'Thank you, that was our best night out in the country.'"

A family with finicky kids needs a restaurant recommendation? No problem. If they like bowling, he makes sure his staff takes them out for a night of fun at the lanes. If they need a tour, he points them in the right direction and splits his commission with them. As a result, his guests return again and again.

"My goal for the guests is to give them the best deal possible," Auvil said. "I'm not going to make any money on it ... but I want to get them the best tours, the best guides, at the best price."

One gets the sense that Auvil sees everyone as a potential

friend. It starts with his employees, whom he views as part family, part staff. "The staff is mentioned by name on TripAdvisor," Auvil said, referring to the popular travel Web site. "I've got two families working for me. I don't have any relatives here, so they're kind of like family."

The guests get the same treatment. He has developed relationships far exceeding that of guest to owner with several of his regulars. He even attended one frequent visitor's high school graduation.

"They were my first guests, my very first week," Auvil said. "Dave is helping me out; he's a contractor. He was walking around with a clipboard, telling me, 'You need this.' I get e-mails all the time. (Dave's daughter) Olivia was like, 'You have to come to my high school graduation.'"

The beach is a five-minute walk down the road, and for those who are not looking to be knee-deep in tourists, it is a part of the beach that is more popular among locals than visitors.

The pool, though small, offers guests the option of a post-beach dip, and the lounge chairs are perfect for the tanning crowd.

Rooms range in size from the two-guest Posada Room to the six-guest Casa. In the more basic rooms, the amenities include comfortable beds, air conditioning, cable TV, bathroom and hot-water shower and free WiFi. In the more luxurious several-bedroom house, guests have access to a living room with big-screen TV, kitchen, hammock-strung balcony and personal bar.

Don't expect this small hotel to expand; Auvil is happy with what he has. "I came down here to semi-retire," Auvil said. "I'm perfectly content."

So if you are in Manuel Antonio and are looking for an instant friend base, both within the local and expat communities and with Bambi and other fauna, La Posada may be the spot for you.

Getting There, Rates, Info

From San José, take the Inter-American Highway west and take the La Garita exit toward the central Pacific beaches, through Atenas and Orotina. Once heading south, head on to Quepos. In Quepos, cross a little bridge and at the third corner, turn left and head uphill to Manuel Antonio and all the way to the beach.

Turn left at Restaurant Marlin, go 100 meters to Hotel Villabosque and then go right. La Posada is at the end of the road on the left, next to the exit of the national park. Bus: Transportes Delia Morales (2223-5567), Ca. 16, Av. 3/5 (Coca Cola).

Rooms, inc. tax, breakfast, range from $113 to $254 per night, high season and $57 to $170, low season. For info: 2777-1446, or **laposadajungle.com**

One of three bedrooms and a kitchen inside "The Tower."

Photos by Patrick Fitzgerald

By Patrick Fitzgerald

If you haven't been to Mono Azul Hotel and Restaurant in a while, Chip Braman understands if you don't recognize it at first. "Within the past nine years, we've gone from 10 rooms to 32 rooms," says Braman, 62. "We've basically combined three hotels into one."

Braman bought Mono Azul, on the road between Quepos and Manuel Antonio on the central Pacific coast, nearly a decade ago. Over the years, he purchased two neighboring hotels – one adjacent, the other across the street – blending Mono Azul into the eclectic amalgamation it is today.

"Each of the hotels has its own system," Braman explains. "You can see that all three are different."

Each section of the hotel has a unique flavor that may appeal to a different type of traveler. The original Mono Azul features standard rooms, while next door are deluxe rooms with at least two beds, air-conditioning and cable TV. Rooms don't come with phones, however, and Internet access carries a small fee.

Across the street are the villas, a honeymoon suite and massage parlor (sessions cost $49). Each sector has its own pool, and with a restaurant, 2,500-book library and poolside "tiki room," Mono Azul has something for everybody.

"We have this variety," Braman says. "So we can separate. Groups can take over one area of our hotel and be on their own."

Catering to groups is one of the hotel's specialties. Braman, former global marketing director at Avon beauty products company, was born in Argentina and has lived in several Latin American countries. He greets guests by name – "It's all about the people," he says – and can often be found in the restaurant or by the front desk, giving advice on what tours to take or what fishing boat is best.

Like the hotel, Mono Azul's restaurant offers variety, ranging from pizzas (₡4,000-8,100/ $7.20-14.50) to surf-and-turf – filet mignon and mahimahi – for two (₡12,700/$23).

Over the course of our stay, we try the quarter-pound bacon cheeseburger with avocado (₡4,100/$7.30), chicken marsala with mushroom cream sauce (₡4,700/$8.40), grilled mahimahi (₡5,100/$9.10), "The American" breakfast plate (orange juice, home fries, bacon, eggs and toast (₡4,500/$8.10) and a ham and cheese omelet (₡3,900/$7).

The fare is solid and good. If you're from the United States and homesick, the cheeseburger and "American" breakfast combo are particularly good bets.

For our first night, my companion and I stay in "The Tower" across the street, which Braman admits is "kind of unique." Perfect for families and groups up to six, it boasts two downstairs bedrooms, an upstairs living room with kitchen and a loft with a third bed. From the balcony, Braman says, "the bird-watching is extraordinary," looking out over the *guarumo* trees that draw motmots and tanagers. While I don't spot any birds with my untrained eye, I do snap some photos of a lizard before heading to the beach.

Mono Azul is five km from the beach, set back a bit from the road, and the pools, especially the one by the deluxe rooms, offer quiet solitude. The distance, Braman says, is a good thing.

"We happen to like being away," he says. "People come in and they feel comfortable. We're just really fortunate to have this environment around our hotel. This is really a safe haven."

Another feature of Mono Azul is the gift shop, which benefits Kids Saving the Rainforest, a nonprofit environmental organization run by Braman's partner, Jennifer Rice. The two, who found out after they met that their fathers had been old friends,

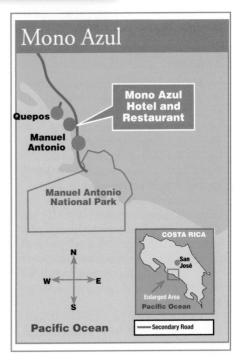

Roy Arguedas Arias | Tico Times

A lizard poses on a branch near a hotel room.

keep their operations separate, but proceeds from the gift shop pay for the foundation's operating expenses. Along with crafts and jewelry made by children involved with the organization, the shop sells work by artists and indigenous artisans.

"They help us," Rice says of Mono Azul. "The store is here, but 100 percent of the proceeds go to saving the rain forest."

Mono Azul's specialty, however, is the personal service you will receive from Chip, Jennifer and the rest of the hotel's 26-member staff. Particularly accommodating for large groups, the hotel also offers packages and is willing to negotiate prices ("We'll always offer a deal," Braman says).

Neither cheap nor luxurious, the hotel is best for travelers looking for friendly comfort and all the assistance you could ask for in booking tours and figuring out what to do or where to go. In that respect, despite its eccentric combination of styles, Mono Azul has managed to forge a clear identity.

"We don't pretend to be any more than that," Braman says. "We think that's our niche."

Getting There, Rates, Info

From San José, take the Inter-American Highway west and take the La Garita exit toward the central Pacific beaches, through Atenas and Orotina. Once heading south, head on to Quepos. In Quepos, cross a little bridge and at the third corner, turn left and head uphill about 1.5 km. uphill toward Manuel Antonio. The hotel is just under 5 km. away from the beaches and the national park.

Standard and semi-deluxe rooms range from $45 to $90, deluxe rooms from $68 to $119, and villas from $68 to $164. Rates are for single occupancy and include taxes. Additional guests cost $10, kids under 8, free. Honeymoon packages and group rates available. Booking online brings a $10 per night discount, and, if you stay a week, you get one night free.

For info: 2777-2572 or 1-800-381-3578 toll-free from the United States, or **hotelmonoazul. com.**

The rustic cabins are basic but clean and comfortable.

Photos by Vicky Longland

A Slice of Rural Tico Life

By Ann Antkiw

For those who want to explore off the beaten track and discover the real Costa Rica, this alternative travel experience is a wonderful choice. Visitors can see the beauty of the country through the eyes of its people and have the chance to share in their daily lives, culture and knowledge of nature, while helping to create more economic opportunities for rural farming, fishing and indigenous communities.

This type of tourism has a positive environmental and social impact, and offers people of all ages – women in particular – new ways of contributing to the economic wellbeing of their families and communities.

Two of us rural tourism devotees recently visited Reserva Los Campesinos in the small mountain community of Quebrada Arroyo, 25 km. from the central Pacific port town of Quepos. After passing through the small town of Londres, we followed signs to Reserva Los Campesinos up a muddy dirt road (four-wheel drive is a must). Along the way we passed a group of *campesinos*, workers from the village, who smiled and waved. They were cheerfully clearing the rubble from a recent landslide; keeping the road passable in rainy season is a never-ending story.

We arrived at a *pulpería*, a small village store that sells all the basics and more. Miguel Mora, our friendly, enthusiastic host and guide, met us and led us down a steep path to the lodge. He showed us to our room, one of two with a private bathroom but no hot water, though it's on the agenda. The basic, comfortable, very clean rooms have a double bed, two bunk beds, shelves and a fan. The lace curtains are an incongruous but delightful touch. Furnished porches offer a wonderful view of the rain forest, while the rushing river below and the thundering sound of a stunning waterfall lulls you to sleep at night.

The lodge can accommodate up to 38 people in cabins with bunk beds sleeping four to eight. Outside shared bathrooms and showers are clean and accessible. Los Campesinos is a popular destination for groups, retreats and national and international students studying ecology and the environment.

Three meals a day are served in the large open-air dining area. The traditional food cooked on a wood stove is superb and would satisfy any appetite.

Cook Yamileth Mora whips up five-star traditional Costa Rican fare on a wood stove.

Cook Yamileth Mora could be rated a five star chef. The fish or chicken *casados* with tasty beans and rice, *picadillo* (a diced vegetable side dish and cabbage salad lightly dressed with lime juice is some of the best Tico fare you'll ever taste.

Breakfast consists of traditional *gallo pinto*, eggs and delicious homemade tortillas, accompanied by *café chorreado*, made by putting coffee in a sock-like bag, pouring hot water over it and allowing it to drip. Alcoholic drinks are not served, but the *refrescos*, tropical fruit blended with spring water, are refreshing and thirst-quenching.

We were amused by our guide Mora's fanatical clock-watching. He had obviously been instructed that punctuality is of the utmost importance for foreigners. Despite cultural differences, our hosts did everything possible to please us and make us feel comfortable.

After lunch we were given an hour's siesta time before setting off for a tour. We crossed a swaying 128-meter hanging bridge, 40 meters above a river and swirling pool under a cascading waterfall. When we reached the pool, we declined taking a dip, as it was a chilly, drizzly afternoon. From there, a 15-minute walk took us to Quebrada Arroyo, where we were given a tour of the village of 16 families.

Before dinner, Mora told us the history of the 33-hectare reserve, on the lower part of the Savegre River. Half the reserve is made up of primary forest; the other half is secondary tropical humid forest, most regenerated from farming and cattle-graz-

Reserva Los Campesinos

← to Jacó

Reserva Los Campesinos

Londres **Quebrada Arroyo**

Quepos

Manuel Antonio

to Dominical →

COSTA RICA

• San José

Enlarged Area

Pacific Ocean

Pacific Ocean

N W E S

■ Inter-American Hwy.
■ Secondary road

Roy Arguedas Arias | Tico Times

Campesinos' 128-meter-long hanging bridge offers a spectacular if swaying view of a waterfall and river 40 meters below.

ng land.

In 1994, Quebrada Arroyo was a bustling vanilla-producing community, but when disease killed the crops, many families left. The remaining 16 families, concerned about the endangered forest, purchased the land with help from various organizations.

They have now found an alternative way of earning a living through grassroots rural tourism, preserving the environment and working toward sustainability. On our second day, Mora took us on a fascinating two-and-a-half-hour hike through the forest to a lookout with panoramic views stretching to the Pacific Ocean. It wasn't as strenuous as it sounds, as we constantly stopped along the way while Mora pointed out medicinal plants and explained their uses. We saw many colorful frogs and birds but no animals – only tracks. On our way back to the lodge, we had an exciting river crossing aboard a platform attached to a pulley.

More hikes on seven km of forest trails and horseback riding tours are also offered, in addition to rafting on the Savegre River. The really adventurous can try rappelling down the waterfall.

A visit to Los Campesinos is a delightful experience and highly recommended if you want to spend a couple of days living the simple life. You can also request an English-speaking guide. You will gain insight into Costa Rican rural life and are guaranteed a wonderful welcome and genuine hospitality.

Getting There, Rates, Info

From San José, take the Inter-American Highway west and take the La Garita exit toward the central Pacific beaches, through Atenas and Orotina. Once heading south, pass Herradura and Jacó. Before entering Quepos, turn at gas station on left toward Londres. Follow signs to Reserva Los Campesinos (10 km.). Four-wheel drive is essential from Londres to the reserve. Otherwise, leave your vehicle in Londres and arrange for transport. Non-residents pay $73, residents $52, inc. tax, for a two-day, one-night package including three guided hikes and three meals.

For info: Costa Rican Association for Community-based Rural Tourism (ACTUAR), 2248-9470, **info@actuarcostarica.com,** or **actuarcostarica.com.** The ACTUAR office is on Av. 9, Ca. 3/5, San José. The group publishes an excellent guidebook on rural tourism in Costa Rica.

Catering to Comfort-Craving Surfers

The Surf Inn Hermosa, south of Jacó on the central Pacific coast, welcomes guests with a colorful mural.

Photos by Lindy Drew

By Elizabeth Goodwin

Christina Truitt used to hang out with her friends on a beautiful beachfront lot in Playa Hermosa, five km south of Jacó on the central Pacific coast. The vacant lot sloped gently down onto the beach, so she and her friends would park there, talk and go surfing.
Just a few years later, Truitt has opened her own hotel, Surf Inn Hermosa, on that very lot.

"I started looking and … one time I saw a 'for sale' sign for this lot, and I was like, 'Wow. I'll just call.' They wanted something ridiculous for it," she recalls. "So I said, 'Why don't we just throw out a number and see what happens?' It was about 50 percent of what was on the sign, and the guy took it."

Truitt has been many things, but never a business owner. She worked in finance and then as a teacher. After she came to Costa Rica about five years ago, began teaching at a private school and working as co-director and now treasurer of the Central Pacific Chamber of Commerce.

At first, she was wary of taking the plunge into business ownership. "Last year I just finally decided, 'OK, I'm going to do it,'" she says.

Her boyfriend, Mike Cruden, is a Web

esigner who has lived there more than ive years. The two lived next door to the ot while the hotel was being constructed nd have since moved into one of the second-floor rooms, with a view of the ocean vhere they both like to surf.

Cruden says part of the reason Truitt vas able to get her hotel up and running in only a year is the respect she has earned in he community as a teacher.

"There were definitely days we'd walk over here and say, 'Wow! It's really happening,'" Cruden says.

The three-story hotel emphasizes simplicity and elegance. Clean, cool woods set off cream walls that blend inconspicuously nto the tropical surroundings. Each room emphasizes comfort.

The four one-bedroom studio apartments feature one queen bed with a single bunk above, stove, refrigerator, TV, air conditioner and leather couch, while the two wo-bedroom apartments have two queen beds and two single bunks, with a larger kitchen that includes a washer and dryer. Everything looks new and clean, like the kind of place someone seeking comfort in paradise would gravitate to. In fact, Truitt had just such a person in mind when she built the hotel.

"One of my good friends is an older guy who surfs," she says. "He got tired of traveling around and staying in places that weren't comfortable. And he loves to surf – he comes down here five, 10 times a year. He's traveled the world, but now he wants comfort and he's got the money to pay for it."

Roy Arguedas Arias | Tico Times

Perhaps the best part of the hotel is its incredible oceanfront view and access. Truitt and Cruden plan to put up a webcam on one of the walls to offer a perennial online view of the talented surfers who gather in front of their hotel, at **crsurfcam.com**.

Unlike most nearby hotels, Surf Inn doesn't have a pool between the hotel and the ocean. Instead, Truitt decided to artfully include the pool by the stairway, where it provides an oasis-like feel to the middle of the hotel. This also means there is no obstruction between the rooms and the ocean. A rolling green lawn stretches for about 50 meters, and then opens onto the sand and ocean.

Truitt hopes the hotel offers the cozy and inclusive feel of a U.S. Eastern Shore bed-and-breakfast.

"I'm from around Annapolis and the Chesapeake Bay (Maryland) area, which has a lot of really quaint bed-and-breakfasts where you go and stay and have a nice time and nice meals. And you kind of feel included. You're entertained," Truitt says. "Here in Costa Rica, I haven't found too many places like that. So that's what I wanted to create."

Because of that vision, Truitt decided to make the third floor an open and spacious café, despite her architect's desire to build more rooms there. Hermosa Café serves tasty treats such as coconut French toast, Asian sesame chicken and curries to guests and the public. The couple's neighbor and friend, Juan Vega, the café's chef, offers delicious beach fare guests can enjoy while watching the ocean crash in front of them.

The hotel is full of personal touches, such as the tropical murals done by the couple's friends, Gary Lynn and Danielle Ciminero (**www.unytedmovement.com**), which brighten the outdoor showers and front wall.

Truitt and Cruden are attentive but relaxed hosts who know the area well and are eager to guide their guests to the best the region has. Whether you're there to surf or just lie on the sand, Surf Inn Hermosa is a comfortable and beautiful place to do it in. You might never leave the hotel's back porch.

Getting There, Rates, Info

Surf Inn Hermosa is 200 meters north of the Backyard Bar in Playa Hermosa, about two hours from San José on the Pacific coastal highway. From San José, take the Inter-American Highway west and take the La Garita exit toward the central Pacific beaches, through Atenas and Orotina. Once heading south, pass Herradura and Jacó and continue five km. to Hermosa Surf Inn, on the right, 200 meters before the Backyard Bar.

Buses to Jacó leave San José from the Coca-Cola Terminal at 6, 7, 9 and 11 a.m. and at 1, 3, 5 and 7 p.m. (Transportes Jacó, 2223-1109, ₡1,935/$3.50 one-way). From Jacó, take a taxi to Hermosa for about ₡3,000 ($5.50).

Rates range from $113 to $283, inc. tax. Rates jump to $170 and $339, inc. taxes, over holidays and July 1 to 20. For the World Surfing Games, rates to be announced. Weekly, monthly rates available. For info: 2643-7184 or (410) 734-2687 in the United States, **surfinnhermosa@yahoo.com** or **surfinnhermosa.com**.

Palm-lined beaches abound in Costa Rica.
Photo by Ronald Reyes

Threatened by habitat destruction, the Scarlet Macaw (ara macao) is arguably the most magnificent bird of the parrot family.

Photo by Ronald Reyes

Southern Zone

Photo by Ronald Reyes

Playa Ventanas is known for its interesting rock formations, such as this tunnel that can be walked through at low tide.

Photos by Lindy Drew

Ballena Marine Park Teems With Wildlife

By Elizabeth Goodwin

Beaches

Beautiful Ballena National Marine Park on the southern Pacific coast has an isolated, pristine beauty to it that makes it seem much more secluded and hard to reach than it is. The park, which first opened in 1990, is about 190 km. southwest of San José and includes 110 hectares of coast and 5,400 hectares of protected ocean territory. Its beaches stretch for 10 km., providing a rich coastline for sun worshippers and surfers alike.

The park is packed with unique natural formations that make its beaches out of the ordinary, even for a place as geographically diverse as Costa Rica. Its waters overlooked by the lush green mountains of the Fila Costeña Range, the park also contains a mangrove estuary. Admission is $6 for foreigners and ₡1,000 ($1.70) for residents.

Playa Ventanas (Windows Beach) is surrounded by tunnels in the cliffs that look like impressive windows into the surrounding landscape – hence the beach's name. At low tide, visitors can walk through the tunnels. At high tide, the beach all but disappears. To the north of Playa Ventanas are pretty **Playa Ballena**, where surfers ride the waves, and expansive, tranquil **Playa Arco**. A little farther north, **Playa Uvita**, near one of the park's entrances, is the site of the stunning tombolo and Moses' Pass. Here, at low tide, the ocean parts, leaving dry a long stretch of sand that reaches far into what is usually covered by the sea. Walking along this stretch of sand, called Whale's Tail, or Moses' Pass after the Biblical Hebrew leader's feat of parting the Red Sea, feels a little unreal. The large expanse of beach dwarfs visitors

Dolphin-watching tours reward visitors with sightings of the playful cetaceans, such as this pantropical spotted dolphin.

and makes it seem as if one were walking straight into the ocean. At the very end of the pass sits a rectangular structure made of stone, possibly the foundation of an old lighthouse.

Climbing atop for an even better view of the mountainous shore is an exhilarating way to experience the beach. Ask the park guards for a tide schedule so as not to miss the tombolo.

Wildlife and How to See It

One of the advantages of the area is the quantity of wildlife one can see in just a single day. I saw spotted dolphins, frigate birds, a host of tropical fish and a scarlet macaw in the space of only a few hours. Humpback and pilot whales can best be seen from January to March, and bottlenose dolphins, toucans, turtles and white-faced monkeys also make appearances.

If you want to get up close and person-

Getting There

By car, head south from San José on the Inter-American Highway about 135 km. to San Isidro de El General, from where you head southwest to Dominical. Once in Dominical, turn south and go 16 km. to Uvita. The center of Uvita is about 3 km. from the main park entrance. The trip takes about four and a half hours.

By bus, Musoc (2222-2422, Ca. Ctrl., Av. 22/24), hourly departures from San José to San Isidro de El General. From there, Transportes Blanco (2771-2550) makes the trip to Dominical and Uvita twice a day (¢400). The trip takes about five and a half hours total. Call for schedules, fares.

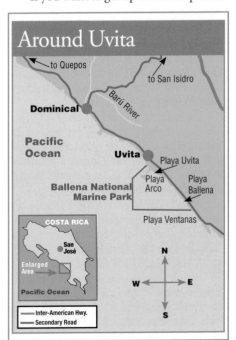

Around Uvita

Roy Arguedas Arias | Tico Times

al with the marine wildlife, some six companies offer boat tours of the park's waters. I went with the family-owned **Dolphin Tour** (8825-4031, dolphintourcostarica.com), at $65 per person for a four-hour spin around the park, including snorkeling on the coral reefs and a trip through one of the cliff-windows at Playa Ventanas. The company also provides sportfishing and kayaking tours. The guides provide fresh fruit and a refreshing lack of ceremony. They let the stunning mountainous scenery speak for itself, but are quick to answer any questions (see sidebar for other tour companies).

My tour guide, Ronald Monge, 21, has been working boat tours since he was 12. He found dolphins for us through a series

Where to Stay and Eat

Uvita offers simple but good food and lodging. I stayed at **Hotel Nido del Halcón** (2743-8373, ilmaja@ice.co.cr) 100 meters from the entrance to Playa Uvita. Rates: $70 dbl, inc. tax. Swimming pool, cable TV, air conditioning, WiFi. Attached restaurant serves affordable fare, including fresh lobster, fish and shrimp.

Or stay at new **Hotel Luz de Luna**, 2743-8271, hotelluzdeluna@racsa.co.cr), 200 meters southeast of the Río Uvita Bridge in the town of Uvita, 12 rooms ($80, inc. tax and breakfast), pool, parking, air conditioning. Its restaurant in front, **La Fogata** (2743-8224), serves delicious oven-baked pizzas. I tried the Pizza Margarita, tomatoes, basil and melted cheese on a crispy crust (average ₡5,000/$9 for a medium). The restaurant's oven-roasted chicken is also tasty.

Other Uvita restaurants recommended are the **Marino Ballena Restaurant** (2743-8104), across from Banco Nacional in Uvita, and the fancier **The Chef's Table** (8838-3378), attached to the Villas de Las Aves Hotel, boasting gourmet pizza and six-course menus on special nights, reservation only.

Also in Dominical, **ConFusione** (2787-0244) offers sophisticated Italian food right on the beach, **La Parcela** (2787-0241) serves up inexpensive seafood with a view, and the **San Clemente Mexican-American Grill** (2787-0055) is a surfer hangout offering tacos and other cheap eats.

Places to stay in Uvita include **Villas de Las Aves** (8838-3378, villasdelasaves.com), a luxury hotel with great views, $85 per night, and **Finca Bavaria** (8355 4465, finca-bavaria.de), six high-quality bungalows, $72-84 dbl., inc. tax. Breakfast, $8, home-made bread and jams, meats, cheeses, tomatoes, avocados, gallo pinto, eggs and pancakes, home-made yogurt, organic fruit. 15 hectares, trails, hikes, 5 mins to waterfall, fabulous birding, pool.

North of Uvita in Dominical, dozens of hotels are yours for the choosing.

The beachfront **Coconut Grove** (2787-0130, coconutgrovecr.com), three cabinas $75, inc. tax, cottages $75-$85, houses, sleep four/six, $120-$135.

Hotel Cuna del Angel (2787-8012, cunadelangel.com) is a pricier option offering 25 "jungle rooms" within the hotel grounds where guests can animal-watch. Rates, inc. tax and buffet breakfast: standard, $110, deluxe, $201.

At **Pacific Edge** (2787-8010, pacificedge.info), enjoy sweeping and affordable views of the beach from 600 feet up. Standard cabin, $60, inc. tax; two deluxe cabins, $70, inc. tax; two-bedroom, two-bath bungalow, sleeps two-four, $90-$125, extra person $10. A la carte breakfast, $5-$10.

The **DiuWak** (2280-8907, diuwak.com), room, deluxe, bungalows, $75-$110, inc. tax, breakfast, fan or air conditioning, terraces, phones, kayaks, tours, private terraces, pool with waterfall, restaurant, bar, laundry, transport, mini market, WiFi. At Km. 169, is **Cristal Ballena** (2786-5355, cristal-ballena.com), mansion style, enormous pool, 19 equipped suites, $234-$293, inc. tax, luxurious buffet breakfast, air conditioning, TV, WiFi, phones, fridge, spa, views, forest lodges , $84-$113, inc. tax, breakfast). **Mar y Selva Ecolodge** (2340-5132, maryselva.com) 10 bungalows, in jungle, beautiful ocean views, $110, inc tax, breakfast, semi-olympic lap pool, fans a/c, WiFi, TV, hair dryer, fridge, safes, babysitting, massage services, kayaks, bikes, security, tours.

Other area tour operators include **Southern Expeditions** (2787-0100), offering whale- and dolphin-watching tours and expeditions to Isla del Caño, an island biological reserve southwest of Ballena, off the Osa Peninsula. **Caverna Tours** (8894-9952) offers tours and snorkeling. **Pacific Whales and Kayak Tours** (8827-8705) has traditional boat and kayak tours available.

The Uvita tombolo, below, a rocky platform jutting out into the sea and exposed at low tide, is joined to Playa Uvita by a narrow strip of sandy beach. Above, low tide at Playa Uvita, right after sunrise.

of rapid cell phone conversations with fellow boaters, who call each other when they spot whales or dolphins. The group of six sleek creatures seemed to enjoy our company, sticking close to the boat for at least 15 minutes before swimming off.

Tourism

The area gets fewer visitors than big-name destinations such as the northwestern Guanacaste province's beaches. However, Manuel Valverde, owner of **Hotel Nido del Halcón**, said he fell in love with it when he first visited and decided to build a hotel here.

"Ten years ago, I came here, and it struck me as a totally different beach from anything I had seen," he said.

Valverde and tour guide Monge said that people don't know of Ballena Park and its surroundings as a tourist destination. Monge blames the Environment, Energy and Telecommunications Ministry

(MINAET) for charging foreigners $6 to enter the park, yet not providing basic services such as bathrooms.

Though the region around the park is underdeveloped, Valverde said Uvita, the town closest to the park, is booming with construction projects and already has several supermarkets and banks.

Take a Hike in Monkey-land

Nature guide José Huertas leads visitors through Corcovado National Park.

Photos by
Blake Schmidt

By Blake Schmidt

It was her first day in *Tiquicia*. She didn't know about monkeys. My mom hadn't yet learned that it wasn't cool to gasp and gawk at the sight of them (she would later learn her lesson as a six-foot-tall, blonde Gringa parting a sea of smaller, gawking Ticos on San José's Avenida Central).

Not unlike a reckless San José *taxista* dodging through traffic and potholes with little regard for life, our boat driver was charging full-speed through swaths of mangroves on chokingly narrow canals along the Sierpe River, in the Southern Zone.

Which is about when Mom freaked. Not at the crazy boat conductor – at the monkey she (allegedly) saw. Squinting and huffing, she informed me that she thought she might have seen a monkey up in the tree we had just passed at 40 miles per hour.

Drake Bay is the jumping-off point for travel to the park, considered the 'crown jewel' in the national park system.

She didn't know what she was in for. We were headed to the land of monkeys: Corcovado National Park.

The Guide of Guides

When I first saw José Huertas, I had my doubts about following him into the rain forest.

A tall Tico with Coke-bottle glasses, a scope slung over his shoulder and a scar the length of a ruler straight across his neck, he galumphed round with what appeared to be a permanent wedgy.

But he had character. And the heady Guanacaste native had a knowledge of Costa Rican ecology and wildlife that would slaughter the flora and fauna section in any Lonely Planet guide.

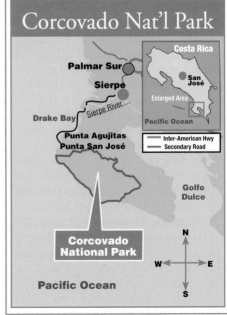

Roy Arguedas Arias | Tico Times

Huertas, we later learned, had been clotheslined as a youngster. Not the innocuous kind of clothesline you see hanging in back yards, in World Wrestling Federation matches, or even on "Monday Night Football." He was clotheslined with barbed wire, while riding full-speed-ahead on an ATV. And lived.

Though it sounds like the stuff of a Darwin Award, to the contrary, Huertas would probably be able to survive much longer than I if dropped off, "Survivor"-style, on a remote island. So, we followed him into Corcovado National Park.

He taught us about how leafcutter ants have all different kinds of roles, from queen to warriors to the quality-control ants that inspect leaves other ants are carrying to make sure they can feed the fungus the ants harvest to eat. He taught us about how white-faced monkeys are attracted to menstruating women. He taught us how to listen to the forest.

As for monkeys, we had a run-in with a family of the white-faced variety swinging through the canopy. Later, we spent several minutes with a spider monkey that descended to perch on a branch just above our heads in an Indian-style squat. Motionlessly, the monkey stared down at us like a furry little Buddha, and we stared back until our necks hurt.

On our day-long guided trip, we saw Jesus Christ lizards, falcons, dart frogs (not poisonous) and lots of monkeys. The tour was a quick boat ride from Drake Bay, and the $65-per-person trip included a relaxing picnic in the shade at the beachfront, with a view of Caño Island (area hotels coordinate tours for guests). We

Selection of Area Hotels

Aguila de Osa Inn (2296-2190, **aguiladeosa.com**), at mouth of Agujas River, 13 luxury cabins ($300, inc. tax, meals), most for up to four, overhead fans, Internet, stunning views, gourmet buffet-style restaurant, sportfishing, scuba, 24-hour electricity, horses, birding, whale/dolphin tours.

Casa Corcovado Jungle Lodge (2256-3181, **casacorcovadolodge.com**, toll-free 1-888-896-6097), beyond San Josecito, closest to park, very beautiful, 14 secluded, romantic luxury bungalows, four honeymoon suites, family suites, tiled bathrooms, screened porches, fans, two pools, two restaurants, two bars; trails into Corcovado or through reserve, tours, dolphin-watching, snorkeling, sportfishing, diving, kayaking. Rates, inc. tax, are $575-865/person, two-night min., inc/air transfer from San José, boat from Sierpe with lifejackets, meals, one tour to Corcovado or Caño Island, park fees.

Corcovado Adventures Tent Camp (384-1679, **corcovado.com**), across Agujas River, 16 platform tents ($80/per person double/triple room, $90, single, inc/meals, kayaks, boogie boards, surf boards, snorkeling gear); very basic, shared bathrooms; three-, six-night packages, inc. tours, boat for fishing, snorkeling, tubing, transportation..

Drake Bay Wilderness Resort (2770-8012), **drakebay.com**), on headland just across Agujas River, 19 rooms ($113/person, inc. tax, full breakfast (reserve for meals), laundry, kayaks, overhead/table fans, ocean views, reading chairs, coffee maker, porches, solar-heated water, bar, international restaurant, homemade chocolate chip cookies, saltwater pool, Internet, tours, fishing, PADI diving, indigenous crafts in shop.

Jinetes de Osa (2231-5806, **jinetesdeosa.com**), at west end of Drake beach. Rates, inc. tax, all meals: Standard rooms per person, $85 single; $75 dbl. Ocean-view rooms, per person: $87 triple; $99 dbl; $130 single. Hammocks, int'l restaurant, beautiful hardwood bar; overhead fans, coffee at your room at dawn; home to branch of **Original Canopy Tour,** seven platforms ($55); also **Costa Rica Adventure Divers** PADI center.

Punta Marenco Lodge (8877-3535, **punta marenco.com**), past Agujas River on hill overlooking ocean, 15 screened, thatched-roof rustic bungalows ($130 inc/meals, dbl. four-day, three-night package $500/person), with porches, ocean views, cold water, ecofriendly.

Capuchin monkeys live high in the treetops.

Photo by Matt Wyczalkowski

also bathed in the foot of a waterfall deep in primary forest before heading back to our cabin.

There, we fell asleep to raindrops on the roof and woke up to sunshine and tropical birds flying over our heads at the breakfast table. As we snapped photos of a toucan that had come to rest on a branch in front of us, Huertas continued eating breakfast quietly.

He wore the rain forest comfortably, like a pair of old, worn jeans.

Getting There

By Plane:

Sansa (2290-4100, **flysansa.com**) and Nature Air (2220-3054, **natureair.com**) make the 45-minute flight from San José to Drake Bay daily. Hotels/taxis offer transport from landing strip to bay. Flights also go to Palmar Sur, from which taxis and hotel vans transport guests 17 km. south to Sierpe for the one-hour boat trip to Drake Bay.

By Bus:

Take the 5 a.m. bus (Tracopa, 2223-7685) from San José to Palmar Norte, then taxi or bus to Sierpe to reach the water taxis, which leave at 11:30 a.m. only. Warning: Water taxis in Agujitas (Drake Bay) also leave at 11:30 a.m. only. The Agujitas taxis and most hotels have wet landings.

The blue Pacific is steps away.

Photos Courtesy of Finca Exotica

Off-the-Grid Garden of Delights

By Dorothy MacKinnon

Finca Exótica is a garden paradise that lives up to the promise of its name. At the very end of the bumpy road from Puerto Jiménez to Carate on southwestern Costa Rica's Osa Peninsula, this combination organic farm, botanical garden and eco-lodge is notable not only for its focus on sustainable living, but also for the delightful contrast between its remote setting and its sophisticated hospitality.

The finca, on about 90 hectares, is the creation of Markus Wehrmeister, a German architect turned caterer turned organic gardener, who had a quasi-Utopian vision seven years ago of transforming a worn-out subsistence farm into a model of organic farming, sustainable living, hospitality and natural beauty.

Wehrmeister sums up the guiding principle behind his vision with this aphorism: "They say, 'If you want to be happy for a day, kill a pig and share it with friends. If you want to be happy for a year, get married. If you want to be happy for a lifetime, plant a garden.'"

And plant a garden he did. Over the last seven years, Wehrmeister has planted more than 125 species of tropical fruits, 1,000 trees, including more than a dozen different species of palms, 15 species of bananas and plantains, seven species of bamboo and countless flowering ornamentals and edible plants.

But Wehrmeister didn't stop at plants.

With the goal of being as self-sufficient as possible, he also built a duck house, a henhouse and a pig enclosure. An architect, Wehrmeister couldn't help infusing even these farmyard structures with elegant design elements. The realities of jungle farming made some adjustments necessary, however. During a heavy rain period last year, a hungry ocelot broke into the poultry houses, ate the ducks and killed most of the chicks and hens. The pig survived with just a *chicharrón* bitten off one flank. Now each is totally enclosed and, Wehrmeister hopes, ocelot-proof. A tour of the organic farm and gorgeous garden includes tastes of edible plants along the way. Wehrmeister introduced me to katuk, a spicy salad green reminiscent of spinach.

Another tasty leaf comes from the *limón criollo* tree – a handful will wake up your taste buds in the morning. The lodging here is as exotic as the garden and just as carefully designed. Five quintessentially tropical cabins are built of bamboo, thatch and screening, affording privacy while remaining as open to the garden as possible. The feeling

A quintessentially tropical cabin at Finca Exótica.

is more *tiki* than *tico*: Each cabin looks as though it belongs on a South Seas island, a feeling reinforced by the steady sound of the surf, steps away. Bathrooms have elegant ceramic sinks and an open window to the garden. Showers are in separate bamboo-cane enclosures in private gardens.

Stunning flower arrangements, beautiful batik fabrics and woven-palm hangings add a touch of sophistication. They're the handiwork of Costa Rican artist, potter and teacher Gabriela Madriz, who makes her home here with Wehrmeister.

For the more adventurous – and budget-minded – six platform tents are scattered around two garden areas, sharing open-to-the- sky showers and bathrooms. These are not your standard camping tents. Wehrmeister's innovative design uses translucent nylon that lets in lots of light, with interestingly shaped, zippered windows screened with aphid-proof netting to allow for maximum air flow and privacy.

Wehrmeister set his tents on light bamboo frames, topped with thatch roofs. Bamboo decks and entries pebbled with washed-up beach stones complete the idyllic, castaway-island look. Inside, though, these thatched huts have comfortable queen or single mattresses, draped in fresh linens.

Wehrmeister also practices what he preaches when it comes to food. The first time I dropped by, a visiting chef had just butchered and cooked up the farm pig. I joined other guests to feast on tender, barbecued pork ribs.

Finca Exotica

COSTA RICA

San José

Enlarged Area

Pacific Ocean

— Inter-American Hwy.
— Secondary Road

Chacarita

Mogos

Rincón

Golfito

Puerto Jiménez

Golfo Dulce

Carate

Agua Buena

Finca Exotica

N
W   E
S

Pacific Ocean

Roy Arguedas Arias | Tico Times

My next, longer visit was a culinary extravaganza. The first night, guests gathered in Wehrmeister and Madriz's handsome house, perched high atop what Wehrmeister calls "Edible Hill," with 360-degree views of ocean and coastline. Designed by Wehrmeister, the wooden house is built on horizontal planes reminiscent of Frank Lloyd Wright and Charles Rennie Mackintosh, with built-in cabinetry and cushioned seating. Wehrmeister and Madriz worked in the open kitchen to produce an exotic meal, starting with appetizers of fresh tuna sashimi and seared tuna chunks, followed by red snapper cooked in a spicy Indian paste, accompanied by a medley of spinach and kale braised in a sake, sesame oil and mirin sauce, atop jasmine rice. Dessert was a spicy

Cabin interior, with garden view.

fruit compote of banana, pineapple and caramelized *carambola* (star fruit). All ingredients were grown on the finca, except for the fish, courtesy of a local fisherman.

The next night's dinner was in the garden, a cooperative effort by Madriz, Wehrmeister and his brother Wieland, a chef from Germany, in addition to U.S. volunteer Amory Tarr, an organic farmer. The meal was proof that organic doesn't mean boring. We started with a hot and sour Mexican soup, a favorite of Wehrmeister.

Next came a savory coconut curry chicken padang, flavored with lemongrass, turmeric and ginger, topped with tender curry-plant leaves.

Dinner features a tropical salad concocted by Madriz and served on a wooden platter decorated with flowers. This night, the salad included colorful chunks of watermelon, avocado, tomato and carrot atop a bed of cabbage and crispy katuk leaves, dressed in a balsamic and honey vinaigrette. Dessert was caramelized carambola and bananas in red wine and coconut milk.

Breakfasts include coffee, fresh eggs, home-baked raisin bread, pancakes, *gallo pinto*, yogurt-and-fruit smoothies and, of course, fresh fruit. Even the picnic lunch we took on a hike into Corcovado was out of the ordinary, with chunks of spicy tuna and sautéed onions wedged between grilled slices of dense homemade bread.

Wehrmeister's ultimate dream for Finca Exótica is to create not only a model of sustainable living, but also an educational environment, offering seminars on bridge building and organic farming, for example, in addition to English lessons. The reception area has a Spanish-language library and a huge pool table, which is a real draw for locals, helping to turn Finca Exótica into Carate's de facto community center.

The key concept, Wehrmeister says, is to provide a place where people can expand their horizons. For visitors, that can be as simple as taking time to listen to the surf, soak up the natural beauty, sleep well and eat exotically.

Getting There, Rates, Info

Finca Exótica is 100 meters east of the Carate Airfield on the Osa Peninsula. There's accommodation for every budget, from $42, inc. tax, per person in a Tiki tent to $62, inc. tax, per person in a cabin with private bath, breakfast included. Add $40 per person for inclusive meal package. For info: 2735-5164, **fincaexotica.com.**

Whole New Barú

A family goes exploring in the Hacienda Barú National Wildlife Refuge.

By Dorothy MacKinnon

Huff, puff. My sister and I are climbing steep steps dug into a hillside, on the heels of our guide, Pedro Porras. He signals us to stop, sets up his scope and aims at the trees. Bingo! We see it: a common potoo, aka "stick bird," sitting absolutely still in what is known as its "cryptic" pose. It does indeed look like an extension of the dead tree it's nesting in. But wait – in front of the adult potoo, there's a wide-eyed, white chick wedged between parent and stump, pink mouth gaping wide as it surveys the brand-new world.

This sighting of parent and chick was the icing on the cake of a recent seven-hour hike at Hacienda Barú National Wildlife Refuge, a 330-hectare reserve near the mouth of the Río Barú, north of Dominical on the southern Pacific coast. It's the kind of unique wildlife experience that has given this refuge a worldwide reputation. It's so popular, in fact, that Hacienda Barú Lodge owner Jack Ewing says he's had to turn away guests in the last few years.

The six cabins Ewing built in the 1990s were suited to families. But a lot of visitors come here in groups. So, Ewing set to work building six new spacious guest rooms, facing a brand-new swimming pool.

Strung together on a slope behind the original cabins, the new rooms are fresh, comfortable and, above all, flexible. Each can sleep up to four, with room to spare. A king-size bed can be separated into twins, plus one or two other twin beds as needed, each topped with an orthopedic mattress. Each has a huge bathroom with good lighting, thick towels and shower fed by plentiful solar-heated water.

Ewing built with a keen eye to sustainable practices. All the wood used in the construction is plantation pine and teak, and all the furniture is made from plantation cypress.

From the recycled plastic in the roof to the microorganisms at work in the septic tank, the cabins are as eco-friendly as possible. Guests might not be interested in how their wastewater is being treated, but they will definitely appreciate how cool and comfortable these new cabins are. High ceilings with screened windows for cross-ventilation and ceiling fans work wonderfully to keep you cool day and night. Even when the temperature soared to 38 C during my visit, the room was comfortable during the day and cool enough for sleeping at night, even without the fans.

The swimming pool was a long time coming, Ewing says. Although the reserve fronts Playa Barú – a wide sweep of beach boasting the Ecological Blue Flag award – the three-km. expanse is also notorious for its riptides. Ewing learned this the hard way when his wife, Diane, was swept away years ago and had to be rescued.

"The determining factor was to have a safe place to swim," Ewing says.

The new pool has become the social hub, especially at the end of the day, when almost every guest arrives at the "watering hole" to bob, chat and cool off. This pool uses an ozone-generator system, rather than chemicals, to kill bacteria and algae.

Another welcome change is the revamped El Ceibo Restaurant. Along with the dining rancho bordered with foliage, tables sit in the garden, each under its own thatch roof, perfect for romantic candlelit dinners. A new menu offers healthy choices such as brown rice, along with fresh, varied salads and vegetarian options.

Chef Rodney Mora knows how to cook fish perfectly. It's always fresh, and you can have it cooked any way, sauced with garlic, lemon or tomato (about $10). The lemon sauce is a standout, tart and salty, as are the sides: a homemade *picadillo* of corn, squash, peppers and potatoes; an al dente vegetable medley; and mountains of real mashed potatoes. Breakfasts are hearty and wholesome. The coffee and fresh-fruit drinks are excellent.

What hasn't changed at Hacienda Barú is what has always made it a premier eco-destination: seven km. of trails wending through a landscape that includes primary rain forest and secondary forest, mangrove, swamp forest, wetlands, seashore, river bank and estuary, an old cacao plantation and pastures.

With so many habitats, this refuge is a treasure trove of wildlife, including more than 350 recorded species of birds, plus crocodiles and spectacled caimans, coatis,

Roy Arguedas Arias | Tico Times

Getting There, Rates, Info

By car, head south from San José on the Inter-American Highway about 135 km. to San Isidro de El General, from where you head southwest to Dominical. Hacienda Barú National Wildlife Refuge and Lodge is three km. north of the Dominical Bridge.

By bus, Musoc (2222-2422, Ca. Ctrl., Av. 22/24), hourly departures from San José to San Isidro de El General. From there, Transportes Blanco (2771-2550) makes the trip to Dominical and Uvita several times a day. The trip takes about five and a half hours total. Call for schedules and fares.

Double-occupancy rates, inc. tax and breakfast, range from $30-$50. Cabins are $40 to $60. Park admission for a self-guided walk costs $6; guided walks start at $20 per person. For info: 2787-0003, **info@haciendabaru.com,** or **haci endabaru.com.**

monkeys, sea turtles and more than 25 species of snakes. You can walk the trails on your own, with a map. But you'll get much more out of a visit if you take advantage of the excellent, bilingual naturalist guides.

You can also swing through the tree-tops on the Flight of the Toucan Zipline, climb a tree with ropes, or overnight in a platform in the canopy or in a beach camp-site. You can take part in the refuge's turtle-nesting project, learn about butterflies in the lovely *mariposario*, visit the orchid gar-den, or just swing on a hammock chair in the shaded El Hangout.

When Ewing and partner Steve Stroud, who owns the refuge, first envisioned an ecotourism project here, they assumed most visitors would be attracted by the beach.

"But people kept showing up at the gate, saying, 'We just want to walk in the park,'" Ewing says. So they switched their focus from beach to nature refuge. And a walk in this fascinating, flora-and-fauna-filled "park" is still the main attraction.

Challenges

Even after 23 years of conservation and regen-eration, Hacienda Barú still isn't out of the woods.

The most recent threat to wildlife and habitat is the planned paving of the road between Quepos and Dominical. Trucks, cars and buses barreling along a wider, smoothed-out road will have an enormous impact on habitat and wildlife.

Along with other conservationists who support the Paso de la Danta (Path of the Tapir) biological corri-dor, Jack Ewing has worked hard to negoti-ate a compromise with road builders. After commissioning an envi-ronmental-impact study, the Public Works and Transport Ministry (MOPT), in a laudable spirit of environmental-ism, agreed to build tunnels under the road and bridges above, to reduce the anticipated increase in roadkill.

MOPT will also limit its tree-cutting along the sides of the widened road to 20 meters instead of the usual 50 meters, making it easier for animals to scoot across. "We

worked with MOPT on where to place the tunnels and bridges. We focused on spots identified by a universi-ty researcher as places where animals are already crossing," Ewing says. Along the two km. of road that border Hacienda Barú, will be an animal crossing built almost every 100 meters. Interestingly, most of the tunnels will be square, Ewing says, based on research showing that animals – in particular, the Florida panther – won't enter round tunnels. It remains to be seen whether mon-keys will cross the bridges or animals will actually use the tun-nels.

But it also remains to be seen when this section of road will actually get paved. "The first promise of a paved road was made to me by President Daniel Oduber – that was in 1974," Ewing says. "So I tend to be skep-tical. I think the road will eventually get paved. It just may not be in my lifetime."

Jack Ewing, owner of Hacienda Barú Lodge, is also a prolific author and columnist with the local Dominical Days magazine. His first col-lection of stories, "Monkeys Are Made of Choc-olate," includes entertaining accounts of wild-life and his experiences transforming Hacienda Barú from cattle ranch to biological reserve.

Photos by Dorothy MacKinnon

Iguana Lodge's Pearl of the Osa Building, with Club Rooms above and La Perla Restaurant below.

Photos by Dorothy MacKinnon

Bouquets for a Refreshed Beachfront Hotel on the Osa Peninsula

By Dorothy MacKinnon

One of the Osa Peninsula's lesser known natural havens is Playa Platanares, only seven km. south of the Puerto Jiménez airfield. This miles-long, all-sand beach stretches along the southern Pacific coast's Golfo Dulce, looking east across serene waters, to the rolling hills of Piedras Blancas National Park.

The beach boasts calm waters perfect for swimming and kayaking, with occasional swells big enough to make boogie-boarders happy.

Playa Platanares also encompasses the Preciosa Platanares Wildlife Refuge, a 249-hectare, privately owned mangrove estuary teeming with wildlife and accessible by kayak, horseback and a beachfront path.

A great place to stay is Iguana Lodge, an upscale family-friendly lodge, with eight elegantly decorated rooms in four private *casitas* on a beachfront garden, along with a three-bedroom villa with kitchen.

Iguana Lodge recently added eight luxurious Club Rooms to its roster, in the totally refurbished Pearl of the Osa Hotel, just a stone's throw away along the beach.

Since 1999, the Cleaver family – Toby, Lauren and their two younger children, Rio and Lakota – have owned Iguana Lodge and made it their home. They saw the potential in the neighboring, two-story Pearl of the Osa, and bought it in 2001.

They renovated the guest rooms with verve and style. Shaded by a balsa tree, the hotel faces the beach across a palm-studded lawn strung with hammocks. Club Rooms look out onto a wide, wraparound veranda edged with wrought-iron railings and furnished with bent bamboo chairs with cushions in a tropical foliage pattern. Ceiling fans above chairs have individual controls.

The four front rooms have beach views and breezes, and the four back rooms look out on the jungle. The best rooms are the four corner rooms, each with a queen bed (the four inside rooms have twins that can be made up as king beds). The downside is when the restaurant/bar is hopping on Friday nights, you won't get much sleep until the party is over. Usually, though, it quiets down by 9 p.m.

The look is elegant and uncluttered: white walls, large, screened windows with white venetian blinds, bamboo headboards, white bedspreads piped with pale green and piled with plenty of pillows. Reading lamps on bedside tables and wicker easy chairs complete the furnishings. Screened windows and overhead fans keep the rooms cool, and breezes off the gulf never let you forget you are right on the beach.

In the bathrooms every detail is delightful: spacious, marble-clad showers with invigorating rain-forest showerheads, diamond-shaped sinks with faucets in the shape of a stick of bamboo, a closet with plenty of storage space, a safety box and two fluffy terry robes.

There's one focal point in each room: an oversize canvas of a single, exotic flower painted by Lauren Cleaver (see box).

Guests can enjoy yoga decks, hammock shack, Japanese soaking tub, complimentary boogie boards and kayaks, rental bikes, free Internet and WiFi in the Rancho Grande, also the setting for the lodge's excellent break-

Roy Arguedas Arias | Tico Times

fast buffet of homemade yogurt and granola, fresh-squeezed juices and coffee. The kitchen in the Rancho is always a beehive of activity. You place your order at the window and the chef whips up your eggs on the spot. There's also coffee cake, toast, platters of fresh fruits and sliced tomato and avocado.

Buffet dinners in the Rancho Grande are by reservation only. The upstairs dining room, under a high thatched roof, is illuminated by candles. Food is inventive and international. The night I dined with them, there was an excellent, spicy shrimp étouffée, New Orleans-style, followed by a scrumptious pecan pie.

Lunch and dinner at the lively La Perla de la Osa Restaurant are open to the public. The lunch menu has a Mexican flavor; the taco plate, for instance, features sautéed mahi-mahi, chicken or tenderloin with roasted peppers, onions and chipotle sauce on flour tortillas, with all the trimmings and sides. There are also salads, sandwiches and pizzas and a kids' menu.

Dinner features more substantial courses: coq au vin, steak *au poivre* and fresh fish with sauces, such as a balsamic reduction or tropical *chimichurri* .

One of the best features of the lodge is its proximity to the nearby wildlife refuge. Guests wake up to a cacophony of birdcalls, perhaps orangechinned parakeets cruising the balsa blossoms. On a morning walk, you may spot klatches of cackling gray-headed chachalacas and get close-up views of scarlet macaws.

Everything Is Possible

For the past years, Lauren Cleaver has been painting eye-catching, large-scale canvases of Georgia O'Keefe-style flowers. Her paintings are everywhere: hung on the walls of the reception and the Club Rooms, gracing the menus of La Perla de la Osa Restaurant, and propped up against walls as she runs out of hanging space.

Lauren's studio is the lodge's Rancho Grande veranda, with paints, brushes and palettes artistically arranged on windowsills and tables. In the midst of guests, Lauren happily dabs on paint. It's cheering to watch her, with the sun backlighting her canvases.

Lauren, a criminal defense lawyer in her former life, will tell you that she has no formal artistic training. But the story of how she found her inspiration to paint is inspiring in itself. Several years ago, Lauren suffered a fall. Her long, painful recuperation was frustrating for an active, athletic woman. Throughout her convalescence, she read voraciously. When she was finally able to hobble around, husband Toby took her to Paris. While they roamed the streets and visited galleries and museums, Lauren was struck with the idea that she wanted to paint. She happened to be reading a book, written by a woman whose philosophy she admired. Simply stated, it was: Nothing ever comes naturally. You have to work hard every day to be great at whatever you do. Encouraged by Toby, Lauren started painting, learning as she went and poring over art books for inspiration.

She has already painted more than 100 huge canvases. Lauren's newfound talent has also inspired her to spearhead the Todo Es Posible (Everything Is Possible) program, helping high school graduates develop their potential by coaching them to apply to university and raising money for scholarships.

To see Lauren's paintings, visit **iguanalodge. com.**

View of Playa Platanares from a restaurant lounge area.

Paradise for Quetzals and Humans

The rustic, welcoming main lodge.

Photos by
Dorothy MacKinnon

By Dorothy MacKinnon

In a highland cloud forest just off the Inter-American Highway near Cerro de la Muerte, south of the capital, Paraíso del Quetzal Mountain Lodge definitely delivers on the promise of its name: It *is* a paradise for resplendent quetzals, as it is for visitors who come to catch sight of this most famous of Central American birds.

If you're driving south from San José through the mountains, you can't miss the giant quetzal painted on the sign for Mirador de Quetzales, at Kilometer 70 of the Inter-American Highway. Formerly known as Finca Eddie Serrano, the Mirador's A-frame cabins are a landmark lodge on the Cerro de la Muerte road.

Eddie Serrano was the first homesteader on this mountain, arriving in 1948. In 1992, by then the father of four daughters and four sons, he opened the Mirador, pioneering nature tourism in this mountain zone. After Eddie Serrano's death 10 years

ago, his youngest son, Jorge, managed the Mirador for seven years. But he was itching to move forward with his own ideas, without having to consult the entire family. "It was the biggest decision – and the saddest – of my life, to leave behind all that my father and I had built together," Jorge says. Three years ago, he and his wife Bertillia, along with their four children, moved slightly downhill from the Mirador and created their own version of a paradise for quetzals, now recognized as a model of sustainable development (see box).

Eight red-roofed, wooden cabins are sprinkled around the steeply inclined property, most with a maximum of privacy. The farthest cabin, with the longest hike and the most spectacular view, juts out over the valley.

Three cabins are closer in and on a level with the main lodge and restaurant. My favorite is No. 4, just downhill from the lodge, hidden in a lavish garden of ferns, fuchsia and "poor man's umbrella" plants, and within sound of a trickling stream.

The cozy cabins have a double bed and a bunk tucked into an alcove. The interior blond wood looks and smells fresh, and each cabin has large windows and a private deck. Jorge has wielded his brush in most of the cabins, painting birds on headboards and walls. The small tiled bathrooms provide the most essential thing you look for at this chilly altitude (2,600 meters): showers with really hot water. Beds are piled high with fleecy blankets, and for really cold nights, when the temperature can

Cozy family cabin in the woods.

drop into the 40s Fahrenheit, Bertillia hands out hot water bottles, which will keep your toes warm the entire night.

The rustic main lodge is welcoming, with an old-fashioned wood stove and long, wooden tables embellished with colorful local birds painted by Jorge. The entire back wall consists of windows framing a view of mountains, forest and valley.

But you hardly notice the view at first because your eye is caught by magnificent and fiery-throated hummingbirds mobbing the feeders just outside the windows. You can easily sit for hours observing hummingbirds in action.

To find the quetzals, though, you have to hit the trail. Within five minutes of setting off on the steep, four-km. El Robledal trail in early May, my birding partner and I caught sight of our first resplendent quetzal of the day, trailing his extravagantly long, greenish-blue tail feathers. By the time we retraced our steps two hours later, with the help of guide Fabio Salazar, we had seen seven more and heard the calls of countless more.

Sprinkled around the forest are *agua-catillo* (wild avocado) trees, the food of the quetzal and the reason you are almost guaranteed to see one here.

After wolfing down a hearty breakfast of *gallo pinto*, eggs, fried plantains, toast, marmalade and coffee, we headed out on another trail, this time with Jorge Junior.

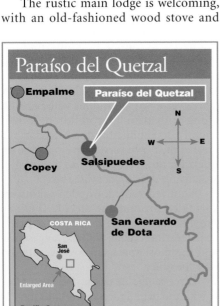

Paraíso del Quetzal

Empalme

Paraíso del Quetzal

Copey

Salsipuedes

COSTA RICA

San José

Enlarged Area

Pacific Ocean

San Gerardo de Dota

Inter-American Hwy.
Secondary Road

San Isidro de El General

Roy Arguedas Arias | Tico Times

Getting There, Rates, Info

Paraíso del Quetzal is at Kilometer 70 of the Inter-American Highway, heading south from San José past Cartago and toward the Southern Zone town of San Isidro de El General. The per-person rate of $50, inc. tax, dinner and breakfast, guided hiking or birding tour. Additional tours, $30. Non-guests can walk the trails for $10 per person, with or without guide. Credit cards are accepted. For info: 2200-0241, **paraisodelquetzal.com**.

Along the way we had excellent views of other highland species, including ochraceous pewees, endemic to this zone, hairy woodpeckers, buffy tuftedcheeks and both long-tailed and black-and-yellow silky-flycatchers.

Even if you're not a birder, the vistas of cloud-enshrouded mountains and valleys here will thrill you, as will the hiking trails through ancient oak forest, dripping with moss and epiphytes and burnished by slanting rays of the early-morning sun.

Along with towering oak trees – many of them 400 to 600 years old – are magnificent mountain cypresses. At the top of the El Robledal trail, on a clear day, you can see three volcanoes: Irazú, Turrialba and, more rarely, Arenal. The morning we climbed the trail, we saw Turrialba smoking away. Other trails lead to waterfalls, rivers, an old plane wreck and fossils. Along the trails, you may encounter mountain goats, rabbits and squirrels, along with myriad mountain birds. If you're lucky, you might see a tapir or at least tapir tracks. Tucked into the forest are a dozen or more round tables with tree-stump stools where you can spend some time relaxing.

If you are really ambitious, you can hike 14 km. over the next hill to reach the village of Copey. Ask for a hiking map at the lodge if you want to set out on your own.

Most visitors arrive in the afternoon, admire the hummingbirds and have an early supper – simple and traditional, with a choice of chicken, pork chop or trout (which has a tendency to be overcooked, so ask for it "*suave*"), along with rice and beans, vegetable *picadillos* and fruit juices. Then it's up at the crack of dawn for the main event: the early-morning search for a quetzal. As Jorge proudly states, "We are 100 percent about birds here."

The Model of a Mountain Eco-lodge

When Jorge Serrano set out to build his own lodge from scratch, his goal was to be as eco-friendly as possible, using only plantation wood to build, minimizing water and electricity use, recycling, regenerating open areas of the forest and planting trees. His vision paid off when Paraíso del Quetzal received the first-ever Blue Flag ecological award to be granted in this zone.

Jorge isn't resting on his laurels. He wants to make improvements to the lodge to make it more comfortable, while retaining its rusticity. The Quetzal Education Research Center (QERC) in nearby San Gerardo de Dota may set up research here, protecting and studying quetzal nests, and Jorge is working with the new Costa Rican Ornithologists Union, which plans to offer birding courses here.

The Jungle Has an Ocean View at Río Magnolia

Photos by
Meg Yamamoto

By Meg Yamamoto

They say Canadians are nice. In the case of John and Maureen Paterson of Río Magnolia Lodge, it couldn't be truer. The Ontario couple have built a beacon of hospitality on a hilltop in the Fila Costeña mountains, between the crossroads town of San Isidro de El General and Playa Dominical on the southern Pacific coast.

The Patersons, both engineers, moved to Costa Rica several years ago and bought the 110-hectare property swathed in rain forest and boasting sweeping views of the Pacific slope and ocean beyond. They built the lodge in a year and a half and moved in last December.

The grandeur of the main house, perched on its ocean-view hilltop, seems to belie the mom-and-pop nature of this operation. In addition to making guests feel welcome, John, 55, keeps busy maintaining the infinity pool and the 12-kilowatt hydroelectric system that powers the lodge, while Maureen, 53, ensures that a constant stream of delicious meals ema-

nates from the kitchen. A small staff and canine companions, Molly, Darcy and Palomo, round out the hospitable crew.

The main house is a grandiose affair. Floor-to-ceiling windows and doors take advantage of the view, while a large central fireplace, open on all sides, adds ambience. Wood furnishings, antique doors and a ceiling lined with *caña brava* reeds round out the decor. Inviting sitting areas abound here, and a large bar beckons guests to gather around it and chat with the congenial hosts.

Accommodations in the main house consist of three guest rooms, the star of which is El Cielo, featuring panoramic ocean and jungle views, a private wraparound terrace, queen-size canopy bed, cozy sitting area and a large bathroom with a shower that lets bathers enjoy the view.

A short walk from the house is Mono Congo, a private cabin nestled at jungle edge. A handsome deck welcomes guests to the wooden cabin. Amenities include a queen-size canopy bed piled high with fluffy pillows, in addition to a comfortable sitting area surrounded by large, handmade windows that open directly onto mossy trees, with a peek-a-boo view of the ocean beyond.

The bathroom features a gas-heated shower open to the scents and sounds of the jungle. Down a steep hillside from the main house, three are three rustic A-frame cabins, with one double or two twin beds and appealing bathrooms completely lined with river stones.

El Cielo features a private terrace and a view down to the Pacific .

For longer stays, the Amapola Cottage, a short distance past the main house, is equipped with a king-size bedroom, separate living, dining and kitchen area with wood-burning fireplace, a high-ceilinged bathroom and a private garden Jacuzzi. A lovely stone patio is fronted by a large garden with a wide view down to the ocean.

With the nearest restaurant three bumpy km. away on the main road, meals come included in the room rates. Dinners might consist of tender trout in lemon-tarragon sauce or grilled chicken skewers, while as-you-like-it breakfasts may include fresh fruit, granola and yogurt, eggs and bacon or some of Maureen's mouthwatering fresh-baked banana muffins.

The Patersons call Río Magnolia Lodge an ecotourism project, and their commitment to protecting the environment includes a recycling program they established for the community, La Alfombra, in addition to a solar drier for laundry and their sustainable hydroelectric system. Most of the property remains protected in its natural state and forms part of a biological corridor for wildlife movement. Nature lovers will find no shortage of activities here, with many trails, including

an easy, one-km walk through the rain forest that lets hikers take in ancient trees, the heady scent of jungle flora and the distinctive call of toucans. Anteaters, kinkajous, peccaries, coatis, sloths and white-faced and howler monkeys have been spotted, along with many birds. Guided horseback rides are available courtesy of four happy

Roy Arguedas Arias | Tico Times

View from the infinity pool stretches all the way to the sea.

Photo Courtesy of Río Magnolia Lodge

horses in Río Magnolia's private stable.

For those wanting to venture off the property, the manifold attractions of the southern Pacific coast, about a 40-minute drive away, include surfing at Dominical, whale- and dolphin-watching at Ballena National Marine Park, kayaking at Playa Ventanas and simply relaxing on any number of beaches, some virtually deserted.

Horseback rides to nearby Nauyaca Falls and zipline canopy tours at Hacienda Barú National Wildlife Refuge are also available. Offering an interesting venue for intimate weddings, the lodge hosted the nuptials of the Patersons' son, David. Seventeen guests were accommodated for the event, in what the Patersons hope was a trial run for more to come.

A wedding party – indeed, any guest – couldn't hope for nicer hosts.

Disclosure: Tico Times Weekend Editor Meg Yamamoto is Canadian.

Getting There, Rates, Contact Info

From San José, take Inter-American Highway south to San Isidro de El General (about three hours) and turn right at the sign to Dominical. Pass through town and head west over the mountains toward Pacific Ocean. About 20 minutes from San Isidro, look for Río Magnolia Lodge turnoff on right, 500 meters past Los Chorros Mirador and Restaurant. After the turnoff, take first right and continue for 3 km. The dirt road winds through village of La Alfombra, crosses three rivers and eventually ends at the Río Magnolia gate. Lodge is 1 km. past the property gate along a bumpy but scenic road through lush rain forest. Four-wheel drive is necessary for the last 1.5 km.

Double-occupancy room rates, inc. tax and three meals per day, dbl.: $270 for A-frame cabins; $281 for standard rooms in main lodge; $304 for El Cielo in main lodge; $315 for Mono Congo cabin; and $372 for Amapola Cottage ($236 without meals). Weekly rates available. For info: 8307-1036 or 8868-5561, **info@riomagnolia.com, riomagnolia.com**

Owners John and Maureen Paterson at the lodge stable.

Photo by Meg Yamamoto

Rural Tourism Helps Revive Fading Culture

Cagrú masks range from simple to highly elaborate.

Photos by
Beverly Gallagher

By Beverly Gallagher

Rural community tourism is gaining ground as a way to combine the country's rich natural environment with its equally rich cultural heritage, and 12 women of the Boruca, one of Costa Rica's eight indigenous groups, are picking up on this trend.

These women have formed an artisan's group called *Sô Cagrú*, which in Boruca means "masked warrior." Contributing to what could be coined a Boruca Renaissance; they are leading tours of Brujo, famous for its carved masks and textiles and providing accommodation to visitors.

The Boruca population of 2,100 is divided into two communities, Boruca and Curré, in the southern Pacific end of Puntarenas. Boruca spreads across mountainous terrain at 450 meters above sea level

while Curré sits along the mid-course of the Grande de Térraba River. The Boruca have inhabited the region since pre-Columbian times.

"We are visionary women who believe in what we're doing," says Lourdes Frasser, 40-year-old mother of four and Sô Cagrú founder. "We are the administrators of a dream."

I sit at a long table. The *fogón*, a traditional firewood stove, glows beneath cast iron pots. An array of handicrafts including woven purses, tube drums, bows and arrows and carved gourds hang along the wall.

"This is *sopa de frijoles*," says Frasser, placing an oblong wooden bowl on the table. Beans, a hard-boiled egg and a green banana float in a tasty broth of cilantro, or *guagran* in Boruca. Frasser admits that when she first thought of hosting visitors, she asked the Costa Rican Tourism Board (ICT) what she should serve. To her delight, the ICT replied that she should serve just what she and her family eat.

Giving tourists the chance to see Boruca by day and night, Frasser was the first to build a guest *rancho*. Four other ranchos are now ready for visitors, one for groups of up to 40 people.

I shoo away chickens roosting on the steps as I enter my room,

William García, son of Sô Cagrú founder Lourdes Frasser, paints masks in the downstairs area.

the entire top floor. Furnishings are a queen bed, two double beds and ample stretching room. The beams form a peak and are topped by royal palm fronds. Gazing out at the treetops makes you feel you are in your own private tree house.

Just outside are a toilet and an open-air bamboo-encased shower with cement floor. Our first stop on the artisan route is Marciana Mora's house. Mother of six and fondly known as doña Chana, she invited me over to make rice tamales, or *chari*, and to learn about Boruca weaving traditions.

We spend the morning wrapping rice and chicken in banana leaves and the afternoon talking about textiles. "One thing is to read about someone in a book – their traditions, what they eat – another thing is to come to where they live and see it," says Mora.

Mora brings out a multi-colored bowl of thread and a bag of caramel-colored cotton balls. She rubs the cotton ball between her thumb and forefinger producing a dark brown seed. She attaches the cotton to a spindle and demonstrates how the cotton fibers are spun to make thread. Picking up the bowl of thread, she hands me the purple ball. It smells like seaweed. A Boruca tradition, weavers travel to the Pacific coast beaches to collect murex snails for extracting purple coloring. Blowing on the snail, a liquid is produced which drips

Sô Cagrú

COSTA RICA

San José

Enlarged Area

Pacific Ocean

—— Inter-American Hwy.
—— Secondary Road

El Brujo

Sô Cagrú

Paso Real

Boruca

Palmar Norte

N

Palmar Sur

W ——+—— E

S

To Golfito

A bowlful of colorful yarn dyed with bark, leaves, fruits, seeds, clay and murex snail.

onto the cotton skeins. After sun drying, the thread turns purple. Most of their woven items are made with industrial cotton thread. Some are dyed naturally with plants harvested only during the waning moon, and others chemically. Only a few Boruca women weave hand-spun and hand-dyed thread. This process is time-consuming and costly. The question is how to market the finer pieces to keep age-old textile traditions alive.

Boys cool off at a swimming hole, 30 minutes from town.

"To get people to appreciate their objects more, there is much work to be done," says Paulina Ortiz, Costa Rican textile artist and president of the Iberoamerican Textile Network.

"By rescuing textile traditions, they would discover exquisite ways of finishing objects and many different designs done in pre-Columbian times," she says. "Some of those objects could supply new designs or they might just be a testimony of how things were."

The road to revival is not smooth. "There are no simple answers; the issue is complex," says Ortiz. "It is important to inform the Boruca about what they are doing to rescue their own culture and preserve its traditional textiles by technique and design... how they do some processes only at a certain time of the year and how valuable it is for them, as well as for Costa Rican culture, to be able to rescue that [heritage], otherwise lost."

The Boruca are well-known for their creation of balsa masks, which has surpassed subsistence agriculture as an occupation. These masks are donned for the Little Devils Festival, or *cagrú_rojc* in Boruca, Dec. 30 to Jan. 2. The festival dates back to the Spanish conquest and recreates the battles that took place between the Spaniards and the Boruca.

Frasser wants visitors to walk away with the whole story and not just an outline. "The masks do not represent devils," she says. "They represent good spirits that frighten away evil. The correct word is not devil; it's *cagrú*, which means warriors who defend what is theirs – their land, women, children, rivers, trees, small and big animals."

The battle continues as the Boruca struggle to build pride in their ancestry and to make ends meet.

As the community starts to encourage more tourism, there is a lot to talk about.

Tours include a visit to the museum and a chance to purchase these lovely hand-made objects at prices much lower than in the Central Valley.

Getting There, Rates, Info

Take the Inter-American Highway south past the town of Buenos Aires, in southern Puntarenas. Continuing south on the Inter-American, turn right 50 meters past El Brujo and the gas station. Continue for 8 km. along a fairly smooth, but steep road that begins paved. Turn right at last road before entering the center of Boruca. Sô Cagrú is first rancho on the right.

From Buenos Aires, buses depart for Boruca at 11 a.m. and 3:30 p.m. and take an hour and a half. Per-person rates are $50 a day including breakfast, lunch, dinner, accommodation and guided tours of artists' studios, the area and waterfalls. For info: 8860-8197, 2730-2453, **boruca.co.cr**

Osa Peninsula, Corcovado Nature Reserve.
Photo by Harmony Reforma

The white ibis is a coastal species, seen here at Corcovado National Reserve on the Osa Peninsula.

Photo by Harmony Reforma

Indigenous Cabécar children walking in the mountain, at Puerto Viejo de Chirripó, where Costa Rican Humanitarian Foundation build a cultural ranch.

Photo by Ronald Reyes

Welcome

Photo by Ronald Reyes

Historical Highlights

COSTA RICA is exalted as a tiny oasis of peace and prosperity in a region often plagued by civil strife.

HISTORICAL events, visionary leaders and an enlightened approach to democracy, social welfare and education, plus abolition of the army have contributed to the praiseworthy development of this distinctive nation.

13,000 – 1,000 B.C. Sporadic records of human habitation, little known except Olmec, Mayan, Aztec and Inca trading routes.

1,000 B.C.-1400 A.D. City of Guayabo, estimated inhabitants 10,000-15,000. Aqueducts, causeways, artifacts unearthed. Pottery, jade and gold jewelry show evidence of a civilization more developed than other pre-Columbian settlements in the country. Perfectly-spherical granite balls (some weighing up to 16 tons) uncovered in the south remain a mystery. Researcher Iván Zapp theorizes they may have been ancient navigation markers for seafaring cultures.

1502: Christopher Columbus, on fourth and final odyssey to the "New World," anchors off present-day Caribbean city of Limón. Although he never comes ashore, it is said Columbus named Costa Rica because of gold worn by tribal dignitaries.

1506-1562: The Spanish explore, conquer and sparsely colonize the territory. European diseases deplete indigenous population estimated between 120,000 to 400,000. Resisting groups flee to highlands, escaping enslavement. The few left convert to Catholicism. Costa Rica becomes isolated backwater of Spanish Empire.

1563-1820: Settlers head for Central Valley, small farming communities develop. Juan Vásquez de Coronado founds colonial capital of Cartago in 1563. In the 1700s other cities are founded, including San José (1737). Coffee is introduced and becomes first major cash crop.

1821-1856: Central America gains independence from Spain on September 15, 1821 and becomes a state of the Central American Federation, but Guatemalan dominance leads to unrest. In 1838, Costa Rica proclaims itself an independent republic.

1856: Battles of Santa Rosa and Rivas. U.S. filibuster William Walker invades Costa Rica in an attempt to conquer Central America and establish a slave state. An ill-equipped volunteer force in what is now Santa Rosa National Park defeats him. Walker's mercenary army flees to Nicaragua and is routed at Rivas, where mythical hero Juan Santamaría dies while torching the enemies' barracks.

1869-1890: General Tomás Guardia revises the constitution, establishing free, compulsory education in 1869. He overthrows the government in 1870, rules for 12 years and is responsible for initiating forces that shape the liberal-democratic state. He abolishes capital punishment, curbs the power of coffee barons and uses earnings and taxation to finance roads and public buildings. U.S. entrepreneur Minor Keith is contracted to build a railroad linking San José to the Caribbean coast. It takes 20 years to complete. Keith cultivates bananas using West Indian and Asian laborers brought over to work the railroad. Bananas flourish and displace coffee as major export.

The first democratic elections are held in 1889 and the opposition wins. The country becomes first true democracy in Central America. The railroad is inaugurated in 1890 and nine years later Minor Keith founds the United Fruit Company.

1914-1939: World War I, followed by the Great Depression, cuts short export trade. Social injustice becomes an issue. In

1917 Minister of War Federico Tinoco overthrows the elected president and forms a dictatorship. After opposition, he's exiled. Conditions deteriorate rapidly during the 1930s. The country is on the verge of revolution, and the Communist Party becomes the voice of the workers.

1940-1948: Rafael Angel Calderón is elected president (1940). Radical social reforms undercut Communist support and continue during Teodoro Picado's administration (1944-1948). With support from the Catholic Church and Communist Party, socialized medicine, housing and child-welfare programs, minimum-wage laws, the right to unionize and a university system are implemented.

1948-1949: Calderón, seeking a second term, refuses to hand over power when the election is declared fraudulent. His opponent, Otilio Ulate, accepts defeat. Outraged citizens join "The National Liberation Army," led by still-revered José "Pepe" Figueres. A month of armed conflict ends when Figueres promises to hand over power after 18 months. The Communist Party is banned, Calderón is exiled and "The National Liberation Army" becomes the National Liberation Party. On December 1, 1949, Figueres' interim government abolishes the army. Public utilities and banking system are nationalized and it is declared mandatory that all citizens 18 and over vote in elections. Women and African Costa Ricans get the right to vote.

1950-1999: Solidarity, plus post-war economic boom, result in prosperity, encouragement of private enterprise and expansion of welfare state. Disease hits banana plantations, thousands unemployed. Tensions with Nicaragua reach a climax when dictator Anastasio Somoza and exiled Calderón attempt an armed rebellion but fail. In 1972 during Figueres' third and final presidency, global rise in coffee prices brings influx of capital, infrastructure investment. Coffee market collapses in 1979. Economic crisis ensues when country is unable to meet debt obli-

gations. Stabilization is restored with enforcement of currency regulations, controlled inflation and financial constraints.

Costa Rica resists being sucked into regional civil wars but suffers continuous fallout from neighboring violence in the form of refugees, spies, gunrunners and combatants from both sides hoping to use the country as a staging area.

Prominence hits Costa Rica in 1987, when President Oscar Arias wins Nobel Peace Prize for formulating the Central American Peace Plan. The country is proud: the national soccer team reaches second round of the 1990 World Cup, swimmer Claudia Poll wins country's first Olympic gold medal and famous astronaut Franklin Chang makes return visits to space.

In 1990, Rafael Angel Calderón Jr., son of the 1940s reformer, succeeds Arias as president. In 1994, José María Figueres, Don Pepe's son, succeeds the younger Calderón as president. Both he and his successor, Miguel Angel Rodríguez, face the problem of adapting to the modern world, establishing new social reforms and maintaining traditions.

2000-2009: New millennium brings many changes. Proposed Central American Free-Trade Agreement (CAFTA) with the United States sparks protests and is finally passed in national referendum. President Abel Pacheco, elected in 2002, is plagued by massive demonstrations, ministerial resignations, strikes and demands for higher wages. Opposition grows against his support of U.S. invasion of Iraq. Corruption scandals rock the country, and two ex-presidents, Rafael Angel Calderón, Jr. (1990-1994), and Miguel Angel Rodríguez (1998-2002), are arrested. Scandal forces Rodríguez, the first Central American Secretary General of the Organization of American States, to resign. Both former presidents are given six-month preventive prison sentences, then house arrest for several months. Calderón's trial begins in 2008. He is sentenced to five years imprisonment in 2009 and is appealing the ruling. Former President Arias gets the ban on presidential reelection overturned and is elected for a second term in 2006. In 2007 the Costa Rican government announces plans for Costa Rica to become the first carbon-neutral country by 2021. The country is ranked 5th in the world, and 1st among the Americas, in terms of the 2008 Environmental Performance Index. In 2009, Costa Rica ranks first in the Happy Planet Index and is the greenest country in the world. Costa Rica remains the most economically stable, democratic, peace-loving nation in Central America. (See **Costa Rica Today**.)

The Indigenous Population

THE nearly 70,000 indigenous Costa Ricans, most of whom live in abject poverty on 22 reserves, are gradually assimilating into the national culture.

THE Indigenous are gaining recognition through advocacy groups and revised governmental policies. Eight ethnic groups strive to maintain their heritage and receive benefits from the country's social welfare programs. Remoteness of many villages hinders development of adequate education and health care.

Chorotega descendants of the Maya live on the Nicoya Peninsula and the Huetar live in the Central Valley region of Puriscal. Both are known for their pottery and crafts. The Bribris, Cabécares, Borucas and Téribes live in the Talamanca Mountains; the Guaymis migrate back and forth across the Panamanian border in southern Costa Rica, where they produce crops such as bananas and cocoa. The Maleku live in the area of Los Chiles-Guatuso in the north. Some native villages welcome tourists, sharing their arts and traditions.

In 1939 every indigenous family received 148 hectares of land. A 1977 law prohibited buying land within a reserve. Land takeovers by non-indigenous continue, and in the southern zone Boruca communities remain threatened by a proposal to build a hydroelectric dam and trans-Talamanca highway.

Many indigenous traditions are fading. Spanish is now the predominant language, European-style clothes are the norm and Christian beliefs are replacing native spiritual practices. However, several indigenous festivals have become popular attractions. One is the Fiesta de los Diablitos, an enactment in the southern zone of a war between Spanish conquistadors and victorious Boruca people. Costumes are fashioned from burlap sacks and brightly-painted actors wear beautifully carved balsa wood masks. The Boruca also celebrate the Los Negritos Festival which combines indigenous rituals with Catholicism to honor the Virgin of the Immaculate Conception with costumes, drums, flutes and dancing.

The indigenous received national identity cards (*cédulas*), which gives them the right to vote, in 1990, but remain marginalized. April 19 marks "Indigenous People's Day" and October 12 is "Meeting of the Cultures Day."

Brilliant and beautiful, but don't touch!

Photo by Ronald Reyes

Costa Rica Today

WITH its patchwork of farms and dense tropical forests, its high literacy rate and modern public-health system, its political stability and respect for peace; Costa Ricans have always known their little Central American country is some place special.

YET, their instincts were confirmed in July of 2009, when the United Kingdom's New Economics Foundation named Costa Rica the happiest place on earth.

The study took into account life expectancy and a country's ecological footprint in judging among the 143 countries.

"Well, it's the truth," was the response of many Ticos when they learned their little Central American country topped the list.

Despite Costa Rica's high ranking on the happiness index, it has not been immune to the economic crisis that's gripped the world. In the first quarter of 2009, tourism dropped by 13 percent compared to the first quarter of the previous year, representing a big hit for a country in which the tourism industry accounts for 8 percent of the gross domestic product. Manufacturing slid nearly 17 percent over last year and exports fell 14.2 percent.

But, at the same time, Costa Rica hit some landmarks in 2009, reopening the commuter train between Heredia and San José, approaching a close-out date for construction on the Caldera Highway that will reduce travel time to the Pacific coast to 45 minutes, and securing an $80 million loan from the World Bank to make Limón – the country's Caribbean port town – a more tourist-friendly place.

Other projects underway include the construction of a new soccer stadium in La Sabana Park (courtesy of the Chinese), renovations to both airports, and the expansion of a major oil refinery on the Caribbean coast.

Costa Ricans have a lot to celebrate as a population. According to the World Health Organization, they are becoming healthier (life expectancy has increased to 78.8 years and infant mortality has dropped to 10 per 1,000 births, from 16 in 1990) and they are ranked higher on the overall health index than the United States. At the same time, the poverty line is dropping. In 2000, 20.6 percent of the population was below the poverty line. Today, the poverty line rests at 17.7 percent.

But Costa Rica is continuing to struggle with teen pregnancy (the number of pregnant mothers under 15 has nearly doubled since 1984), and – to some extent – it's behind in certain business-friendly practices, with a recent report by the World Bank ranking Costa Rica 121 after countries such as Colombia (37), Panamá (77) and Nicaragua (117) for ease of doing business.

Yet, the country is still looking for ways to make itself known on the world stage.

In 2009, Costa Rica made headlines for the role its Nobel Prize-winning President Oscar Arias played in mediating the Honduran crisis. When Honduran president Manuel Zelaya was marched from his home at gunpoint, he arrived a few hours later in Costa Rica, still in his pajamas. From that moment, Arias worked with the international community to try to restore the ousted president. As one of the only countries in the region without an army and home to the University of Peace, Costa Rica's role in the mediation process further solidified the country's reputation as the "Switzerland of the Americas." It inaugurated the first Peace Ministry in the Western Hemisphere in September.

Costa Rica is also pushing to become

the first carbon-neutral country by 2021 – a goal President Arias is initiating before he leaves office in May 2010. The country has long relied on renewable energy sources to generate more than 90 percent of electricity consumption, but analysts say the country has a lot of work to do (including a large cutback in emissions) in the next decade.

In part due to its political stability, but also due to active solicitation, more and more international companies are opening offices in Costa Rica. Boston Scientific expanded its role in Costa Rica, creating 2,000 new jobs; call centers, casinos and outsourcing companies are growing; and Intel's microchips have expanded to represent 36.7 percent of all Costa Rica's exports.

Meanwhile, the Legislative Assembly has been busy signing off on new bills to remain current with the changing needs of the country. Fines for drunk-driving, riding seatbelt-less or talking on the phone while driving have skyrocketed to upwards of $300. And be careful with your definition of drunk; Costa Rica considers a blood alcohol level of .5 grams per liter (barely two beers for some) to be worth a $370 fine.

Legislators have also adjusted the immigration laws, allowing foreigners to apply for residency with the purchase of a property worth more than $200,000 and permitting applications to be processed entirely through Costa Rica (instead of communicating with a consulate in one's home country.)

While Costa Rica continues to experience growing pains and deals with myriad serious 21st century issues, its people remain engaging and friendly, guided by the optimistic spirit of *pura vida* (pure life). Visitors marvel at the warmth and hospitality of the Ticos, as well as at the weather and natural beauty of this small, proud country that has become a world-class attraction.

Geography & Climate

GEOGRAPHICALLY a land of extreme contrasts, Costa Rica offers a virtual smorgasbord of fantastic diversity.

STRADDLING a rugged mountain chain, its topography is responsible for constant seismic activity, spewing volcanoes, distinctive climatic zones and immense biodiversity.

Lying within the tropics (between 8 and 11 degrees north of the Equator), the country has two seasons, dry and rainy. However, elevation and temperatures influence this tropical climate and conditions vary considerably. Hot steamy jungles, fertile pasturelands, chilly highlands and mountain peaks make Costa Rica a land of spellbinding and infinite variety.

Shifting Cocos and Caribbean tectonic plates, plus local faults, cause thousands of tremors yearly, some short and jarring, others longer and rolling. Geologists claim this frequency relieves pressure and keeps at bay a "really big one." On November 20, 2004, a prolonged 6.2 Richter scale earthquake in the Central Pacific zone shook the country. Areas near the epicenter suffered serious structural damage and six deaths, five from heart failure were partially blamed on the quake.

In 1991 a devastating earthquake measuring 7.5 on the Richter scale struck the Caribbean coastal regions, killing 47, injuring 109, leaving 7,439 homeless. It caused extensive damage to the port city of Limón and exposed coral reefs when the coastline rose by more than a meter. The Central Valley has suffered several damaging

Arenal Volcano blowing its top sounds like a pride of lions roaring in the distance. Awesome.

Photo Courtesy
Arenal Lodge

quakes since 1910, when most of the colonial capital of Cartago was leveled. Other quakes measuring 4.9 to 6.5 near the Central Valley city of Alajuela, the Caribbean slope town of Turrialba, Puriscal, west of San José, in the Los Santos area, plus the Central Pacific communities of Parrita and Quepos resulted in varying degrees of damage. On December 18, 2008, an earthquake measuring 6.2, killed 20 people, left thousands homeless, brought down hillsides and destroyed homes and schools around Poás Volcano

Seismic activity has been recorded since 1638, but predictions are still ambiguous. Together with Central American scientists, Costa Rican scientists are working on a regional warning system on both coasts.

Major hurricanes causing havoc in North America also affect Costa Rica, mostly in the form of torrential rain and flooding, causing death and destruction on both coasts.

Mountain chains from the northwestern Nicaraguan border to the southeastern Panamanian border divide the country.

The Cordillera de Guanacaste, the northernmost range, boasts the steaming volcano Rincón de la Vieja. Further south in the Cordillera de Tilarán, the most active and famous volcano, Arenal, continually spews rocks and lava. These eruptions are a major tourist attraction.

In the Cordillera Central, active volcano Poás still belches sulfurous gases and bubbles menacingly. Irazú last erupted in 1963, showering the Central Valley with ash for two years. Turrialba, part of the same range, has been showing activity recently. Sleeping volcanoes – Tenorio, Miravalles, Orosí, Santa María, Cacho Negro, Platanar, and Barva – could grumble to life at any time. Extinct volcanoes number 200.

Geologically older but non-volcanic, the southeastern Cordillera de Talamanca is the largest, most rugged massif in the country. The highest peak, Mt. Chirripó (3,819 m., 12,529 ft.), experiences temperatures below freezing and occasional light snowfalls. South of Cartago, the Inter-American Highway starts to climb the Cerro de la Muerte, rising from some 5,000 ft.

to 11,450 ft., where temperatures range from 5-20°C (41-68° F). The Bustamente in the central Los Santos area and the Costanera running along the southern Pacific coast are lower-altitude undulating regions.

Over half the population live in the fertile Central Valley, known for its abrupt changes in altitude, temperature and landscape. It is home to the capital, San José (1,160 m.), the Orosí Valley and major cities Alajuela, Heredia, Cartago and Turrialba. Rolling countryside and fertile volcanic soil make the upper elevations a prime coffee-growing area. Dairy farming and produce also flourish.

Multiple changes in altitude and temperature create amazing micro-climates, responsible for the country's incredible biodiversity. San José averages 18-27° C (64-80° F) year round. Other nearby communities can be five to six degrees warmer or colder. Surrounding the Central Valley, inland hills and mountain ranges tumble down in the northwest to the Province of Guanacaste and the Nicoya Peninsula. Scorching daytime temperatures between 31° C (88° F) and 38° C (100° F) drop to around 20° C (72° F) at night. Ten hours of sun during the dry season and six hours in the wet are the norm for this region of dry tropical forests and flat grassy plains famous for beef cattle.

The lush, sodden rainforests of the Caribbean slope descend to the flatlands and major banana-growing regions. Year-round rainfall, with October traditionally the driest month, produces a greater humidity level than the Pacific coast with temperatures averaging 25°-27° C (77°-80° F).

The Central Pacific zone's palm oil plantations cover a huge area, and the Southern zone's dense steamy jungles border the rugged coastline of the remote Osa Peninsula. The Northern zone's diverse topography results in an amazing variety of microclimates. The scenery includes Lake Arenal's verdant pasturelands and Monteverde's misty cloud forests.

Two seasons – the rainy or "winter," May to November, and the dry "summer," December to April, mostly affect the Central Valley, Guanacaste and Central Pacific, although climate change and phenomena like *El Niño* and *La Niña* have made weather patterns less predictable. In the rainy season cloudless skies and intense sun make this the hottest time of the year. Around noon, clouds roll in and thunderous downpours occur. Lighter rain continues into the night. Rain often ceases during *veranillo* (little summer) that lasts for a couple of weeks in late June – early July.

In the Southern Pacific rain starts a month earlier, but the Northern and humid Caribbean zones are less affected by the seasonal cycle, where showers or torrential rains alternate with blazing sun.

Biodiversity & National Parks

THIS is where the wild things are. Thanks to its geographical position as a land bridge linking North and South America, Costa Rica is one of the most biologically diverse countries in the world.

ALTHOUGH the country covers only about 0.03% of the earth's area, it contains an astonishing 4% of the world's estimated 13 to 14 million species of flora and fauna. Costa Rica's abundant biodiversity on land is more than matched by the undersea life teeming along both Atlantic and Pacific coasts

Varying levels of altitude and rainfall make for 12 distinctive tropical life zones.

in which a natural treasure chest of flora and fauna thrives. The most popular zones visited by tourists and scientists alike are tropical rainforest, cloud forest and low-land dry and wet forests.

There is, however, trouble in paradise. Frogs, the harbingers of environmental stress, are disappearing at an alarming rate all around the world and Costa Rica is no exception. About 40 frog, toad, salamander and wormlike caecilian species are threat-ened here. Monteverde's golden toad already is believed extinct and the harle-quin frog hasn't been spotted for years. The cause appears to be the chytrid fungus running wild in the Americas, which, in turn, is caused by climate change.

The Ministry of Environment and Energy and Telecommunications (MINAET) lists 38 animal and bird species officially in danger of extinction, including all the country's wild cats, three of the four monkey species and both the Green and the Scarlet Macaw.

How can so many species be endan-gered in a country renowned abroad for its conservation policies and high environ-mental consciousness? Deforestation is the main culprit, along with illegal hunting, pollution, infrastructure growth; roads, dams, etc., illegal commerce in exotic pets, indiscriminate use of pesticides, misuse of river systems and large-scale, non-sustain-able commercial developments.

Within MINAET, the National System of Conservation Areas (SINAC, 2233-4533, **joaquin.calvo@sinac.go.cr**) is responsible for administering and protecting flora and fauna in 11 vast conservation areas across the country. It is limited by lack of finan-cial resources, personnel, and coordination among ministries and private sector with overlapping responsibilities. However, SINAC reports that illegal logging has been reduced by 10%.

Fifty new rangers have been hired in Corcovado National Park, crown jewel of the national park system. Nevertheless, there are still not enough park rangers to patrol an area of 172 sq. mi. Although data on illegal hunting of peccaries (wild pigs), depriving jaguars, the park's most famous

La Casona de Santa Rosa: a landmark to Costa Rica's defeat of foreign invaders.

Photo by Blake Schmidt

residents, of vital food, is scant, the perception is that it has diminished.

Other positive signs exist. Nationwide, public awareness and action are growing. Non-profit conservation and environmental groups, along with hotel owners and tour operators, are raising money to buy land for conservation and educating the public to the dangers of unchecked development.

The **Instituto Nacional de Biodiversidad (INBio** 2507-8100, for the park 2507-8107), a non-profit research organization, collects and identifies every species of plant and animal nationwide.

According to the INBio head of conservation efforts, Vilma Obando (**vobando@inbio.ac.cr**), biologists at INBio and a host of researchers, estimate that only 18% of the country's more than 500,000 species — 300,000 of which are insects — have been identified to date, so there are still new frontiers for biologists to explore. INBio maintains an online database of identified species at: **inbio.ac.cr.**

National Territory

Protecting this rich natural legacy is not easy. Some 26.25% of national territory and 0.87% of marine wildlife are protected officially in 28 national parks, two pristine nature reserves, eight biological reserves, 73 wildlife refuges, 31 protected zones, 13 wetlands and 9 forest reserves. More than 186 private refuges also serve as biological corridors between publicly protected areas.

The national parks and reserves system is a major reason visitors come to Costa Rica. They walk jungle trails, climb mountain peaks, camp in the wilderness and explore the pristine shores of the mostly well-maintained parks (check out the National Parks Foundation site at **fpncostarica.org** or visit: **minaet.go.cr**).

Many Costa Ricans recognize the value

of environmental protection as a tourist attraction.

Still, some unscrupulous tourism operators "greenwash" less-than-ecological hotels and attractions, hoping to ride the "green" bandwagon to profits without true environmental responsibility. Tourists should do some research before they book a "green" hotel or tour. Check out the many hotels that are truly "eco" in this guidebook.

The most pressing problem is full-throttle development of mega-resorts, condominiums and golf courses, especially in water-starved areas of the Pacific northwest. Overdevelopment is one of the main threats to dry forest habitats, mangroves and turtle-nesting beaches. And sometimes success spells eco-stress, when too many visitors put pressure on sensitive sites. A few years ago, MINAE severely restricted the number of visitors per day to Chirripó National Park.

The most successful public initiative is the **Ecological Blue Flag** program, an effort to clean up the country's beaches and tourist areas. In 2009, 61 beaches passed stringent tests and are proudly flying the blue flag. The program also now includes communities and schools that organize conservation programs. And, in 2006, nature reserves were added to the program.

Another government initiative is the **Green Leaf** program, run by the National Tourism Institute, which rates hotels on the basis of sustainable development and environmental friendliness.

These two programs have become models for ecotourism worldwide. But environmentalists agree that more programs, more money and more awareness campaigns are needed.

Raising national consciousness about protecting this biological treasure and finding the funds to finance environmental safeguards remain two of Costa Rica's biggest challenges.

Blue Flag Beaches & Communities

COSTA RICA'S Ecological Blue Flag (Bandera Azul Ecológica) program assesses the cleanliness of beaches and inland communities and nature reserves.

MONTHLY or bi-monthly inspections by teams of engineers evaluate ocean and drinking water, waste disposal, environmental education and security. Communities passing with a score of 90% or greater can fly the coveted Blue Flag.

In 2009, institutes were added to the list of places that can hoist the sanitary symbol.

The National University in Heredia was the first to raise one.

The program is a joint effort of the National Water Authority (AyA), the Costa Rican Tourism Institute (ICT), the National Chamber of Tourism (Canatur) and the Ministry of Health. Communities dare not rest on their laurels, however, and flags do get pulled on occasion: In 2009, the hot Guanacaste tourist beach, Tamarindo, lost its flag along with a handful of others in the province.

After receiving the Blue Flag, communities, institutes and beaches can earn extra points for higher scores and more wide-ranging sanitation plans and policies.

These extra efforts are indicated by A's on the flag. Up to 4 A's can be earned.

So far, Blanca Beach in Puntarenas is the lone zone to achieve such an ecological honor.

On the Pacific coast in Puntarenas province:

Playas: Ballena, Barú, Bejuco, Blanca, Blanca (Jiménez), Dulce Vida, El Carmen (Cóbano), El Rey, El Roble (Puntarenas), Espadilla Sur, Gemelas, Isla Tortuga, La Colonia Limoncito, Mal País, Mantas (Punta Leona), Manuel Antonio, Matapalo, Pochote, Puerto Escondido, Piñuela, Puntarenas, Punta Uvita, Quitzales, San Pedrillo, Tulemar.

On the Pacific coast in Guanacaste province:

Playas: Avellanas, Bahía Junquillal, Buena, Bonita, Camaronal, Carillo, Coco Norte, Conchal, Flamingo, Grande, Guacamaya, Guiones (Nosara), Hermosa, Junquillal, Langosta, Mansita, Monte de Barco, Ostional, Pan de Azúcar, Panamá, Punta El Madero, Punta Islita, Santa Teresa, Ventanas, Zapotal.

On the Caribbean coast in Limón province:

Playas: Blanca, Chiquita, Cocles, Gandoca, Mile Creek, Need Creek, Negra (Cahuita), Negra, Puerto Vargas, Punta Uva.

Inland Communities:

Aquiares (Turrialba), Barva de Heredia, Carrizal (Alajuela), Dulce Nombre (Naranjo), EARTH, El Guisaro (Atenas), El Rosario (Naranjo), Heredia, La Fortuna, La Legua (Aserrí), La Luisa (Sarchí), La Suiza (San Rafael, Heredia), Las Horquetas (Sarapiquí), Los Angeles (San Rafael, Heredia), Los Lagos (Heredia), Mercedes Sur (Heredia), Pejibaye (Jiménez), Puente Salas (Heredia), Punta Leona (township), San Gabriel (Aserrí), San Gerardo (Rivas), San Juan (Ciudad Quesada), San Marcos (Tarrazú), San Miguel (Santo Domingo, Heredia) San Rafael (Heredia), San Roque (Grecia), San Vicente (Ciudad Quesada), Santiago (San Rafael, Heredia), Varablanca (Heredia).

A Touch of Tico Culture

FOR the culturally bewildered, this section will help you under-stand the traditions and idiosyncrasies that make Tiquicia unique.

Bombas!

Bomba can mean a service station, a pump or a bomb. But that's not all. Another bomba is an earthy, sometimes amorous couplet or four-line rhyme. Heard through-out the country, they are deeply rooted in Guanacaste's cowboy culture. Bombas are part of every festivity. People try to "out-bomba" each other with a funnier, more sexual or downright rude rhyme invented especially for the occasion or on the spot.

Bullfights

"Bullfighting" in *Tiquicia* is actually bull "teasing." The bull is never killed but is taunted by throngs of agile young men and an occasional woman. The cocky *impro-visados*, improvised bullfighters, run around the ring shouting and waving brightly colored shirts and caps. When the bull charges, they head for safety and vault over the barriers in the nick of time. These popular events, part of many local carni-vals, are often televised nationally.

Cafecito Anyone?

Coffee, once the backbone of Costa Rica's economy, has taken a back seat to tourism. Nevertheless, the tasty coffee grown in the highlands on rich volcanic soil is justifiably world renowned and remains the staff of life for Ticos.

Central Markets

Every major city has one, and you can find food, flowers, leather goods, knick-knacks and almost anything your heart desires. A maze of stalls and typical restau-rants, these markets date back to when farm-ers brought their goods to town by oxcart. The crowded, narrow aisles also attract adept pickpockets, so watch your wallet.

Cimarronas and Mascaradas

Cimarronas, which means "wild," are Tico bands with trumpets, saxophones, trombones, cymbals and big drums. At fes-tivals and parades they accompany the *mascaradas* (clowns) who support on their shoulders enormous papier-mâché heads depicting animals, devils, giants and famous personalities.

Dichos: Tico Colloquialisms

While a few books are dedicated to *Tiquismos*, Costa Rican slang, you won't find them in most regular Spanish diction-aries. But Ticos will be happy to explain that *adiós*! means "hi" unless you're leaving for a long time, in which case it means "good-bye." *¿Upe?* Is anybody home? A *chunche* (thing) can refer to almost any-thing, and if you are going to *Chepe*, you're off to San José. It's all *pura vida* and *tuanis mae*, or super and cool, buddy.

Directions, Tico Style

Who said they are confusing? There's nothing difficult about trying to find a place that's 300 meters south and 50 meters west of the fig tree that fell down 10 years ago! First, get down to basics. Buy a com-pass. Next, remember that 100 meters is equivalent to one block and 50 meters is about half-way down the street. Also, know

Mascaradas (clowns) wear giant heads of papier maché that depict animals, devils, giants and famous people.

Photo by
Mónica Quesada

that street numbers and names are rarely visible. It's good to remember that city streets (*calles*) run one way (north-south) and avenues (*avenidas*) run perpendicular to them. Numbers east of Calle Central are odd and numbers west are even. Numbers north of Avenida Central are odd; numbers south are even. Buildings are known by name or color. Your best bet is to ask for directions and write them down. If in doubt, take a taxi, but give the driver directions "Tico style" to avoid confusion.

Don & Doña

These respectful titles precede first names to address anyone from the president, Don Oscar, to the owner of the corner store, Doña Anita.

Farmers' Markets

Ferias are held on Saturdays or Sundays throughout the country, including in San José's neighborhoods. The fun starts around 5 a.m. when farmers arrive with their bounty of fresh, cheap produce. Friendly vendors are happy to chat about the exotic tropical fruits, explain how to cook weird-looking veggies or offer you a sample of their cheese. Freshly-squeezed juice, coffee and breakfast treats are also on hand.

Festejos Patronales or Turnos

Ticos love to *pachanguear* (party), and virtually every month there's a carnival to celebrate their patron saint's day. The custom dates back to Colonial times and brings together everyone for religious services, merrymaking and to raise funds for community projects. *Turnos*, fun for the whole family, offer soccer matches, *cabalgatas* or *topes* (horse parades), games, music, dancing and typical food. They are usually relatively tourist free. (See **Festivals**.)

Livin' & Lovin'

Ticos, amorous by nature, often show public displays of affection. Hand-holding and passionate embraces are acceptable and often seen on buses, street corners and in parks.

The "Running of the Bulls" in Costa Rica is dnagerous for the people, but not the bull, which tends to get pretty grouchy at being teased.

Photo by Ronald Reyes

Names, Last and Last Again

All Ticos tack both their fathers' and mothers' last names to their given names. The first *apellido*, or surname, is the principal one and comes from their father. The second *apellido* comes from their mother. People are identified by both names, and women keep their own last name when they marry.

Nicknames

Ticos are known for their good humor and are surprisingly straightforward about race and physical characteristics. "*Gorda*" or "*Gordo*" (fatty) are common endearments among friends and family, as are "*Flaca*" or "*Flaco*" (skinny) and "*Negro*" or "*Negra*." Anyone with slanted eyes is referred to as "*China*" or "*Chino*."

Oxcarts and Oxen

Symbols of the nation. In 2006, UNESCO declared Costa Rica's oxcarts a Masterpiece of Oral and Intangible Heritage of Humanity. These colorful wooden carts pulled by teams of stately oxen played a crucial role in the country's economy by hauling coffee from the mountain slopes to the port of Puntarenas. The oxcarts, with their intricate hand-painted designs, have become a source of pride, and their cultural/historical significance is celebrated at the annual Oxcart Parade in San José (last weekend in November) and at many other festivals including an annual parade (second Sunday in March) in San Antonio de Escazú, where there is also a monument to the oxcart driver. In Sarchi, where oxcarts are made in every size, you can also see the world's largest oxcart.

Piropos

Comments made by men to women on the street can be yelled, hissed or said innocently in passing. Many are flattering, like *guapa* (pretty) and *reina* (queen). But others can be vulgar or sexually offensive. Whether you are flattered or offended by *piropos*, you can't stop them, so dress appropriately and keep moving.

"Suicide" Showers

Hot water tanks are a rarity in middle-class homes and cheaper hotels. Never fear, hot water's there. It comes from an electrical contraption that heats water in the showerhead. These are known as "suicide showers" by many foreigners, but they work well. Just remember, the slower the flow, the hotter the water.

Tico Time

This drives visitors crazy. It means events never start on time and could be more than an hour later than scheduled. If you arrive for dinner or a party on time, you'll likely find your hosts totally unprepared. Ex-pats usually specify *hora Gringa*, meaning be punctual. When doing business, remember "*ahora*" (now) = in a little while, and "*ahorita*" (soon) = anything from minutes to hours. You're in *Tiquicia*, so be patient, take a book and relax.

Accommodations

COSTA RICA offers multiple choices for the more than 1.6 million annual visitors. Whether your budget is for a rustic beach cabin, city B&B, simple eco-lodge or five-star resort, you'll find it here.

When to Go & Cost:

PRICES can vary considerably between high season (Dec.-Feb. and Easter Week), and low season.

Some hotels charge higher rates for non-residents; it's worth trying to negotiate. Book ahead for high season and holiday weekends.

During the rainy, or "green" season, from May-Oct. (except the Caribbean, which is driest during Sept.-Oct.), prices can drop and, though an umbrella is a must, the compensation is fresh, lush scenery.

Prices vary tremendously according to location and tourist traffic.

Options in the lower price range ($10-30) abound throughout the country. Rooms often have cold showers and/or shared bathrooms.

Shop around, as quality can vary enormously for the same price. Website: **backpackers.com** offers over 100 budget lodgings with online booking.

The ($30-70) range usually offers private bath w/hot water, a huge choice of beach cabins, B&Bs, boutique hotels, and eco-lodges. Some include breakfast; most will have a restaurant, parking and attractive setting.

The next category ($70 and Up) includes anything from upscale cabins in the jungle to high-end city hotels to swanky international chain resorts, often themed around golf, horseback riding, spa treatments.

Many times you'll find all-inclusive amenities in stunning surroundings by the ocean or high in the hills. Room rates, based on high-season (Nov.-Apr) double occupancy, include 13% sales tax.

On-Line Information

The Costa Rican Hotel Association (2248-0990, **costaricanhotels.com**) has 250 hotels with clear info, online reservations for mid-to high-end accommodations.

Vacation City (2290-0798, **vacationcity.com**) provides extensive listings in the mid-range, plus B&Bs and other tourist info.

Costa Rica Innkeepers (**costaricainnkeepers.com**) specializes in small hotels, clearly marked on regional maps.

Hostels

Hostels can provide reliable word-of-mouth updates on what's hot and what's not, in addition to the usual kitchen and laundry facilities, luggage storage and shared bathrooms. Check **youth-hostels-in.com/costa-rica-hostels.html** for over 100 hostels. Site offers online reservations, ratings and descriptions.

Homestays

Often combined with Spanish courses, homestays are an ideal way to practice the language and enjoy a first-hand taste of Costa Rica.

Many language-school Websites give contact details. Stays can vary from one week to a month and can include meals and laundry service.

Bell's Home Hospitality (2225-4752,

homestay.thebells.org) has a list of approved home-stay families around San José and years of experience in providing travel hints and general info.

Guests are met at the airport and driven to their 'families' with stay lengths tailored to needs. Per night w/breakfast and private bath ($50); monthly rates $550/person includes dinner.

Eco-Lodges

From the 400 or so hotels in the country, only 61 can tout the **ICT – Costa Rican Tourism Board**'s (2299-5800, ext. 346 or 371, **visitacostarica.com**) Certificate of Sustainable Tourism Program at any of the five levels (a **Green Leaf** per level).

Care should be taken with the 'eco' label, as some environmentally invasive hotels think it enough to offer biodegradable shampoo and clever, if inaccurate, claims to conserve both natural and village surroundings.

Community Tourism

More travelers are opting for community-based rural tour packages, giving

Shy Capuchin monkey snacks in the jungle.

Photo by Matt Wyczalkowski

visitors an authentic insight into village community life and culture, plus the satisfaction of knowing their tourist dollars are reaching the people in need.

Several tour operators give info on lodges and multi-day tours that, although rustic, will promise a wealth of unforgettable memories and photo ops.

The Rural Tourism Association – ACTUAR (2248-9470, **actuarcostarica. com**) works with community-tourism enterprises developing sustainable tourism.

Single-night lodging or multi-day packages to experience mangrove fishing, birding, riding through organic farms, even meditation trips.

The Talamancan Association of Ecotourism and Conservation – ATEC (2750-0191, **atec.org**) arranges visits to indigenous communities throughout the Caribbean with opportunities to camp, go birding, watch dolphins and hike over the Talamanca mountains.

COOPRENA (2290-8646, **turismoru ralcr.com**) through its agency **Simbiosis Tours** (2290-8646, 2290-8651 or **info@ turismoruralcr.com**) specializes in multi-day excursions to rural cooperative-managed lodges focusing on organic coffee and cheese production, nature hikes, whale watching.

Cultourica (2249-1271, **cultourica. com**) based in Hotel El Marañón, west of San José, offers one- to two-week tours around the country with cycling and trekking options.

Its Flexi-Drive Program coordinates car rental with selected hotel vouchers. Spanish classes, day trips and expert eco-information, available.

Wellness Tourism

Spas, nature retreats, yoga weeks and innumerable ways to relax and rejuvenate are increasingly popular and offered throughout the country. See "**Alternative Healing**" in this guidebook.

Banks

ALTHOUGH competition from more foreign banks creates pressure for those locally owned, industry observers say this encourages all banks to improve technology and customer service.

FACTORS to consider when choosing a bank include where you plan to live and how much you plan to travel; whether you need to access your account abroad, an option not all banks offer; and whether you speak Spanish (if you don't, an international bank may be a good choice).

Requirements to open accounts vary and may include personal references from other bank clients. In most cases, you'll need to have on hand your original passport for any bank transaction.

Under the new exchange-rate system, banks are free to set their own exchange rate within a narrow range; therefore, prospective clients looking to perform any transaction that involves currency conversion would do well to shop around and determine which bank offers that day's best rate.

The Tico Times publishes the Central Bank Reference Rate, an average of the bank rates during a given week, along with other economic indicators, in its weekly print edition and online edition, **tico times.net**.

Be sure to call ahead for bank hours, and plan ahead before Costa Rican holidays, when banks are closed.

Public Banks

Banco Central de Costa Rica (2243-3333, **bccr.fi.cr**) establishes monetary and banking policy, supervising both public and private banks, not a commercial bank.

Banco Nacional (2212-2000, **bncr.fi.cr**) 150 branches and some 350 ATMs, ideal for those planning to travel extensively, live or work in remote areas of the country.

Banco de Costa Rica (2287-9000, **bancobcr.com**) even wider coverage, 220 offices and 300 ATMs throughout the country, telephone and Internet banking.

Banco Popular (2211-7000, **bancopopularcr.com**) offers Banca Fácil phone service (2202-2020), 79 offices nationwide.

Banco Crédito Agrícola de Cartago, or Bancrédito as it is known (2550-0202, 2550-0620, **bancreditocr.com**), smallest public bank.

Private Banks

Scotiabank (2287-8743, 800-1SCOTIA – inside Costa Rica only –**scotiabankcr. com**) leads the private-bank market; its acquisition of Banco Interfin gave it 41 branches, 75 automatic-teller machines and 13% of the loan market.

BAC San José (2295-9797, **bac.net**).

HSBC (2287-1000, **banex.com**).

Citi (2299-0200).

Banca Promérica (2258-2212, **promerica.fi.cr**).

Credomatic (2295-9898, **credomatic. com/costarica/index.html**).

CNB S.A. (Citibank) (2201-0800, **citibank.fi.co**) in Costa Rica, corporate bank only, no personal banking services.

Photo by Leland Baxter

Bus Schedules

REGULAR buses (indirectos or corrientes) stop along the route. Busetas and microbuses charge a more, but all riders must be seated, making the trip more pleasant. In the list below, "RT:" means "return trip."

FARES change frequently, so ask someone in line or call ahead. When you are ready to get off, press the red button (on sides, seats or posts), pull the string or simply shout, "*La parada, por favor.*"

SAN JOSE and ENVIRONS

San José – Alajuela, Juan Santamaría International Airport

Every 5 min., 4 a.m.-10 p.m. **RT:** same, Av. 2, Ca. 12/14, 35 min. (1+ hr./rush hr.), **TUASA** (2442-6900) ¢400, also to Heredia ¢320; **Station Wagon** (8388-9263) every 5 min., 5 a.m.-midnight, Av. 2, Ca. 2/4, after midnight, every hour, Av. 2, Ca. 2/4 **RT:** same, ¢400.

Alajuela – Laguna de Fraijanes

Hourly, 6 a.m.-10:10 p.m. **RT:** same through 9 p.m., 50 min., 100 m. south of TUASA bus stop, Alajuela, **Coopetransasi** (2449-5141), ¢660.

San José – Anonos - Escazú

Hourly 5-11 a.m., noon, 2, 4, 5 p.m. **RT:** hourly 5-8 a.m., 10, 11 a.m., 2, 3, 5 p.m., Weekends hourly 5-8, 10, 11 a.m., 2, 3, 5 p.m., Ca. 16, Av. 3/5 (Coca-Cola), **Compañía de Inversiones La Tapachula S.A.** (2288-2025, 2203-4212, citapachula.com), ¢240.

San José – San Antonio de Escazú

5-6 every 20 min.; 6-8 every 10 min.; 8 a.m.-1 p.m., every 15 min.; 2-5 p.m. every 10 min.; 6-7 p.m. every 15 min., 8-9 p.m., every 20 min.; 9-10 every 30 min., 11 p.m., midnight. **RT:** 4, 5 a.m.-7 p.m. every 15 min.; 7-8 p.m. every 20 min.; 9-11 p.m.,

every 30 min., Ca. 16, Av. 3/5 (Coca-Cola), **La Tapachula S.A.** (2288-2025, 2203-4212, **citapachula.com**), ¢295.

San José – Escazú Center

5 a.m.-11 p.m. every 10 min. RT: same, Ca. 16, Av. 3/5 (Coca-Cola), **La Tapachula S.A.** (2288-2025, 2203-4212, **citapachula.com**), ¢240.

San José – Santa Ana (via the highway)

5 a.m.-8 p.m., every 10 min.; 8-11 p.m. every 20 min., **RT:** same, Ca. 16, Av. 3/5 (Coca-Cola), **La Tapachula S.A.** (2288-2025, 2203-4212, **citapachula.com**), ¢260. Via Calle Vieja, goes to Piedades, ¢245.

San José – Ciudad Colón

5:10 a.m.-10:30 p.m., RT: 4:10 a.m.- 9:25 p.m., every 30 min.; 40 min., Ca. 20, Av. 3-5, **Contrasuli** (2248-1703, 2249-2706), ¢305.

San José – Poás Volcano

8:30 a.m. **RT:** 2:30 p.m., 2 hrs., Av. 2, Ca 12/14, **TUASA** (2442-6900), ¢3,190 **RT**.

San José – Cartago

Direct every 7 min., 4:45 a.m.-11 p.m.; night shift midnight-3 a.m., every 25 min. **RT:** same; 45 min., Ca. 3, Av. 2, **Lumaca S.A.** (2537-0347), ¢410.

Cartago – Orosi Valley

Mon.-Fri., 5:15-8 a.m., every 15 min.; 8 a.m.-2 p.m., every 30 min.; 2-7:30 p.m. every 15 min.; 7:30-10:25 p.m. every 30 min. **RT:** 4-8 a.m., every 15 min., 8 a.m.-2 p.m., every 30 min., 2-7 p.m., every 15 min., 7-9 p.m., every 30 min.; 9 p.m.: Sat. no 8 p.m., Sun. no 8, 9 p.m.; Sat., 5:30 a.m.-10 p.m., every 30 min., 10 a.m.-7 p.m. every

20 min.; then 7-10:25 p.m., every 30 min. **RT:** 4:30 a.m.-10 p.m. every 30 min.; 10 a.m.-6 p.m., every 20; 6-8 p.m., every 30 min.; 9 p.m. Sun., 7 a.m.-9 p.m., every 30 min., 9-6 p.m., every 20 min. **RT:** 5:30 a.m.-8 p.m., every 15 min., 8 a.m.-1 p.m., every 30 min., 1-7 p.m., every 30 min., 45 min., 200 m. east and 125 m. south of the Municipality, **Auto Transportes Mata** (2533-1916), ¢385, to Palomo and Río Macho ¢445, to Purisil and La Alegría ¢475.

Cartago-Lankester Gardens-Paraíso

Every 10 min., 5 a.m.-11 p.m. **RT:** 4:30 a.m.-10 p.m., 25 min., ask driver to stop, then walk 800 m. **Coopepar** (2574-6127), ¢165.

San José – Grecia

Every 25 min., 5:40 a.m.-10:10 p.m. **RT:** every 25 min., 4:25 a.m.-8:30 p.m., (Sun., 5 a.m.), every 40 min., 8:30-8:30 p.m., 70 min., west side of Abonos Agro, Barrio México, **TUAN** (2258-2004), ¢770.

San José – Sarchí

Mon.-Sat., 12:15 p.m. **RT:** 1:45 p.m. Sun. no bus, 90 min., east side of Abonos Agro, Barrio México, **TUAN** (2258-2004), ¢795.

Alajuela – Naranjo

Every 25 min., 6 a.m.-10 p.m. **RT:** same, 90 min., behind TUASA bus stop, Alajuela, **TUAN** (2451-5847), ¢655 (check first: bus goes through different towns and driver charges different prices for each).

San José – Palmares

Hourly, 5 a.m.-10 p.m. **RT:** 5, 5:20, 5:35, 6:15 a.m., every hour through 8:10 p.m., Ca. 16, Av. 3/5 (Coca-Cola), **Transportes Palmareños** (2453-3808), ¢750. Also, hourly, 5:45 a.m.-9 p.m. **RT:** 4:30 a.m.-6:30 p.m., Ca. 16, Av. 3/5 (Coca-Cola), 75 min., **Auto Transportes Palmares** (2452-0518), ¢790.

San José – San Ramón

4, 5:50, 6:30-9 a.m. every 30 min.; 9 a.m.-

10:30 p.m. every 30 min. **RT:** 5 a.m.-8:30 p.m., every 30 min., 75 min., Ca. 16, Av. 10/12, **Empresarios Unidos** (2222-0064), ¢925.

San José – Atenas

Mon.-Fri. 5:40, 6:30, 7, 7:30, 8, 8:30, 9, 10, 11 a.m., noon, 12:30, 1:30, 2:30, 3:20, 3:35, 4, 4:30, 4:45, 5, 5:15, 5:30, 5:45, 6, 6:30, 7, 8, 8:50, 9:15, 10 p.m. **RT:** 4:30, 5, 5:10, 5:30, 5:35, 6, 6:10, 6:20, 6:30, 6:50, 6:55, 7, 7:50, 8, 8:50, 9, 10:20, 10:30 a.m., 11, noon, 1, 2, 2:30, 3, 3:30, 4, 4:35, 5, 5:30, 6:30, 7, 8:30 p.m.; **Sat./holidays,** 6, 6:30, 7:15, 7:45, 9, 10, 11 a.m., noon, 1, 1:30, 2, 2:30, 3:30, 4, 4:30, 5, 5:30, 7, 8:30 p.m. **RT:** 4:30, 5:50, 6, 6:50, 7, 8, 9, 10:20, 10:30, noon, 1, 2, 2:30, 4, 5:30, 6:30 p.m.; **Sun.,** 7:45, 8:30, 9:15, 10:30 a.m., noon, 12:30, 1:30, 3, 4:30, 5:30, 6:30, 7 p.m. **RT:** 6, 7, 8, 9, 10:30 a.m., noon, 1, 3, 4, 5, 5:30, 7 p.m., Ca. 11, Av. 10/12, **Coopetransatenas** (2446-5767), ¢660.

San José – San Ignacio de Acosta

Hourly 5:30 a.m.-10:30 p.m. **RT:** hourly 4:15 a.m.-9 p.m., until 8 p.m. weekends, Ca. 8, Av. 10/12, across from Baptist Church, 90 min. (75 min., via Aserrí, Tarbaca), **Transportes San Gabriel S.A.** (410-0330), ¢630.

San José – Turrialba

Hourly 5:45 a.m.-10 p.m. (regular) 8 a.m.-8 p.m. (direct) **RT:** 4:45 a.m.-9 p.m.; Sat., 4:45 a.m.-9 p.m. (regular) 5 a.m.-5 p.m. (direct), Sun., 5 a.m.-9 p.m. (regular) 7 a.m.-7 p.m. (direct), direct 1 hr. 40 min., regular 2 hrs. 10 min., Ca. 13, Av. 6/8, **Transtusa** (2556-4233), ¢1,105.

San José – Irazú Volcano

Daily, 8 a.m. **RT:** 12:30 p.m., 2:30 hrs., Av. 2, Ca. 1/3, across from Gran Hotel Costa Rica, **Buses Metrópoli** (2530-1064), ¢3,820 **RT.**

San José – Heredia

Every 5 min., 5:02 a.m.-midnight **RT:** 4:30 a.m.-11:30 p.m. (after midnight Sun.-

Thurs. 1, 2, 3 a.m.) **RT:** 12:30, 1:30, 2:30 a.m.; Fri.-Sun. Every 30 min., midnight-3 a.m. **RT:** every 30 min. 12:30-3 a.m. (stops Ca. 1, Av. 2), 30 min., Ca. 1, Av. 7/9, stops in Tibás and Santo Domingo, Microbuses **Rápidos Heredianos** (2233-8392), ¢320. Every 5 min., 5 a.m.-10 p.m. **RT:** same, 30 min., Av. 2, Ca. 12/14, **Busetas Heredianas** (2261-7171), ¢390. Every 5 min., 5 a.m.-11 p.m. **RT:** 4:20 a.m.-10:30 p.m., via La Uruca, Ca. 4, Av. 5/7, 30 min. **Transportes Unidos La 400** (2222-8986), ¢320.

NORTHERN ZONE

San José – Ciudad Quesada

5 a.m.-7:30 p.m., every 45 min. **RT:** 5 a.m.-6:15 p.m., 3 hrs., via Zarcero, Ca. 12, Av. 7/9, **Autotransportes San José-San Carlos** (2255-4318), ¢1,365. Direct bus depends on demand.

San José – La Fortuna

6:15, 8:40, 11:30 a.m. **RT:** 12:45 p.m., 2:45 p.m., 4 hrs., Ca. 12, Av. 7/9, **Auto Transportes San José-San Carlos** (2256-8914), ¢1,955.

San José – Pital

7:40 a.m., 12:45, 3, 7:30 p.m. **RT:** 6:30, 7:30, 11 a.m., 1, 5 p.m., 4 hrs., Ca. 12, Av. 7/9, **Auto Transportes San José – San Carlos** (2256-8914), ¢1,660.

Ciudad Quesada – Pital

5:30, 5:55, 6:30, 7:30, 8, 8:30, 9:30, 10, 10:30, 11:30 a.m., noon, 12:40, 1, 1:40, 2, 2:30, 3:30, 4:25, 4:35, 5, 5:30, 6:30, 7, 7:30, 8:30, 9:30 p.m. **RT:** 4:30, 5, 5:20, 5:40, 6, 7, 8, 8:30, 9, 9:30, 10, 10:30, 11:30 a.m., noon, 1:30, 2, 2:40, 3:15, 4, 4:30, 5:30, 6, 6:30, 7, 8 p.m., 75 min., Plaza San Carlos, **Transportes Pital** (2460-3554), ¢485.

Ciudad Quesada – La Fortuna

6, 6:30, 9:30, 10:30, 11:40 a.m., 12:15, 1, 2:30, 3, 3:30, 4:45 5:15, 6 8, 9:30 p.m. **RT:** : 4:50, 5:10, 5:40, 5:40, 6:30, 7:30, 8:30, 10:30 a.m., 12:15, 3:15, 4:40, 5:30 p.m., 90 min.

Municipal Bus Terminal, **Transpisa** (2461-0934), ¢525.

Ciudad Quesada – la Tigra

7, 9:15 a.m., 12, 2, 4:30, 5:30, 6:30 p.m. RT: 6, 6:30, 11:30 a.m., 2, 4:30 p.m. 1 hr. Municipal Bus Terminal, **Transpisa** (2461-0934), ¢450.

Ciudad Quesada – Puerto Viejo de Sarapiquí

Via highway, 4:40, 6, 10 a.m., noon, 3, 4:30, 5:30, 6:30 p.m. **RT:** 5:30, 8:30, 10:30 a.m., 12:15, 2:30, 4, 7 p.m., 2 hrs. 30 min., Ciudad Quesada main terminal, **Empresarios Guapileños** (2766-6141), ¢1,230.

San José – Bagaces – Fortuna – Guayabo – Aguas Claras

5:30 a.m., 2 p.m. **RT:** 4:30 a.m., 1:45 p.m., 4 hrs. 30 min., Ca. 12, Av. 7/9, **Transportes Upala** (2221-3318), ¢2,885.

San José – Monteverde Cloud Forest

6:30 a.m., 2:30 p.m. **RT:** same, 5 hrs., Ca. 12, Av. 7/9, **Transportes Monteverde** (2222-3854), ¢2,350.

San José – Río Frío de Sarapiquí

8:30, 11 a.m., 1, 4, 5:30 p.m. (through farms) **RT:** 5:45, 8:25 a.m., noon, 2:30, 3:30, 6:15 p.m., 11 a.m. (via La Victoria) **RT:** noon, 2:30 p.m. (via La Victoria), 90 min., Caribbean Bus Terminal, Ca. Ctrl., Av. 11, **Empresarios Guapileños** (2710-7780), ¢875.

San José – Guatuso

5, 8:40, 11:30 a.m. **RT:** 8, 11:30 a.m., 3 p.m., 5 hrs., Ca. 12, Av. 7/9, **Auto Transportes San José-San Carlos** (2255-4318), ¢2,445.

San José – Los Chiles (Nicaragua border)

5:30 a.m., 3:30 p.m. **RT:** 5 a.m., 3, p.m., 5 hrs. 30 min., Ca. 12, Av. 7/9, **Auto Transportes San Carlos** (2255-4318), ¢2,085.

San José – Puerto Viejo (Sarapiquí)

Via highway to Limón, 6, 7:30, 10, 11:30 a.m., 1:30, 2:30, 3:30, 4:30, 6 p.m. **RT:** 5:30,

7, 8, 11 a.m., 1:30, 3, 5:30 p.m., 2 hrs., Caribbean Bus Terminal, Ca. Ctrl., Av. 11, **Empresarios Guapileños** (2710-7780), ¢1,230.

San José – Upala (Nicaragua border)

Via Cañas 10:15 a.m., 3, 5:10 p.m. **RT:** 4:30, 5:15, 9:30 a.m., 5 hrs., ¢3,525. Vía San Carlos, 3:45 p.m. **RT:** 9 a.m., 5 hrs. 30 min., Ca. 12, Av. 7/9, **Transportes Upala** (2221-3318), ¢3,665.

CARIBBEAN

San José – Cariari – Tortuguero

6:30, 9, 10:30 a.m., 1, 3, 4:30, 6, 7 p.m. **RT:** 5:30, 6:30, 7:30, 8:30, 11:30 a.m., 1, 3, 5:30 p.m., 2 hrs., Caribbean Bus Terminal (Gran Terminal del Caribe), Ca. Ctrl., Av. 11, **Empresarios Guapileños** (2710-7780), ¢1,310. For Tortuguero, get off at last stop in Cariari, catch bus to La Pavona at 11 a.m., 2 p.m., take boat at 12:40 p.m. **RT:** 1, 4 p.m., Boats, 6:30, 11:30 a.m., 3 p.m., bus, **Rubén Bananeros** (2709-8005), bus ¢1,000, boat ¢1,600.

San José – Guápiles

(Braulio Carrillo National Park)

Leaves when full, 5:30 a.m.-10 p.m. **RT:** 5 a.m.- 7 p.m., (Sat., Sun./holidays, 5:30 a.m.-7 p.m.) 90 min., stops at Rainforest Aerial Tram, Caribbean Bus Terminal, Ca. Ctrl., Av. 11, **Empresarios Guápileños** (2222-2727) ¢1,075.

San José – Limón

Hourly, 5 a.m.- 7 p.m. **RT:** same, 3 hrs., direct & regular, via Guápiles, Siquirres, Caribbean Bus Terminal, Ca. Ctrl., Av. 11, **Transportes Caribeños** (221-2596), ¢2,470.

San José – Cahuita National Park – Puerto Viejo – Sixaola (Panamá border)

6, 10 a.m., noon (Manzanillo, ¢4,825, **RT:** 7 a.m.), 2, 4 p.m. **RT:** from Sixaola, 6, 8, 10 a.m., 3 p.m., 6 hours., ¢5,265. From Cahu-

ita, 7, 8, 9:30, 11:30 a.m., 4:30 p.m., 4 hrs., ¢3,690. From Puerto Viejo, 7:30, 9, 11 a.m., 4 p.m., 4:30 hrs., ¢4, 290. Caribbean Bus Terminal, Ca. Ctrl., Av. 11, **Transportes Mepe** (2257-8129).

San José – Siquirres

6:30, 9:30 a.m., then hourly until 6 p.m. **RT:** same, 2 hrs., Caribbean Bus terminal, Ca. Ctrl., Av. 11, **Tracasa** (2768-6731) ¢995.

GUANACASTE

San José – Liberia

Hourly 6 a.m.-8 p.m., 7 p.m. (only Fridays), **RT:** 3-8 a.m., hourly; 8 a.m.-8 p.m., every 2 hours, 4 hrs. 30 min., Ca. 24, Av. 5/7, **Pulmitan** (2222-1650), ¢2,750.

San José – Santa Cruz

6:30, 10 a.m., 1:30, 3, 5 p.m. **RT:** 5:30, 7:30, 10 a.m., 12:30, 3 p.m., Ca. 14, Av. 5, 5 hrs. 30 min. **Alfaro-Tracopa** (2222-2666), ¢2,630. Via Friendship Bridge (Tempisque), 7, 9, 10:30 a.m., 1, 4 p.m. **RT:** 3, 5, 6:30, 10:30 a.m., 1:30 p.m., 4 hrs. Via Liberia, 8, 9 a.m., noon, 2, 3, 3:30, 6 p.m. **RT:** 4:30, 5, 8:30, 11:30 a.m., 2 (leaves from Flamingo), 5 p.m., 4 hrs., Av. 3/4, Ca. 20, 6 hr., **Tralapa** (2223-5859), ¢4,190.

San José – Tilarán

7:30, 9:30 a.m., 12:45, 3:45, 6:30 p.m. **RT:** 5, 7, 9:30 a.m., 2, 5, p.m., 4 hrs., Ca. 12, Av. 7/9, **Auto Transportes Tilarán**, (2695-5611), ¢1,855.

San José – Canas – Upala

5:30, 8:30, 11:50 a.m., 12:20, 1:45, 3:30, 5 p.m. RT: 4, 4:50, 5:40, 6:30, 8:30, 11:20, 1:30 p.m., 3 hr. 30 min., 1,440. To Upala, 6 a.m., **RT:** 2 p.m., 6 hrs., 2,60. Av. 2/4, Ca. 14/18, **Auto Transportes Tilarán**, (2695-5611).

San José – La Cruz – Peñas Blancas (Nicaragua border)

4, 5, 7, 7:45, 9:30, 10:45 a.m., 1:20, 4:10 p.m. **RT:** 5:15, 7:30, 10:30, 10:45 a.m., noon, 3:30 p.m., Sunday starts 3:30 a.m., 6 hrs., Ca. 10/12, Av. 9/11, next to Hotel Cocorí, **Transportes Deldú** (2256-9072), ¢4,325, La Cruz, ¢3,110.

San José – Tamarindo

11:30 a.m., (via Friendship Bridge, 5 hrs.), 3:30 p.m. (via Liberia, 5 hrs. 30 min.) RT: 3:30, 5:45 a.m., 2 p.m. (via bridge), Av. 5, Ca. 14, **Alfaro** (2222-2666), ¢4,360. 7:15 a.m., 4 p.m. RT: 6:30 a.m., 2:15 p.m., 6 hrs., Ca. 20, Av. 3/5, **Tralapa** (2221-7202), ¢4,370.

San José – Playas del Coco

8 a.m., 2, 4 p.m. RT: 4, 8 a.m., 2 p.m., 5 hrs., Ca. 24, Av. 5/7, **Pulmitan** (2222-1650), ¢3,280.

San José – Coyote Beach, Bejuco Beach and Caletas Beach

6 a.m., 3:30 p.m. RT: 2:30 a.m.-12:30 p.m. 6 hrs., Ca. 12, Av. 7/9, **ARSA** (2258-3883). ¢3,980.

San José – Brasilito/Conchal – Flamingo – Panamá Beach

To Brasilito/Conchal and Flamingo, 8, 10:30 a.m., 3 p.m. RT: 2:45 a.m., 9 a.m., 2 p.m., 5 hrs., Flamingo. To Panama Beach, 3:30 p.m., ¢4,160 RT: 5 a.m., 5 hrs., Ca. 20, Av. 3/5, **Tralapa** (2221-7202), ¢4,795.

CENTRAL PACIFIC COAST

San José – Puntarenas

Direct 6 a.m.- 7 p.m. every hour, regular service 4, 6, 8, 10 a.m., 12, 2, 3:30, 5, 6,7:30, 9, 10:30 p.m. RT: same but no 6 p.m., no 10:30 p.m.; 4 a.m.-7 p.m. direct RT: same, 3 hrs. 30 min., direct 2 hrs. 20 min., Ca. 16, Av. 10/12, **Empresarios Unidos** (2222-0064), ¢1,720.

San José – Quepos – Manuel Antonio

Direct 6 a.m., 9, noon, 2:30, 6, 7:30 p.m., 3 hrs. 45 min., ¢2,495. Regular, 6 (to Uvita and Bahía), 7, 10 a.m., 2, 3 (to Uvita and Bahía) 4, 5 p.m. (Mon.-Fri.), ¢3,450 RT: 4

a.m. (Mon.-Fri.), 6, 9:30 a.m., noon, 2:30, 5 p.m. Via Puriscal, 5:30 a.m., noon. RT: 4:30 a.m., 1 p.m., 5 hrs., ¢1,800, Ca. 16, Av. 3/5 (Coca Cola), **Transportes Delio Morales** (2223-5567).

San José – Jacó Beach

6 a.m. (Fri.-Mon.), 7, 9, 11 a.m., 1, 5, 7 p.m. RT: 5, 7, 9, 11 a.m., 1, 3, 5 p.m., 3 hrs., Coca-Cola Bus Terminal, Ca. 16, Av. 1/3, **Transportes Jacó** (2290-7920), ¢1,970.

NICOYA PENINSULA

San José – Nicoya

Via Friendship Bridge (Tempisque), 5:30, 7:30, 10 a.m., 1, 3, 5 p.m. RT: 3, 4:30, 5:15, 7, 8 a.m., 1:15, 2, 2:45, 3, 5 p.m., 4 hrs.; via Liberia 7 a.m., 3 p.m. RT: 7 a.m., 3 p.m., 6 hrs., Av. 3/5, Ca. 14, **Empresa Alfaro** (2685-5032), ¢3,130.

San José – Sámara

12, 4:30, 8 p.m. RT: 4, 8 a.m., Sun., 8 a.m., 3 p.m., 5 hrs., 30 min., Ca. 14, Av. 3/5, **Empresa Alfaro** (2685-5032), ¢3,580.

Nicoya – Sámara – Carrillo Beaches

To Sámara, 5, 6, 8, 10, 11 a.m., noon, 1:30, 2:30, 3:30, 4:30, 6:30, 8, 9:45 p.m. RT: 4:15, 5, 5:30, 6:30, 8, 10, 11:30 a.m., 12:30, 1:30, 3, 4, 5, 6 p.m., main station in Nicoya, 400 m. east of southeast corner of park, **Empresa Rojas** (2685-5352), Samara ¢780, Carrillo ¢1,035.

San José – Nosara

5:30 a.m. RT: 12:30 p.m., 6 hrs., Ca. 14, Av. 3/5, **Empresa Alfaro** (2222-2666), ¢3,845.

Nicoya – Nosara – Garza – Guiones

4:45, 10 a.m., noon, 3, 5:30 p.m. RT: 5, 7 a.m., 12, 3 p.m., 400 m. east of Nicoya Park; Nosara, 90 min., Garza 2 hrs. 15 min., Guiones 2 hrs. 30 min., **Empresa Rojas** (2686-9089), ¢1,115.

San José – Mal País – Montezuma

6 a.m., 2 p.m., 5 hrs., Bus to Puntarenas,

take Paquera Ferry. (See **Ferries.**) >From there, Cóbano- Paquera,. 4:30, 5:50, 8:30, 10:30 a.m., 12:30, 2:30, 4:30 p.m., **RT:** 6 a.m.-6:30 p.m., every two hours, 90 min., **Transportes Rodríguez** (2642-0219), ¢1,100. In Cóbano, catch a mini-bus or taxi to either beach – end of line, ¢6,200 (including ferry ticket).

SOUTHERN ZONE

San José – Los Santos

6, 7:15, 9 a.m., 12:30, 3, 5, 7:30 p.m. **RT:** 5:15, 7:15, 9:15 a.m., 12:40, 3, 6:15 p.m., Av. 16, Ca. 19/21 (Barrio Luján) 2 hrs., via Santa María de Dota, San Marcos de Tarrazú, San Pablo de León Cortés, **Empresa Los Santos** (2546-7248), ¢1560.

San José – San Isidro de El General and Chirripó National Park

Every hour, 5:30 a.m.-5:30 p.m. **RT:** 5, 5:30, 6:30, 7:30 a.m., every hour through 5:30 p.m. (Mon.-Sat.); every hour 5:30 a.m.- 6:30 p.m., Sun., Ca. Ctrl., Av. 22/24, 3 hrs. 30 min., **MUSOC** (2222-2422), ¢2,410. From San Isidro, catch connecting bus to San Gerardo de Rivas (park entrance), 5 a.m., leaves from the Church; and 2 p.m., leaves from the Municipal Market, **RT:** 7 a.m., 4 p.m., 2 hrs., ¢800, (2742-5083). Or taxi, rates negotiable.

San Isidro – Coronado de Osa

4 p.m. **RT:** 5 a.m., 3 hrs., 300 m. south of Court Building on Inter-American Highway, **Transportes Blanco** (2771-4744), ¢2,100.

San Isidro de El General – Uvita

9 a.m., 4 p.m., from main terminal. **RT:** 5:45 a.m., 1:45 p.m., 2 hrs., 300 m. south of Court Building on Inter-American Highway, **Transportes Blanco** (2771-4744), ¢1,420.

San Isidro de El General – Dominical

7, 9, 11:30 a.m., 3:30, 4 p.m. **RT:** 6:30, 7 a.m., 1, 2:30, 5 p.m., 1 hr. 30 min, 300 m.

south of Court Building on Inter-American Highway, **Transportes Blanco** (2771-4744), ¢1,170.

San Isidro de El General – Quepos

7 a.m., 11:30, 3:30 p.m. **RT:** 5 a.m., 1:30 p.m., 1 hr. 30 min., 300 m. south of Court Building on Inter-American Highway, **Transportes Blanco** (2771-4744), ¢1,900.

San José – Ciudad Cortés – Palmar – Buenos Aires – Ciudad Neilly

8:30 a.m., 2:30 p.m. **RT:** 5:45, 9:15 a.m., 4:15 p.m., 7 hrs., Ca. 5, Av. 18/20, **Tracopa** (2221-4214), ¢4,780.

San José – Palmar Norte

5, 7, 8:30, 10 a.m., 1, 2:30, 6:30 p.m. **RT:** 4:55, 6:15, 7:45, 10 a.m., 1, 3, 6 p.m., 6 hrs., Ca. 5, Av. 18/20, **Tracopa** (2221-4214), ¢4,550.

San José – San Vito

6, 8:15 a.m., noon, 4 p.m. **RT:** 5, 7:30, 10 a.m., 3 p.m., 7 hrs. 30 min., Ca. 5, Av. 18/20, **Tracopa** (2221-4214), ¢5,505.

San José – Paso Canoas (Panamá Border)

5, 7:30 a.m., (to David, Panamá, $30 round trip, **RT:** 7:30 a.m., one way ¢7,315), 1, 4:30, 6:30 p.m. **RT:** 4, 8, 9:30 a.m., 4:30 p.m., 8 hrs., Ca. 5, Av. 18/20, **Tracopa** (2221-4214), ¢6,100.

San José – Golfito

7 a.m., 5:30 p.m. **RT:** 5 a.m., 1:30 p.m., 8 hrs., Ca. 5, Av. 18/20, **Tracopa** (2221-4214), ¢5,490.

San José – Puerto Jiménez

8 a.m., noon, **RT:** 5 a.m., 8 hrs., Ca. 12, Av. 7/9, Transportes Blanco-Lobo (2771-4744), ¢5,900.

INTERNATIONAL SERVICES

(Note: Prices are for round trip; services do not include lodging or meals unless tagged as "executive." Check with the bus line for info

on return trips.)

Tica Bus (2221-0006, 2223-8680, **tica bus. com**) leaves San José daily from Av. 3, Ca. 24/28 for Central America.

Tica Bus Destinations:

Note: Executive service (includes meals, pillow and blanket) offered only to Nicaragua ($32), Panama ($37, leaves at 11 a.m.), and El Salvador ($58). No executive service to Tapachula ($89) or Guatemala ($74),

Tapachula, Mexico: 6, 7:30 a.m., 12:30 p.m., overnight in Nicaragua and El Salvador, $84.

Guatemala: 6, 7:30 a.m., 12:30 p.m., overnight in Nicaragua and El Salvador, $68.

Honduras: Tegucigalpa, 6, 7:30 a.m., 12:30 p.m., overnight in Nicaragua, $42. **San Pedro Sula:** 6, 7:30 a.m., 10:30 p.m., overnight in Nicaragua, $55.

El Salvador: 6, 7:30 a.m., 12:30 p.m., $53.

Nicaragua: 6, 7:30 a.m., 12:30 p.m., $21.

Panamá: 10 p.m., $26.

Throughout the country, beauty everywhere.
Photo by Ronald Reyes

King Quality (2258-8190) Ca.12, Av. 3/5. All buses leave from Costa Rica at 3 a.m. going to **Managua, Nicaragua** ($36); **San Salvador, El Salvador** ($112, round trip); **San Pedro Sula**, **Honduras,** ($124), overnight at El Salvador, leaves next day at 7 a.m.; **Tegucigalpa Honduras,** ($115); **Guatemala**, ($124), overnight at El Salvador, leaves next day at 6 a.m. and 3 p.m.

Transnica (2223-4920, 2223-4242, fax: 2221-6853, **transnica.com**), Ca. 22, Av. 3/5. Leaves for Nicaragua (Granada, Masaya, Managua) 4, 5, 9 a.m. ($42, round trip; $21 one way); executive, noon ($63 round trip, $31.50 one way); and to **Honduras**, overnight in Managua, w/8 a.m. connection in Managua ($90 round trip, $45 one way).

PRIVATE BUSES & SHUTTLES

Costa Rica Shuttle (2289-9509, **costaricashuttle.com**), groups 1-6 passengers, covers the country, prices depend on distance, larger buses for up to 30 passengers, San Rafael de Escazú.

Gray Line (2220-2126, **graylinecosta rica.com**), one-day trips, multi-day pkgs., ground transfers all over the country, hotel reservations, airport (San José and Liberia) shuttles, operates throughout Central America, La Uruca, San José.

Interbus (2283-5573, **interbusonline. com**), airport or hotel-to-hotel shuttle throughout the country, regular buses w/ numerous tourist routes, max. 8 passengers, price depends on destination, San Pedro, Montes de Oca.

Transport Costa Rica Monteverde (2645-6768, 2290-7307, **transportcosta rica.net**), fleet of vans/mini-buses, door-to-door service all over the country, price depends on destination, 100 m. north of Hotel Las Orchideas, Monteverde.

Costa Rica Van Go (2441-7837, **costa ricavango.com**), picks up travelers at the airport and delivers them to their destination. Reservations.

Day Trips

DON'T let a tight schedule limit your exploration of Costa Rica. One day can find you beach hopping in the Pacific, standing at the edge of a volcano in the Central Valley or getting lost on a banana plantation in the Caribbean.

THE best part? The only planning you have to do is make a phone call. Most tour companies offer door-to-door transport, meals and friendly guides who speak English and Spanish.

ALL-IN-ONE TOURS

(including hotel pickup)

AVENTOURS (2538-5900, **aventourscostarica.com**) Offers customized, private guided tours with visits to indigenous Cabécar villages in the Talamanca Mountains, agri-tours of sugarcane, coffee, pineapple, macadamia crop processing. *Based out of San Antonio, 12 km. north of Turrialba.*

COSTA RICA TEMPTATIONS (2508-5000, **crtinfo.com**) Tours include visits to Arenal Volcano, a butterfly farm, national parks, along with rafting opportunities, $25 to $100. *With offices in San Antonio de Belén, Guanacaste and the Central Pacific Coast*

ECOSCAPE NATURE TOUR (2239-8333, from U.S. 310-945-5335 or 866-887-2764, **ecoscapetours.com**), after suspending tours for several months due to an earthquake in January 2009, the "highlights" is scheduled to resume in Dec. 2009. Tour includes visits to a coffee plantation, volcano, canopy adventure, Braulio Carrillo National Park, breakfast and lunch. Adults $99, kids 5-11, $79, kids 4 and under, free.

EXPEDICIONES TROPICALES (2257-4171, **expedicionestropicales. com**), from adventure packages to visits to craftsmen's workshops to trips to Tortuguero, this agency offers a long list of day tours to match any interest, $32 to $110.

IL VIAGGIO TRAVEL (2289-8225, from U.S.: 306-283-5266, **ilviaggiocr. com**) Specializes in all-inclusive trips, custom-designed tours, day excursions, personalized service. *Near San Miguel Catholic Church in Escazú.*

SWISS TRAVEL COSTA RICA (2282-4898, **costaricaonedaytours.com**), tours range from visits to botanical gardens and national parks, to a hanging-bridge experience, guided shopping trips, to rafting.

SPECIALITY TOURS

BRAULIO CARRILLO NATIONAL PARK (2268-1038), primary forest trails northeast of San José. Begin with hiking/birding from Quebrada González station on highway, 17 km. past tunnel, 8 a.m.-3:30 p.m.; or hike forested Barva Volcano starting at ranger station above San Rafael de Heredia. Tourists $8, residents $1.75.

HACIENDA TAYUTIC (2538-1717, **tayutic.com**), offers three types of tours including an Agrotour, in which travelers can see coffee, macadamia, sugarcane production, $75 inc. breakfast, lunch, guide, coffee tasting.

RAINFOREST AERIAL TRAM (2257-5961, from U.S.: 866-SKY-TRAM, **rfat. com**), an all-inclusive eco tour includes park entrance fee, guided walking tour, canopy experience, butterfly and frog gardens and aerial tram, among others. Adults $104, students and children $57.50. Transportation can be requested for an additional fee (45 minutes from San José.)

*If it's a caiman,
not to worry.
If it's a crocodile,
best get your foot
back into the boat!*

Photo by Ronald Reyes

SAN JOSÉ

COSTA RICA ART TOUR (8359-5571, 2288-0896, **costaricaarttour.com**), visit five artists in their studios, also private tours, $125 inc/lunch. Group discounts available by calling in advance.

CENTRO ECUESTRE VALLE DE YOSOY (2282-3222), equestrian classes ($95) and guided tours through mountains of Santa Ana ($25/hour). Specializes in classes for children.

EL ENCANTO DE PIEDRA BLANCA (2228-0183), in mountains of Santa Ana, 20 min. west of San José, mask-making, sugar mill, organic farm. $36 and up.

TICO WALKS (2283-8281, 8914-3429), visits museums, parks and monuments on a two-hour guided tour. Leaves from the National Theatre at 10 a.m., on Tues., Thurs., Sat., Sun. $25. Private tours available.

ALAJUELA

BOTANICAL ORCHID GARDEN (2487-8095, **orchidgardencr.com**), 30-year-old garden on an old coffee plantation, views of a variety of orchids, cedar trees, bamboo and a panoply of other plant life. Tourists $12, residents $3.50.

THE BUTTERFLY FARM (2438-0400, **butterflyfarm.co.cr**), educational tours to view 40 species of butterflies in tented garden. $15 or $35 with transportation from San José. Also combined tour with Café Britt for $63 (lunch included.)

POAS VOLCANO NATIONAL PARK (2482-2165), a short hike up unique dwarf-forest trail to a crater lake and views of the wide-mouthed volcano. 8 a.m.-3:30 p.m., but arrive early or volcano may be clouded in. Tourists $10, residents $1.75.

ZOO AVE (2433-8989, **zooave.com**), view rescued wild animals, birds in natural habitats, biological reserve and gardens. 9 a.m.-5 p.m. Tourists $15, residents $6, children $3.

COFFEE TOWNS
(Atenas, Grecia, Sarchí, San Ramón)

ELSE KIENTZLER BOTANICAL GARDEN (2454-2070, 2454-4956, **elsekientzlergarden.com**), in Sarchi, more than 17 acres of grounds with magnificent trails and plants from all over Central America. 8 a.m.-4 p.m. Tourists $15, residents $4, students get discounted rate, children under five, free.

JOSE FIGUERES FERRER HISTORICAL AND CULTURAL CENTER (2447-2178), in San Ramón, just north of church. Features concerts and poetry readings. Also check out San Ramón Central Market. 10 a.m.-7 p.m., closed Sun. Free

HEREDIA

CAFÉ BRITT COFFEE TOUR (2277-1500, 2277-1699, **coffeetour.com**), humorous tour with play on the history of coffee and how it's produced, with samples. 11 a.m. year-round. Also 3 p.m. tour in high season (Nov.-April). Lunch option and transportation available. Minimum: $20

INBio PARQUE (2507-8100, **inbioparque.com**), walk though grounds to see snakehouses, frogs, ants, lakes, butterfly house, restaurant and bookstore. Take bus to Santo Domingo de Heredia via Tibás or call for hotel pickup. 8 a.m.-2 p.m., Tues.-Fri.; 9 a.m.-3:30 p.m., weekends. Tourists $23, residents $5.50, children and students get discounted rate.

LA PAZ WATERFALL GARDENS (2482-2720, **waterfallgardens.com**), after a 6.2 magnitude earthquake in Jan. 2008 closed the gardens for months, the park has been open and renovated. Trails lead to series of spectacular waterfalls, a butterfly observatory, hummingbird garden, and trout lake, 8 a.m. -5 p.m., daily. Last entrance 3 p.m. for trail walk. Tourists $35, residents $15, discount rate for children.

CARTAGO AND OROSI VALLEY

IRAZU VOLCANO NATIONAL PARK (2200-5025), walk to top to view green crater lake with stunning views of Central Valley. *How to get there*: Bus leaves from National Theater in San José, 8 a.m. Tourists $10, residents $1.75, discounted rates for children.

LANKESTER GARDENS (2552-3247, **jardinbotanicolankester.org**), huge garden with bamboos, heliconia, palms, butterflies, birds and orchids. 8:30 a.m.-4:30 p.m. Adults $5.

NORTHERN ZONE

The Puerto Viejo de Sarapiquí bus will take you near these attractions:

ARENAL BUNGEE (2479-7440, **www.arenalbungee.com**), experience the thrill of a free-fall in a series of different jumps. $50 per jump (packages available.).

ARENAL HANGING BRIDGES (2290-0469, **hangingbridges.com**), explore a network of trails and bridges in a 250-hectare private reserve in La Fortuna. Bridges range between 8 and 22 meters long, offering dramatic views of ravines and a ledge from which to observe plants and birds. $22.

CENTRO NEOTROPICO SARAPIQUIS (2761-1004, **sarapiquis.org**), ecological center and biological reserve and museum of indigenous cultures. $8.

COLLIN STREET BAKERY AND FINCA CORSICANA (2761-1300, **www.collinstreet.com**), view the entire pineapple process from start to finish on a 3,000 acre farm and then enjoy a slew of baked goodies at farm just two hours north of San José.

LA SELVA BIOLOGICAL STATION (2524-0628, **threepaths.co.cr**), full- and half-day guided tours through jungle and arboretum. Half-day tours (three hours), 8 a.m. and 1:30 p.m. Full-day tours at 8 a.m. with a lunch break. Half-day for tourists $30, residents $22, full-day for tourists $38, residents $28.

LAS TILAPIAS (2768-8683, 2768-

9293), 1 km. from Siquirres, show by Chito and Poncho (a man and his domesticated crocodile), other animals, pool, restaurant, $2.

GUANACASTE NORTH

AFRICA MIA (2666-1111, **africamia. net**), boasting 150 animals from native monkeys, wild rabbits and birds to "African safari" animals such as giraffes, warthogs and zebras, this newly-opened park has become a must-see in Liberia. Adults $15, children $10.

DIVING SAFARIS DE COSTA RICA (2672-1259, **costaricadiving.net**), off Playa Hermosa and with some of the best diving in the region at their fingertips, this outfit offers daily diving and snorkelling trips, including night time dives.

ELEVEN-WATERFALL CANOPY TOUR (2639 8303, **adventureparkcostarica.com**), begin climbing through the mountains on horseback, zip down 25 lines and over 11 waterfalls in one of the most stunning canopy tours in Costa Rica, stop for a dip in an icy pool and finish the day with a typical lunch. Also, ATVs, ropes course and trail rides available. Tours begin at 9 a.m. during off-season and 11 a.m. during high season. *Cost:* $89

SAIL SAMONIQUE III (2654-5280, **costarica-sailing.com**), enjoy good food, drinks and music against the backdrop of a volcanic peninsula. Tour Potrero Bay, often called Bio-Bay by marine biologists for the quantity of life there.

CENTRAL PACIFIC

AQUAHOLIC MARINE ADVENTURE (2237-2953, 8875-6264, from U.S. 805-880-1270, **aquaholics.co.cr**), offers sportfishing tours (from $350 to $999), mangrove tours ($65) and scuba-diving adventures.

BAY ISLAND CRUISES (*2258*-3536, **bayislandcruises.com**), cruise Gulf of Nicoya to Tortuga Island aboard 55-ft. boat. Tourists $95, residents $65, children

2-11 $55, inc/breakfast/snack/lunch and transportation.

CALYPSO CRUISES TO TORTUGA ISLAND (2256-2727, **calypsocruises. com**), cruise on luxury catamaran to Nicoya Gulf islands, leaves from Puntarenas, inc/transportation from San José, Jacó, Manuel Antonio. Tourists $119, residents and tourists (7 to 17 years old) $109, children 6 and under $65.

CARARA NATIONAL PARK (2637-1080 or 2637-1054), park with trails, wildlife, birds.

$20 per person for two-hour guided tours, $10 without guide, residents $1.75.

JUNGLE CROCODILE SAFARI (2241-1853, **junglecrocodilesafari.com**), on Río Tárcoles 1.5 hrs. southwest of San José, pontoon boat tour to see crocodiles and other wildlife. $25. Hiking in Carara National Park or horseback rides also. Transportation from San José upon request.

KAYAK JACO (2643-1233, **kayakjaco. com**), ten-year-old company offers sea kayak tours, snorkeling and fishing among other activities.

PURA VIDA GARDENS AND WATER-FALLS (2645-1001, **puravida garden.com**), four waterfalls, garden, wild and injured birds, gift shop and restaurant. $20.

TICO TRAIN TOUR (2233-3300, **ticotraintour.com**), scenic ride from San José to port of Caldera, departs at 7 a.m. and returns at 8:30 p.m. $39. Also offers a scenic trip to a farm leaves San José at 8 a.m. $39 (lunch included)

TURUBARI TROPICAL PARK (2250-0705, 2250-8643, **turubari.com**), in Turrubares, tropical park with cable, canopy, aerial tram, horseback riding. Nature tour plus one activity. Adults $99, children 3-11 $79; packages with transport.

GUANACASTE SOUTH

CABO BLANCO NATURE RESERVE (2642-0093), established in 1963, this reserve was the first protected area of the country. At the southern tip of the Nicoya, Peninsula, it ranks among the most beautiful nature reserves.

FLYING CROCODILE (2656-8048, **flying-crocodile.com**), sail on an ultralight over the ocean, beaches and jungle. Flying lessons also provided upon request. $75 for 20 min.

PAPAGAYO EXCURSION (2653-0254, **tamarindo.com/papagayo**), from a jungle boat safari, to visits to turtle nesting sites, to a river float, Papagayo Excursions is one of the oldest tour operators in the area.

PROYECTO MONTEZUMA (8312-0815, **proyectomontezuma.com**), **a** socially responsible tour operator, Proyecto Montezuma offers volunteer opportunities, boat tours, snorkeling trips and horseback riding.

SOUTHERN ZONE

TROUT-TILAPIA FISHING ponds along Inter-American Highway near Empalme. Catch/eat farm-raised trout or tilapia, mostly weekends, look for signs or try **Lago Santa Ana** (at Km. 61), **El Yugo**, 1 km. west of Empalme on road to Santa María.

CARIBBEAN

CACAO TRAILS (2756-8186, **cacaotrail.com**), Puerto Viejo (Home Creek), Package includes visits to chocolate museum, botanical garden, canoe trip, snorkeling, and visit to indigenous village. 8 a.m.-4 p.m., daily.

DOLE BANANA TOUR (8383-4596, 2768-8683, **bananatourcostarica.com**), Puerto Viejo de Sarapiquí or Limón. See bananas picked, washed, labeled and packaged. $100 for group of 1-15 people, $7 per person.

THE PINEAPPLE TOUR (2765-8192, **agritourscr.com**), family-owned farm that features tours and a gift shop, $19.

Dialing & Dollars

CALLS, Currency and Credit Cards

CALLS

Most public telephones require a phone card available for purchase at many shops, grocery stores, pharmacies and some street vendors. Look for blue-on-gold TARJETAS TELEFÓNICAS signs.

Colibrí 197 card: (¢500) Use with any touch-tone phone, domestic calls only. Dial 197, then long number on the card.

Viajero 199 card: (¢3,000- ¢10,000) Use with any touch-tone phone, domestic or international calls. Dial 199, then 2 for instructions in English. A ¢3,000 card gets about 11 minutes to the U.S., eight minutes to Europe.

Chip card: (¢500): Use in special blue public phones. Insert card -- phone reads value – follow screen instructions. Not popular, Chip cards and phones are hard to find.

"Multipago" public phones accept all three types of phone cards, as well as newer coins.

"Country direct" numbers connect you with an English-speaking operator in your home country to place calls at international rates: **AT&T** (0800-011-4114), **British Telecom** (0800-044-1044), **Canada Direct** (0800-015-1161), **MCI** (0800-012-2222), **Sprint** (0800-013-0123).

Want to rent a cell phone while you're here? Nope, not yet.

Legal residents may obtain cellular phone lines from the Costa Rican Electricity Institute (ICE), the state telecom monopoly. For visitors, ***ask your mobile carrier back home*** if it provides roaming in Costa Rica. U.S. carriers **AT&T** and **Sprint** do; most others do not.

CURRENCY

The *colón*, Costa Rica's currency, with prices denoted by a ₡ sign, comes in ₡1,000, ₡2,000, ₡5,000 and ₡10,000 bills. Gold-colored coins have ₡5, ₡10, ₡25, ₡50, ₡100 and ₡500 values; lightweight aluminum ₡5 and ₡10 coins were introduced in 2006; older, bulky silver coins (₡5, ₡10 and ₡20) are being withdrawn from circulation.

At press time, the exchange rate was ₡585 to US$1 if you SELL dollars; ₡595 if you BUY dollars. ₡630 to Can$1 if you SELL Can$; ₡640 if you BUY them. ₡860 to Eu1 if you SELL Euros; ₡875 if you BUY them, and ₡955 to UK£1 if you SELL UK£ and ₡972 if you BUY them.

Fabulous scarlet macaws flourish in the Southern Zone.

Photo Courtesy of Rodolfo Orozco

MONEY EXCHANGE

Most banks have ATM machines (*cajero automático*) and accept international cards. Check with your home bank for transaction charges and if your PIN needs to be converted for use here. State banks (**Banco Nacional, Banco de Costa Rica, Bancrédito, Banco Popular**) perform currency exchange, but with long lines. (Bring a book.) Things move faster at private banks (**BAC San José, Scotiabank, Citi group, HSBC**), but branches are fewer.

CREDIT CARDS

Most large businesses take credit and debit cards. Visa and MasterCard are widely accepted with American Express, Diner's Club and Discover catching on. Some businesses may levy a fee for card use or offer discounts for cash payment. Your card issuer may also charge a fee for card use in a foreign country. Check before you leave home.

SENDING MONEY

Western Union (2283-6336, westernunion.com) operates from their own outlets and many Más x Menos supermarkets. **Moneygram** (2295-9595, **moneygram. com**) operates from BAC San José, Banex and Fischel Pharmacies. Sender pays fees; receiver does not. Bring your passport or *cédula* to retrieve your cash. Banks arrange transfers more cheaply, but much more slowly.

ELECTRICAL CURRENT

Two- and three-prong plugs and 110V current are used here, both the same as seen in the U.S. European adapters and converters are hard to find; bring your own with you. Power surges are common, especially during electrical storms. Hook valuable appliances to a surge protector, or unplug during storms.

Disabled Travelers

PLENTY of resources are available in Costa Rica for disabled travelers, making a wide range of destinations and activities accessible to everyone.

NEAR San José, wheelchair-accessible attractions include the **Rainforest Aerial Tram** (2257-5961) and you'll find many others throughout the country.

The **International Institute of Creative Development**, where Canadian Monic Chabot creates personalized itineraries for disabled travelers (2771-7482, **empowermentaccess.com**), or **Serendipity Adventures** (2558-1000, U.S./Canada 1-877-507-1358, **serendipityadventures.com**) can help you design a trip that fits your needs. **Costa Rica Dream Travel** (2289-4812, **costaricadreamtravel.com**) arranges tours staffed by hearing-impaired and deaf guides certified in U.S. and international sign language.

Safaris Corobicí, S.A. (2669-6091, safaris@racsa.co.cr, safaricorobici.com) offers tours on the Tenorio and Corobicí Rivers, Cañas, Guanacaste; boats are designed to accommodate wheelchairs. Once your destinations are arranged, you'll find various traveling options. The equal-access law has led to some improvement and a gradual increase in attention to issues affecting the disabled.

Vaya con Silla de Ruedas (Go with a Wheelchair, 2454-2810, 8391-5045, **gowithwheelchairs.com**) offers a/c vans with up to three wheelchair stations. Advance reservations are recommended during high season, and a 10% discount is available for booking directly with the company.

Emergency Contacts

All Emergencies 9-1-1

FOR emergencies, call 911. Operators will guide you to the correct service. This service is available nationwide to summon ambulances, police, firefighters, killer-bee busters, and to report domestic violence and traffic accidents.

THE Red Cross provides ambulance and emergency-rescue service even in the smallest towns, but poor roads and rural distances can slow arrival times.

For medical emergencies in remote towns it is usually faster to appeal to the nearest person with a vehicle.

24-Hour Pharmacies

Clínica Católica, Guadalupe, 2283-6616.
Farmacia Clínica Bíblica, 2522-1000, ext. 1, San José.
Farmacia CIMA 2208-1080, Escazú.
Farmacia Sucre Los Angeles, 2262-3111, across from Más x Menos, Heredia.

Auto Accidents

Call the Transit Police in San José (800-872-6748) and, if the vehicle is insured, call the National Insurance Institute (INS) (800-800-8000, ext. 1). Do not move the car until the traffic cop arrives. In case of a broken-down car, forgotten keys or keys locked inside the car, 800-800-8001 (only for cars with INS insurance).

Credit Cards

Credomatic, American Express, Master Card (2295-9000, 2295-9589, credomatic.com), the local issuing agent for most major credit cards, can usually be contacted directly in the case of a lost or stolen credit card.

You can also contact your specific card company directly:

Visa International, 0-800-0110030.

Master Card, 0-8000-11-0184. 24 hours, 2295-9898.

For a local credit card, apply at a national or private bank. In case of loss, contact bank where you opened account.

Government Abuse/Corruption

Report it to the Ombudsman's Office, 2258-8585.

Embassies

Canadá	2242-4400
France	2234-4167
Germany	2290-9091
Great Britain	2258-2025
	(office hours)
Holland	2296-1490
Israel	2221-6444
Italy	2234-2326
Japan	2232-3787
Spain	2222-1933
Switzerland	2221-4829,
2222-3229, 2233-0052	
United States	2519-2000

Hospitals (See **Medical: Hospitals.**)

Household Emergencies

Maridos de Alquiler (handymen): 2293-2096, fax: 2291-2829, **maridos-dealquiler.net**, 300 m. west of the American Embassy, Pavas, San José.

Medical

Red Cross Ambulance, 2233-7033.

National Insurance Institute, 800-800-8000. *Note: All hospitals have answering machine in Spanish, except Clínica Bíblica which offer an option in English.*

Money Transfers
See **Dialing & Dollars.**

Police

Crimes must be reported in person, as soon as possible, to the nearest office of the Judicial Investigative Police (OIJ) (2295-3643) Av. 4/6, Ca. 15/17, San José. If you need a cop in a hurry, ask for the nearest Fuerza Pública (beat cops).

Taxis
(See **Getting Around: Taxis.**)

Telephone Service
International Collect Calls:
USA, Mexico, Canada and most countries around the world, 175.
Costa Rica to Nicaragua, 0-800-505-1505.
All others (to charge in C.R. or in the other country), 116.
Local directory assistance, 113.
Cellular problems, 193.
Telegram by phone, 123.
International phone calls assistance, 124.

Tourist Information

192 offers information on national parks, reserves, conservation areas and tourist areas (no info on theaters, lodging, other tourist issues).

Veterinarians

Dr. Bitter's Clinic, Escazú, 2228-1753, emergencies, 2225-2500.
Dr. Adrián Molina, 2288-1716, 2228-1909, Escazú. emergency beeper, 2225-2500.
Drs. Echandi, 2223-3111, Av. 6, Ca. 13/15.
Dr. Starke, 2253-7142, San Pedro, Montes de Oca, emergencies, 2225-2500.
Dr. Carol Miranda, 2237-1312, 325 m. north of Hipermás, Heredia, emergencies, 8311-0647.

Gay & Lesbian Travelers

COMPARED to elsewhere in Latin America, Costa Rica is reasonably open for gay, lesbian, bisexual and transgender (GLBT) people.

YOU'LL be welcomed, but Ticos take "don't ask, don't tell" approach to the subject, and they frown on public displays of affection between same-sex couples.

In 2006, the Constitutional Chamber of the Supreme Court (Sala IV) turned down an appeal to permit same-sex marriage, but it did leave the door open for the possibility of civil unions.

The Legislative Assembly is evaluating bill that would establish a Law of Civil Union for Same-Sex Couples.

A few resources of support and information do exist, primarily in San José and gay-friendly Manuel Antonio.

Both places have a couple of hotels exclusively for gay and lesbian clients, and a few others get the "gay friendly" seal of approval.

The **Sexual Diversity Cultural Center of Costa Rica** (2280-7821, **cipacdh. org**) offers support groups and counseling, hosts weekly workshops for GLBT persons and their friends and families, sponsors the annual June pride festival and organizes Dec. 1 World AIDS Day activities.

The **Agua Buena Human Rights Association** (2280-3548, **aguabuena.org**) counsels on human rights, focusing on AIDS activism and access to anti-retroviral medications.

The **Diversity Movement** (**movininetodiversidad.org**) promotes political awareness among Costa Rica's GLBT community.

The non-denominational **Comunidad Arco Iris** (**comunidadarcoiris.org**) provides a place of religious and spiritual gatherings for the country's GLBT community.

Colours Destinations (2296-1880, **coloursoasis.com/tours.htm**), based at San José's predominantly gay Colours Oasis Resort, specializes in gay and lesbian travel to and around Costa Rica.

Gay Travel Costa Rica (8844-9476, **costaricagaytraveler.com**) puts together *à la carte* package tours for gay and lesbian travelers.

The International Gay and Lesbian Association (**ilga.org**) gives advice worldwide.

Tiquicia Travel (2248-9728, **tiquicia travel.com**) focuses on gay and lesbian travel to and around Costa Rica.

Aventuras Yemaya (2294-5907) specializes in gay and lesbian group and individual trips with birding, cultural, volunteer and environmental focuses.

Yemaya is affiliated with **Journey Weavers** (607-277-1416 in North America, **journeyweavers.com**) in the U.S.

Pick up copies of **Gente 10** (2280-8886, **gente10.com**) magazine with directories of services, at Casa de las Revistas bookstores around San José. Pick up bimonthly **Urbano Circuit** at gay-friendly outlets in Quepos.

Several Websites exist, most in Spanish: **travelcostaricanow.com/index.php/Gay**, **gaycostarica.com** (links to gay-friendly lodging, travel tips, nightlife, general info); **Doingaycostarica, OrgulloGayCR. com** (offers a great catalogue of resources and political information for GLBT community, in addition to lively columns by regular writers).

Also check out: **ticosos.com** (activities for older gay men); **mujerymujer.com** (info for Costa Rica's lesbian community); Website: **rincontranscostarica.blogspot. com** (info for transgender people).

Getting Around Costa Rica

By Air

Local Travel: Flying to Costa Rica's domestic airstrips saves many hours on the road. The country has two domestic airlines:

Nature Air (2299-6000, **natureair.com**), flies from the small Tobías Bolaños Airport (SYQ) in Pavas, west of San José.

SANSA (2290-4100, **flysansa.com**) uses an adjoining terminal at Juan Santamaría.

One or both serve Barra del Colorado (BCL), Coto 47 (OTR), Drake Bay (DRK), Golfito (GLF), La Fortuna (FTN), Liberia, Limón (LIO), Nosara (NOB), Palmar Sur (PMZ), Puerto Jiménez (PJM), Punta Islita (PBP), Quepos (XQP), Sámara (PLD), Tamarindo (TNO), Tambor (TMU) and Tortuguero (TTQ). **Nature Air** also flies to Bocas del Toro, Panamá. One-way domestic fares range $60-100 with discounts for residents and children.

Charters are available:
Aero Bell
  (2290-0000, **aerobell.com**).
Paradise Air (2231-0938,
  flywithparadise.com),
  Helicopter service is rare.

By Bus

You can go virtually everywhere by bus. Bus travel is inexpensive and quite good. Fares are usually posted in the front window or inside above the driver's head. Carry small change. Drivers will not make change for large bills. Direct buses are more expensive and rarely stop until they reach their destinations.

Riders of city buses pay the driver upon boarding. Urban routes cost less than $0.50. Most buses are equipped with a cable to pull or buttons to push when you want to get off. You can also whistle or call out "*Parada, por favor*" (next stop, please).

Customer-counting devices in the form o two floor-to-ceiling electronic bars ar mounted just up the steps. Don't block th bars and do have fare ready.

Some stops are marked with the rout name. Some drivers are flexible and wil pick up and drop off passengers betwee stops (not during rush hour, and mor likely in rural areas); wave them dow Longer trips range from $1-10.

On routes that connect San José wit rural areas, most companies allow ticke purchase in advance. Other companie wait until the bus leaves the station an then send a "collector" down the aisle. Bu your ticket ahead of time, especially dur ing high season or on weekends, or if trav eling to a popular tourist destination. Tr to get a *directo* ticket to avoid frequen stops. Buy your return ticket soon afte reaching your destination; sometimes yo can do it while buying your outboun ticket in San José.

San José is the hub for the long-distanc bus system. That makes travel frustratin when you're trying to go from one region al town to another without returning firs to the capital. However, regional bus rout head to urban centers and run at least onc a day and some routes exist between out lying areas, although stops can be frequen (See **Bus Schedules**).

San José has no central bus station rather, buses to destinations both near an far leave from all over downtown. Th largest, busiest station is the so-calle Coca-Cola Bus Terminal (Av. 1/3, Ca. 16 which serves most Central Pacific loca tions. The station has a market and littl restaurants.

The Gran Terminal del Caribe serve Caribbean destinations. The Termina Atlántico Norte serves many routes goin to the Northern Zone. Other bus compa nies have private terminals. Most terminal are in dicey neighborhoods. Take a taxi t and from. Be fanatically aware of your belongings in all terminals, especially the Coca-Cola. Pickpockets and thieves frequent the areas. Most stations and some shops will guard your bags for a fee and can generally be trusted while you shop in the city.

Also be very careful about putting belongings in overhead containers on buses. Thieves have been known to grab backpacks and slip out the back door at a mid-route stop without the owners' ever noticing. John R. Wood's "Costa Rica by Bus" contains schedules, tips and humor. It's updated constantly and available for purchase as a PDF file, which can be downloaded from the Internet (**costaricabybus. com**), printed, or installed on a computer.

By Car/Motorbike

Driving Around: Tourists can drive here with valid licenses from their home countries and passports with valid entry stamps. Seatbelts are required.

Renting can be expensive – in the high season, prices start at about $45/day and $300/week for a compact, and $60/day and $350-$800 for a 4WD.

Car Rentals

Adobe   (2258-4242, **adobecar.com**)
Alamo   (2242-7733, **alamo.com**)
Avis   (2293-2222, **avis.co.cr**)
Dollar   (2443-2950, **dollar.com**)
Hertz   (2221-1818, **hertz.com**)
National (2242-7878, **natcar.com**)
Payless   (2257-0026, **payless.com**)
Many fine local companies are here too:
Economy (2299-2000,
        economyrentacar.com)
Europcar (2257-1158, **europcar.co.cr**)
Hola   (2520-0100, **hola.net**)
Mapache (2586-6364, **mapache.com**)
Toyota   (2258-5797, **toyotarent.com**)
Tricolor   (2440-3333
        tricolorcarrental.com)

A 4WD is necessary for exploring the unpaved countryside during rainy season and sometimes during the dry season. Note that automatic 4WDs are harder to find and usually more expensive.

Most companies have multiple branch offices. **Wild Rider Motorcycle** (2258-4604, **wild-rider.com**) rents dual sport bikes (dirt bikes).

Take care when driving – road conditions can be terrible, with crater-sized potholes, hairpin turns, unmarked and narrow lanes and steep hills. Torrential rains, fog, mudslides, animals and pedestrians on the road, traffic jams and some notoriously bad Tico drivers further make driving a challenge.

Be particularly careful when driving at night. Roads often are unmarked and unlit, and bridges in the boonies sometimes lack railings. Many bridges are one-way – the direction that has the "yield" (*Ceda el paso*) sign must wait until oncoming traffic crosses, but always check for on-coming cars before crossing a narrow bridge. Often intersections have both stoplights and stop (*Alto*) signs. If they're working, obey the lights. If not, the stop sign rules. Watch out for turning cars, which rarely allow pedestrians their legal right of way.

Beware of parking your car in an unguarded lot, and NEVER leave anything of value inside it anywhere, even for a moment. (See **Safe & Secure**.) When eating, try to park the car where you can see it. Speed limits range from 45-90 k.p.h. and are posted on signs and/or painted on the road. Traffic cops have radar and use it; speeding tickets cost from $12 to $150.

If pulled over, don't let them scare you into paying a fine. Insist on being given a ticket ("*Deme el parte*"); traffic police are forbidden to accept money. If in an accident, don't move your car or let the other driver talk you into "making a deal." Wait for police and an insurance inspector. (See **Emergency Contacts**.)

By Ferry

Crossing over the water via ferry is a fun part of the journey to some pristine beaches on the Nicoya Peninsula and in the Southern Zone. Travelers need only slap on some sunscreen, grab a cold drink and be sure to watch over their belongings. Cars and trucks of various sizes can also be driven aboard some ferries; the price of the driver is included in the fares.

Playa Naranjo Ferry (2661-1069) leaves Puntarenas at 6:30, 10 a.m., 2:30 and 7:30 p.m. Return ferry leaves Playa Naranjo at 8 a.m., 12:30, 5:30 and 9 p.m. One-way adults ¢860, children under 12 ¢515. Motorcycles ¢1,850 and cars ¢6,050. Prices for larger vehicles depend on size.

Puntarenas to Paquera, (2661-2984) ferries run at 5, 9, 11 a.m. and 2 and 5 p.m. Adults ¢810, children 3-12 years old ¢485, bikes ¢1,300, cars ¢6,300. From Paquera, you can access Guanacaste South beaches, including Malpaís, Montezuma and Tambor.

Tambor Ferry (2661-2084), two ferries running between Puntarenas and Paquera, operated by Naviera Tambor. Leave Puntarenas at 5, 9 and 11a.m., 2, 5 and 8 p.m. Leave Paquera at 6, 9 and 11a.m., 2, 5 and 8p.m. One-way adults ¢810, kids 12 and under ¢485, bikes ¢1,300, motorcycles ¢1,900, cars ¢6,300. Bigger vehicles depend on size.

Golfo Dulce Two passenger ferries travel from Puerto Jiménez to Golfito and back, leaving from public docks. Leave Puerto Jiménez at 6 a.m., noon, 3 p.m. Return 10:30, 11:30 a.m., 1:30, 4 p.m., smaller ferry ¢2,000 (30 min.), larger ferry (1.5 hrs.) ¢850. Private boats also available for hire.

By Taxi

The most convenient way to travel around the city, but an expensive option for traveling out of the city. Though still affordable for most visitors, high fuel costs continue to increase taxi rates. Cabs can be hailed – evening rush hour, Friday and Saturday nights, and rainstorms usually mean longer waits – or call ahead.

Licensed cabs are red with a yellow triangle on the door, whose number matches its plates. They should be equipped with

Taxis

Alfaro, 2221-8466);
Coopetaxi, 2235-9966.
Coopetico, 2224-7979.
Taxis Coopeguaria, 2226-1366.
Taxis 5 Estrellas, 2228-3159 (based in Escazú). Hourly, daily service (2228-3159); or when going to the airport,
Taxis Unidos Aeropuerto, 2221-6865 (airport service).

working meters, colloquially called *marías*. If the driver doesn't turn on the meter (which sometimes happens), say "*Ponga la maría, por favor*" (please, turn on the meter). If the driver refuses, ask to be let out and hail another cab.

Taxis often don't use meters on trips outside the city, such as to the airport or to Heredia. This is illegal (call the Public Services Regulatory Authority, 2220-0102, to make a complaint) but arguing can sometimes be more problematic – or even dangerous – than just agreeing on a fare beforehand.

The current fare to central San José from Juan Santamaría Airport is a fixed $19 (¢10,000). Cabs in front of nicer hotels often charge fixed minimum rates, more expensive than on the street. This is also an illegal practice for official red taxis, though sometimes hard to avoid.

Illegal taxis, called *piratas*, also patrol the streets. Some look like regular cars, others like taxis (minus the yellow triangles). They can be cheaper, but don't have meters and many don't carry insurance; riders run the risk of being overcharged, or worse. Use only piratas recommended by locals.

A few unscrupulous drivers reset meters

to run up the fare. If you know how much the trip usually costs, dispute the amount diplomatically.

Anger gets you nowhere and can be dangerous.

Cabbies balk at large bills; try not to use anything larger than a ¢2,000 bill for short trips. They often complain about the door-slamming habits of North Americans – be gentle.

Seatbelts are required by law for drivers and passengers. Cab drivers may ask you to use your *cinturón* (seatbelt).

By Train

More trains and tracks are in the works, but for now, **Incofer** (2221-0777) operates a commuter train between San José and Heredia. Departs Heredia at 5:30 a.m. and runs every half hour until 9 a.m. (Mon.-Fri. only). Re-starts at 4:30 p.m., leaving from the Atlantic RR Station, in front of the Parque Nacional in San José. Train runs every half hour until 8 p.m.

Another commuter train runs from San José to Pavas, leaving at 4 p.m. and to Ulatina in San Pedro, leaving at 4:28 p.m., both from the Pacific RR station. For the tourist train that runs to down to the Pacific (weekends only), see **Day Trips.**

Getting to Costa Rica

CITIZENS of all countries must have a passport to enter Costa Rica. Children must also have passports; they may not enter on their parents' documents.

NO visas are required of citizens of the United States, Canada, the European Union, Australia, New Zealand, Japan, Israel and South Africa. They are allowed to stay 90 days as tourists.

In Central America, only Nicaraguans need visas to enter Costa Rica. Panamanians may stay 90 days. All other isthmus citizens receive initial 30-day admittances.

Passports should have at least one-month remaining validity, but computer systems at most airline check-in counters in foreign countries flag Costa Rica as requiring six months and deny boarding to passengers whose documents don't comply. To be safe, renew your passport before that cutoff time approaches.

All arriving air passengers who are non-resident foreigners must possess a paid plane ticket out of Costa Rica. Those arriving by bus must show a bus or plane ticket out. If you travel to a neighboring country, carry your flight itinerary with you to show you satisfy that requirement upon reentering Costa Rica.

The much-practiced "perpetual-tourist" routine – stay 90 days, leave 72 hours, back another 90 days, over and over – carries risks. Tourists are subject to deportation if Immigration catches them living here year-round. The immigration law has stiffened penalties for people who violate the law.

If your child was born in Costa Rica, and you reside here, you must get advance departure permission from Immigration. For more info on immigration policies, visit **migracion.go.cr** or call 2299-8100.

By Air

Some 1.6 million people traveled to Costa Rica last year; most arrived by plane at one of the two international airports.

Prices vary by season and departure city. Generally, tickets are $400-$800 from U.S. and Canadian cities. Flights from Europe are $700-$1,000, but fall at low season.

Most flights arrive at Juan Santamaría International Airport (arrival/departure info: 2437-2626, airport code: SJO) outside Alajuela, a half-hour northwest of San José. The ever-improving terminal offers several shops, a food court, a VIP lounge w/Internet, TVs, DVDs (day/year passes available, **viploungecr.com**), and WiFi access in the food court and at boarding gates.

BAC San José in the check-in area gives good rates on money exchange; Global Exchange windows in the boarding and baggage-claim areas give distinctly poorer rates. ATMs are here too. Taxis accept dollars and charge a uniform $18 to points in San José. Flight schedules vary by season.

Air Canada (0-800-052-1988, **aircanada.com**) flies three times weekly from Toronto.

Air Comet (**aircomet.com**) flies three times weekly from Madrid.

America West (0-800-011-0888, 8363-2957) **americawest.com**) one daily flight from Phoenix.

American Airlines (2248-9010, **aa.com**) flies three times daily from Miami, daily from Dallas. High season: also daily from Los Angeles, and Fort Lauderdale. Low season: daily from Miami, once weekly from Dallas.

Condor (2243-1818, **condor.com**) flies twice weekly from Frankfurt.

Continental (0-800-044-0005, **continental.com**) flies twice daily from Newark, three times daily from Houston. Low season: daily from Houston.

COPA (2223-2672, **copaair.com**) flies twice daily to Panama City and other Central American countries.

Cubana (2221-7625, **cubana.cu**) flies twice weekly from Havana.

Delta (0-800-056-2002/2241-4141) **delta.com**) flies twice daily from Atlanta and five times weekly from New York (JFK). Low season: daily from Atlanta and twice weekly from New York (JFK).

Frontier (1-800-432-1359, **frontierairlines.com**) flies daily from Denver during high season, starting December 18. Low season: discontinued.

Iberia (2431-5633, **iberia.com**) flies daily from Madrid.

Mexicana (2295-6969, mexicana.com) offers flights from numerous North American cities, connecting Mexico City.

Spirit Air (0-800-756-7117, **spiritair.com**) flies daily from Fort Lauderdale.

TACA (2299-8222, **taca.com**) flies from Chicago, Houston, Los Angeles, Miami, New Orleans, New York (JFK), San Francisco, Washington, D.C. (Dulles), Toronto, Mexico City, Santo Domingo and Havana, in addition to all Central American and some South American countries.

US Airways (**usairways.com**) flies daily from Charlotte, also on weekends. Charter flights also fly to Liberia.

Flying into Daniel Oduber International Airport (2668-1010, LIR) in Liberia is an ever-growing option for those planning to head straight to the beaches of Guanacaste, an hour from the airport. Recent years have seen huge growth for the airport. Further expansion is expected.

<u>Exit Taxes</u>: When leaving by air, all travelers pay $26.

<u>Various</u>: Juan Santamaría Airport allows only ticketed passengers inside the terminal. Arrive three hours before your international flight. Costa Rica follows the liquid carry-on restrictions used in North America and Europe.

Baggage limits are usually a maximum of 50 lbs. each, with dimensions (length + height + width) of 62" (160 cm.) in one or two bags, plus one carry-on, weighing no more than 40 lbs. and a purse, briefcase, laptop computer or diaper bag. Check with airlines.

Policies on surfboards vary widely, with additional charges ranging from $80-$100. Check before buying your ticket. Domestic airlines use seven- to 40-passenger planes, and impose baggage limits of 25 lbs. (12 kg).

By Land

<u>Driving Here</u>: The overland route from the U.S. or Canada to Costa Rica takes you through five countries. It's a long haul and

Cruise ships bring thousands of passengers to Costa Rica's shores, even if only for a day.

Photo by
Mónica Quesada

the road conditions can be poor, but the scenery and experience are breathtaking. Anyone considering going it alone, especially women, should consider the risks, including carjacking. Don't drive after dark. Before heading out, get a tune-up/inspection and buy spare tires and parts.

Like you, your vehicle gets a three-month visa upon entering Costa Rica. Make sure you have documentation for all drivers and that they're noted on the paperwork. You can renew this visa once, after that you have to pay steep import duties and follow bureaucratic "vehicle-nationalization" procedures. Have your original title and a notarized letter from vehicle's lien holder.

The fastest way to drive from the U.S. is along the Inter-American Highway from Texas through Mexico, Guatemala, El Salvador, Honduras and Nicaragua. It's possible to do the trip in eight days, but more enjoyable if you take more time.

Sanborn's Insurance (800-222-0158, sanbornsinsurance.com) has offices all along the U.S.-Mexican border and specializes in overland travel though Mexico. They can update you on driving conditions, proper insurance and give advice.

Border crossings can be time-consum-ing and tricky. Call the embassy or consulate of the country you're going to pass through to get updates on customs procedures and fees. Even so, rules and fees may be different at the border – some officials are looking for bribes.

The books "You Can Drive to Costa Rica in 8 Days," by Dawn Rae Wessler, "Central America by Car," by Mike Nelson, and "Driving the Pan-American Highway to Mexico and Central America," by Raymond and Audrey Pritchard, are valuable resources.

Busing Here: Let someone else do the driving. Most international buses are comfortable and equipped with toilets and TV. Keep an eye on your luggage, even if it's in the overhead bin. (See **Bus Schedules.**)

Border Crossings: The principal border crossing to and from Nicaragua is **Peñas Blancas** (Immigration, 2677-0064) on the Inter-American Highway. The Costa Rican side is open 6 a.m.-10 p.m., Mon.-Fri.; 6 a.m.-8 p.m., Sat.-Sun. People leaving Costa Rica by land need a passport. If driving, make sure you have all vehicle documenta-tion (see above). Buy mandatory car insur-ance, $10 for three months, at the border.

Another northern crossing at **Los Chil-es** (2471-1233), for pedestrians, provides limited access to the rest of Nicaragua. Immigration and Customs, 8 a.m.-4 p.m. Further travel north involves a boat ride across the San Juan River ($7); departures are usually at 11 a.m., 12:30, 3:30 p.m.

Three border crossings connect Costa Rica and Panama, although only two are open to foreigners. **Sixaola** (2754-2044), on the southern Caribbean, is the gateway to the popular Bocas del Toro Archipelago in Panama, 7 a.m.-5 p.m. **Paso Canoas** (2732-2150), on the Pacific side, is the main border crossing into Panama on the Inter-American Highway, 6 a.m.-10 p.m. The isolated crossing at **Sabalito** (2784-0130) is open to Costa Ricans and Panamanians only. Don't forget that Panama is one hour later than Costa Rica.

Residents who wish to drive their Costa Rica-plated cars across the border must apply for an "Exit Request" (*Solicitud de salida del país*) from the National Registry (2224-8111). The solicitud can be obtained for $1 at the National Registry offices in Zapote, southeast of San José, across from MultiPlaza del Este, or in the registry's office in Liberia, in Guanacaste, at the Banco de Costa Rica, on the way to Nicaragua. Bring ownership documents, passport or *cédula*.

The vehicle must be free of liens and have no outstanding traffic tickets. If the car isn't in your name, a certified note is required from a lawyer.

Tourists driving cars with foreign plates, permitted to be in the country under a three-month (renewable up to six months) vehicle-entry visa, do not have to go through this procedure. They can drive in and out of the country with no previous approval.

No rental car agencies in Costa Rica allow their vehicles to be driven out of the country.

By Sea

More than 200 large cruise ships carrying more than 300,000 passengers docked here last cruise season. About two-thirds of the visitors stopped in the Caribbean port of Limón; with the others visiting the Pacific ports of Puntarenas and Caldera, with a few stopping at the Southern Pacific port of Golfito. Smaller ships make stops at beach towns such as Playas del Coco in Guanacaste.

Ships usually stop here as part of a larger tour, with most passengers spending a day on short sightseeing trips.

Limón and Puntarenas have cruise terminals with banking, phones, Internet, tourist info and crafts markets.

Marinas also are sprouting up along the Pacific coast, with many in various planning or construction stages. Papagayo Peninsula and Golfito marinas are open. The ones in Quepos and Puntarenas are still under construction.

All complement the country's only official marina, **Los Sueños Marina** (2630-4000, **lossuenosresort.com**) at Playa Herradura.

Flamingo Marina, near Flamingo Beach, is still being renovated.

Ports of Entry

Official ports of entry, usually open 8 a.m.-4 p.m., Mon.-Fri., are:

North Pacific: Playas del Coco, Port Captain coordinates immigration (2670-0216) from Coco and customs from Liberia (2667-0068).

Radio ahead (VHF16) before arrival. The usual wait is an hour.

Central Pacific: Puntarenas has immigration (2661-4263) and Caldera has customs (2634-4055). Radio ahead (VHF16). Quepos has only immigration (2777-1331), obliging boats to go to Caldera.

South Pacific: Golfito has customs (2775-0273) and immigration (2775-0423).

Caribbean Coast: No formal yacht facilities, but boaters go through customs at Limón (2798-3836) and immigration (2798-2097). Radio ahead (VHF16).

ICT Info Offices

FREE Maps and More!

THE Costa Rican Tourism Institute (ICT) (2299-5800, **visitacostarica.com**) has kiosks with free general information, inc/free maps, tourist attractions, bus schedules, brochures for special tours, procedures, etc., in San José, under Plaza de la Cultura (2222-1090), Ca. 5, Av. Ctrl/2, 8 a.m.-4 p.m., Mon.-Fri., and at ICT administrative offices (2299-5800, **info@visita costarica.com**), east side of the Juan Pablo II Bridge, La Uruca, 9 a.m.-5 p.m., Mon.-Fri. Puntarenas: 2661-6408, Nicoya: 2685-3260, Liberia: 2666-2976, San Carlos: 2461-9102. Quepos: 2777-4217.

Offices at the main entry points to the country: Peñas Blancas (2677-0138), border crossing with Nicaragua on Inter-American Highway; Paso Canoas (2732-2035), southern border to Panamá, and Juan Santamaría International Airport (2443-1535).

For info on tours, contact a tour operator. (See **Tour Operators.**)

Internet Services

THE second-highest rated country for Internet (after Chile) in Latin America, Costa Rica offers reasonably fast, reliable connections throughout most of the country.

FREE public hotspots can be found in the Central Valley to date, at Plaza Colonial, Best Western, Intercontinental Real, some mall food courts, Bagelman's, Denny's and TGIF in Escazú and the Juan Santamaría and Liberia airports.

In San José, try **CyberCafé Las Arcadas** (2233-3310), next to Gran Hotel Costa Rica, 7 a.m.-9 p.m., $0.50 hr., 2x1 after 7 p.m., plus laundromat, book exchange, restaurant. (See **Living & Working Here** and **Websites About Costa Rica.**)

Investing

EVEN in the economic crisis year of 2009, the investment scene in Costa Rica continues to bulge, particularly in the foreign direct investment area.

IN August 2009, Foreign Direct Investment Magazine ranked Costa Rica as the second most attractive foreign direct investment market in the Central American and Caribbean region.

Investing in Costa Rica remains high due to benefits offered by the land and people of the country. Costa Rica's biggest investment draws include: a well-educated populace, commitment to environment maintenance and sustainability, sound and reliable business practices and free-trade zones, which continue to garner more and more investment. Though some investors remain wary of investment here due to an increasingly high exchange rate, a lack of raw materials and high inflation rate, overall, the Costa Rican investment market remains attractive, active and fertile.

No matter what the exchange rate, the most important rule for would-be investors remains the same: be skeptical, be skeptical, and be skeptical. In a phenomenon sometimes referred to as the "sunshine syndrome," many visitors or foreign residents of Costa Rica mistakenly assume that the country's friendly people and laid-back style mean investors don't have to take the same precautions they would back home. If anything, the opposite is true, because scam artists abound. It's essential that you do your homework and get good advice, particularly if you aren't fluent in Spanish and, thus, have limited access to the investor resources available.

In order to publicly solicit investments in Costa Rica, a company must be registered as a "*Sociedad Anónima*" (S.A.) with the Superintendence of Financial Entities (SUGEF) or the Superintendence of Securities (SUGEVAL), both dependencies of the Central Bank. Their Web sites, **sugef.fi.cr** and **sugeval.fi.cr,** provide information about registered companies, their audited financial statements and the investments they offer. Stock and bond trading takes place at the fledgling National Stock Market (**bnv.co.cr**).

SUGEVAL's National Securities Registry also offers information about the types of investments available on the stock market, including Costa Rican companies offering stocks.

SUGEVAL has been working for several years to improve the quality of information available to investors and has launched new efforts to educate would-be investors with seminars and fairs. This was prompted, in part, after a combination of dropping C.R. bond prices and investor panic due to international factors resulted in total capital and accumulated interest losses exceeding $123 million in 2004. At the time, some U.S. investors in Banco Nacional's dollar investment funds said they had not understood clearly some terms of their investments until it was too late. To learn more about SUGEVAL's activities, visit its Web site or call its Information Center (243-4700).

Non-Spanish speakers need to do some extra legwork to find translated background information on potential investments. The SUGEVAL Web site offers some translations, but the best approach for those needing assistance in English is to call the Information Center, which has some bilingual operators, or contact SUGEVAL at **correo@sugeval.fi.cr** to request an English speaker.

For more guidance, contact a brokerage house. The SUGEVAL Web site lists the registered brokerage houses where potential investors can find an advisor. These can help experienced investors find options abroad; it is increasingly easy to maintain a diverse, international portfolio in Costa Rica as globalization takes root.

Among the multinational firms, attracted by the country's free-zone regimen which gives businesses tax exemptions and incentives, is high-tech giant Intel. Gone are the days when bananas and coffee were the country's export mainstays. Though Costa Rican bananas and pineapples remain heavily exported, in 2009, Costa Rica's most lucrative exports were microchips and medical equipment, which were produced here in free-trade zone areas. Boston Scientific and St. Jude's are two of the biggest producers of medical equipment in the country.

However, while it may be easier now to manage investments both here and abroad, it is crucial that all investors new to the country increase assets here gradually and keep their home advisors informed of their activities in order to maintain a well-balanced overall portfolio and avoid undue risks.

Options include Central Bank or Finance Ministry bonds (which make up a huge percentage of the overall investment market), certificates of deposit, investment funds and real estate, as well as stocks in the small National Stock Market.

The booming real estate market, particularly in the northwestern province of Guanacaste, makes buying property another way to invest. Again, doing your homework is especially important in this area, as the industry is unregulated. Many brokers recommend real estate funds as a good choice for foreign investors in Costa Rica. Real Estate Investment Trusts (REITs or *fondos inmobilarios*) are publicly traded companies which buy and rent out real estate and distribute the profits among investors. Since the first REITs became available here in 1999, they have become one of the country's most lucrative investment options.

Another option is investment funds, which tend to offer returns that are relatively low, but higher than what is available in the U.S.

Laundromats

HOTELS have laundry service or recommend nearby dry cleaners. Check under lavanderías in the Yellow Pages. Most are closed Sundays.

HERE are a few mainstays for clothes washing and dry cleaning.

San José Area:

Alajuela: Más x Menos, (2443-4947). Sixaola, Av. 2 (2221-2111). Martinizing (2443-1390),
Ciudad Cariari: Dryclean USA (2293-0928). Express Service (2220-1572),
Curridabat: Sixaola (2234-0278), Plaza del Sol. Dryclean USA, (2225-5297) Plaza Crystal. Martinizing, (2224-6480), Vida Nueva (2280-4432), repairs, too.
Escazú: Martinizing (2289-5201). Dryclean International (2228-4482), next to Banco Nacional, friendly, helpful, guarantees work. Express Service (8344-8219). Dryclean USA, Los Anonos (2228-4763), also clothing and shoe repairs, Dryclean USA, Atlantis Shopping Center (2588-1820).
Guachipelín: Dryclean USA (2215-0301).
Guadalupe: Sixaola (2225-7284), Lava Sola (2253-4665.
Guayabos: Dryclean USA (2271-5394).
Heredia: Sixaola (2260-8083). Hipermás, Mall Las Flores, (2237-3194). Martinizing (2260-7808). Sixaola La Magnolia (2237-0729), ironing, repairs. Dryclean USA (2260-0919).

La Sabana: Lavandería La Sabana, three-hour service, 300 m. west of Pop's (2232-5302).
Los Yoses: Martinizing (2253-8776).
Moravia: Sixaola (2240-7667). Martinizing (2240-8574). Dryclean USA (2297-3472). Lavandería Aqua Matic (2235-9174).
Rohrmoser: Martinizing (2231-6275). Dryclean USA (2231-7396). Plaza Mayor, Lavandería Aqua Matic (2291-2847).
Sabanilla: Sixaola (2283-7332). Lavandería Aqua Matic (2283-7844).
San Francisco: Martinizing (2226-2114).
San José: Economy Lavatex, Paseo Colón (2257-3590), ironing, repairs.
San Pedro: Martinizing (2224-4183), Burbujas (2224-9822), charges regular clothes by the kilo but dry cleaning by single piece. Lava Sola (2234-6311) near the American Mall.
San Sebastián: Sixaola (2286-2207), Hipermás.
Santa Ana: Martinizing (2282-3327). Dryclean USA (2203-4790).
Tibás: Sixaola (2240-1968).

Caribbean Coast:
La Caribbeña (2759-9043), first two story yellow house at the entrance of Manzanillo, and Mr. Big J (2755-0353, 8887-4695)

in Cahuita, south side of the park.

La Fortuna, Near Arenal:
Lavandería Alice (2479-7111) across from Hotel San Bosco. La Fortuna (2479-9737) across from Hotel & Pizzería Luigi's.

Quepos:
Casa Tica (2777-2533) in El Mercado.

Jacó: Lavandería Aqua Matic (2643-2083).

Clothing Repairs:
Retoucherie de Manuela (2281-1653), in Mall San Pedro, Terra Mall, Pavas, Escazú, Multiplaza del Este, Santa Ana. Julio the Tailor (2201-8247) alters clothes in Multiplaza, Escazú.

Living & Working Here

WHETHER you've come here to sink your feet into the sands of permanent retirement or you're passing through on an extended visit, you are one in the thousands of foreigners who have made Costa Rica their home.

IF you plan on staying longer than three months, take the time to understand the rules for being here, otherwise you could be surprised with an unwelcome fine.

Residency

Costa Rica just undertook an extensive revision of its immigration law, changing some of the country's antiquated practices to make applying for residency less complicated, but at the same time, increasing fees for those who are here illegally.

The new law does not affect the "perpetual tourist," a popular but risky method employed by foreigners who don't want to go through the complications of achieving residency. Foreigners can remain in the country for three months as a tourist, at which time they must leave the country for a period of 72 hours so that their status as tourist is renewed. Those that get caught doing this too often face deportation.

Be careful about flying to Costa Rica on a one-way ticket. Airlines have become increasingly vigilant about requiring tourists to present proof of outbound travel before they board the plane. In some cases, they require travelers to purchase a ticket on the spot.

Residency falls into four main categories: *Pensionado* (retiree) requires proof of $1,000/month fixed pension income; *Rentista* (investor) must prove permanent fixed income of $2,500/month (the proof of income covers immediate family members); *Inversionista* (large investors) must invest $50,000-$200,000 in approved sectors such as tourism or reforestation; *Representante* (company director) must employ a minimum number of local workers and present certified financial statements.

Resident or not, you can get a driver's license and you can purchase property.

Recent changes allow for foreigners who own a home of more than $200,000 in Costa Rica to apply for residency under investor status. The new law also provides foreigners the opportunity to go through the application process for residency within Costa Rica.

Basic documents needed for application for residency include a notarized and certificated birth certificate and police report from your home city or town, copies of your passport, fingerprints conducted at the Public Security Ministry in Desamparados in San José and – just recently – immigration officials require a written document from your embassy in Costa Rica, indicating you have registered with them. US citizens can register at the embassy ($30 per person) or online **https://travelregis tration.state.gov** (free). Another change is that applications or renewal requests must show proof of contributions to the Costa Rican Social Security System and registration with one's embassy. Be wary of higher fines for employing undocumented workers. Immigration officials reserve the right to fine employers between two and 12 times the employee's base salary.

Getting Help

The ground rules for obtaining residency change often, and paperwork, lines and delays are inevitable. Therefore, a healthy dose of patience is prescribed for would-be residents.

The Association of Residents of Costa Rica (2233-8068, **arcr.net**) has over 20 years' experience in helping newcomers. The last Thurs./Fri. of each month (except December) seminars are held on laws, real estate, residency, banking, insurance, moving and health, $65 non-members, $45 members. Annual membership is $100 non-residents, $50 residents, spouses and dependents $10 each. Services include residency processing, shipping and customs, real estate, medical plans, courier to U.S., vehicle and home insurance.

For chat rooms, blogs and all kinds of info on the country, see **Costa Rica on the Web**.

Moving & Shipping

Home-furnishing stores, with plenty of styles and prices, can be found everywhere, and many people visit the duty-free zone in Golfito to buy electrical appliances at bargain prices.

Goods accompanying future residents by plane tend not to be charged duty. Shipped goods - if basic household items,

sports equipment and books - are rarely charged duty, but beware of bringing in antiques or items in bulk. Contact a reliable shipper, as tax rates are variable. Freight costs are included in the duty levied, so use the closest possible port.

Starting a Business

Anyone can form a new company or buy an existing one. Owning a company means a fast-track to residency and work permits, with a few glitches. Foreigners can be owners and managers of B&Bs, restaurants and language schools, and there is no problem with Immigration as long as they are not observed physically working in those businesses. Investing in and running a business, especially with the challenges of a different legal system and language, take hard work and dedication. Scams abound and finding a trustworthy legal advisor is essential.

Finding Work

Numerous foreigners work as teachers, call operators and in tourism. Their wages usually are relatively low and in local currency. Tourists and temporary residents cannot be employed without a work permit approved by Immigration. Ticos generally are well educated and they easily fill executive and specialized positions in national and multi-national companies, so opportunities are scarce for foreigners unless contracted from abroad. Self-employment is possible, but you must pay all Social Security and income taxes.

Technology & Utilities

Even remote villages boast an Internet café with capability to burn CDs, download photos and make cheap international calls. In San José and smaller towns prices are around $1/hr. but rise to as high as $3/ hr. in high-tourist centers.

The telecommunications market was opened to competition in 2009 with the passing of the Central American Free Trade Agreement (CAFTA). With the signing of CAFTA, the longstanding monopoly of the **Costa Rican Electricity Institute (grupoice.com)** was toppled, and the telecommunications market was suddenly a manifest-destiny scenario for market share. The resulting changes in the telecommunications market have made for a dramatic shakeup in 2009.

According to the Superintendent of Telecommunications, the governing body that permits companies to compete in the telecommunications market, more than 500 applications for entry into the telecommunications market were received in 2009. At the beginning of September, SUTEL had officially welcomed over 30 companies into the telecommunications market, and the number is expected to continue to rise.

Possibly the largest name in the Internet-provider market is **Amnet** (2210-2929, **amnet.co.cr**), which ended its long-term partnership with **Radiográfica Costarricense (Racsa)**, (800-628-3427, **racsa.co.cr**). For 10 years, the two companies had teamed to offer dial-up and broadband cable modem Internet connections. With the split, the two are now competitors in the market, as both aim to provide Internet and cable services across the country. Current cable modem rates range from $17-$168/month (64 kbps – 4 mb). Set-up costs are about $70, including modem.

Racsa also offers a no-contract pre-paid system using cards. Their basic dial-up service costs $15 for unlimited connectivity. ICE is increasing its broadband ADSL Internet access using existing phone lines throughout the country. Costs are $22-$169/month (128-4096 kbps) plus $45 installation fee, but it is important to contact ICE first to make sure a specific area has coverage.

Other companies have already joined the telecommunications market. They are: Dodona SRL, Intertel Worldwide S.A., Worldcom de Costa Rica S.A., Call My Way NY S.A., Redes Inalámbricas de Costa Rica S.A., JASEC Companies CableTica, Costa Rican Internet Service Provider (CRISP) and Cablevision and Super Cable. Though all of these companies do not provide Internet access, it is evident that the increasing number of companies offering software, infrastructure, calling networks and Internet service, represent the changing face of the telecommunications market in Costa Rica.

Cell Phones

Costa Rica has a relatively modern telecom structure with one of the highest Internet usage rates in Latin America and comprehensive land line and mobile telephone systems, but GSM lines sell out fast and are currently scarce. They can be rented – at an inflated price – from most car rental agencies or **cellphonescr.com**.

Money Exchange

Money exchange is easy from banks, hotels and many Western Union outlets. Travelers' checks are accepted in many hotels, but cashing them can involve long waits in banks. This applies to just about any transaction in crowded state banks or municipal departments unless you are a pensioner, pregnant, disabled or can tote a baby, in which case 'fast track' lanes are available. ATMs, which are just about everywhere, take major credit/debit cards.

Post Offices

The mail service works well and offers a guaranteed Express Mail Service (EMS) similar to DHL and UPS. Most residents rent a PO box. Courier services charge a monthly fee and operate mail boxes in Miami for documents and purchased goods. **Starbox** (2289-9393, **starboxcos** tarica.com), JetBox (2253-5400, **jetbox. com**), **Mail Boxes Etc.** (2289-3696 **mail boxesetc.co.cr**), **Aerocasillas** (2208-4848, **Aerocasillas.com**).

Drivers' Licenses

Foreign drivers' licenses can be used up to 90 days from the date of entrance into the country. If you plan on driving a car 90 days, you should obtain a Costa Rican drivers' license, a straightforward process that requires a morning to complete.

A drivers' license can be used almost like a *cédula* – as proof of identity – which is useful if you don't have residency. The licensing office (2257-7371, at COSEVI in La Uruca, requests a medical and eye test ($30) issued at any of the doctors' offices along the street. Bring along a copy and the original of your passport and foreign drivers' license. Once inside, simple procedures take about an hour and cost about $8. (**See Getting Around in Costa Rica: By** car.)

Shopping

Malls are sprouting up everywhere, but expect to pay more for imported brand names. Hand-crafted wood furniture from Sarchí, low-cost clothing from *ropa americana* thrift shops, farmers' markets for fresh produce, garage sales advertised in local newspapers all offer great savings.

Car prices are rather steep here, but so are import duties on new and old vehicles (nearly 60 percent on a three-year-old or less); new cars cost about 20 percent over listed price in the United States. Great care must be taken when looking at second-hand vehicles; many recently imported cars have been in accidents or had their odometers turned back. Check the VIN number and check its online car history at carfax.com. Gas prices fluctuate against international market prices, but average $3-4/gallon for regular.

Eating out in high-end restaurants averages $25 without alcohol, but informal Tico *sodas* prepare fresh meals for around $4-5.

Maps

A city map is essential to get your bearings. Beyond the city, more road signs have been put up, but a good map is still basic survival gear.

REMEMBER some place names are repeated around the country, so it's important to specify which Playa Hermosa, you're heading to - the one in Guanacaste or the one near Jacó.

In San José you can get free maps at the **Costa Rican Tourism Institute** (ICT) kiosk under the Plaza de la Cultura (2222-1090, **visitacostarica.com**, Av. Ctrl., Ca.5), also ICT offices at: Juan Santamaria Airport 2443-1535, **ictaeropuerto5@ice.co.cr**; Puntarenas 2661-6408, **ictpuntarenas@ ict.go.cr**; Nicoya 2685-3260, **ictnicoya@ ict.go.cr**; Liberia 2666-2976, **ictliberia@ ict.go.cr**; San Carlos 2461-9102, **ictsan carlos@ict.go.cr**; and, Quepos, 2777-

4217, **ictquepos@ict.go. cr**. Better maps, including up-to-date National Geographic maps, are for sale at **7th Street Books** (2256-8251), Ca. 7, Av. 1/Ctrl., and **Boutique Annemarie** (2221-6707), Av. 9, Ca. 7/9, in the Hotel Don Carlos in Barrio Amón. The book departments of the downtown branches of **Universal** (2222-2222), Av. Ctrl., Ca. 3, and **Lehmann** (2522-4848), Av. Ctrl., Ca. 1, have inexpensive, basic national maps.

For national parks, the **Fundación Neotrópica** (2253-2130), 300 m. east of Plaza del Sol in Curridabat, publishes and sells official national parks map.

The most detailed maps, are the 1:10,000

and 1:200,000-scale, topographical maps ($2) available at the **National Geographic Institute** (2523-2000, ext. 2630, Av. 20, Ca. 5/7 in the Public Works and Transport Ministry's (MOPT) huge complex on the southwest side of Plaza Víquez, 7 a.m. - 3 p.m., weekdays.

In Escazú, **Librería Las Palabras** (250 m. east of Banco Nacional in central Escazú) sells highway maps. In Heredia, the best source for maps is the gift shop at **INBioparque/INBio Park** (2507-8107), 400 m. west of Shell station on road from Santo Domingo to Heredia (follow signs), 9 a.m.-5 p.m., Tues.-Sun.

Media and the Message

MAGAZINES and newspapers are sold throughout the country.

Newspapers & Magazines

Most notable as the leader for national news coverage in English is **The Tico Times**, (2258-1558, **ticotimes.net**), with prizewinning in-depth reports on everything from politics to the environment, plus thoughtful editorials and a lively letters section. The 'Weekend' section covers travel, culture and happenings.

A weekly Nica Times insert covers Central America. Also, the paper carries periodic supplements on topics, including tourism, real estate, shopping, investing.

The Tico Times comes out on Fridays and is sold for ¢600 in supermarkets, hotels, bookstores, souvenir shops and its home office, Av. 8, Ca.15, where you can subscribe to both the print and daily online (**ticotimes.net**) editions. The Tico Times also publishes this annual tourist guide and a bilingual restaurant guide.

Costa Rica Outdoors (1-800-308-3394, **costaricaoutdoors.com**), bimonthly, attractive tourist-oriented magazine with info on everything from sportfishing to history. Available in magazine stores, gift shops and hotels, or purchased online.

Mesoamérica (2253-3195, **mesoamericaonline.net**), monthly coverage of human rights, economics, politics and the environment in Central America. Published since 1982 by the Institute of Central American Studies. Available through subscription and where English-language publications are sold.

Business Costa Rica (2220-2200, **amcham.co.cr**), monthly business magazine put out by the Costa Rica –America Chamber of Commerce. Order online or contact the main office.

Regional Publications

The Howler (2653-0545, **howlermag.com**) and **The Mountain Howler** (8881-6084, mountainhowler.com), monthly magazines based in Tamarindo & Grecia, tourist info, news, articles on regional culture and updates on area events. Free.

Quepolandia (2777-1113 or 8811-4961, **quepolandia.com**), monthly guide focusing on the Quepos-Manuel Antonio area. Articles plus useful info: tide charts, public transportation schedules, maps, telephone numbers. Owners also publish an annual bilingual guide, **La Guia**. Free.

Peninsula de Nicoya (8369-6687, **peninsuladenicoya.com**), monthly regional, bilingual guide with tide tables, maps, business directory, hotels, ferry schedules, points of interest. Free.

Costa Rica Today (2520-0303, **costaricatoday.cr**), monthly bilingual newspaper, tourism. Free.

Nature Landings (2299-6039, **naturelandings.com**), Nature Air's inflight magazine. Six issues/year. Free.

In Spanish

Spanish-language publications are easy to find on almost every street corner in the city and in neighborhood stores. For sports, check out the Monday editions that recap weekend soccer.

La Nación is the largest and most influential newspaper. Sunday editions include a magazine and supplements. **Al Día**, run by the same company, is a smaller, tabloid heavy on sports. Popular **Diario Extra** features more sensationalist fare. **La República** is more business-oriented, and **El Financiero** covers business. **La Gaceta** is the official government gazette, listing all bills and legislation. **La Prensa Libre** and **El Heraldo** are smaller, popular dailies.

The brilliant jewel-like colors of the poison-dart frog warn predators to "beware."

Photo by Michelle Bezanson

On the Air in Costa Rica

Both radio and TV have many options for listening to English-language programs.

Radio

Radio Dos 99.5 FM (2224-7272, online stream at **radiodos.com**), highly popular station, '70s-'90s music. English news every hour, Morning Show, 6-9 a.m. and evening show n7-9 p.m.

Rock Radio 107.5 FM (2289-9222, online stream at radio1075.com) All English 24/7. BBC news at 8 a.m., noon, 5 p.m. Request songs at 2228-2167.

95.5 Jazz (2225-8955) for jazz, concerts, and events. Weekly programs include the Dave Koz show from the U.S. daily at 2 p.m. and Jazz Beat, a history of jazz, Fri. at 6 p.m. Also plays related genres in Spanish, including traditional and flamenco guitar.

Super-Radio 102.3 FM (2240-3940) plays oldies in English, including an hour of Beatles, "*Los Cuatro Grandes*," 4-5 p.m. daily. Sounds of the '80s, 5-6 p.m., Mon.-Fri., and Black Light soul music, 6-7 p.m.

Radio Universidad 96.7 FM plays classical music.

Spanish-language stations feature music, news and general information, including sports coverage. **Radio Reloj 94.3** is one of the most popular, playing classic and modern hits. The *Manicomio de la Risa*, or Insane Asylum of Laughs show, is unavoidable due to its popularity and can

be heard in taxis, stores and buses. Featuring jokes, imitations and satire, you can catch it on **Estereo Omega, 105.1 FM**, 6-9 a.m. weekdays.

Television

Cable Tica (2210-1450, **cabletica.com**) offers 73 channels and 'pay per view' movies. Service is available in most of the country but check with the company. International shows include Chinese, French, German and Italian channels. Variety of package prices including cable, Internet, and digital. **Amnet** (2210-2929, **amnet.co.cr**) offers similar service and a more expensive package, including Internet cable modem. **DirecTV** (2205-5151, **directv.co.cr**) offers packages, rents or sells equipment and covers the entire country.

Local TV leader is Teletica Channel 7 with news at 6 a.m., noon, and 7 p.m. Also offers a popular news show, *Siete Días* (Seven Days), at 8 p.m. Mondays, plus many local programs. Mexican **Repretel** owns Channels 4, 6 and 11, with news in the mornings and evenings. These channels also air children's shows throughout the day. State-owned **Channel 13** has good cultural and news programs and nightly news. You can catch international news from Europe on **Channels 14** and **15** in the evenings. Channels and news times subject to change based on your cable provider.

Pets

COSTA RICA is a pet-friendly country, with plenty of pet stores and veterinarians to meet the needs of your best buddy.

YET, bringing your pet to Costa Rica can be complicated and those wishing to bring a pet to Costa Rica should prepare well in advance.

To keep things simple, experts recommend your pet fly from its country of origin as "baggage," accompanied by a person (owner, friend or family member). All that is needed is a health certificate issued by a licensed veterinarian and endorsed by a Veterinary Services (VS) veterinarian. The certificate should affirm that an exam was conducted within two weeks of travel and that the animal is healthy and free from any clinical signs of infectious disease, cats were vaccinated against rabies and dogs were vaccinated against distemper, hepatitis, leptospirosis, parvovirus and rabies. Pet owners traveling from the United States can use a State or Federal (VS Form 18-1) U.S. Interstate and International Certificate for Small Animals. The health certificate does not need to be signed by an attorney at law, nor does it need to be stamped by the Costa Rican Consular office, but a rabies vaccination certificate should accompany the health documents.

However, if the pet flies unescorted, even on a commercial airline, it's a different story. You'll need to prepare well before the arrival of your pet by contacting the **Agriculture Ministry** (2260-9046, **mvarela@senasa.go.cr**, attn: María Varela). At minimum, you should expect to provide customs with a bill of sale for the pet, a cargo bill of landing (obtained from the airline) and the pet's health certificate. The fee is $16. These documents must be personally shuffled between ministries *before* the arrival of your pet to ensure that it does not have to swelter in a customs storage facility while you attempt to unravel the red tape.

If all of this seems too overwhelming, help is available. In Costa Rica, the **Association of Residents of Costa Rica** (2233-8068) offers information on importing animals. In the U.S., try **Jet-A-Pet** (888-538-2738, jet-a-pet.com) and **Delta Airlines'** international pet service (888-736-3738, **delta.com**), both of which serve Costa Rica.

Before going home, you will need to go through a more abbreviated authorization process that requires a health certificate from a Costa Rican vet. Authorization can take several days, so don't put it off until the last minute. You must also be in compliance with all regulations for re-entering your home country.

While the import of certain types of birds is now legal, the process requires patience and a good deal of paperwork. To make a request, contact Dr. Manuel Vargas Chavarría (2260-8300, ext. 2110) with the Ministry of Agriculture and Livestock. Exporting birds requires permission from the Environment Ministry. Exporting large animals, such as horses, requires approval from the Agriculture Ministry (see above).

Airline Requirements

On international flights, pets (except for service animals, such as guide dogs) usually are not allowed to travel in the cabin. They are normally accepted as checked baggage or shipped as cargo. The cost for importing pets varies, depending on how you send them and their size. Expect to pay at least $80 each way. More airlines, with cost cutting in mind, are restricting international travel with animals, particularly during the high-travel season, May 15-Sept. 15. Most will not transport pets when temperatures are above 85°F (29.5 °C) or below 20°F (-6.7°C) in the city of origin, connection or destination.

Some Restrictions

Certain airlines have restrictions on Rottweilers, Doberman pinschers, pit bulls and bull terriers. Most also have separate guidelines for short-nosed dogs and certain cats, refusing to transport them in warmer weather. Airlines also reject animals which behave aggressively. Check with the airline for prices/regulations.

For flight, pets should be in well-ventilated, leak-proof, lockable kennels that provide space for the animal to lie down, turn around and stand up freely. U.S. regulations require that you provide feeding instructions for 24 hours and state, in writing, that your pet has been offered food and water in the preceding four hours. To help make your pet more comfortable, you may want to place a toy or blanket in the kennel, but never include a muzzle or leash. Many vets advise against giving pet sedatives for air travel.

To travel with your pet in country, call ahead.

Pet Culture in Costa Rica

The number of dogs freely roaming the streets may surprise visitors new to Latin America. While most of these dogs are not aggressive, be cautious in approaching them. Regulations have been enacted in an effort to increase owner liability and reduce problems caused by animals.

By law, guide dogs are permitted in buses and taxis; otherwise, pets usually are not welcome on public transport. Always keep your dog on a leash when in public.

Although many Costa Ricans keep dogs, especially for security, they usually are not allowed in the house. Never enter a person's yard or property without the owners' permission if there is an unleashed dog.

Pet Care

Supermarkets, grocery stores and many vets sell pet food. Larger markets have familiar brands imported from the U.S.

There are numerous veterinarians in Costa Rica; check **Emergency Contacts** in this guide and the Yellow Pages for clinics near you.

Many vets will board pets for $8-$12 per day. In Heredia, **Mi Amigo Fiel** (2260-1791), $6/night, bring own food. Also in Heredia is **Pets Paradise** (8381-8285), $12, bring own food, vet available, outdoor area. In Escazú, **Clínica Veterinaria Escazú** (2228-6880), $12, offers pet sitting. Home pet sitting in Central Valley: **Fur and Feather Pet Care** (8381-8285) or. **furandfeatherpetcare.com**.

Shelters

Many cats and dogs need homes in Costa Rica. If you have room in your heart and your home for a pet, there are numerous choices. Contact the **Refugio de Animales Shelter** (2267-7158 or 267-6374, **animalsheltercostarica.com**), which is associated with **The Humane Society** and is located in San Rafael de Heredia, for a variety of puppies, dogs, kittens and cats. Adoption is usually free; donations are welcome. Also, check the classified section of The Tico Times for free pets and those for sale.

Vets can spay or neuter your pet, or contact the **National Association for the Protection of Animals** (2233-0779). Av. 8, Ca. 17/19, cost ₡7,000 ($12). Additionally, **The McKee Project** (**mckeeproject.org**) is a U.S. non-profit dedicated to animal health in Latin America via spay and neuter services and community education.

Practical Packing

PACKING for Costa Rica is a challenge, considering the country's variable weather conditions – from mountain-top night temperatures near freezing to blistering heat on the coast.

CONDITIONS can vary greatly in a single trip, so multi-purpose layering is the trick. While most essential travel items can be found here, do bring your favorite must-have's.

Ticos generally dress well and are conscious of appropriate attire; only foreigners wander around in shorts in Central Valley cities. That's fine if you don't mind being labeled a 'tourist,' but remember standing out from the crowd can bring unwanted attention to you and your valuables. Be respectful of what is culturally acceptable.

Bear in mind that May-Nov. is the rainy season. The Caribbean, however, is fairly wet all year except during Sept.-Oct.

Clothing: easy-care layers. Comfort is the key. Bring your favorite beach gear with robust sandals, sun hat, sarong. Also, you'll need a cold-climate sweatshirt, pants and waterproof windbreaker. Bring a smarter outfit for more formal outings. (Jackets and ties are rare). And if you plan to hike or explore on foot, pack some good-quality trainers and boots and plenty of socks.

Also bring: camera/binoculars, iPod, flashlight, sun block (15 or over) and insect repellent. A dry bag is excellent for protecting mechanical valuables like watches, music and cameras, etc., and sturdy plastic bags for wet clothes. Bring a basic first-aid kit, prescription drugs, travel insurance. Many items like batteries, film, toiletries, T-shirts are often cheaper here.

A smaller daypack doubles as 'handbag.' Hotels normally store bulky luggage. Money belts keep your cash and documents concealed.

Recycling

REDUCE, Reuse (Recycle If You Can). In 2007, Costa Rica adopted a program sponsored by the German governmental group GTZ to help augment the country's recycling plans.

ONLY about 15 percent of Costa Rica's material is recycled. A few independent collection centers exist around the country.

Some communities (and a few businesses) offer collection centers where you bring your recyclables; a few will even pick them up at your home. If you live anywhere offering recycling, separate your materials and take advantage. "Glass" and "plastic" in the list below generally refer to bottles only.

Alajuelita (2252-4016), collection center, east side of church. Glass, plastic, aluminum, paper, newspaper, cardboard.

Curridabat (2272-0126), Wed. pick-up. Place materials in plastic bags. Glass, plastic, aluminum.

Desamparados (2227-2942), collection center, 200 m before cemetery. Glass, plastic, aluminum, paper, newspaper, cardboard, metal, batteries.

Escazú (2228-5757), fixed routes, pick-up every week. Six collection barrels around town. Glass, plastic, aluminum, paper, newspaper, cardboard, batteries.

Esparza (2636-7878), collection center, Municipality. Glass, plastic, aluminum, paper, newspaper, cardboard.

Grecia (2444-2885), collection center next to former Warner factory. Glass, plastic, aluminum, paper, newspaper, cardboard, batteries.

Naranjo (2451-5858), collection center at Municipality. Glass, plastic, aluminum, paper, newspaper, cardboard.

Playa Hermosa, Guanacaste (2672-0108), barrels, second entrance to beach and at bus stops. Glass, plastic, aluminum.

Puerto Jiménez, collection center next to Colegio Técnico. Glass, plastic, aluminum, paper, newspaper, batteries.

Puerto Viejo, Limón (2750-0347), *Recicaribe* barrels around town. Glass, plastic, aluminum.

San Antonio de Belén (2293-5944) in the Municipal Building: paper, plastic, aluminum, and boxes, glass. First Thursday, Friday of each month

San Isidro de El General (772-3472), collection center, Barrio La Cen2iza. Glass, plastic, aluminum, newspaper, cardboard, metal.

San José Channel 7 in Sabana West, 6 a.m.-8 p.m. collects paper, plastic, aluminum, boxes, glass. First Thursday, Friday of each month

San Marcos, Tarrazú (2546-6879), collection center, 25 m. west of high school. Glass, plastic, aluminum, paper, newspaper, cardboard.

San Rafael, Heredia (8845-6293), fixed routes, pick-up. Collection center next to Hogar de Ancianos. Glass, plastic, aluminum, paper, cardboard, metal.

San Ramón, Alajuela, (2447-2181, coferene.tripod.com), collection center, 700 m. north, 300 m. east of hospital. Glass, plastic, aluminum, paper, newspaper, cardboard.

Santa Ana (2203-5559), collection center, 200 m. north, 100 m. west of main entrance to town. Glass, plastic, aluminum, paper, newspaper.

Sarchí (2454-4001) Recycling pick-up. Plastic, aluminum, glass.

Tibás (2240-7155), collection center, next to Puente Tibás. Glass, plastic, aluminum, paper, newspaper, cardboard.

Tortuguero, collection barrels around town. Glass, plastic, aluminum.

Safe & Secure

PAY attention! Common sense and a few precautions should result in a wonderful, hassle-free vacation.

IT'S easy to let your guard down, and it takes a clever street thief mere seconds to lift your property. Watch your belongings closely at all times, especially at bus stations/stops and at the airport, and don't sleep on public transport with bags left overhead. If someone bumps into you, spin round fast, create a distance and do not accept 'help.'

Don't go out alone after dark or act lost. Consult your map inside a shop or café then proceed with confidence, even if you haven't a clue. Spread money among different pockets. If you are mugged, don't fight back and risk being injured. Things can be replaced.

Passports: A photocopy of the identification page and entry stamp in your passport is legally sufficient for traveling. Keep the original locked safely away if possible; theft of U.S. passports in Costa Rica is the highest in the world. If police stop and query this, ask to go to regional headquarters (*unidad policial*) and insist on your rights. If your passport is stolen or lost, report it immediately to your embassy or consulate.

Adventure Tourism: Most whitewater rafting, canopy and rappelling tours are run by professional, organized agencies, but unregulated operators do work without licenses and care must be taken when choosing a tour.

Driving: Rental cars, especially the Daihatsu Terios, are targeted by thieves, so leave nothing unattended inside, park in guarded lots and if you get a surprising flat, don't accept any offers of 'help.' One scam is to slash tires and rob occupants on the roadside. Rentals from the Juan Santamaría airport also have been held up at night. If you have a cell phone, call 911 for help (even if you are pretending), flag down another car or lock yourself in the car and drive on the flat tire to a better-populated area. These warnings apply to ALL cars.

Seatbelts are obligatory, and defensive driving is recommended. Poor road conditions and slapdash driving standards make driving a challenge. Road signs are improving, but San José can be confusing.

Walking:
Pedestrians beware!
Don't walk on highways at night, as oncoming traffic won't always swerve to avoid you.
Turning cars in cities rarely give way even if you do have the 'right of way.' either.

Public Transport: Buses go everywhere. Be highly vigilant of luggage at busy bus stations or bags on crowded city buses. "Pirate" taxis abound, but official red taxis with a yellow triangle are advisable, especially if single and moving around at night.

Harassment: Tico men's *piropos* (cat calls) to women are entrenched behavior, but *machismo* is less annoying here than other Latin countries. Women should not venture out in revealing clothing at night on lonely roads or touristy hotspots if they want to avoid undue attention.

Water hazards: Riptides, waterfalls and rivers all take their toll on human life. If swept out to sea, do not fight the current, don't panic, swim parallel to the shore and come in gradually further down. It's hard, but it will save your life. Surf within your capabilities and ask about local conditions. Don't jump into welcoming river rock pools unless you are certain no dangerous obstacles lurk underwater.

Natural hazards: Keep to marked trails and wear closed footwear to protect against gashes or bites, and don't steady yourself on steep paths by grabbing at supporting tree trunks – they may have nasty thorns. Costa Rica's active volcanoes are impressive and they can kill; don't be foolhardy about getting too close. Rainy season flash floods are fast and sudden.

Be careful if bathing in rivers or attempting to drive across a deceptively shallow river after a storm; levels can rise in minutes. Also, crocodile attacks do happen in rivers, lagoons and river mouths.

Dengue, carried by mosquitoes, is on the rise. Use a good repellent and nets on your bed. Check shoes and bags for scorpions in rural areas.

If you disturb bee or wasp nests and the insects give chase, run in a zig-zag fashion as far as you can (at least 300 m). Cover your face and eyes just enough to be able to see. If you find a beehive near your home, call 911. They will alert firemen who will come to get rid of it. Earthquakes are frequent and usually low-scale. Don't panic, follow exit routes if in a hotel or calmly head outside if the tremor seems too intense.

Taxes & Tipping

IN Costa Rica, a 13% sales tax at restaurants and a 10% tip for your waiter or waitress is automatically included in the bill. Yes, service is always included, but extra is nice.

IF the service is really good, you're always welcome to leave a little extra. Prices on menus may or may not include the sales tax, so look for a note on the menu or ask your server.

For accommodations, you'll pay the 13% sales tax (included in the rates listed in all this guidebooks' selections). Use common sense in tipping for hotel services. At mid-range to upscale hotels, maids should get a couple of dollars per day and porters count on $1 per bag. Tipping, like extra services, is rare in cheap hotels. Tour guides should receive ¢1,000 to ¢2,000 ($2-4) extra per person in your party.

When leaving a parking space, you may notice the presence of a self-appointed car guard who has been watching over your vehicle. They expect at least ¢200 (35 cents) per hour. At cab stands and malls, young boys sometimes will "hail" a cab for you in exchange for small change (maybe ¢100, or 17 cents). Taxi drivers do not expect tips unless they've had to struggle with heavy bags or perform extra tasks. It's always nice, however, to tip the pleasant, helpful drivers.

Tour Operators

TOUR operators can take the stress out of vacation preparations. The following are just a few of the many agencies that can arrange your stay in Costa Rica, guiding you both to the country's hidden gems and along well-traveled routes.

FOR more complete listings, try the Internet or for travel agents, check the Yellow Pages under "Agencias de Viajes." (See **Day Trips**.)

Aventours (2538-5900, 8870-7766, **aventourscostarica.com**), in San Antonio, 12 km. north of Turrialba, private guided tours, visits to indigenous Cabécar villages in Talamanca mountains, agri-tours of sugarcane, coffee, pineapple, macadamia-crop processing.
About Costa Rica Tours (2268-6515, **ACRtours.com**), San Luis de Santo Domingo, Heredia.
Agencia de Viajes Virtual Costa Rica (2479-7215, **agenciadeviajesvirtual** costarica.com), La Fortuna, San Carlos.
Association for the Conservation & Sustainable Development of the Escazú Mountains (CODECE), (2228-0183, **codece.org**).
Asociación Costarricense de Turísmo Rural Comunitario (ACTUAR) (2248-9470, **actuarcostarica.com**), San José.
Asociación Talamanqueña de Ecoturismo y Conservación (ATEC) (2750-0398, **greencoast.com**), Puerto Viejo, Limón.
Caravan Tours (1-800-227-2826, **caravantours.com**), based in Chicago, IL.
Catch Travel (2231-6341), **info@catchtravels.com**, San José.
Coast to Coast Adventures (2280-8054, **coasttocoastadventures.com**),

Lourdes de Montes de Oca.

Corporación de Viajes TAM (2256-0203, **tamtravel.com**), San José.

Costa Rica Expeditions (2257-0766, **costaricaexpeditions.com**), San José.

Costa Rica One Day Tours (2282-2792, **costaricaonedaytours.com**), Santa Ana.

Costa Rica Sun Tours (2296-7757, **crsuntours.com**), San José.

Costa Rica Nature Escape (2257-8064, 24-hr. tel: 2381-7178, **crnature.com**), San José.

Costa Sol Rafting (2431-1183, **costasolrafting.com**), Alajuela.

Desafío Adventure Company (2479-9464, **desafiocostarica.com**), La Fortuna, San Carlos.

DestinosTV (2289-0707, **destinostv.com**), Escazú. One-day tours, adventure, int'l trips, restaurant tours.

Expediciones Tropicales (2257-4171, **expedicionestropicales.com**), San José.

Explore Nicaragua Tours (1-800-800-1132 in US, **explorenicaragua.com**), Chicago, IL.

Grupo Cedrela (2286-5216, **ecoturismo.co.cr**), educational and ecotourism tours.

Hacienda Pozo Azul Adventures (2438-2616, **haciendapozoazul.com**), La Virgen de Sarapiquí.

Horizontes Nature Tours (2222-2022, **horizontes.com**), San José.

Il Viaggio Travel (2289-8225, **ilvaggiocr.com**), specialists in all-inclusive trips, custom-designed tours, day excursions, personalized service.

Latii Express Tours (2296-0806, **costaricalatiiexpress.com**), San José.

Costa Rican Beauties (2258-7840, 2258-2293, **costa-rica.us**), Las Arcadas Bldg., Suite 9, Plaza de la Cultura, San José, tours to Tortuguero, Monteverde, Northern Zone.

Lynch Travel (2777-1170, **lynchtravel.com**), Quepos.

Miki Travel (2291-4455, **mikitravel.net**), San José.

Out Of Bounds (2288-6762) Also has hotel. Escazú.

Ríos Tropicales (2233-6455, **riostropi cales.com**), San José.

Swiss Travel (2282-4898, **swisstravelcr.com**), San José.

The Travel Store (2279-8927, **costaricatravelstore.com**), San José.

Volunteering

TRAVELING can be infinitely rewarding for those who dedicate time to humanitarian work and environmental- improvement projects. Spanish is not always a must.

THE following is a partial listing of organizations that place long-or short-term volunteers. Some offer stipends; most require volunteers to pay their own way.

MOST hospitals have a group of **Damas Voluntarias** (volunteer women) to care for the sick. (See **Hospitals** for hospital numbers.)

Amigos de las Aves (2441-2658, **hatchedtoflyfree.org**), Alajuela, must be 18 or older, caring for endangered macaws, feeding them, making toys, observing babies, cleaning and more.

Amor en la Calle (2256-2009, **info@ ascrigere.org**), Av. 12, Ca. 3/5, Casa #319, street children and teens-at-risk communities, teens in jail and in the drug-recovery program, food delivery to San José high-risk areas twice a week, Spanish is a plus but there is a translator if necessary. Volunteers must a attend preparation course before going to street to serve, proposals for projects/donations accepted.

APREFLOFAS (2240-6087, 2236-3210,

apreflofas.or.cr), Moravia, Los Colegios, wildlife protection, environmental education, community support.

Asociación ANAI (2224-3570, **anaicr. org; anaivol@anaicr.org**), Barrio Vargas Araya, San Pedro experimental organic farming/rainforest conservation projects, for the physically fit.

Asociación Lucha Contra el Cáncer Infantil (2255-0231, **asolcancer@ice.co. cr**), Ca. 20, Av. 6/4, Spanish a must, Feb.-May, preparation of materials for school campaigns against cancer.

Asociación Obras del Espíritu Santo (2226-0303, **obrasdelespiritusanto.org**), Cristo Rey Church office, Ca. 24, Av. 26/28, 1 km. south of La Merced Church, San José, humanitarian work, street kids, teens at risk, soup kitchen three times daily, food delivery to street people.

ASVO (Association of Volunteers Working in Protected Areas) (2223-4260, 2258-4430, **asvocr.org, info@asvocr.org,** Ca. 36, Av. 3/5, San José, nat'l. park trail maintenance/construction, marine turtle conservation, teach English, basic Spanish required, minimum commitment of two weeks.

Caribbean Conservation Corporation (2297-5510, 2709-8091, **cccturtle.org**), protect turtle-nesting areas, help tag turtles and w/research: 15 days, all meals, March-June (Leatherback turtle season), June-Nov. (Green turtle season).

Caño Palma Research Station (2709-8052, **coterc.org**), Tortuguero, education, research, conservation activities, volunteers.

Club Activo 20-30 (2233-2030, **ayudemos.com**), Barrio Carit, 100 meters south of Hospital de las Mujeres, poor schools, help in flood/earthquake emergencies, telathon (48-hour TV shows to raise money for the National Children's Hospital).

Costa Rica Multilingüe (2207-8485, **volunteer@casapres.go.cr**), Resident Volunteer Program, which pairs native English-speaking volunteers with Costa Rican's interested in learning English. Speaking sessions are coordinated for volunteers to speak English with Tico's.

Cruz Roja (Red Cross) (2233-7033, **cruzroja.or.cr**), Av. 8, Ca. 14, international. medical/humanitarian organization, youth (for people 14-25), donations accepted especially after a disaster, HIV/AIDS-awareness and disaster-prevention programs, drivers need five years experience and updated B1 license.

Damas Voluntarias de Escazú (2228-0279, **cguerra@racsa.co.cr**), Escazú, library/daycare for children, help with homework.

La Flor de Paraíso Agroecological Farm (2534-8003, **la-flor-de-paraiso.org**), on road to Cervantes de Alvarado (Southern Zone), turn 100 m. before La Casita Restaurant, go 1 km. At La Flor, farm is 100 m. from church, in front of school; organic farm, medicinal plants, art, environmental education.

Fundación Paniamor (2234-2993, **paniamor.or.cr**), Av. Ctrl., Ca. 29/33, child-abuse prevention, adolescent education.

Habitat for Humanity (2296-3436, fax: 290-7112, **habitatcostarica.org**), La Uruca, construction of houses for low-income families, individual or group volunteers, foreigners $100 participation fee per person, residents no fee, maximum two weeks.

Humanitarian Foundation (8390-4192, 2282-6358, **gnystrom@racsa.co.cr**), 100 m. south of Super Piedades Grocery Store, Piedades, Santa Ana, nationwide programs help at-risk populations including elderly, indigenous, orphans, former street children, immigrants.

The McKee Project (8821-0581, 2440-3293, **mckeeproject.org**), spays/neuters street dogs, cats. Needs vets.

Monteverde Butterfly Garden (2645-5512, **monteverdebutterflygarden.com**), Monteverde, environmental education, garden tour guides.

National Parks (192), maintenance, park stays nationwide.

The Salvation Army (2257-7535, **lan_ leadership@lan.salvationarmy.org**), shelters for abused women, children, rehab for recovering alcoholics. Volunteers Dec. only, help w/parties for poor children.

Tropical Adventure (2574-4412, 1-800-832-9419 in U.S., Canada, **tropicaladventures.com**), cultural immersion w/volunteer projects, $995, Central Valley and Caribbean, 1-wk. min., airport pick-up, accommodations, some meals, tours, Spanish classes.

Sarapiquí Conservation Learning Center (2766-6482, **learningcentercostarica.org**), English, computer, environmental education, community development and outreach, Spanish required, commitment from one to six months.

Websites About Costa Rica

News

The Tico Times Online (**ticotimes.net**) provides the top news, business and weekend section stories from the weekly print edition in addition to daily news, including the exchange rate and weather (**ticotimes.net/daily.htm**), for free. The Tico Times has joined the blogosphere with the launch of its blog at **theticotimes.wordpress.com**. The blog – like this book – is written by TT staff and contributors and offers an insider's look at the ins and outs of life in Costa Rica. Topics range from where to live in San José to how U.S. health reformers could take some lessons from little Costa Rica, and readers are invited to participate in the discussion.

The Tico Times has also added several new components to its online edition, **tico times.net**, including Web-exclusive feature stories and restaurant reviews, in addition to a surf forecast, with up-to-date charts illustrating wave and wind conditions. These features join the mass of other interactive ingredients TT has been adding to the mix: video reports, photo slideshows, reader comments, Twitter, Facebook, the Fishing Forum, the list goes on.

Also, the most complete classified advertisement section (**ticotimes.net/classified.htm**) is available at no cost. Subscriptions to an expanded daily news page (including the calendar of events and a weekly columnist from the print edition) are available for $5/month and electronic subscriptions to the complete newspaper are available for $8/month. The Nica Times, with weekly news of Central America, is also online (**nica times.net**).

Inside Costa Rica (**insidecostarica. com**), news coverage, travel and real estate info, classifieds.

La Nación (**nacion.com/ln_ee/english**) has weekly news review in English, updated every Friday.

Other Spanish-language dailies have online editions: La República (**larepublica.net**), Al Día (**aldia.co.cr**), Diario Extra (**diarioextra.com**), La Prensa Libre (**www.prensalibre.co.cr**).

Forums

Info Costa Rica (**infocostarica.com**), living, traveling, volunteering, news, articles, useful links.

Costa Rica Living (**costaricaliving.org**), subscription e-mail list for info exchange about living in Costa Rica. Separate lists for job opportunities and chat for Spanish learners.

Costa Rica Forum (**costarica.com/ forum**), travel, retirement, investment, scams, gambling, chat rooms in Spanish.

Living Life in Costa Rica (**http://livinglifeincostarica.blogspot.com**) – Helpful blog site that provides several Costa Rican links and information.

Advice for living on the west side: **esca-**

unews@yahoogroups.com

All kinds of advice, questions answered; CostaRicaCentralValleyLiving@yahoo groups.com

General Information

Costa Rica In Focus (**zurqui.co.cr/crinfocus/info.html**), health, language schools, real estate, maps, weather.

U.S. Embassy (**usembassy.or.cr**), visa information, general info on Costa Rica.

1-Costa Rica Link (**1-costaricalink.com**), comprehensive A-Z menu of all aspects of living and traveling in Costa Rica.

My Costa Rican Guide (**mycostarican guide.com**), info, hotels, restaurants.

www.TicoLinks.net – An Index of links that can assist to find out information about travel, education, news, learning Spanish, museums and much more.

Directories

Costa Rica Pages (**costaricapages. com**), hotels, real estate, tourism, education, surfing, fishing.

Costa Rica Click (**costaricaclick. com**), art, business, computers, environment, government, shopping links.

Costa Rican Directory (**directorycostarica.com**) – tourism, travel, real estate, arts & entertainment, science and environment, news and media, business and economy, transportation and more

Travel

Costa Rica No Artificial Ingredients (**visitcostarica.com**), the Costa Rica Tourism Board (ICT) official site with info on hotels rated for quality and sustainable tourism, news, travel agencies, maps, bus timetables, FAQ.

Central America.com (**centralamerica. com**), member of National Tourism Chamber, mostly high-end accommodations, travel plans, one-day and multi-day

packages, transport.

Costa Rican Chamber of Hotels (CCH), (**costaricanhotels.com**), official hotel site, 300 hotels, reservations, promotions.

Costa Rica Outdoors (**costaricaout doors.com**), online edition of hardcopy magazine, trip itineraries, travel agency, sport fishing specialists.

Costa Rica Hotels (**hotels.co.cr**), concise, easy-viewing information on hotels with links for regions, attractions.

Costa Rica Guides (**costaricaguides. com**), hotel and tour reservations, general info.

Talamanca Discovery (**greencoast. com**), ecotourism in Caribbean, accommodation for all budgets, tours, bus timetables, maps, cuisine scene, wildlife, history and culture of the Caribbean

Costa Rica Bureau (**costaricabureau. com**), top-10 destinations, tours, airfare search, comprehensive hotel list, online booking.

Costa Rica Discover (**costaricadiscov er.com**), car rentals, cruises via Panama Canal, wide variety of tours, selected high-end hotels.

Greenway Nature Tours (**costarica-ec otourism.com**), student, gay, nature, adventure tours, general info, accommodations, services.

Costa Rica By Bus (**costaricabybus. ocm**), good budget travel tips and up-to-date news, free travel advice, complete bus guide/e-book for $9.50.

1CostaRicaLink.com – offers information about hotels, travel ideas and packages, restaurants and activities throughout the country

Wedoitallcostarica.com – Offers information about hotels, locations, activities to do in locations around the country

Business & Investing & Living

Costa Rica Investment Board (CINDE) (**cinde.org**), investment promotion agency.

Costa Rica - American Chamber of

Commerce (AmCham) (**amcham.co.cr**), business guide, exchange rate, magazine.

Export Promotion Office (PROCOMER) (**procomer.com**), English site under construction, market info., stats, regulations, news.

Residents' Association of Costa Rica (ARCR) (**arcr.net**), seminars, tips on residency, legal resident applications, insurance, shipping and customs, title searches.

Costa Rica Real Estate Brokers Board (CBR) (**camaracbr.or.cr**), accredited brokers, appraisers, info., multiple listing.

Doing Business In Costa Rica (**business costarica.com**), directory of business organizations, real estate, links to crica. com for travel, hotels.

We Love Costa Rica (**welovecostarica.**

com), comprehensive info on ins and out of living, buying property, forum, investments, news.

Puravida.com – Site offers hotel and travel information throughout the country, as well as real estate listing and photo of available homes, condos and villas in various areas

Top Sites in Spanish

Tiquicia (**tiquicia.com**), articles, classifieds, forum, news, entertainment & TV guides.

Informa-tico (**informa-tico.com**) weekly online news, editorials, downloadable version.

Entretenimiento (**entretenimiento.co cr**), comprehensive guide to theater, music TV, restaurants, bars, tourism.

Art in All its Forms

COSTA RICA has been, for centuries, a generous host to her own artists and those from other countries looking for a welcoming place to work and exhibit.

HERE, alcohol factories have been turned into art galleries and prisons into museums for children; all speak to Costa Rican resourcefulness when it comes to art and culture.

If you don't speak Spanish, there is always an alternative: dance, circus performances, visual art exhibitions or English-language theater. (See **Museums, Art Galleries, Theaters, Movies** and **Dance** for more complete listings.) Meanwhile, for a little bit of everything, check out the following:

Note: More than 30 art galleries and many small museums are scattered around San José. Musicians, painters, photographers and indigenous artists often are seen working to preserve Tico traditions. Check The Tico Times Weekend Calendar for updates on the cultural agenda.

Art: Festival of the Arts Costa Rica (2223-4752, **teatronacional.go.cr**), in March, theaters, galleries and open-air venues are filled with national and international talent. Concerts usually are staged indoors, but there are many open-air performances as well; try both! Many free activities, too.

The Museo de Arte Costarricense (2257-5224) housed in the old airport terminal, Ca. 42, Sabana, the best overview of Costa Rican art; everything from the Colonial period to modern art, look for paintings, prints and sculptures by Juan Manuel Sánchez, also an outdoor sculpture garden, 10 a.m-5 p.m. Tues.- Sun., free on Sun. Also, check out exhibitions and program of **Museum of Art and Contemporary Design** (2222-2974, **madc.ac.cr**), Centro

Nacional de la Cultura, Old National Liquor Factory, Av. 3, Ca. 15/17.

Gold: below the Plaza de la Cultura check out **The Gold Museum** (2243-4202, museosdelbancocentral.org) with Latin America's second largest collection of pre-Columbian gold artifacts with nearly 2,000 pieces in artful, educational display, as well as temporary art exhibits, Ca. 5, Av. Ctrl../2, 9 a.m.- 4:45 p.m., daily.

Music in town: the world-class **National Symphony Orchestra** (2240-0333, ext. 206) represents the country abroad. During its March-Nov. season the symphony performs on Fri. evenings, Sun. mornings in the National Theater, a gem and worth visiting, Av. 2, Ca 3/5, San José. The **National Youth Symphony** (2236-6669) plays Feb.–Dec. at the **Teatro Melico Salazar** with enjoyable performances, excellent acoustics. Other excellent groups include: **The National Choir** (2236-6669), the **National Dance Company** (2256-4838). The **Auditorio Nacional** (2258-4929) at the **Children's Museum**, which has superb acoustics, stages concerts and rotating art exhibitions.

Music in the wilderness: Monteverde Amphitheater (2645-6272, bromeliasmusic@gmail.com), national and international musicians play in this inspiring wild environment high in the Tilarán Mountains.

Music on the beach: The **South Caribbean Music Festival** (2750-0062, 2750-0428, playachiquitalodge.com), annual festival of Caribbean beats to support children's music programs and community projects, Mar.-Apr. at Playa Chiquita Lodge, Puerto Viejo.

Dance and Theater: The National Cultural Center (CENAC) (2222-2974, mcjdr.go), at the former liquor factory, is a thriving art center, and hosts performances in **Teatro 1887** (2221-6325). The historic building also houses an open-air amphitheater, a contemporary art gallery and a museum. Come on Saturday afternoon to play board games and to see rehearsals in the amphitheater.

Dance: The University of Costa Rica Dancers (2511-4000) includes modern dance groups, folklore and ballet companies with performances all year.

Movies: Sala Garbo (2222-1034) shows international films, hosts film festivals in many languages, slightly more expensive than the other movie houses, around $4, but absolutely worth the extra quarter if you are looking for independent and quality films. (Note: foreign-language films are usually subtitled in Spanish.)
The Costa Rican Film Association (Asociación Costarricense de Cinematografía), in the fashionable Barrio Amón, offers Latin American movie festivals, many free activities also.

Theater: Some 16 small, independent theaters are active throughout the year in San José. Most offer light-hearted comedies. Watch for anything the **National Theater Group** performs, especially at their alternative space, the **Vargas Calvo Theater** (2221-1329, teatronacional.go.cr), Av. 2, Ca. 3/5. Plays are excellent and brilliantly performed.

English-language theater: offered by the 60-year-old **Little Theatre Group** (8858-1446, littletheatregroup.org) in the Laurence Olivier Theater in San José. Many professional directors and actors generously give time and talent to the group. Offers modern, classical and farcical plays. The younger **Dominical Little Theater** (2787-8007, dominical.biz/theater), on the Pacific Coast, is another option for English-language entertainment.

Art Galleries

Artwork abounds in numerous galleries in San José and prices range from very reasonable to astronomical. Even if you're no shopping, browsing through galleries is a great way to spend a rainy afternoon.

SOME cultural centers and museums also offer temporary exhibitions (check the Calendar Section of The Tico Times for current shows).

Alternativa (2232-8500, **galeriaalternativacr.com**), Condominio Industrial de Pavas, store #21.

Andrómeda (2223-3529, **materika. org**), Ca. 9, Av. 9, Barrio Amón.

Café de Artistas (2288-5082, **café_de_artistas.com**), San Rafael, Escazú, 125 m. southeast of Plaza Rolex.

Casa Real (2234-1616,), Av. 10, Ca. 43, Los Yoses.

El Marañon Hotel, Restaurant and Gallery, (2249-1271, **cultourica@racsa. co.cr**), Barrio La Trinidad, old road between Piedades de Santa Ana and Ciudad Colón.

Enmarcarte (2228-4853, **enmarcarte. com**), old road to Santa Ana, facing Scotiabank. Also in Escazú, Multiplaza Escazú.

Flor Alvarado Gallery (2280-4568, **floralcr@yahoo.com**), José María Zeledón, Curridabat, west of soccer field.

Galería Dau al Set (2281-2260, 8820-4033, **botica@amnet.co.cr**), Los Yoses, 200 m. south and 125 m. east of Subaru.

García Monge (2221-3756, **teatronacional.go.cr**), Ca. 3/5, Av. Ctrl./2.

Jacob Karpio (2257-7963, **jacobkarpiogaleria.com**), Av. 1, Cuesta de Núñez, #1352.

José Luis López Escarré (2221-3756, **teatronacional.go.cr**), in National Theater Café, Av. 2, Ca. 5.

Kandinsky (2234-0478, **artkandinsky@yahoo.com**), San Pedro, Centro Comercial Calle Real, #20.

Klaus Steinmetz (2289-5403, **artcontemporaneo@racsa.co.cr**), San Rafael Escazú, 25 m. south of Plaza Rolex (left hand side).

Mata (2253-6473, **galeriamata@racsa co.cr**), 200 m. south, 10 m. west of Banco Nacional, San Pedro.

Namú (2256-3412, **galerianamu.com**) Av. 7, Ca. 5/7, art, crafts of indigenou groups of Costa Rica.

National Gallery (2258-4929, **museoc com**), Children's Museum, Ca. 4/Av. 9.

Oasis Gallery (8307-2264, **galeriaoa sis@hotmail.com**), Pérez Zeledón, acros from the Cultural Complex.

Octágono Gallery (2267-6325, **galeri aoctagono.com**), San Rafael, Heredia, road to La Condesa Hotel, next to Ave del Paraí so Residence, permanent textiles and woodworks exhibits.

Pueblarte (2552-1276, **pueblarte.com**) exclusive original works of Fernando Car ballo and other renowned national/inter national artists, Cartago, 25 m. west of Sa Luis Gonzaga High School, at Centro d Modas Shopping Center.

Sophia Wanamaker (2207-7554, **cccn cr.com**), CR-North American Cultura Center, Av. Ctrl., Ca. 37, Barrio Dent.

Sylvia Laks (2267-6350, **sylvialaks com**), San Rafael, Heredia, permanen stained-glass exhibit.

Taller del Artista (2278-3594, **arte@ calirivera.com**), Tres Ríos, 250 m. west o cemetery.

TEORética (2233-8775, teoretica.com) Barrio Amón, Ca. 7, Av 9/11, house #953.

Valanti (2253-1659, **galeriavalanti com**), Barrio Escalante, Ca. 33/35, #3395.

Valanti Los Sueños (2637-8412), Mari na Los Sueños, Herradura.

Bands & Music

Music can be found all over town. Reggae and hip-hop are popular at some dance halls, but for Latin rhythms try El Tobogán in Barrio Tournón.

TWO bands entertain and an enormous dance floor fills with people dancing salsa, merengue, cumbia and bachata. Sunday afternoons are especially fun. Both men and women on their own can invite others to dance. Don't know the steps? Take classes at one of the many dance schools in the country.

The **Jazz Café** (2253-8933) in San Pedro hosts many excellent bands, such as Parque en el Espacio, Editus, Calacas Blues, Escats and Arabika, or sweet listening in a pub-like atmosphere. Toku in Escazú has live music and, for electronic music with DJs mixing a great blend of music, try **Vertigo** (2258-5189) in the Centro Colón on Paseo Colón.

Music, music music! It's everywhere in Costa Rica.

Photo by Robert Goodier

Editus, winner of two Grammies for its work with Rubén Blades, is Costa Rica's most famous popular band. Don't miss a chance to hear Editus perform its mix of Latin and new-age sounds combined with lots of percussion: fabulous and unique. Also, watch for **Malpaís,** with its fusion of blues, jazz and other genres, and for **Cantoamérica** for Afro-Caribbean and Latin rhythms.

The **Orquesta de la Papaya,** under the direction of pianist Manuel Obregón, brings traditional and classical Central American musicians together for a powerful sound. Other danceable groups include **Kalua, Marfil** and **Timbaleo.**

For Afro-Caribbean flavor, **Mekatelyu** is an excellent reggaeton group; **Native Culture** also is very good. Be there when **Walter Ferguson,** Calypso legend who lives in Cahuita, entertains. **Luis Angel Castro** is also popular for his mellow Caribbean music.

Humberto Vargas brought Costa Rican Nueva Trova into the limelight when he won the esteemed *Gaviota de Plata* at the Viña del Mar Festival in Chile.

Gandhi, another favorite, plays socially-conscious music and energetic rock. **Evolución** has a catchy, alternative sound; **Kantera** hits a tropical Flamenco beat.

For punk and underground rock, look for **Vieja Escuela, Días de Agonía, Mac Beth, Esimple** and **U.F.O.**

In Manuel Antonio, be sure to hear rhythm and blues queen **Fuzzy Rojas** when she sings with her band at **Bambú Jam** or **Gato Negro.**

Mariachis & Marimbas

Originally from Mexico, the sombrero-wearing musicians usually number seven men who belt out traditional love songs as they strum guitars, play violins and blow trumpets. They are popular here and loads of fun to invite to a special occasion.

MARIACHI Colonial (2280-3131) will sing some six *serenatas* for ₡65,000 ($115) in downtown San José. They perform anywhere in the country. Transportation costs more and is adjusted depending on the distance.

Longtime favorite **Mariachi Internacional Hermanos Calderón** (2272-0614) also offers six typical songs and an additional birthday song for the occasion. Cost varies from ₡60,000 – ₡140,000 ($105 - $240).

Listening to the marimba is also a delightful cultural activity. Legend says the keyboard, carved out of hardwoods, came with slave ships from Africa. Guatemalans insist it is indigenous in origin. Wherever it's from, the music is unique and a pleasure to watch performed.

Marimbas sometimes can be heard in the plaza in front of the Gran Hotel Costa Rica (Av. 2, Ca. 5).

In addition, at **Chicharronera Cacique Aserrí** (2230-4022), in the hills of Aserrí south of San José, marimbas start up around 7 p.m. on Fri. and Sat. The marimbas kick off the music and give way to cimarronas, before bouncing back to marimbas to close the show. The music runs until midnight Friday and Saturday.

Uphill, the **Ram Luna** (2230-3060) hosts a folkloric Wednesday evening show that includes a buffet, traditional Costa Rican dances and the music of marimbas and cimarronas. Cost is $34 per person. Dinner and dancing runs from 7-10 p.m.

The marimba is most popular in Guanacaste. There, **Gregorio Duarte** (8355-6315) carries on the art taught to him by his father and performs at social events throughout the area.

Books

LEARN *about Costa Rica via a wealth of literature available in stores and online. The following is only a small sampling of what's out there.*

TRAVEL GUIDES

The Costa Rica Traveler: Getting Around in Costa Rica, Ellen Searby, 2003, 416 p.

Fodor's Costa Rica 2010

Frommer's Costa Rica 2009, Eliot Greenspan, 416 p.

Lonely Planet Costa Rica, Mara Vorhees, Matthew Firestone, 2009, 608 p.

New Key to Costa Rica, the pioneer guidebook, Beatrice Blake, Anne Becher, 2006, 500 p.

H2O Surf Travel Guide: Costa Rica, Jonathan Yonkers Chavarría, 2007, 208 p.

CULTURAL REFERENCE

The Ticos: Culture and Social Change in Costa Rica, Mavis, Richard and Karen Biesanz, 1998, 295 p. A must.

"What Happen," Paula Palmer, 2005, 286 p., fascinating folk history of Talamanca Coast and Caribbean culture, illust.

Butterfly in the City: A Good Life in Costa Rica, Jo Stuart, 2006, charming tale about a retiree's life in San José.

CHILDREN'S BOOKS

Fernando's Gift, photos by Douglas Keister, 1998, 32 p., family life in Costa Rica.

The Monkey Thief, Aileen Kilgore Henderson, 1998, 110 p., boy learns responsibility during rainforest visit.

Song of La Selva: A Story of the Costa Rican Rain Forest (Nature Conservancy), Joan Banks, 1998, 27 p.

FOOD & COOKING

Feasting and Foraging in Costa Rica, Lenny Karpman, 2008, 320 p., extensive food guide.

My Kitchen, Nelly Urbina, 1999, 132 p., simple recipes for traditional meals.

The Best Recipes of Costa Rica, Tatiana Coto, photos, Mike Blum, 2005, 87 p.

The Tico Times Restaurant Guide to Costa Rica, Eliot Greenspan, 2009

Tropical Fruits of Costa Rica, Ellen Rancho and Marcia Barahona, 152 p.

DRIVING TO & THROUGH

Driving the Pan-American Highway to Mexico and Central America, Raymond and Audrey Pritchard, 2002, 170 p.

You Can Drive to Costa Rica in 8 Days, Dawna Rae Westler, 2000, 250 p.

Central America by Car, Mike Nelson, 1997, 197 p.

GARDENING

Medicinal Plants of Costa Rica, Ed Bernhardt, 2008, 140 p.

The Costa Rican Organic Home Gardening Guide, Ed Bernhardt, 1998, 128 p.

HISTORY

The Green Republic: A Conservation History of Costa Rica, Sterling Evans, 1999, 320 p.

The History of Costa Rica, Iván Molina and Steven Palmer, 2001, 174 p.

Place in the Rainforest: Settling the Costa Rican Frontier, Darryl Cole Christensen, 1997, 216 p., frontier life.

BUSINESS, HEALTH, LAW

The Legal Guide to Costa Rica, Roger A. Petersen, 2005, 347 p.

Choose Costa Rica: Travel, Investment and Living Opportunities for Every Budget, John Howells, 2004, 320 p.

The New Golden Door to Retirement and Living in Costa Rica, Christopher Howard, 2005, 360 p.

Official Guide to Costa Rican Real Estate, Christopher Howard, 2007, 500 p.

Living Abroad in Costa Rica, Erin Van Rheenen, 2004, 424 p.

NATURE/ENVIRONMENT

A Guide to Tropical Plants of Costa Rica, Willow Zuchowski, photos by Turid Forsyth, 2005, 529 p.

Costa Rica: National Parks Guide, Mario Boza, 2002.

Costa Rican Natural History, Ed. Daniel H. Janzen, 1983, 816 p.

A Field Guide to the Mammals of Central America & Southeast Mexico, Fiona A. Reid, 1998, 400 p.

A Guide to Amphibians and Reptiles of Costa Rica, Twan Leenders, 2001, 305 p.

Field Guide to the Wildlife of Costa Rica, Carrol L. Henderson, 2002, 345 p.

Field Guide to Orchids of Costa Rica and Panama, Robert L. Dresseler, 1993.

A Guide to the Birds of Costa Rica, Gary Stiles & Alexander Skutch, 1990, 511 p.

Hummingbirds of Costa Rica, Michael and Patricia Fogden, 2005, 153 p.

The Birds of Costa Rica, A Field Guide, Richard Garrigues, illustrated by Robert Dean, 2007, 408 p.

The Natural History of Costa Rican Mammals, Mark Wainwright, 2003, 384 p.

Tropical Nature: Life and Death in the Rainforests of Central and South America, Adrian Forsyth and Ken Miyata, 1995, 248 p.

NOVELS & SHORT STORIES

Costa Rica: A Traveler's Literary Companion, Barbara Ras, 1994, 256 p.

The Stories of Tata Mundo, Fabián Dobles, 1998, 245 p.

PHOTO BOOKS

Costa Rica: Wildlife of the National Parks and Reserves, Michael and Patricia Fogden, for Neotrópica Foundation, 166 p.

Costa Rica, Ricardo Zúñiga, 2001, 114 p.

Costa Rica: National Parks, Mario Boza, 2004, 224 p.

Costa Rica: The Forests of Eden, Kevin Schafer, Alvaro Ugalde, 2000, 100 p.

Passion for the Caribbean, Yazmín Ross, 2003, 279 p.

LEARNING SPANISH

Berlitz Latin American Spanish, 2001, 224 p.

Lonely Planet's Costa Rica Phrasebook, Thomas B. Kohnstamm, 2000, 260 p.

Guide to Costa Rican Spanish, Christopher Howard, 2005, 200 p.

Madrigal's Magic Key to Spanish, Margarita Madrigal, 1989, 512 p.

Bookstores & Newsstands

YOU can find reading material in English (and Spanish, too) at the following outlets.

THE good news is that despite the plethora of TV shows and chat rooms, people are still reading, and many new bookstores have opened. And, of course, a book is still the very best gift of all.

BOOKSTORES

7th Street Books (2256-8251, **marroca@racsa.co.cr**), Ca. 7, Av. 1/Ctrl. New and used.

Beith-Zvi Bookstore (2291-6772, **beithzvi.com**), 800 m. west of Pops, west Sabana. Judaica.

Goodlight Books (2430-4083, good-lightbooks@ice.co.cr), 100 m. north, 30 m. west of La Agonía church, Alajuela Used books, new books on Costa Rica.

Librería Francesa (2283-4242, **libreriafrancesa.net**), Curridabat, 25 m. sout of Indoor Club. Also French books.

Librería Internacional (**libreriainternacional.com**), Barrio Dent (2253-9553), A Ctrl. (2257-2563), Terramall, Tres Río (2278-1522), Real Cariari (2239-5056), Rohrmoser (2290-3331), Plaza Cemac (2280-8065), Multiplaza, Escazú (2201 8320), Plaza Atlantis, Escazú (2588-1817 Mall Internacional, Alajuela (2442-3800, Paseo de las Flores, Heredia (2237-2887,

Resource Centers

Libraries and research centers are open to visitors, but it's a good idea to bring along an official I.D. Reference materials usually must be used on the premises.

THE National Library (2221-2436), Av. 3, Ca 5/7, north side of National Park, full service archives of Costa Rica, multilingual collection, 8 a.m.-4 p.m., Mon.-Fri.

Archivo Nacional (2234-7223, **archivonacional.go.cr**), in Curridabat, 900 m. south of Plaza del Sol, then 150 m. west. Historical/legal info dating to 1600s, photos, maps, wills, family histories, 8 a.m.-3 p.m., Mon.-Fri. Take Barrio Pinto de San Pedro bus from Av. Ctrl., in front of Más x Menos; look for modern flying saucer-style building.

Museo Nacional (2257-1433, **www.museosdecostarica.com**), Ca. 17, Av. Ctrl/Av.2, magazines, books, documents on natural history, archeology, indigenous tribes, culture in English and Spanish. Free entrance to library; $4 entrance museum, 9 a.m.-noon, 1-3 p.m., Tues.-Fri.

Centro de Investigación y Conservación del Patrimonio Cultural (2223-2533, **patrimonio@mcge.go.cr**), housed in Ministry of Culture's CENAC complex in old National Liquor Factory, Ca. 15, Av. 3/7, books, magazines, documents on traditions, architecture, history, in Spanish, 7 a.m.-3 p.m. Mon.-Fri.

Mark Twain Library (2207-7575, **cccncr.com**) at

C.R.-North American Cultural Center, Ca. 37, 150 m. north of AutoMercado, Los Yoses. U.S. newspapers, English-language magazines, newspapers, videos, audio books; annual membership for tourist students, $18/yr., plus $25 deposit for check-out rights; regular tourists, $30/yr., plus $25 deposit; C.R. residents, $20/yr.; 8 a.m.-8 p.m. Mon.-Fri., 8 a.m.-5 p.m., Sat. La Sabana campus (2207-7501), same hours/fees. In Cartago, branch in Metrocentro Mall (2207-7506), 1-8 p.m. , Mon.-Fri., 8 a.m.-5 p.m., Sat.

Topsy (2642-0576), in Montezuma, diagonally across from school. Buy/rent/exchange books, many languages; also, magazines, newspapers, mail service, 8 a.m.-4 p.m., Mon.-Fri., 8 a.m.-noon, Sat.

Biblioteca David Kitson (2682-0211), **bibliodk@racsa.co.cr**), bilingual books in Nosara, behind EBAIS clinic, 9 a.m.-noon, 1-6 p.m., daily.

Kids Saving the Rain Forest Library (2777-2592, **kidssavingtherainforest.org**), hosted by Hotel Mono Azul in Manuel Antonio, mostly English, Internet, 7 a.m.-9 p.m.

Puerto Jiménez Library, next to post office in Puerto Jiménez, Osa Peninsula. English/Spanish books for kids and adults, 9 a.m.-noon, 1-3 p.m., Mon.-Fri. Donations.

San Pedro (2253-9553), 300 m. west of Taco Bell, Santa Ana (2203-3590), Moravia, next to Automercado (2241-4838).

Librería Lehmann (2522-4848, **librerialehmann.com**), Av. Ctrl. Ca. 1/3; Plaza Mayor, Rohrmoser; east side of stadium, Tibás; next to Catholic church, San Pedro.

Librería Motivos (2289-9808, libreriamotivos.com), phone, Internet orders, home delivery.

Librería Universal (**universalcr.com**), Av. Central, Ca. 1/Ctrl. (2222-2222), Sabana Sur (2296-1010), Zapote (2234-8070), Guadalupe (2234-0314), Real Cariari (2239-2414), San Isidro de El General (2772-6770), Liberia (2665-1212), Heredia (2263-7070), Desamparados (2251-0000), Lindora (2282-0019).

LibroMax (800-542-7662, **libromax. com**), Av. Ctrl., Ca. 5; Mall San Pedro; American Mall, San Pedro; Multiplaza Escazú.

Mora Books (8383-8385, **morabooks. com**) Ca. 5, Av. 5/7. Used books, comics, CDs, DVDs.

Rincón Educativo (**rincon-educativo. co.cr**), San Pedro (2283-5810), Escazú (2288-5161). Books, games, puzzles.

MAGAZINES AND NEWSPAPERS

Canadian company **NewspaperDirect** (**newspaperdirect.com**) and local firm **Europrensa** (2232-6682) bring digitally printed, same-day delivery of 1,000 newspapers of 40 different languages from 84 countries to Costa Rica.

Agencia de Publicaciones de Costa Rica (2283-9383, **agenciadepublicaciones. com**), Zapote. Distributes periodicals and has 23 stores: **La Casa de las Revistas**, Ca. Ctrl., Av. 4/6 (2222-0987), Ca. 5, Av. 1/3 (2256-5092), Plaza del Sol, Curridabat (2283-0822), Multiplaza, Escazú (2201-5858), Novacentro, Moravia (2224-4941), Guadalupe (2283-7211), next to Llobet, Alajuela (2442-0968), Mall Internacional, Alajuela (2442-7770), 75 m. north of La Cartaginesa Bakery, Heredia (2237-6660), El Dorado, Cartago (2551-6925). Also inside Maxi Bodega stores in Ciudad Quesada, Liberia, Más x Menos supermarket in Guápiles, Hipermás Guadalupe, Hipermás San Sebastián, Hipermás Escazú, Hipermás Santa Ana (2582-0191). **Papyrus**, Ca. 5, Av. Ctrl./2 (2221-4664), next to Más x Menos, north Sabana (2221-4664).

Cheapies & Freebies

THERE'S lots to do that's easy, cheap and fun. Many entertainment options exist for about ¢1,000 ($1.70) or less in San José and its suburbs. Also, check out the daily La Nación's Viva section and The Tico Times' Calendar page for the latest low-budget happenings.

SEVERAL museums have free or cheap admission days. The **Peace Museum** (2223-4664), Av. 2, Ca.13, run by Nobel Peace Prize-winning President Oscar Arias' Foundation for Peace and Human Progress, is free. Mail a postcard from the old Central Post Office and then pop upstairs to visit the **Stamp Museum** (2223-6918), Ca. 2, Av. 1/3, (adults ¢150, ¢100 children) to view some delightful postal relics.

The Museum of Costa Rican Art (2222-7155) in La Sabana Park, featuring artists from Costa Rica and abroad, is free on Sundays, but closed for renovation. Call first.. The **Costa Rican Jewish Community Museum** (2520-1013), in the western suburb of Rohrmoser, houses photos and documentary films and is free, appointment only.

Art Festivals are another fun way to

check out talent without spending money (unless you're compelled to make a purchase!) **La Sabana Park** lights up with performances and crafts during two weeks in March, and the **San Pedro Art Fair** in December draws national and international sculptors, painters and jewelry makers, in addition to food and performances. The same organizers hold open-air **Exporte Escazú** during March, again drawing international artists.

Town Fairs are also free. Check out Festivals and Holidays in this guidebook. Something's happening almost every day, celebrating just about everything from milk, to mutts to solar energy. Hop on a bus and go.

Take advantage of San José's great weather and go on a walking tour of its parks. You'll find several oases of greenery with benches and tables ideal for sharing a picnic, reading or people-watching. The **Plaza de la Cultura** (Av. Ctrl./2, Ca. 5) spreads out beside the National Theater. Kids of all ages enjoy ice cream and feed pigeons. The **Parque Nacional** (Av. 1/3, Ca. 15/19) is perhaps the capital's greenest park, with fountains, statues and several spots on which to plop. Nearby **Parque Morazán** (Av. 3/5, Ca. 5/9) and **Parque de España** (Av. 3/7, Ca. 9/11) are popular with young lovebirds.

City Churches

Visiting the city's churches is another way to eye architecture and get a glimpse of Catholic culture. Admission is free, including the **Metropolitan Cathedral** (Av. 2/4, Ca. Ctrl.), where a statue of Pope John Paul II by famous Costa Rican sculptor Jorge Jiménez Deredia proudly stands outside. Visit also **La Soledad** (Av. 4, Ca. 9), **El Carmen** (Av. 1/3, Ca. Ctrl.) and **La Merced** (Ca. 12, Av. 2/4).

When downtown gets too intense, hop on the **San José Urban Train** (2221-0777) and head west to La Sabana Park. The ride is ¢200 from downtown San José to either Pavas (west) or ¢300 to San Pedro (east) side of the route. You'll find **La Sabana Park** a true respite of nature on the west side of San José. Families flock there for weekend soccer games, kite-flying, jogging, baseball and picnics. On weekend mornings, look for free aerobics classes to get your blood pumping to some Latin-inspired moves.

Parque de la Paz, on the east side of town, offers a similar recreational experience.

When bargain hunting makes you hungry, the best cheap eats throughout the country are **sodas**, where the traditional plate of rice, beans, meat, salad and plantains are served up without fail for about $2,000 ($3.50).

If you're looking for intellectual inspiration, inquire about free lectures, concerts and exhibits at the **University of Costa Rica** (UCR) (2511-4000) in San Pedro, and **Universidad Nacional** (UNA) (2277-3000) in Heredia.

For books, check out the **Mark Twain Library** (2207-7575) on the lower level of the C.R./North American Cultural Center, Ca. 37, 150 m. north of AutoMercado, Los Yoses. **Mora Books** (8383-8385), Ca. 5, Av. 5/7, 75m north of Hotel Aurora Holiday Inn, Barrio Amón, 11 a.m.-7 p.m. **7th Street Books** (2258-1223), Ca. 7, Av. 1/Ctrl., also has books in English.

At the **National Cemetery's** (Av. 10/Ca. 24) immense grounds, where many of the city's wealthy families bury their loved ones, a quiet walk offers a look back at history though elaborate tombstones, Av. 10, Ca. 24.

Movie tickets are half-price at many theaters on Wednesdays. Finally, for soccer games at **Ricardo Saprissa Stadium** (2240-6158) in the northern suburb of Tibás, bleacher seats start at ¢2,000 for non-playoff games. Get there early to see what the country's soccer craze is all about as fans, clad in their team's colors, arrive with painted faces and team flags.

Dance Schools

DANCE with the stars -- and the stars really are Latin-Americans, who start learning all about music and rhythm while still just babes in arms.

DANCE schools teach you how to bend your knees, move your hips and slide your feet to those marvelous Latin rhythms. Many language schools also offer dance classes. (**See Schools.**)

NATIONAL COMPANIES:

Compañía de Danza Universitaria (2511-4595, **casiotea01@gmail.com**), University of Costa Rica, San Pedro.

Danza UNA Chamber Company (2277-3393, **danza@una.ac.cr**), Universidad Nacional Campus, Heredia.

National Dance Company (2256-4838, **comdanza@mcj.go.cr**), CENAC, Av. 3/7, Ca. 11, San José.

Taller Nacional de Danza & Conservatory El Barco (part of the Taller) (2222-9398, crtallernacionaldedanza.com), Barrio Escalante. Contemporary, popular, ballet, flamenco, jazz, urban jazz, hip-hop, break dance, belly dance, creative dance for children, pre-ballet (for pre-schoolers).

INDEPENDENT COMPANIES:

Ballet

Abend (2236-0700, **danzaabend.com**), Calle Blancos. Also hip-hop.

Academia Superior de Ballet (2272-5163, **academiasuperiorcr@yahoo.com**), Concepción de Tres Ríos.

Atellier Arts Institute (2232-9801, **ficoher@hotmail.com**), Rohrmoser. Classic ballet, jazz.

Ballet Academy Magnificat (8816-3055, 2259-2404, **balletmagnificatcr.com**), San Francisco de Dos Ríos.

Escuela de Ballet Clásico Ruso (2290-2886, **escuela_ballet@yahoo.com**), La Uruca.

Layin Sing Academy (2225-2576, **la yins@racsa.co.cr**), Desamparados. Classic ballet, jazz.

Ballet Estudio Maureen Rivera (2552-3798, **balletstudio.maureenrivera@ gmail. com**), Cartago, Paraíso, Tres Ríos and Heredia. Classic ballet, baby ballet, ballet therapy, jazz and popular dances.

Flamenco

Flamenco de Paulina Peralta (8376-4122, **paulina.peralta@gmail.com**), Zapote, Centro de Artes Promenade.

Latin Dance

Academia de Baile Kinesis (2440-0852, **kinesis7@racsa.co.cr**), Alajuela. Salsa, merengue, bolero, paso doble, tango, cumbia, ballet, belly, hip hop, breakdance and zumba.

Merecumbé (2224-3531, **merecumbe. net**), schools in Escazú, Alajuela, Heredia, Tibás, San Pedro, Pérez Zeledón, San Carlos, San Ramón, Guápiles, Desamparados, Grecia, Guadalupe, Hatillo, San Ramón and Cartago, all styles.

Dance Force Center (2290-2293, **dan cecr.com**), Pavas. Ballet, jazz, flamenco, belly dance, hip-hop, tap, tango.

Fantasía de Tango (8336-1616, **fanta siadetango.com**), 50 m. north of the Il Pomodoro Restaurant, San Pedro, tango.

Contemporary Dance

Condanza (2233-1124, 8386-5175, **estu diocondanza@hotmail.com**), Av. 3, Ca.

25/29. Also, dancetherapy for stress.

Various Styles

Academia de Bellas Artes Sin Front-eras (2270-5757, 8853-1270), in front of La Salle High School, southwest Sabana Park. Flamenco, tango, belly dance.

Academia de Baile Popular Malecón (2223-8122, **academiasmalecon@yahoo.com**), Plaza Víquez. San José. Salsa, merengue, cumbia, tango, bolero, rumba, Flamenco, belly dance.

Academia de Danza O, Fusión Cultural (2296-2022, **odineya@racsa.co.cr**), in front of Irazú Hotel, La Uruca. Ballet, hip-hop; Middle Eastern classical and folkloric dances, artistic belly dance, Flamenco, popular dance.

Cascanueces Dance Studio (2228-6458), San Rafael, Escazú. Ballet, hip-hop, tap, jazz.

Danceworks (2288-5490, **danceworkscr.com**), Escazú. Jazz, ballet, tap, hip hop.

Danzale Studio (2440-1540, **danza le@ yahoo.com**), Alajuela. Ballet, modern.

Giro Danza (2241-4424, **introdanza@hotmail.com**), Moravia. Modern, ballet, belly, jazz and hip hop.

Margarita Esquivel Program (2277-3529, **pmesq@una.ac.cr**), Dance School of Universidad Nacional, Heredia. Creative movement, early stimulation, ballet, contemporary dance, body movement. For children, teens, adults, elderly.

Piruetas Danza (2262-0647), 75 m. south of Iglesia de los Ángeles Catholic Church, Heredia. Ballet, baby ballet, Flamenco, Jewish dances, contemporary.

Promenade Arts Center (2283-6660, **artespromenade.com**), Zapote. Ballet, belly dance, flamenco, folklore, jazz, hip-hop, tango.

Signos Teatro Danza (2255-0618, 8876-0541), San José. Hip hop, modern, contemporary.

Zingari Dance Studio (2282-1127, eszingari@yahoo.com), 350 m. north of Red Cross, Santa Ana. Flamenco, ballet, belly, modern dance.

Festivals & Celebrations

MANY occasions are celebrated in Costa Rica. Most of the fiestas include turnos (small fairs), exhibits of food, animals, and art, carnivals and days off. Read on for a calendar of the most important events. Check The Tico Times for dates and locations.

JANUARY

New Year's Day, Jan. 1 – holiday.

Palmares Fiestas, first two weeks – carnival, rides, bingo, horse parades, concerts.

Alajuelita Fiestas, week of 15th – honor Guatemala's Black Christ of Esquipulas, Alajuelita's Patron Saint, oxcart parade, pilgrimage to cross on mountain.

Santa Cruz Fiestas, week of 15th in Guanacaste – honor Black Christ of Esquipulas, folk dancing, marimbas, more.

Fiestas Carrizal, 2nd-15th, mascaradas, carnival, bands, Carrizal, Alajuela.

Copa del Café, week-long, int'l. tennis tourney at Country Club, Escazú, players under 18. See tennis greats before they become famous.

Jorge Debravo's Day (Poetry Day), 31st, dedicated to Costa Rica's most famous poet, readings/cultural events at cultural centers, special event at National Culture Center (CENAC).

National Games, week-long competition for athletes younger than 21, rotates change annually.

National Conference for Teachers of English, last week, C.R.-North American Cultural Center, Barrio Dent, 2207-7500.

In mid-July, just about everything that can float gets decorated and joins in the parade in honor of the Virgin of the Sea.

Photo by Mónica Quesada

FEBRUARY

Expo-Feria Pérez Zeledón, first week, cattle show/sale, cowboy demos, rides, concerts, livestock show, agricultural/industrial fairs, bullfights, Pérez Zeledón, 2771-3758.

La Fortuna Fair, first week, cattle shows and turno, 2479-9185.

Puntarenas Carnival, first two weeks, fun in the sun, 2661-0250.

Orange Expofair, 2nd week, citrus sales, crafts, traditional food, dances, song festival, Campo Ferial, Ciudad Colón.

Expoferia Orosi Colonial, 2nd week, contests, crafts, food, in front of Colonial Church.

Sculpture Symposium, 3rd week, sculptors make their pieces for a week, 9 a.m.-5 p.m., each year the material changes, nightly cultural events, Barva Park, Heredia, 2237-3262.

Fiesta del Sol, last week, solar energy tools inc/light systems, pumps, toys, ovens, also celebrates Maya New Year. Casa del Sol, Santa Bárbara, Santa Cruz, Guanacaste, 2681-1015.

MARCH

Expo-Alfaro Ruiz, 1st week, contests, crafts, food, 500 m. east of Zarcero Park, Alajuela, 2463-3306, 2463-1330.

Annual Canine Festival, 1st week, SASY event honors Costa Rican mixed-breed dogs, all breeds welcome, contests, raffles, prizes, costumes, flea market, Curridabat, 2228-2397.

Liberia Fiestas, 1st week, Guanacaste folklore, rides, concerts, 2666-0169.

Sandcastle Contest, 1st week, depends on tides, Playas del Coco, Guanacaste, (**peninsuladenicoya@hotmail.com**)

International Women's Day, 8th, gatherings, cultural shows, San José.

Día del Boyero (Oxcart Driver's Day), 2nd Sunday, San Antonio de Escazú, colorful oxcart parade, priests bless animals/crops, 2208-7500.

International Arts Festival, 3rd week, San José, international theater, dance, concerts, exhibits.

Milk Fair, 2nd-12th, cattle exhibit, food, concerts, dances, bullfights, March 2nd-12th, fair site, Zarcero, Alajuela, 2463-3673.

Commemoration of Santa Rosa Battle, 20th, assemblies in schools to remember when Costa Rican troops repelled the entrance of filibusters to the country, national symbol of the fight against William Walker.

Chiverre Fair, 2nd and 3rd weeks, inc/ food made of the huge fruit (squash family, traditional during Holy Week), sports, cultural events, dances, karaoke, Alfaro Ruiz, Zarcero, Alajuela, 4 km. towards San Carlos, 2463-3673.

Annual International Food Fair, 3rd weekend, proceeds help poor, at IICA, 2216-0222, Coronado.

Festival of Music and Arts of the South Caribbean, Feb-April, usually week before Holy Week. Playa Chiquita, Limón.

Fruit Festival, 2nd and 3rd weeks, Orotina, exhibit, sale of fruits, vegetables, lectures, rides, concerts, food, craft, sports, cultural activities.

National Orchid Show, some 1,500 local, foreign species, hybrids on display in San José. Check The Tico Times for dates, venue.

Pilgrimage to Ujarrás, mid-month, religious procession from Paraíso Church to ruins of first church in Costa Rica, cultural events.

Saint Joseph's Day, 19th, namesake neighborhoods celebrate with fairs, parades, special masses.

San José Obrero Artisans' Fair, 19th-28th, San José, huge crafts fair, FERCORI, Ca. 23, Av. Ctrl. 2297-1449.

Feria Nacional de la Mascarada, last weekend, mascarada and cimarrona competitions, cultural events, Park, Barva, Heredia. 2260-3292.

National Sports Day, last Sunday, talks, competitions, exhibits, sales at Sabana Park, San José, around country.

APRIL

Sol & Arena Athletic Race, call for date, 4 p.m., 10 km. on the beach, Puntarenas, from the Hospital to the dock on the beach, entrée fee, ¢5000, fun, surprises, motorcycles, raffles, 2663-2512.

Holy Week, 16th-23rd, dramatic street processions depict story of Christ's passion, San José shuts down Thurs.-Sun.; many head to the beach.

Luz de Luna Festival, a week after Holy Week, cultural events, inc/folklore, dance, concerts, plays, organized by the Munici-

pal School of Integrated Arts, Santa Ana, 2282-8662.

Juan Santamaría Day, 11th, commemorates Costa Rica's national hero, mythical, legendary soldier (also known as *El Erizo*) who died in battle against William Walker's troops in 1856.

Festival del Erizo, 11th-23th, week-long celebration, parades, concerts, dances, carnival, horse parade, especially in hero's birthplace, Alajuela, 2443-2255.

University Week, 3rd week, University of Costa Rica, carnival, concerts, exhibits, parades, 2207-5634.

Anniversary Abolition of the Army, 26th, students of San José attend public act with government officials, Parque de la Democracia, in front of statue of ex-President José ("Pepe") Figueres Ferrer.

MAY

Labor Day, 1st, marches, President's annual "state of the nation" address. Congress elects leaders.

Hike to the Cross on top of Cerro La Cruz, Nicoya, 3rd, 100-year-old tradition, people hike to hilltop, believing that by celebrating mass there, a snake that supposedly inhabits the place will not awaken. Others believe that a volcano will not erupt if people visit.

San Isidro Labrador's Day, 15th, all namesake towns honor this patron saint of farmers and farm animals with blessings of animals, crops, parades, fairs.

Corpus Christi Day, 29th, national holiday, religious celebration.

JUNE

Father's Day, 3rd Sun., dads get presents in Costa Rica, too.

Carrera de San Juan, 18th, long-distance foot race on 22.5-km course.

International Music Day, 21st, concerts in parks, theaters, cultural centers.

JULY

Virgin of the Sea, Sat. closest to the 16th, Puntarenas, parade of decorated fishing boats, yachts in Gulf of Nicoya salute Puntarenas' Patron Saint, the Virgin of Mt.

Carmel; masses, parades, dances, sports events, fireworks, 2661-0387.

Annexation of Guanacaste, 25th, celebrates Guanacaste's decision to be part of Costa Rica instead of Nicaragua in 1824; some public and private institutes have their employees dressed as campesinos.

II Cultural Festival of the Annexation, 19th-25th, fiestas in Liberia, folk dances, parades, cattle shows, bullfights, concerts, tourism fair.

AUGUST

Virgin de Los Angeles, 2nd, nationwide pilgrimage to Basílica in Cartago to honor Costa Rica's Patron Saint, the miracle-working black Virgin of Los Angeles (*La Negrita*).

Expo-Feria del Queso, date might change, cow milking competition, biggest cheese contest, cattle, sports, cultural events, Santa Cruz, Turrialba, 2538-8355.

Mother's Day, 15th, national holiday, flowers, candy, flowers for moms.

Día de San Bartolomeo, two weeks inc/ Aug. 24, mascaradas with clowns hitting people w/dried pig bladders, cimarrona bands, cultural shows, Barva Park, Heredia, 2260-3292.

San Ramón's Day, 31st, townspeople parade to San Ramón church bearing their districts' patron saints; "San Ramón" dances in streets; parades, fun.

Día del Negro, month-long celebrations including the **Festival de la Cultura Negra and Festival Cultural Limón Roots and Festival Diáspora Africana**, honors Afro-Costa Rican culture with lectures, dances, theater, Limón and San José. 2758-0020.

International Music Festival, musicians of many genres perform; dates vary.

SEPTEMBER

Independence Day, 15th, gigantic relay race over entire Central American isthmus. Student runners carry "Freedom Torch" from Guatemala to Costa Rica. Torch arrives at colonial capital of Cartago at 6 p.m. on the 14th, when everyone, nationwide, sings national anthem. Kids go out for nocturnal homemade-lantern parades.

Drum-beating, uniformed schoolchildren parade the next day.

Fiesta de San Miguel, 29th, in San Miguel de Escazú, 2208-7500, weeklong celebration with fireworks, turno, music.

OCTOBER

San Isidro de El General, 9th, celebration of the southern hub city's founding.

Limón Carnival, week-long street dances, parades, concerts – "Mardi Gras" to a Caribbean beat.

Cultures Day, 12th, commemorates Spanish conquest, schools celebrate with assemblies.

Virgen del Pilar's Day, 12th, masses, rosaries, serenade in San José district of Tres Ríos celebrating Patron Saint.

Fiesta del Maíz, 12th, in Upala, costumes made of corn husks, grains, silks, food made of corn, 2470-0157.

International Guitar Festival, best classical guitar players, date varies.

Palmito Fair, 14th-16th, sales of dishes made of palmito, Horquetas, Sarapiquí, 2764-3124.

Expo-Feria del Pejibaye, 19th-29th and Nov. 4-6, sales of products made of pejibaye fruit, wood, Tucurrique, Cartago.

Traditional Day of the Costa Rican Mascarada, 31st, mascaradas and cimarrona parades in around the country.

NOVEMBER

All Soul's Day, 2nd, "Day of the Dead," families visit cemeteries to remember loved ones.

National Baroque Festival, 2nd week, Santa Ana Church, 2203-3344.

Oxcart Parade in San José, last Sunday, oxen owners camp in La Sabana Park day before, hold a Campesino Song Festival, firecrackers, next day, parade along Paseo Colón, Av. 2, finish at Plaza Víquez, 2282-8662.

Day Against Violence Towards Women, 25th, marches/vigils for victims of domestic violence, San José.

DECEMBER

Teletón, 1st weekend, 27-hour perform-

Carnaval *in Limón on the Caribbean Coast, was back in full force in 2009 with dancing in the streets, bands, yummy food and more.*

Photo by Keely Kernan

ing marathon, with nat'l., int'l. musicians, reporters, actors/actresses, benefits Children's Hospital, organized by Club Activo 20-30, 2233-2030.

Nativity Scene of Los Heraldos del Evangelio, 20-minute presentation of small figures in moving dioramas with special effects, through Jan. 12, Mon.-Sat., 3-7 p.m.; Sun., 3-8:30 p.m., green house, 200 m. west, 75 m. south of main entrance to Club La Guaria, Moravia, 2235-5410.

Chicharrón Fair, first two weekends, Puriscal, 2416-6026.

Christmas Choir Festival, 1st week, choirs from around country perform at National Theater.

Fiesta de Los Negritos, week of the 8th in the indigenous village of Boruca, ancient rituals combine with Catholicism to honor Virgin of Immaculate Conception, costumes, drums, music, dance.

Dance Festival, 1st two weeks, acclaimed national/international dancers, seminars at National Theater.

Festival of Lights, 2nd week, parade through San José with floats adorned with lights, concert and fireworks.

Fiesta de la Yegüita (Little Mare), week of 12th, Nicoya, blends ancient indigenous rituals to honor Virgin of Guadalupe, processions, concerts, fireworks, special foods.

Christmas Celebrations, homes, businesses set up Nativity scenes. Competition for best scene through the 22nd. Season's foods include cookies, eggnog, corn liquor or wine, tamales, apples, grapes. Las Posadas begin Dec. 15 – carolers go house to house and are treated to refreshments. At 8 and 9 p.m., Dec. 24, Catholic churches celebrate the *Misa del Gallo* (Rooster Mass).

Festejos Populares (year-end festivals), 25th-31st, at San José fairgrounds, Zapote, amusement park, rides, food, music, fireworks.

Tope, 28th, major horse parade, downtown San José.

Carnival, 27th, downtown San José, huge parade with colorful floats, music. (May be cancelled. Check newspapers.)

Fiesta de Los Diablitos, Dec. 31st-Jan. 2nd, indigenous of southern Boruca region enact a fight/dance between the indigenous (little devils) and Spaniards (bulls) amid flute, drum music; crafts sale, fireworks.

Food

COSTA RICA boasts international and fast-food cuisine, but yummy typical meals are still the order of the day at home and in many restaurants and sodas, small family-run eateries, at very low prices.

MOST cooks rely on the basic staples of beans, white rice and veggies, with an addition of chicken, meat or fish. Fresh cilantro and garlic add flavor, and although hot spices and sauces are shunned, a bottle of Tabasco is on every table. Strange names can be baffling.

The following are Tiquicia's "daily specials" and special feasts, when Costa Rica's most treasured culinary delight, the tamal, is served (see **Holidays**).

Gallo pinto, a breakfast standby, is day-old rice fried with beans, chopped onions, sweet peppers and fresh cilantro. A splash of *Salsa Lizano*, a tangy fruit-and-cumin-based sauce, often is added. *Gallo Pinto* is served with tortillas, scrambled eggs, a chunk of mild white cheese or a dollop of *natilla* (sour cream). *Café con leche* (coffee with milk), often served in a glass in rural areas, accompanies breakfast.

A cheap and satisfying lunchtime favorite is *casado*, which means "marriage," and it certainly is a partnership on a platter. It combines rice, beans, beef, chicken or fish, plus fried ripe plantain, *picadillo* (finely chopped cooked vegetables sometimes mixed with ground beef) and shredded cabbage salad.

Other popular dishes are *arroz con pollo* (seasoned rice with chicken), *olla de carne* (a hearty beef and vegetable soup), *sopa negra* (black bean soup served with a poached egg), *pozol* (a Guanacaste specialty of pork and corn) and *sopa de mondongo* (tripe soup).

Gallos are corn flour tortillas folded around anything – shredded beef, chicken, sausage, potato or cheese. Similar ingredients are found in *arreglados,* tiny puff pastries spread with refried beans, and *empanadas*, deep-fried or baked turnovers. *Tacos* – fried tortillas stuffed with chicken or beef

and brimming with shredded cabbage, mayonnaise and ketchup – are very different from their Mexican cousins. *Chorreadas*, sweet corn fritters, are served with sour cream. *Ceviche*, fresh fish or seafood marinated in lime juice with onions and fresh cilantro, and *palmito*, heart of palm, are much-loved classics.

Other typical treats include *chicharrones*, crispy fried pork rinds; *patacones*, mashed fried plantain; and *pejibaye*, a nutty palm fruit boiled and served with mayonnaise. Costa Rica also offers many options for vegetarians.

Topping the dessert popularity poll are the traditional *queque de tres leches*, a moist sponge cake drenched in evaporated milk, condensed milk and cream and topped with meringue; *flan*, a caramel or coconut custard; and *torta chilena*, an extremely sweet multi-layered cake filled with condensed milk.

Many fresh tropical fruits, including cas, from a species of guava unique to Costa Rica, are blended with water to make the famous *refrescos naturales* served with every meal. For thirst-quenching *pipas*, street vendors bore holes in the tops of green coconuts and insert straws.

The Caribbean coast's flavors and aromas are different. Dishes tend to be far spicier and many, such as *rondon* (a fish and vegetable stew), are cooked in coconut milk. *Pan bon*, a rum-spiked fruitcake, is a regional favorite.

The law controls hygienic conditions wherever food is served, and even tiny eateries are spotlessly clean. Do not buy cooked food from street vendors, but packaged munchies present no problem.

Before eating or when you see others eating, it is polite to say *"Buen provecho."* Good appetite!

Holidays

THESE are the times to do what you love best: gather for family, food and fun.

CHRISTMAS and Holy Week are times to be with families and celebrate traditions with food and festivals, and many head to the beaches. Religious fervor charges the atmosphere in towns and cities, and Good Friday processions depicting the Passion of Christ are performed by local townsfolk dressed in elaborate costumes.

Holiday foods feature sweet empanadas stuffed with *chiverre* (a squash-like vegetable), homemade bread and *flor de itabo* (the flower of the Itabo tree) dipped in egg and bread crumbs and fried. The country virtually shuts down from Thursday through Easter Sunday; there's no bus service on Good Friday and most supermarkets are closed.

The Christmas goody is the tamal, and making tamales is a family affair. Seasoned cornmeal is stuffed with diced pork, chicken, beef, rice, chopped vegetables, prunes, etc., then wrapped in banana leaves and boiled. Every household has a special recipe handed down through generations, and families give each other tamales as special gifts.

Apples and grapes are synonymous with Christmas. While Costa Rica now produces these fruits, the most popular are expensive imported red apples and purple and green grapes. A Tico tradition holds that people who consume 12 grapes before midnight on New Year's Eve will enjoy 12 happy months in the coming year!

24-hour Restaurants

San José has a choice of safe, friendly, clean eateries open 24/7 to satisfy your late-night munchies or early-morning hunger pains.

INTERNATIONAL fare indoors or on the patio at **Cafetería 1830** (2221-4000, ext. 263), Gran Hotel de Costa Rica, Av. 2, Ca. 5/7. A dive with character is centrally located **Chelles** (2221-1369), Av. Ctrl., Ca. 3, late-night drinking and light bites. **Denny's** (2431-5050), Hotel Best Western Irazú, General Cañas Highway, local franchise of U.S. chain, diner-style setting. The **Del Mar** (2257-7800), opposite Hotel del Rey, Av.1, Ca. 9/11, serves breakfast all day and night from its U.S.-style menu. **Hotel Europa** (2222-1222), Ca. Ctrl., Av 4, offers cafeteria-style fare. **Magnolia** (2258-2807), a fashionable place in the Casino Club Colonial, serves yummy food and drinks. **Manolo's** (2221-2041), Av. Ctrl., Ca. Ctrl/2, a downtown classic on the pedestrian mall, offers a typical menu. Try its famous churros, fried dough tubes coated in sugar or fabulous black-bean soup. **Nuestra Tierra** (2258-6500), Av.2, Ca.15, rustic décor, typical food, munchies. **Soda Tapia** (2222-6734), east side of La Sabana Park, a traditional family landmark, open 24-hours Friday only, to midnight Sun. offers hearty Tico menu, outdoor tables and parking.

Other 24-hour eateries exist, but for safety it's best to stick to those listed above.

In the eastern suburb of San Pedro, **Subway** custom-builds subs all night Fri. and Sat. For fast food to go, some **Select** mini-markets at 24-hour Shell gas stations stay open round the clock Fri. and Sat.,.

In the Central Pacific town of Jacó, late-nighters can fill up on Mexican and Tico fare at **Pancho Villa** (2643-3571).

Houses of Worship

COSTA RICA a Catholic country, but freedom of religion is alive and well and many faiths flourish here. The following houses of worship offer services in English.

Anglican Episcopal Church (2222-1560, **ibuenpastor@gmail.com**), Ca. 3/5, Av. 4, north side of Colegio de Señoritas.

Bahá'i Faith Firesides (2249-1231, **juliemckinney9@gmail.com**), La Uruca.

Beach Community Church, (2653-1864, 8868-0871, **johnwadmaniii@hotmail.com**), next to Country Day School, road to Brasilito, Tamarindo, 10 a.m., Sunday.

B'Nei Israel (2231-5243, **congbnei@racsa.co.cr**), 800 m. west of Pop's, La Sabana, on old road to Escazú.

Chabad Lubavitch (2296-6565, **hspalter@jabadcr.com**), in front of Antojitos, Rohrmoser. Also, in Trejos Montealegre, 50 m. west of Banco General.

Christian Center (2494-0970, 2444-5212, **laterrazagrecia@msn.com**), San Roque, Grecia.

Church of Christ (English 8834-8825, **jmcrealtimes.net**, Spanish 8839-4331), Quircot, Cartago.

Church of Jesus Christ of the Latter Day Saints (2224-9401, **2015218@ldschurch.org**), Curridabat, 500 m. south of Pop's, Edificio Trebol, store #6.

Costa Rican Lutheran Church (2227-8080, **comunicacion@ilco.cr**), Barrio El Carmen, San José, 600 m. southeast of San Cayetano Church. Interpretation services available in English, Russian, German, and Swedish.

Episcopal Diocese of Costa Rica (2225-0209, **anglicancr@racsa.co.cr**), 75 m. north of Plaza Cemaco, Zapote.

Escazú Christian Fellowship (8395-9653, **info@ecfcr.net, ecfcr.net**), at International Baptist Church, Guachipelín, Escazú, 5 p.m., Sunday, interdenominational.

Guadalupe Missionary Baptist Temple (2222-4757, 8848-3987, **kerawa@racsa.co.cr**), three blocks east of the cemetery, corner church, Guadalupe.

Hare Krishna Center Gaudiya Math (2256-8650, **haribol@racsa.co.cr**), Cuesta de Núñez, #1331, Av. 1, Ca. 15/17.

Harvest Vineyard Church (2291-4383, **info@harvestvineyard.info**), West Sabana Park, 200 m. north, 100 m. east, 75 m. north of USIMED, at the Lexicon Library.

Iglesia Sion de Costa Rica (2524-2058, 8919-0328, **sanghkeum@hotmail.com, pastorkeum@hanmail.net**), Korean spoken, San Pedro.

International Baptist Church (2215-2117, 8365-1005, **paul_dina@hotmail.com**), west of Multiplaza, north side of the Santa Ana Highway, Guachipelín, Escazú.

Jehovah's Witnesses (2293-2943, crhisid@racsa.co.cr), La Asunción, Belén, across from Avis Rent-a-Car.

Muslim Center (2240-4872, omarhemeda@hotmail.com), Guadalupe, Calle Blancos-Montelimar, 100 m. east, 80 m. south of Escuela Santa Mónica.

Nondenominational Christian Church (2447-6765, trandall360@gmail.com), El Empalme, San Ramón, 8:30 a.m., Sunday.

Quaker Meeting (2222-1400, friends@racsa.co.cr), Friends Peace Center, San José, Ca. 15, Av. 6/8, 11 a.m., Sunday; in Monteverde, Monteverde School, 11 a.m., Sunday.

Roman Catholic Mass (2221-3820, 2221-7692), Cathedral, Ca. Ctrl./1, Av. 2/4, San José, 4 p.m. , Saturday.

San Pedro Christian Fellowship (2267-6038, 2235-6052, **sleves@racsa.co.cr**), Centro Comercial Calle Real, San Pedro.

Science of Mind Study Group and

Potluck (8378-6679, **scienceofmind incostarica.com**), Escazú, 10 a.m.-1 p.m., Tuesday.

St. Mary's Roman Catholic Chapel (2209-9800), mass, 4 p.m. Sunday, Ramada Plaza Herradura Hotel, Ciudad Cariari, Heredia.

Tibetan-Costa Rican Cultural Association (2258-0254, **tibetencosta rica.com**), 400 m. north and 80 m. west of the Kiosk in Parque Morazán, Barrio Amón.

Union Church (2235-6709, **info@ iglesiaunion.net, iglesiaunion.net**), 100 m. east, 500 m. north, 100 m. east of Lincoln School, San Rafael, Moravia.

Unity Community (2203-4411, **unitycostarica.org**), 350 m. south of Shang Hai Restaurant, Piedades, Santa Ana.

Zen Buddhism (2244-3532, **casazen. org**), Casa Zen, Santo Domingo, Heredia.

Wine, Beer & Spirits

Cervecería Costa Rica, the country's beer monopoly, brews a good choice of flavorful suds, each with a distinctive character that will keep beer drinkers happy.

IMPERIAL tops the popularity list. This smooth lager is easily recognized by its black eagle trademark.

Some bars sell a lighter version on tap, cerveza cruda, often served by the jug.

When you order beer bien fría (good and cold), it's always frosty. But if you don't want ice added, ask for it sin hielo (without ice).

Other flavorful suds include **Pilsen**, **Rock Ice** and the slightly pricier **Bavaria**. There's a low-calorie variety, **Bavaria Lite**, and **Bavaria Dark** is a delicious malty brew.

Heineken, with a character resembling its Dutch cousin, is bottled here but is a little more expensive, and **Kaiser**, a non-alcoholic brew, is refreshing.

Beer and liquor prices fluctuate with the exchange rate. The best beer prices are found in grocery stores.

For a stronger tipple, the state-monopoly, **Fábrica Nacional de Licores (FANAL)**, offers the well-known **Cacique**-brand. **Guaro** sold under that brand name, is a sugar cane-based spirit.

A shot or two is fine, but overindulgence can produce a terrific hangover. Among FANAL's various products you'll find **Magallanes** and **Marqués** rums, as well as **Zar** vodka.

Ron Rico and **Ron Abuelo** are nice rums, but the classy **Centenario** and Nicaraguan **Flor de Caña** are far more commendable.

Local vodkas **Rostov** and **Nikolai** are okay, but the cheap **Ginebra** is a questionable gin.

Salicsa S.A., in Escazú, offers popular liqueurs, including **Café Rica** and **Golden Cream**.

It also produces a high-quality rum called **Bucanero Special Reserve**.

Another liqueur that enjoys wide acclaim is **Liqueur de Café Britt** offered by **Café Britt**, a major coffee producer. All of these are export quality.

Costa Rica is not a wine country, and local wines tend to be sweet and fruity.

Very reasonably priced to expensive top-quality Chilean and other imported wines are available, as are imported whiskeys and other liquors. And very good-tasting organic wines from Argentina are also now on the market.

Most bars serve bocas, tasty treats to curb the appetite.

Chicharrones (fried pork rinds), refried beans, ceviche (raw fish marinated in lime juice), patacones (deep-fried plantain) and fried cheese are all popular.

No alcohol is sold Easter Thursday-Saturday or on election days. This applies to stores, as well as bars and restaurants.

Remember that drinking and driving don't mix. Laws are strict and danger is real, so don't do it.

Movie Theaters

MOVIE houses are primarily found in malls: lots of small theaters with small screens. For the best large-screen viewing head over to Magaly in Barrio California and for the best movies, check out what Sala Garbo is offering.

THE Magaly chain, **Cinemark, Cinépolis** and **Sala Garbo** dominate the local cinema business. The first three show the latest Hollywood offerings, while **Sala Garbo** and **Arte Cine Lindora** specialize in international films.

Centro de Cine stages discussions after showing films. The **University of Costa Rica** also shows occasional flicks. Check The Tico Times for schedules.

Movie are usually in English with Spanish subtitles. Most theaters have comfortable seats, air conditioning and digital surround sound. Wednesdays are half price nights at **Magaly** theaters. **Cinépolis** offers VIP theaters with lounge seats and food service. Tickets, $4-6; before 4 p.m., $2.

ALAJUELA

Grecia #1-2 (2495-6000, 2494-3737, **info@fabrica.co.cr**), Centro Comercial Fábrica, 800 m. west of the Shell station.

Internacional #1-4 (2442-6100), Mall Internacional, Alajuela, near airport.

Multicines San Ramón #1-3, (2447-7120), Plaza Occidente, San Ramón.

CARTAGO

Multicines Plaza Paraíso #1-3 (2592-3133), Mall Paraíso, Paraíso de Cartago.

Cinépolis Terramall (2278-3586, 2278-3631, **c_terramall@cinepolis.com.mx**), Terramall, Tres Ríos.

CIUDAD QUESADA

Multicines Plaza San Carlos #1-3 (2460-8110), Plaza San Carlos, town center.

CURRIDABAT

Cinemark del Este #1-8 (2280-0490, **cinemarkca.com**), Multiplaza del Este, next to PriceSmart, Curridabat.

ESCAZU

Cinemark #1-8 (2201-5050, **cinemarkca.com**), Multiplaza Mall, Guachipelín.

GUANACASTE

Multicines Plaza Liberia #1-4 (2665-2335, 2666-4512), Plaza Liberia Shopping Center, Liberia entrance.

HEREDIA

Cariari #1-6 (2293-3300), Plaza Real Cariari, 15 min. northwest of San José, General Cañas Hwy.

Flores #1-5 (2237-6263), Paseo de las Flores Mall, Heredia, road to La Uruca.

PAVAS

Plaza Mayor #1-2 (2232-0621), Plaza Mayor Shopping Center, Rohrmoser, reservations accepted.

SAN JOSE

Alliance Française (2222-2283, **llin@afsj.net**), Barrio Amón, Av. 7, Ca. 5, also, 300 m. south of Librería Universal, south Sabana Park and Heredia, 100 m. east of Liceo Samuel Sáenz (2262-7182).

Centro de Cine, (2223-2127, 2223-0610, **centrodecine.go.cr**), Barrio Otoya, Av. 9, Ca. 11.

Cinépolis Desamparados (2218-0802, **c_desamparados@cinepolis.com.mx**),

Multicentro Desamparados, Desamparados.

Magaly (2223-0085, **www.ccmcine mas.com**), Ca. 23, Av. Ctrl./1.

Sala Garbo (2222-1034, **garbfilm@ racsa.co.cr**), Av. 2, Ca. 28.

Variedades (2222-6108, 2222-6018, **jinestaurbini@ice.co.cr**), Ca. 5, Av. Ctrl./1.

SAN PEDRO

Cine Universitario (2511-4717, 2511-5322, **accionsocial.ucr.ac.cr**), UCR Law School auditorium shows movies during school year, 6:45 p.m., Thurs., Fri., March-Dec. except in July (mid-term vacations).

San Pedro #1-5 (2283-5716), **#6-10** (2280-9585), Mall San Pedro.

SANTA ANA

Arte Cine Lindora (2205-4130, **info@ artecinelindora.com**), Centro Comercial Vía Lindora.

SOUTHERN ZONE

Pérez Zeledón (2772-6179), Monte General Shopping Center.

Museums & Science Centers

MUSEUMS offer more than displays of art, history and science. Visitors can also participate in workshops, concerts and plays.

MOST are in the Central Valley. Learn, enjoy and be sure to ask permission before taking flash photographs inside.

HISTORY, ART, SCIENCE

San José

Dr. Rafael Angel Calderón Guardia Museum (2255-1218, **musecal@mcj. go.cr**), Ca. 25/27, Av. 11, Barrio Escalante, 9 a.m.-5 p.m., Mon.-Fri.; 9 a.m.-noon, 1-5 p.m. Sat., in former Calderón Family mansion, historic building, exhibits life of President Rafael Angel Calderón, 1948-war documentation, student library, temporary exhibitions, films, theater, dance shows in auditorium, parking. Free.

Gold Museum (2243-4202, **museos delbancocentral.org**), below Plaza de la Cultura, Ca. 5, Av. Ctrl./2, 9:30 a.m.-4:30 p.m., Mon.-Sun. Over 1,000 pre-Columbian gold artifacts, temporary art exhibits. Residents $3, tourists $7, children under 11, free.

Jade Museum (2287-6034, **ins-cr.com**), outside INS building, Av. 7/9, Ca. 9/11, 8:30 a.m.-3:30 p.m., Mon.-Fri.; 9 a.m.-1 p.m., Sat. Pre-Columbian jade, stone, and ceramics. Residents ₡1,000, tourists $7, kids under 12 and elders, free.

Museo Filatélico Numismático de Costa Rica (2223-6918, **correos.go.cr**), Ca. 2, Av. 1/3, 2nd floor of Central Post Office, 8 a.m.-5 p.m., Mon.-Fri., stamp collection, history of telegraph, mail. Adults ₡150, kids ₡100.

Museo Histórico Tecnólogico del Grupo ICE (2220-6054, 2220-6497, **grupoice.com**), 400 m. north of ICE, 8 a.m.-4 p.m., Mon.-Fri., temporary art exhibits, documents, photos, story of electricity and telecommunications in Costa Rica. Free.

Museum of Liceo de Costa Rica (2233-6784, **generacionlcr96@yahoo.com**), Boulevard de Liceo de Costa Rica, Av. 18, photos, art collection, trophy room, alumni objects, books. Free. Appointments required.

National Museum (2257-1433, **museo-costarica.go.cr**), Ca.17, Av. Ctrl./2., 8:30 a.m.-4:30 p.m., Tues.-Sat., 9 a.m.-4:30 p.m., Sun. History of the nation housed in Bellavista Fortress built in 1870, pre-Co-

Subtly lit figures show off the beautiful, pre-Columbian gold work on display at the Gold Museum.

Photo by Harmony Reforma

lumbian art (pottery, stone, gold). "Colonial Room" w/period art, furniture, charming natural history exhibits and a recent discovery of a tunnel running underneath the old fort. Temporary art, photo exhibits. Residents ₡1,000, tourists $6, children under 12, free, students w/ID, $2.

Sala Magón (2221-2022, **mcj.go.cr**), CENAC, Av. 3/5, Ca. 11/15, call for appointment, 8 a.m.-3 p.m., Mon.-Fri., photographs of renowned Costa Ricans who have won the Magón Award since 1962-2004. Free.

Provinces

Ecomuseo Minas de Abangares (2662-0033, **puebloantiguo.com**), La Sierra, Abangares, Guanacaste, 7 a.m.-4 p.m., closed Mon. Gold-extraction machines, tunnels, wagons, photos, tours, night walks, thermal pools, lodging, restaurant, residents ₡800, tourists ₡1,500.

José Figueres Ferrer Historic and Cultural Center (2447-2178, **centrojose figueres.org**), San Ramón de Alajuela, north side of San Ramón Church, 10 a.m.-7 p.m., Mon.-Sat., photos, documents

1948 Civil War, documents on C.R., country without army, cultural activities, temporary exhibits. Free.

Juan Santamaría Museum (2441-4775, **museojuansantamaria.go.cr**), Alajuela, Av. 3, Ca. Ctrl./2, 10 a.m.-5:30 p.m., Tues.-Sun. Highlights battles against William Walker in 1856-1857 and life of legendary hero Juan Santamaría. Free.

Museo de Cultura Popular (2260-1619, **mcp@una.ac.cr**), Santa Lucía, Barva, Heredia, 8 a.m.-4 p.m., Mon.-Fri. (reservations), closed, Sat., 10 a.m.-4 p.m., Sun. Old *bahareque* house built 1885-1887 by the parents of former President Alfredo González Flores, furniture, domestic/work tools of the era. Tourists $2, residents ₡500, kids ₡200.

Museo Ferroviario (8810-0660), former train station, Atenas, 7 a.m.-6 p.m., Sun., exhibits photos, tools and AEG German locomotive. Donations.

Museo Histórico Etnográfico Elías Leiva Quirós (2551-0895, **gameio4@hot mail.com**), north side of Colegio San Luis Gonzaga, Cartago, by appointment, archeology and history collection from 1932.

Donations.

Museo Regional Omar Salazar (2558-3733, fax: 2556-7020, **museoturrialbau cr@ gmai.com**), University of Costa Rica Campus, Turrialba, 9 a.m.-noon, 1-4 p.m., Mon.-Fri. Archaeological exhibits from 10,000 BC-1,500 AD, temporary art exhibits. Free.

Santa Rosa Battle House (2666-5051), Santa Rosa National Park, Guanacaste, 8-11:30 a.m., 1-4 p.m. Site of skirmish with U.S. filibusterer William Walker. Tourists $10, tourist kids $1, residents ₡1,100, children 6-12 ₡400.

PAINTING & SCULPTURE

Contemporary Art & Design Museum (2257-9370, **madc.ac.cr**), CENAC, Av. 3/5, Ca. 15/17, 9:30 a.m.-4:30 p.m., Mon.-Sat. $3, tourists ₡700, residents, kids and seniors, free, students w/ID ₡500. Mondays free.

Joaquín García Monge Museum (2259-9705, **gomarin@racsa.co.cr**), across from the north-west side of Desamparados Park, noon-4 p.m., Mon.-Fri., temp. exhibits, workshops, painting classes, objects of the writer (Joaquín García Monge). Free.

Museo de Arte Contemporáneo al Aire Libre de Punta Islita (2290-4259, 2661-4044, **museo.dir@hotelpuntaislita.com**), Islita de Bejuco, Nandayure, Guanacaste, tours (2661-4044, 10 a.m., Tues.-Sun., temporary exhibits.

Museum of Costa Rican Art (2222-7155, **musarco.go.cr**), La Sabana Park, 9 a.m.-5 p.m., Tues.-Fri., 10 a.m.-4 p.m., Sat.-Sun. Extensive collection, temporary exhibits. Closed for Remodeling.

Regional Costa Rican Art Museum (2240-9044 ext. 146, **coopsain@racsa. co.cr**), at Clínica Integrada, Tibás, south side Ricardo Saprissa Stadium, 7 a.m.-4 p.m., Mon.- Fri. Temporary exhibits. Free.

CHILDREN & NATURE

San José

Children's Museum (C.R. Science and Cultural Center) (2258-4929, **info@ museoocr.com**), end Ca. 4, Av. 9, 8 a.m.-4:30 p.m., Tues.-Fri., 9:30 a.m.-5 p.m., weekends (closed Christmas, Easter week). Buy tickets at museum box office. Children's rights, universe, earth, living creatures, many interactive exhibits, gallery, National Auditorium, youth complex, guided tours. Children under 18 ₡800, adults ₡1,100. Kids under 3 and elders, free.

INBioparque (2507-8107, **inbio parque.com**), Santo Domingo de Heredia, 8:30 a.m.-4 p.m.; 9 a.m.-3 p.m., weekends. C.R.'s biodiversity featured via interactive exhibits, live ecosystems, butterfly garden, fishpond, aquarium, boa station. Residents ₡3,250, kids 4-12 ₡2,250, tourists $23, students $14, kids 0-4, free.

Insect Museum (2207-5318, **hlezama@ cariari.ucr.ac.cr**), basement of U. of Costa Rica Music School, San Pedro, 1-5 p.m., Mon.-Fri. More than 500 insects. From Ca. 5, take San Pedro bus along Avenida 2. Tourists ₡1,000, children ₡200, residents ₡500. Ring bell to gain entry.

Museum of Natural Sciences La Salle (2232-1306, **moisobeso@yahoo.com**), southwest corner of La Sabana Park, 8 a.m.-4 p.m., Mon.-Sat., 9 a.m.-5 p.m., Sun. More than 65,000 specimens of zoology, paleontology, archaeology, mineralogy. Terrific dinosaur. Adults $2, kids $1.

Provinces

Puntarenas Marine Park (661-5272, **parquemarino.org**), Puntarenas center, 9 a.m.-4:30 p.m., Tues.-Sun. Aquariums w/ marine life from as far away as Cocos Island National Park, salt- and fresh-water species. Residents ₡1,600, kids 4-12 ₡1,000, students w/ID ₡900, tourists $7, kids 4-12 $4, disabled and seniors ₡600.

Museo Vulcanológico Noche Buena (2530-8013, **nochebuena.org**), Cartago, 5 km. before Irazú Volcano entrance, history of Irazú Volcano, info on the planet and Costa Rican volcanoes, legends, restaurant. Adults ₡2,000, kids ₡1,000.

RELIGION

Museo de la Comunidad Judía de Costa Rica (2520-1013 ext. 129, **museo judio-decostarica@yahoo.com**), Centro Israelita Sionista de Costa Rica, Rohrmoser, 10 a.m.-2 p.m., Mon.-Fri.; 2-6 p.m. ,Weds., by appointments, photos, documents, films of the Jewish community in Costa Rica and Holocaust. Free.

Provinces

Museo de San Blas de Nicoya (2685-5109), next of San Blas Park, Nicoya, 8-11 a.m., 2-4 p.m. Mon.-Fri., 8-11 a.m., Sat.

17th, 18th century, religious artifacts in an adobe building. Free.

Our Lady of Ujarrás Museum (2574-7258), basement of Catholic Church, Paraíso de Cartago. 2:30-5:30 p.m. Thurs.-Sat., 9 a.m.-noon, 2:30-5:30 p.m., Sun. History of Ujarrás, religious and Indian artifacts, books, photo collection. No flash photos. ₡100.

Religious Art Museum San José de Orosi (2533-3852), Orosi Church, southeast of Cartago,1-5 p.m., Tues.-Fri., 9 a.m.-5 p.m., Sat.-Sun. Colonial religious art. No flash photos. Adults ₡350, children ₡200.

Orchids

FROM vanilla to tiny plants that grow underground, orchids are exotic and everywhere.

COLLECTING and growing orchids is a veritable national hobby. Many towns have clubs that offer shows in dry season, when the majority of orchids bloom. Here are some helpful leads on the orchid trail:

The Monteverde Orchid Garden (2645-6565), dedicated to investigation and documentation of orchids in the Monteverde region, contains some 500 species of orchids classified in 22 groups. Here, you will find Costa Rica's national flower, the *Guaria Morada,* and the smallest orchid in the world.

Botanical Orchid Garden (2487-8095, **orchidgardencr.com**), La Garita, Alajuela, tropical trails, varied gardens, exhibitions, nurseries, souvenir and coffee shops, 8:30 a.m.-4:30 p.m., Tues.-Sun., adults $12, kids $6, group rates.

Lankester Gardens (2552-3247, **jardin-botanicolankester.org**), educational center sponsored by the University of Costa Rica, extensive collection of orchids, near Cartago, 8:30 a.m.-4:30 p.m.

National Orchid Show, huge yearly event sponsored by the Costa Rican Orchid Association, mid-March, venue varies.

In love with plants of all kinds, including orchids? Try a two-week **Tropical Botany Course** in March, April (Spanish), June, July (English), $1,600 includes, 13-nights' lodging, all meals, transportation all over the country and in depth, fact-filled course. Call 2291-0862 or visit **hjimenez.org** to learn more about the course and read testimonials of enthralled students.

Books: "Vanishing Beauty, Native Costa Rican Orchids," Vol. 1, Franco Pupulin, 2005, and "A Field Guide to Orchids of Costa Rica and Panamá," Robert L. Dressler, 1993.

The National Flower is the Guaria Morada.
Photo by Jeffrey Arguedas

Organic Produce

TOURISTS and residents fond of chemical-free foods will be pleased to note that every year more organic food products are available in Costa Rica.

ORGANIC farming is a growing movement as some small farmers look for alternatives to chemicals. Every day Costa Rica's national hospitals handle at least one case of pesticide poisoning, and recent cases of large pineapple farms letting pesticide run-off enter streams and rivers hasn't helped matters much.

But large scale agro-producers aside, small and mid-range organic farmers in Costa Rica have organized to share technical information, marketing data and organic certification.

The National Association of Organic Farmers emerged as the most important organization, and the government has responded to the organic movement by creating a special department of organic agriculture within the Ministry of Agriculture.

In the '90s organic-food products went big with production of organic bananas, cacao, coffee, pineapple, etc., for export to U.S. and European clients. EARTH University in Guápiles is dedicated to environmentally friendly agriculture.

Costa Ricans and visitors now can choose certified organic produce from two of the largest supermarkets in Costa Rica, Más x Menos and Automercado.

Also, farmers' markets increasingly are offering organic-produce stands. Try to visit one of the many markets where you can get a variety of tropical fruits and vegetables available in Costa Rica.

Farmers in Turrialba, a town on the Caribbean slope, east of San José, host two to three organic farmers' markets per week in the town center (usually on Saturday and Sunday).

In San José, on Saturday mornings, an organic market, with fruits, vegetables, coffee, cheese, even chicken, is north of the Paso Ancho traffic circle on the *circunvaluación* (Beltway). Going around the circle, there are two exits to the north. Take the first one. Go 400 m. north. At T- crossing, turn left, go 100 m., and then right. Go 200 m. It opens at 5 a.m. If you go after 8 a.m., most stuff is gone. Lots of veggies, coffee, cheese, fruits, bread, even chicken.

Kasasana (2224-0432), Ca. 37, a block and a half north of the Costa Rican North American Cultural Center in Barrio Dent), buys from those producers. You can get vegetables and fruit, but no cheese or chicken. You can place the order Friday night on costarica-organica.com and they'll reserve the stuff for you.

One organic shipper says, "Whatever you do, do not buy regular (i.e., non-organic) strawberries and other non-peelable stuff like that. The amount of pesticides used here (and in other countries in Central America) is incredible, and it's bad."

In central Escazú, organic produce can be found at the market held 8-11 a.m., Wednesdays, across from the Red Cross.

The international non-governmental organization Rain Forest Alliance organized an organic, sustainability pact between Nestlé and Costa Rican coffee-bean growers midyear 2009.

Under the new agreement, farmers who grow beans without the use of pesticides will receive a sustainability stamp from the Nestlé Company, which will allow the final product to sell for a higher price in stores.

Some restaurants in Costa Rica offer organic produce and make a note of it on their menus. One such restaurant in San José is the ever-popular Tin Jo, which specializes in Asian dishes.

The bulk of Costa Rica's organic crops includes bananas, cocoa and coffee, most of which are shipped to the United States and the European Union.

Schools

COSTA RICA'S academic and linguistic standards are reflected in its quality public and private schools, universities and language academies.

PRIVATE, ENGLISH-LANGUAGE, U.S. CALENDAR

American International School (2293-2567, **aiscr.com**), Ciudad Cariari, PK-12.

Blue Valley School (2215-2204, **bluevalley.ed.cr**), Escazú, K-11, both programs (U.S./Tico calendars).

Centro de Educación Creativa (2645-5161, **cloudforestschool.org**), Monteverde, Puntarenas, PK-11.

Country Day School (2289-0919, **cds. ed.cr**), Escazú, Daycare-12. Also Playa Brasilito, Guanacaste (2654-5042, **cdsgte. com**), PK-12.

European School (2261-0717, **euro peanschool.com**), San Pablo, Heredia, K-12.

International Christian School (2241-1445, **icscr.net**), Heredia, PK-12.

Liberty Christian Academy (2297-7533, **directora@lca.iglesiaunion.net**), Moravia, PK-9.

Lincoln School (2247-6600, **lincoln. ed.cr**), Barrio del Socorro, Santo Domingo de Heredia, 1,200 students, PK-12.

Marian Baker School (2273-0024, **mbs. ed.cr.com**), San Ramón de Tres Ríos, PK-12.

PRIVATE BILINGUAL, C.R. CALENDAR

Anglo American School (2279-2626, **angloamericano.ed.cr**), Concepción de Tres Ríos, 1.6 years-11th grade.

British School (2220-0131, **britsch@ racsa.co.cr**), K-12, Pavas.

Canadian International School (2272-7097, **colegiocanadiense@ice.co. cr**), Curridabat, Lomas de Ayarco Sur, French, English, Spanish (Latin after 7th grade), PK-11.

Centro Educativo Angloamericano (2279-2626, **angloamericano.ed.cr**), Concepción de Tres Ríos, PK-12.

Centro Educativo Bilingüe Pasos de Juventud (2237-4454, **pasosdejuventud. ed.cr**), Heredia, Daycare-5.

Ciudad Blanca School (International Christian School branch) (2665-0007, **cbscr@icscr.net**), Liberia, PK-6.

Colegio Humboldt (2232-1455, **humboldt.ed.cr**), Pavas, German, English, Spanish, PK-12.

Colegio Internacional SEK-Costa Rica (2272-5464, **sek.net**), Curridabat, Daycare-11.

Complejo Educativo Royal (2215-1742, **mirtabrito@royal.ed.cr**), Escazú, PK-11.

Escuela Santa Mónica (2241-3287, **informacion@santamonica.ed.cr**), Guadalupe, Daycare-6.

Escuela Japonesa (2235-9528, **escuelaj@racsa.co.cr**), Moravia, (7-15 years old), Japanese calendar.

Hebrew Day School (2296-6565, **www. chabadcostarica.com**), Rohrmoser, Daycare-6. English and Hebrew.

Instituto Educativo Moderno (2273-3414, **iemonline.org**), Concepción de Tres Ríos, PK-6.

Kiwi Learning Center (2282-6512, **kiwicr.com**), Santa Ana, English, Spanish, German, violin, piano, Daycare-4.

Liceo Franco-Costarricense (2273-6373, **franco.ed.cr**), road to Concepción de Tres Ríos. Most classes in French, Daycare-12.

Montessori Learning Center (2272-4997, **montessoricostarica.com**), Lomas de Ayarco Sur, Curridabat, Daycare-PK (1-5 yrs.).

Monteverde Friends School (2645-

5302, **mfschool.org**), Monteverde, Puntarenas, PK-12.

Pan American School (2298-5700 **panam.ed.cr**), San Antonio de Belén, Daycare-11.

St. Anthony School (**saintanthony. ed.cr**), Primary: 2297-4500/01/02) PK-6, Tibás; Secondary (2236-6362), Guadalupe.

St. Francis High School (2297-1704,**sfc@stfrancis.ed.cr**), Los Colegios, Moravia, K-11. English, Spanish, French.

St. Gregory School (2279-4444, **sgs. ed.cr**), Curridabat, Daycare-11.

St. Mary Primary School (2215-2133, **admisiones@saintmary.ed.cr**), Escazú, Daycare-11.

St. Paul School (2438-0818, **infoesc@ saintpaul.ed.cr**), San Rafael de Alajuela, Daycare-11.

Sistema Educativo Saint Clare (2279-8816, **saintclare.ed.cr**), San Juan de Tres Ríos, Daycare-11.

St. Patrick American School (2663-3839, **saintpatrick.ed.cr**), Puntarenas, PK-6.

Talarke School (2273-3353, **talarke school.com**), San Ramón de Tres Ríos, Daycare-6.

Teocali Academy (2666-0273, **aca demiateocali.ed.cr**), Liberia, Guanacaste, Daycare-11.

PUBLIC UNIVERSITIES

Costa Rican Technological Institute (**ITCR**) (2552-5333, **tec.cr**), Cartago, four-year, postgrad, also in San Carlos and San José.

Universidad Estatal a Distancia (**UNED**) (2224-1766, **uned.ac.cr**), Sabanilla, four-year, postgrad, study-at-home courses, postgrad, 30 centers around country, main campus in Sabanilla.

University of Costa Rica (**UCR**) (2511-4000, **ucr.ac.cr**), San Pedro, four-year, postgrad, doctorates, C.R.'s largest, campuses in San Ramón, Turrialba, Puntarenas, Guanacaste, Limón.

Universidad Nacional (**UNA**) (2277-3000, **una.ac.cr**), Heredia, four-year, post-

grad. Also in Pérez Zeledón, Guanacaste.

PRIVATE UNIVERSITIES

Universidad Fidélitas (2253-0262, **ufidelitas.ac.cr**), San Pedro Montes de Oca, four-year, postgrad.

Escuela de Agricultura de la Región Tropical Húmeda (**EARTH**) (2713-0000, earth.ac.cr), Guácimo, Limón, agricultural engineering.

Business Administration Institute (**INCAE**) (2437-2000, **incae.edu**), La Garita, Alajuela, Harvard-affiliated MBA.

Inter-American University of Costa Rica (2277-8000, **uinteramericana.edu**), Heredia, four-year, postgrad.

International University of the Americas (**UIA**) (2255-3444, **uia.ac.cr**), San José, four-year, postgrad.

Latin American University of Science and Technology (**ULACIT**) (2257-5767, **ulacit.ac.cr**), San José, four year, postgrad.

Universidad Americana (**UAM**) (2207-7000, **uam.ac.cr**), Los Yoses, Heredia, Cartago, four-year, postgrad.

Universidad Autónoma de Centro América (**UACA**) (2272-9100, **uaca.ac.cr**), Curridabat, Santa Cruz (Guanacaste), San Ramón, Guápiles, Ciudad Neily, four-year, postgrad and doctorates.

Universidad Católica de Costa Rica (2240-7272, **ucatolica.ac.cr**), Moravia, four-year, postgrad and doctorates.

Universidad Centroamericana de Ciencias Empresariales (**UCEM**), (2440-2090, **ucem.ac.cr**), Alajuela, four-year.

Universidad Creativa (2283-6880, **ucreativa.com**), graphic design, fashion design, interior design, architecture, Sabanilla.

University for Peace (2205-9000, **upeace.org**), Ciudad Colón, Master's.

Universidad Iberoamericana (**UNIBE**) (2297-2242, **unibe.ac.cr**), Tibás, four-year, postgrad: medicine, psychology, nursing, pharmacy.

Universidad Latina de Costa Rica (2283-2611, **ulatina.ac.cr**), Lourdes de

Montes de Oca, four-year, postgrad.

Universidad La Salle (2290-1010, **ulasalle.ac.cr**), south Sabana Park, four-year and postgrad: law, education, business administration., doctorate.

University of Medical Sciences (UCIMED) (2296-3944, **ucimed.com**), west Sabana, four-year, postgrad.

Universidad Veritas-Instituto de Español para Extranjeros (2283-4747, ext. 132, **uveritas.ac.cr**), Zapote, four-year, postgrad.

LANGUAGE SCHOOLS

(Note: The following schools are listed according to ambiance: City, Country/Rural, Beach, Mountain/Forest.)

City Schools

Academia Europea (2222-4307, **academia-europea.com**), San José, English, Spanish, French, German, Italian, Portuguese.

Academia Latinoamericana de Español (2224-9917, **alespanish.com**), San José. Also dancing classes.

Academia Profesional del Idioma Mandarín (APIM) (2253-4098, **api mcr@gmail.com**), San Pedro de Montes de Oca.

Alliance Française (2257-1944, **afsj.net**), San José; (2290-2705), Sabana Sur, French and Heredia.

Berlitz Institute (2253-9191, **berlitz.cr**), Santa Ana, San Pedro, San José downtown, Sabana.

Central American Institute for International Affairs (ICAI) (2233-8571, **expreso.co.cr**), San José.

Centro Lingüístico Conversa (2221-7649, **conversa.net**), San José (Ca. 38, Av. 3/5) and Santa Ana.

Centro Goethe de Costa Rica (2290-0958, **centrogoethe.com**), Pavas, German.

Colegio Victoria (2278-2536, **colegiovictoria.com**), Lourdes de Montes de Oca, Mandarin.

Costa Rica-Chinese Cultural Center (2834-7587, 2290-1247), Rohrmoser, Mandarin.

Costa Rican-North American Cultural Center (2207-7500, **cccncr.com**), San Pedro, North Sabana and Cartago.

Costa Rica Spanish Institute (COSI) (2234-1001, **cosi.co.cr**), Zapote.

Costa Rican Language Academy (CRLA) (2280-5834, **spanishandmore.com**), San Pedro.

Escuela Dante Alighieri (2225-3796, **dantealighierisj@racsa.co.cr**), Sabana (tel/fax: 2231-4305).

Forester Instituto Internacional (2225-3155, **fores.com**), Los Yoses.

ILISA Language Institute (2280-0700, **ilisa.com**), San Pedro.

Intercultura Language School (2260-8480, **interculturacostarica.com**), Heredia.

Instituto Británico (2225-0256, **institutobritanico.co.cr**), Los Yoses.

IECR Instituto de Español "Costa Rica" (2280-6622, **iespcr@racsa.co.cr**), homestays, Guadalupe.

Instituto Costarricense de Idiomas MPH S.A. (2431-0912, **iciidiomas.com**), Heredia.

Instituto di Lingua Italiana (2222-1990, **istitutobologna@ice.co.cr**), San José, Italian.

Institute for Central American Studies Mesoamerica Language Program (2253-3195, **mesoamericaonline.net**), internships, road to Sabanilla.

Instituto Profesional de Educación (IPE) (2238-3608), Heredia.

Instituto Universal de Idiomas (2257-0441, **universal-edu.com**), San José and Moravia.

Institute for Central Amer. Development Studies (ICADS) (2225-0508, **org, icads.org**), San Pedro de Montes de Oca.

INTENSA (2281-1818, **intensa.com**), Los Yoses, Escazú (288-4747) and Alajuela (442-3843).

Language Institute (ILERI) Escazú (2228-1687, **ilerispanishschool.com**), Escazú. Cooking/dance.

Lisa Tec (2239-2225, **lisatec1@hotmail.com**), Ciudad Cariari. Also in Northern Zone, Ciudad Quesada.

Schoolgirls line up for the annual parades on Independence Day: September 15.

Photo by Mayra Sojo

New Learning Academy (2283-3385, **newlearningcr.com**), Guadalupe.

Philology & Linguistics (UCR) (2207-4703, **lenguasmodernas.ucr.ac.cr**), San Pedro campus.

Country/Rural Schools

Academia Centroamericana de Español (2444-6161, **acce.co.cr**), Grecia. Also, dance and cooking.

Centro Panamericano de Idiomas (C.P.I.) (2645-5441, **cpi-edu.com**), San Joaquín de Flores, near San José. Also in Mountain Schools (Monteverde, 2645-5448, **montever@cpi-edu.com**) and Beach Schools (Flamingo, 2654-5002, **info@cpi-edu.com**). Also, Chinese.

Centro Para el Potencial Humano (CPH) (2282-9920, **spanishincostarica.com**), Santa Ana. Also, cooking and dance classes.

Montaña Linda Language School & Hostel (2533-3640, **mountanalinda.com**), Orosi Valley. Also, hotels & tours.

Rancho de Español (2438-0071, **ranchodeespanol.com**), La Guácima, Alajuela. Also, lodging, cooking/dance classes.

Spanish Language & Environmental Protection Ctr. (SEPA) (2770-1457, **sabalo@racsa.co.cr**), San Isidro de El General.

Beach Schools

Centro Panamericano de Idiomas (CPI) (2654-5001, **cpi-edu.com**), Flamingo Beach.

Costa Rica Spanish Institute (COSI) (2777-0021, **cosi.co.cr**), Manuel Antonio. Also see **City Schools**. Cooking/dance classes.

Escuela de Idiomas D'Amore (2777-1143, **escueladamore.com**), 3 km., Manuel Antonio. Also dance classes.

La Escuela del Sol (8358-5312, **spanishandsurf.com**), Montezuma.

Horizontes de Montezuma (2642-0534, **horizontes-montezuma.com**), Montezuma.

Sámara Language School (2656-0954, 2656-0127, **samaralanguage school.com**), Sámara, Guanacaste.

Rey de Nosara (2682-0215, **reyde nosara.itgo.com**), Nosara.

School of the World (2643-2462, **schooloftheworld.org**), Jacó, surfing, photography, art.

Wayra Spanish Institute (2653-0617, **spanish-wayra.co.cr**), Tamarindo, Guanacaste.

Mountain/Forest Schools

Centro Panamericano de Idiomas (2645-5441, 2645-6349, **cpi-edu.com**), Monteverde, homestays, volunteer programs.

SPECIAL COURSES

Tropical Dendrology in Costa Rica (2291-0862, 2231-1236, **hjimenez.org**), field identification of tropical plants, 2-wk. course in four different life zones (Central Valley, Monteverde, Guanacaste, Northern Zone), $1,600, inc/all expenses in country.

Shopping

COSTA RICA offers a good selection of quality souvenirs that provide the answer for the folks back home.

TWO of Costa Rica's signature products, such as oxcarts and rocking chairs, may look big but several stores will disassemble them for shipment. Many souvenir stores in the capital dot the streets around Parque Morazán. Another group congregates in the northeastern suburb of Moravia near the Colegio María Inmaculada, two blocks behind the city's church.

At supermarkets, food and beverage items make fine souvenirs, and you'll find better prices than in souvenir shops and way better prices than at the airport. Coffee is a guaranteed crowd pleaser.

The Central Market sells the high-grown Café Poás, will vacuum-pack it for you and it's half the price of quality coffee anywhere else.

The coffee stall also sells those yummy chocolate-covered coffee beans -- again at a great savings. Café Rica is the Costa Rican response to Kahlúa coffee liqueur.

A bottle of tangy Salsa Lizano lets you take a bit of Costa Rica to your kitchen. It comes in light-weight plastic bottles -- all sizes. Refried beans come in very small, easy-to-pack sizes.

Hot sauces are also a nice *típico* purchase. The following are a few shopping options in and around San José. Unless otherwise specified, stores are open daily.

Amir Art Gallery (2256-9445, **amirart. com**), Av. 5, Ca. 5, across from Holiday Inn. Original paintings, wood carvings, 9-6 p.m., closed Sun., for appointment, 8997-8432.

Arte Latino (2258-3306), Av. 1, Ca. 5. Latin American paintings, weavings and wood sculptures. Focus on primitivism and expressionism.

Artesanías la Rueda, (2297-2736), 50 m. north of Colegio María Inmaculada, Moravia. Beautiful ceramics, woodcarvings, rocking chairs, oxcarts. Helpful staff, 8 a.m.-7 p.m.

Artesanías Morazán (2222-1892), Av. Ctrl., Ca. 7. Hammocks, shirts, jewelry, woods, leathers, 9 a.m.-6:30 p.m.

Biesanz Woodworks (2289-4337, **biesanz.com**), Bello Horizonte, Escazú. Beautiful wood designs. Environmentally conscious, uses wood from own plantation. Works are often gifts from Costa Rican presidents to foreign dignitaries. Closed Sun.

Boutique Annemarie (2221-6707), Hotel don Carlos, Ca. 9, Av. 9. One of the best for wood, jewelry, ceramics, crystal, 8 a.m.-6 p.m., weekdays; 8:30 a.m.-5:30 p.m., weekends. Sells The Tico Times.

Casa Tica, El Cafetal & Morpho, Juan Santamaría Airport, Alajuela. High-quality souvenirs, sells The Tico Times. Managed jointly by Café Britt, Librería Internacional. Open for all departing flights.

Central Market, Av. Ctrl./1, Ca. 6/8, great typical shopping. Go early, have breakfast. Mostly shopping for locals, but a few souvenir stands congregate near entrances. Closed Sun.

Congo (2228-6423, 2201-8017, **cos taricacongo.com**), Multiplaza, Guachipelín, Escazú. (2280-0750), Multiplaza del Este, Curridabat, 10 a.m.-9 p.m. Wood works, sculpture, ceramics, paintings.

El Patio Amón (2258-7740), Ave. 11, Ca. 3bis/5. Good quality souvenirs, woodwork, t-shirts. 9 a.m.-7 p.m.

Galería Namu (2256-3412, **galerianamu.com**), Av. 7, Ca. 5/7. Indigenous and local arts and crafts, supports the artisans.

Panamanian baskets made of black palm-leaf chunga, animals carved from ivory-like tagua nut, Nicaragua, Honduran handicrafts, 9 a.m.-6:30 p.m., closed Sun.

Gold Museum (2243-4217, **museos delbancocentral.org**), Ca. 5, Av. Ctrl/2. Pre-Columbian-themed jewelry, art, t-shirts, exclusive designs, coin-, bill-themed key chains, notebooks, mousepads, vintage currency.

Hotel Grano de Oro (2255-3322, **hotel-granodeoro.com**), Ca. 30, Av. 2/4, indigenous and other arts and crafts, wood carvings, fabrics, distinctive souvenirs.

Inti (2258-7682), Ca. 5, Av. 1/3, 9 a.m.-6:30p.m. Woods, paintings.

Isidro Vargas (2249-0886), 500 m. southeast, 700 m. northwest of Centro de Ancianos, Brasil de Mora, near Ciudad Colón. Beautiful woodwork using recycled or sustainable wood. Also items crafted from palm, lovely pejibaye goblets. Closed Sat.-Sun.

La Casona, C. 2, Av. Ctrl/1. Souvenirs, arts, crafts in rickety two-story building, fun to browse, flea-market atmosphere.

La Ranita Dorada (2256-6808), Av. 1, Ca. 9/11. Oil paintings, wood sculptures, t-shirts, crafts, sells The Tico Times.

Mundo de Recuerdos (2240-8990), across from Colegio María Inmaculada, Moravia. Huge shop, everything under one roof, 9 a.m-6 p.m.

Nico-yatle (2228-7540), 75 m. south of Scotiabank, San Rafael, Escazú. Exclusive jewelry, leather, craft designs, 9:30 a.m.-1:30 p.m., 3-6 p.m. Closed Sun.

Pura Vida (2221-3895), Ca. 5, Av. 1/3, 9 a.m-7 p.m. Woods, Boruca masks, t-shirts.

Randall Rodríguez (2443-2746), La Ribera de Belén. Beautiful custom-made ironwork. By appointment.

Sarchí, an hour's drive northwest of San José, an entire village dedicated to creating artifacts primarily from wood: oxcarts, souvenirs, chairs, tables, bedsteads, etc.

Souvenirs Balmoral (2223-2669), Ca. 7, Av. 1/3., 9:30 A.M.-6 p.m. Woods, t-shirts, sells The Tico Times.

Souvenirs Diana (2255-3606), Ca. 5, Av. 1/3. Woods, art.

Souvenirs Morazán (2222-1892), Ca. 5, Av. 1/3. Fine woods, embroidery, t-shirts.

Suraska (2222-0129), Av. 3, Ca. 5. Oil paintings, delicate porcelain orchids, miniature marimbas.

Theaters

ALL shows are in Spanish except for the English-language Little Theatre Group that puts on plays at the Laurence Olivier Theatre and the Dominical Little Theatre Group on the Pacific. Theaters are in the San José area unless otherwise noted.

Dionisio (2277-1600, 2237-1750) Café Britt, Heredia, 500 m. north, 400 m. west of Automercado, road to Barva.

Dominical Little Theatre (8308-8855, **dominical.biz\theater**), Dominical.

Eugene O'Neill Theater (2207-7554, **centrocultural.cr**), Costa Rican-North American Cultural Center, Ca. 37, Av. 1/3, Barrio Dent.

Little Theatre Group (8858-1446, **lit-tletheatregroup.org**), community theatre, open to all, four to five plays a year. Open House, 7- p.m., first Monday of month, at Laurence Olivier, Av. 2, Ca. 28.

Melico Salazar (2233-5424, **melico salazar.go.cr**), Av. 2, Ca. Ctrl.

Montes de Oca (2511-4595, **danzau pro-duccion@gmail.com**), across from Carlos Monge Library, University of Costa Rica.

Municipal de Alajuela (2431-5286), Ala-

The National Theater is one of the country's jewels. A must-see, even if you only check out the lobby and visit the charming café inside.

Photo by Lindy Drew

uela, north side of Juan Santamaría Park.

National Auditorium (2258-4929, **museocr.com**), plays, concerts, and dances, Children's Museum, Ca. 4/Av. 9.

Oscar Fessler (Taller Nacional de) 2221-1273, **tallernac@racsa.co.cr**), 200 m. north, 150 m. east of Santa Teresita Church, Barrio Escalante.

Sala de la Calle 15 (2223-7482, **quilodejo@yahoo.es**), Av. 2, Ca. 15, in front of Plaza de la Democracia.

Teatro 1887 (2221-6325, 2257-5524, **direccioncnt@gmail.com**), Ca. 11, Av. 3/7.

Teatro Arlequín (2221-5485, **arlequin-cr@gmail.com**), Ca. 15, Av. 2/6.

Teatro Atahualpa del Cioppo (2277-3386, **producre@una.ac.cr**), 800 m. northeast of Burger King, Heredia.

Teatro Chaplin (2221-0812, 8832-2516), Av. 12, Ca. 11/13.

Teatro de Bellas Artes (2511-8930, **teatro.ucr.ac.cr**), School of Fine Arts, University of Costa Rica, San Pedro.

Teatro de la Danza (2222-2974, **comdanza@mcj.go.cr**), Ca. 11, Av. 3/7.

Teatro de San José (2222-2624), Ca. 15, Av. 8/10.

Teatro del Ángel (2222-8258), Av. Ctrl.,

Ca. 13/15, Cuesta de Moras.

Teatro del Conservatorio Castella (2232-0265), north of Sabana Park, next to Nissan Agency.

Teatro Giratablas (2253-6001, **giratablas.com**), across from Kentucky Fried Chicken, Barrio La California.

Teatro José Joaquín Vargas Calvo (2221-1329, **nacional.go.cr**), Av. 2, Ca. 3/5.

Teatro La Comedia (2233-2170), Av. Ctrl., Ca. 13/15.

Teatro La Esquina (2257-0223, **laesquina@yahoo.com**), Av. 1, Ca. 23.

Teatro La Máscara (2222-4574, 8365-5368), Ca. 13, Av. 2/4.

Teatro Laurence Olivier (2222-1034, **garbfilm@racsa.co.cr**), Av. 2, Ca. 28.

Teatro Lucho Barahona (2223-5972), Ca. 11, Av. 6/8.

Teatro Moliére (2222-5281, **moliere@costarricense.cr**), Av. 2, Ca. 13.

Teatro National (2221-9417, **nacional.go.cr**), Av. 2, Ca. 3/5.

Teatro Torres (2256-4295, **torresvalverde@hotmail.com**), Av. 8, Ca. 11/13

Teatro Universitario (2511-6720, **.ucr.ac.cr**), behind Edificio Saprissa, San Pedro, Montes de Oca.

Medical Overview

THE Costa Rican health-care system founded in 1943, provides good services, and is the envy of much of the developing world.

COSTA Rica's Social Security System, or Caja (short for Caja Costarricense de Seguro Social), the government health-care system, is indeed the envy of much of the developing world. But dwindling resources, long waits and red tape dog the system. It may require a wait, especially if you seek care for a non-threatening condition, but you'll get treated eventually; clinics and hospitals are in most communities.

Many foreigners patronize the superb private health care system, with its large number of providers trained both here and abroad. Services cost more, but you're paying for efficient, personalized service sometimes lacking in the Caja institutions.

The standard of living and hygiene is relatively high, with long life expectancies, low infant-mortality rates, and near-complete access to potable water: hallmarks of the country's devotion to well-being. But the typical diet -- high in sugar, fat and cholesterol -- has led to alarming levels of diabetes and hypertension.

Few tourists bother getting any vaccinations and most do not encounter any major health problems here. Your health-care provider may suggest preventive measures if you plan to stay over six weeks or travel in remote areas or come in contact with animals. The U.S. National Centers for Disease Control (**cdc.gov**) recommends vaccinations against hepatitis A and typhoid in such cases. The most recent concern is the spread of the AH1N1 flu that has caused 37 deaths in Costa Rica, primarily people with poor health or suffering from asthma or lung problems. The Ministry of Health confirmed that as of September, there were 1,315 cases, including the nation's president. Labs around the world are working on creating a vaccine for this flu, in the meantime, wearing a surgical mask when traveling by air or in crowded places, is not a bad idea.

No vaccines exist for Costa Rica's most prevalent public-health problem, dengue.

Dengue fever, transmitted by the Aedes aegypti mosquito, remains the country's most worrisome health concern, although case numbers have shown a reduction. The Ministry of Health concedes that dengue can be controlled, but likely will never be eradicated here. Warning signs include severe body aches and flu symptoms that may last several days. A second infection occasionally can be fatal. Dengue is a slight risk, especially May-Nov. The Caribbean coast, Central Pacific and northern Chorotega regions see the most cases; instances have also popped up in the Central Valley but with less frequency.

Mosquitoes also transmit malaria, much less common here than dengue. Pockets on the Caribbean coast and the Northern Zone are periodic problem areas. Precautions focus on avoiding being bitten in the first place: avoid stagnant water, wear long sleeved clothing, especially at dusk, use a repellent containing DEET, and sleep under mosquito nets. Your health-care provider may recommend a preventive pre/post-trip regimen of chloroquine against strains of malaria that occur in Costa Rica.

It comes down to hygiene and a healthy dose of common sense to avoid traveler's diarrhea, the most common ailment to afflict tourists and, less so, hepatitis. Do NOT buy food from street vendors. Stick with bottled water in remote areas or port cities; the rest of the country has potable water. Peel and thoroughly wash fruits and vegetables with potable water before eating. Stick to hot, well-cooked meals. Wash your hands frequently, especially before eating. If diarrhea lays you low, rest, drink rehydration solution (suero oral, available at pharmacies) and eat light foods.

Alternative Healing

HEALTH, when traveling or living abroad, takes on a whole new meaning and importance. While Costa Rica's socialized health care system and internationally recognized private hospitals serve the needs of many, others may be looking for something different.

FOR those seeking alternative health care, both physical and spiritual, many practitioners, spas, retreat homes, centers and products can be found in the Central Valley and also scattered throughout the country.

Chiropractors: Dianne Rowley, integrated chiropractics and body work (2266-0123, 8382-0519). Yolanda Camacho Kortman, of **Vida Quiropráctica** (2443-3276, qpvida@hotmail.com), Alajuela.

Holistic Centers:
AmaTierra: near Puriscal, offers aromatherapy, massage, yoga, acupuncture, herbology (2419-0110, **amatierra@gmail.com**).
Casa de Cultura Alternativa (2224-5691, gruposiris.com), alternative lifestyle guidance, Feldenkreis method, acupuncture, bioenergetics yoga, Ayurvedic medicine.
Clínica la Paz (2225-2620, **labscholler@hotmail.com**), Dr. Christine Scholler and resident homeopaths, lab, pharmacy.
Clínica Victoria (2224-0654, **yu@clinicavictoria.com**), Dr. Ricky Yu and other specialists in a wide array of fields, onc/acupuncture, nutrition, psychology, gynecology, internal medicine, neurology, and others.
Harmony Center for Holistic Medicine (2288-4658, **harmonycenters.com**), Escazú, holistic facial treatment, acupuncture, massage, all-incl. health and beauty tourist packages.
Kasasana (2253-8322, **kasasana.com**), Barrio Dent, yoga, aromatherapy, meditation, nutrition counseling, massage.
Massage: Bárbara Adams of **Secret Gar-**den Massage (2228-1049, **secretgardenmassage@yahoo.com**), deep tissue, craniosacral therapy, reflexology, Tsu Ya massage, therapeutic massage, physical therapy. Carolyn Reilly (2283-7383, **casa reilly@hotmail.com**), Tsu Ya massage, aromatherapy, reflexology. Rebalancing with Jasmine Isabel Cabrera, certified rebalancer and healer (8916-6564, **jasmin ecabrera@yahoo.com**).

Midwifery: Midwives cannot "officially" manage births; however prenatal care and natural birth information from Uva Meiner (2268-2127, 8383-7326, **uvaearth@ice.co.cr**). Childbirth education at Aman (Natalie and Ansu, 2224-5806, mamasalnacimiento.com), Dr. Carlos Orosco.

Naturopaths: Pedro Bolaños (2253-7974 San Pedro, 2290-2938 Pavas, **pedrobol@yahoo.com**), acupuncture, orthopedics, nutrition, general and natural medicine. Dr. Edgardo Maya Bohorquez (2232-3047, **mayacanconsultores@gmail.com**), natural medicine and psychotherapy. María Hoffmann (2268-4646, **mariahoffmann@yahoo.de**), natural medicine.

Psychology: Ana Luisa Monge (2203-3439, **analu_mn@yahoo.com**), astrologer and psychologist.

Psychotherapy and Body Work: Mercedes Daneri (2289-3687, **mercedesdaneri.com**), Escazú, cranial sacral balancing, Rolfing, acupressure, color hypnotherapy, massage, lymphatic draining.
Reiki: María Jiménez, of the **Magisa Institute** (2272-4279), naturopathic heal-

ing, seminars, lectures.

T'ai Chi: Elliot Greenspan (2282-4973, **eliotg@racsa.co.cr**), classes in t'ai chi chuan and chi gung. **Chen T'ai ji Academy** (001-786-2488-6128, number in U.S., **chentaijiinternational.com**), Pavones, vacations, retreats, training camps. Ligia Salazar (225-4411, **muevete.co.cr** or **taichicr@gmail.com**), t'ai chi chuan classes in San Pedro and Escazú.

Therapies:
Aqua Therapy: Ocean Divers (2253-2198), aqua aerobics, hydrotherapy.

Flower Therapy: Elsa V. Vanegas (2253-8636, 812-8934, **centrotransfor mar.com**). Practitioner Marina Rivera, also psychologist (8377-1983) Ana Orozco (2224-2876), of the **Natural Therapy Association of Costa Rica** (2224-2876): flower therapy, gem therapy, life systems, bio-feedback, Reiki.

Dance therapy: Condanza (2233-1124, 8386-5175, **estudiocondanza@hot mail.com**), Av. 3, Ca. 25/29, for releasing stress.

Nueva Era (2228-6712), physical therapy.

Lotus (2288-4874), personal growth facilitation, re-education for mind, body, spirit.

Yoga: Vimala Joan Martha (8393-0995), yoga/meditation classes, new "gentle yoga" class for people with limited physical abilities and the elderly. **Turya** (2289-7524, **turya.info**), yoga instructor Janine Fafard, Kripalu yoga for relaxation and healing, stress management workshops and soul surrender therapy. **Shivshaktiyoga,** (837-3183, 2235-7215, **shivshaktiyoga.com**, **shivshakti@gmail.com**), yoga center, based on Ashtanga yoga, in Guadalupe.

Kapoli Center (2228-1350), Escazú, yoga/meditation classes, various types of therapy, workshops, Ayurvedic medicine. **Vajra Sol** (2203-2694, **vajrasoltravel.com**), adventure travel company for yoga-minded, outdoor nature enthusiasts, 10-day itineraries, inc/daily yoga sessions in pristine settings, adventure activities, custom-

ized trips for yoga teachers w/own group. **Krama Yoga Center** (2215-3535, **kra may oga.com**), in Escazú, with Esteban Salazar offers Vinyasa Flow, hot yoga, pre-natal yoga, restorative yoga, yoga for kids, t'a chi, etc. . **Sound Body YOGA®** (2203-0082, **relax@soundbodyYOGA.com**), Dr. Free dom and Leela, yoga lifestyle coaches.

Health Supplies: Bio Land, organic cookies, cereal, supplements, toiletries available in supermarkets. **Nature's Sun shine Products,** (2283-5340, San Pedro 2225-8062, Paseo Colón, **nspsanpedro@ice co.cr**), imported vitamins, health and beauty products, free lectures on holistic health and lifestyle topics. **GNC,** multiple locations in San José and Central Valley malls/commercial centers, vitamins and supplements. **Bio Salud**, in Multiplaza Escazú and Plaza del Sol, Curridabat, vitamins, herbs, health foods. **Simbiosis**, Plaza Mayor, Rohrmoser, vitamins, flower remedies, health foods. La Buena Hierba (2233-0363), Ca. Ctrl., Av.6/8, macrobiotic products, herb teas.

Unity Community (2203-4411, **unity costarica.org**), non-denominational, English-speaking, inspirational center offers courses, support, spiritual gatherings in Piedades de Santa Ana. Check out **Miracles** bookstore for self help, esoteric, spirituality titles.

Elsewhere: Holistic health options can also be found in other areas of Costa Rica. Check with hotels for services in the area.

Hacienda del Sol (8828-4080, **become tocostarica.com**), yoga retreats and teacher training course, certified rebalancing bodywork training, cleansing, in San Jua nillo, north of Nosara.

Montezuma Yoga (2642-0076, 8811 7582, **montezumayoga.com**), yoga classes at Hotel Los Mangos.

Nosara Yoga Retreat in Playa Guione (2682-0071, **nosarayoga.com**), yoga instructor training, also offers yoga retreats.

PachaMama (2289-7081, +1 646 863

4 74, call between 11 a.m.-1 p.m., achamama.com), meditation center and co-spiritual community near Nosara, Guanacaste, silent retreats, yoga retreats, ourses in shiatsu massage, ecology.

Posada Nature Mountain Retreat 2779-1053, **posadanatura.com**), Central Pacific Coast, on Naranjo River, river wimming, saltwater pool, saltwater acuzzi, yoga and movement. Vegetarian, egan or local cuisine. Kitchen is stocked or Raw-Food chefs. Retreats include: mandala painting and nature immersion, new moon nature synergy, somadance, raw ood and mandala workshop, theta healing /raw food and music, more.

Pura Vida (2767-7375, **puravidaspa. om**), Alajuela, yoga, meditation, retreats.

Shangri La Bio Spa Costa Rica (8313 0512 **ShangriLaBioSpaCostaRica.com**), yoga, fitness center, meditation, gym, nutrition, counseling, rehabilitation treatment, beach.

Private ecological sanctuary bordering Chirripó National Park, the **Blue Mountain Resort** (2742-5278, **shaolin-wahnam-center.org**) hosts the **Shaolin Wahnam Institute for Latin America**, which offers organic meals, tours, meditations, Qi gong, Tai Chi, Sufu Wong courses, wellness yoga retreats and workshops for corporate events, groups, weddings, vacation travel tours, surgery recovery and individuals seeking personal yoga lifestyle coaching, healthy back and relaxation programs in Costa Rica.

Hospitals

MEDICAL care in Costa Rica is generally good, evidenced in the fact t attracts 25,000 tourists each year looking to take advantage of cheaper medical procedures.

MANY doctors are trained and educated in the United States and Europe and get practice in a wide range of cases in the public hospitals.

Costa Rica offers free medical care to all ax-paying residents. If you don't pay into he Social Security system (*Caja*), you risk unning a high tab for use of the public system, with consultations costing as much as $80 and overnights as much as $770. Patients are usually required to pay all fees up front. In rare cases, those who cannot afford public-hospital fees may be able to pay less.

Consultations at a private hospital begin at $60 and the basic overnight stay ate starts at $260 for a room, $350 for a suite. Tests and medications increase the price. Some international insurance is accepted, but check with the hospital.

Costa Rica's few private hospitals congregate mostly in San José and the Central

Valley. Public hospitals are found in most communities of any size.

PRIVATE HOSPITALS:

Clínica Bíblica, Ca. Ctrl./1, Av. 14/16, San José (2522-1000, **clinicabiblica.com**)

Clínica Santa Rita, Av. 8, Ca. 15/17, San José (2221-6433)

Hospital Católica, San Antonio, Guadalupe (2246-3000, **hospitallacatolica.com**)

Hospital CIMA, Escazú (2208-1000, **hospitalcima.com**)

PUBLIC HOSPITALS:

San José/Central Valle

Hospital Calderón Guardia, San José (2212-1000)

Hospital México, La Uruca
(2242-6700)
Hospital de las Mujeres, San José
(2523-5900)
Hospital de los Niños, San José
(2222-0122)
Hospital San Juan de Dios, San José
(2257-6282)
Hospital San Rafael, Alajuela
(2436-1000)
Hospital San Vicente de Paul, Heredia
(2261-0091)
Hospital Max Peralta, Cartago
(2550-1999)
Hospital San Francisco de Asís,
Grecia (2494-6444)
Hospital de Upala, Alajuela
(2470-0181)
Hospital Carlos Luis Valverde Vega,
San Ramón (2456-9700)

Caribbean Slope

Hospital Dr. Tony Facio, Limón
(2758-2222)
Hospital de Guápiles, Guápiles
(2710-6801)
Hospital William Allen, Turrialba
(2556-4343)

Northern Zone

Hospital de Upala, Upala
(2470-0058)
Hospital de Los Chiles, Los Chiles
(2471-2000)

Guanacaste

Hospital Enrique Baltodano, Liberia
(2666-0011)
Hospital La Anexión, Nicoya
(2685-8400)

Central Pacific

Hospital Monseñor Sanabria, Puntarenas
(2630-8000)
Hospital Dr. Max Terán Valls, Quepos
(2777-0922)

Southern Zone

Hospital de Osa Tomás Casas Casajús,
Ciudad Cortés (2788-8003)
Hospital de Ciudad Neilly, Brunca
Region, (2783-4111)
Hospital Dr. Fernando Escalante
Pradilla, San Isidro de El General
(2785 0700)
Hospital San Vito de Coto Brus,
San Vito (2773-3103)

12 Steps to Sobriety

Alcoholics Anonymous groups meet daily throughout the country. It's a good idea to call first.

Escazú, 2228-1049.
Jacó, 2637-8824.
Heredia, Laura, 2267-7466.
Liberia, 2666-5821.
Manuel Antonio, Jennifer, 2777-2572, 2777-1548, 2777-2592.
Puerto Viejo, Limón, 8811-3448

San José, 2222-1880
(known as Anchor Club also holds Narcotics Anonymous meetings), Av. 6, Ca. 1, 2nd floor, Maryland Building.
Tamarindo, 2653-0897, ellenzoe@aol.com.
Zancudo, 2776-0012.
For more info, check The Tico Times Calendar.

Medical Insurance

OPTIONS for health insurance in Costa Rica are both simple and complex at the same time. You have few choices: the state holds a monopoly on insurance.

THE complexity stems from the same factor: few foreign health insurance plans will cover you in Costa Rica.

All salary-earning Costa Rican residents have access to treatment and coverage extends to dependents in the public health-care system via their contributions through payroll taxes and deductions to the Costa Rican Social Security System (Caja Costarricense de Seguro Social). The **Residents' Association of Costa Rica** (ARCR, 2233-1017, **arcr.net**) can help its members register for services. The **National Insurance Institute** (INS), the state insurance entity since 1924, offers health insurance packages, which can be used to supplement Caja coverage, or as a substitute for those without Caja benefits.

Premiums for all INS policies vary by age, sex and health. Clinics and hospitals can pre-certify care to avoid the requirement to pay upfront and wait for reimbursement. Otherwise, the patient pays outpatient fees and is reimbursed in three to six weeks. INS insurance experts **Garrett y Asociados** (2233-2455, **egurosgarrett.com**) speak English and help clients get coverage. The agency's website offers information in detail. **nsuranceCostaRica.info**.

Foreigners, regardless of residence status, are eligible for **INS Plan 16**, the long-standing, basic *colón*-denominated policy with four levels of coverage, and yearly limits of ₡4-10 million ($7,000-19,000 at current exchange rates, not very high if you require much care). Annual premiums run $330-$2,600. Premiums for workplace policies are about 20% less.

Better coverage (with higher premiums) is available to residents through more

Irises are healthy in the humidity here.
Photo by Chrissie Long

stable dollar-denominated policies: **INS Medical Regional** (up to $200,000 annual coverage; $60,000 for those over 69) is valid for coverage in Costa Rica and Central America. Premiums range from $526-$1,687.

INS Medical Internacional (up to $2 million annual coverage) provides worldwide coverage, with premiums ranging from $323-$3,331, depending also on deductibles chosen.

At age 70, coverage goes down to 30%, i.e., $60,000 for the Regional plan, and $600,000 for the International plan. Group reductions of about 10% apply for workplace policies.

Your home country insurance companies may provide some coverage at private hospitals. Check with the facility.

Pharmacies

COSTA RICAN pharmacies are smaller than the mega-pharmacie found in the United States and deal primarily in medications and health-related items only.

ANTIBIOTICS, drugs for sleep, anxiety or mental disorders, and so-called vanity drugs (for erectile dysfunction, baldness or weight loss) require a prescription; most other maintenance medications are available over the counter at prices comparable to Canada and Western Europe. Bring extra supplies of meds from home if you depend on less-common medications. Some pharmacies, including those in the metro-area private hospitals, keep late hours, offer home delivery or stay open 24 hours. (See **Emergency Contacts**.)

A few of the chain pharmacies in Costa Rica are:

Farmacia Chavarría (2258-6204, **far maciachavarria.com**), Av. 2, Ca. 7/9, San José (2258-8453); Alajuela (2441-1231), Desam-parados (2218-0880), Heredia (2263-4668).

Farmacia Fischel (2519-0000, **fischel.c cr**), Ca. 2, Av. 3, San José, plus 75 branche around Costa Rica under Fischel, Catedr and Farmatica names in: Alajuela, Alajuelit Cartago, Ciudad Quesada, Curridaba Desamparados, Escazú, Guadalupe, Hatill Heredia, La Fortuna, Liberia, Moravi Nicoya, Pavas, Playa Herradura, Puntarena Quepos, Rohrmoser, Sabanilla, San Antoni de Belén, San Pedro, San Sebastián, Sant Ana, Tamarindo, Tibás, Tres Ríos.

Farmacia Sucre (2233-6380, **farmacia sucre.com**), Ca. 1, Av. 2, San José, Guadalup (2258-3028), Pavas (2291-5548), Moravi (2240-8114), Curridabat (2271-1803 Tibás (2241-4018), San Francisco de D Ríos (2286-2191).

Senior Care

MOST Costa Rican communities of any size have an hogar de ancia nos (loosely translated, an "old folks' home"), all licensed by th Ministry of Health.

A few services stand out for their bilingual staff and are accustomed to dealing with foreigners.

Some offer assisted living services (help with activities of daily living, such as bathing, dressing or transportation). Others offer complete skilled-nursing care. Some proffer such services at their own facilities, others through home visits.

Casa Sol (2288-0213, 2288-0209, up hill from Escazú town center), 100 m from Los Balcones, senior day-care center run by Jenny Mora, a psychologist with a degree in gerontology, atmosphere is filled with fun, education and caring staff.

Finca Futuro Verde (2494-5187, **finca futuroverde.com**), Rincón de Salas, Gre cia, in-facility, assisted-living service medical staff on call.

HomeCare (2236-8252, **arnie615@ho mail.com**), 20 years experience in direc patent care including personal groomin medications, assisting with special need taking people to doctor appointment shopping, running errands, etc.

Homewatch Caregivers (2201-526 **homewatchcaregiverscr.com**), hom healthcare, services ranging from compan ionship to 24-hr. skilled-nursing care, fra chise of U.S. corporation.

José Pujol Martí Assisted Living Residence, Ribera de Belén (outskirts of San Antonio de Belén). 2239-0295. Luz, the secretary, does not speak English. $1000/month includes TV, broad band access, utilities, laundry and house cleaning. Apartments are unfurnished, but furniture is available. Also access to Spanish Country Club.

Villa Alegría Skilled Nursing Center (2433-8590, **villaalegria@gmail.com**), Barrio San José, Alajuela, complete in-facility, skilled-nursing and assisted-living care.

Medical Tourism

TEETH to Tummy: from around the world, people come for low-cost, high-quality "renewals."

THE Costa Rican Tourism Institute (ICT) estimates that some 10,000 visitors come here for health reasons, data-based on surveys it has conducted and the number is expected to grow.

With dental insurance a costly add-on option in many countries, and with cosmetic surgery not covered at all by most health-insurance companies, the incentive exists in those two areas in particular to look for lower-cost alternatives.

Rates for malpractice insurance are so low here, few practitioners even carry it. That cost savings is passed on to the patient, but not at the expense of quality; the majority of Costa Rican practitioners in these fields have also studied abroad and are quite capable.

Elective cosmetic-surgery procedures such as rhinoplasty, breast implantation or liposuction performed in Costa Rica often cost one-third to one-half their corresponding North American or European costs. The Internet and the ability to transmit photos online have been a boon to cosmetic surgeons, allowing them to do pre- and post-operative online consultations.

Offering the chance to recuperate anonymously, a cottage industry of small resorts has sprung up to tend to post-operative recovery needs.

Clínica Bíblica (2522-1000, **hospitalbiblicamedicaltourism.com**) has an entire floor dedicated to medical tourists, arranging travel packages for them in conjunction with their treatment.

Dental work can be a bit trickier to fit into a single two-week vacation. Many practitioners will, within reason, work with you to accommodate your schedule if possible. (Some dentists in Costa Rica count 70% of their patients as foreign visitors.) Expect to pay about $85 for a filling, $250 for laser whitening, or $250-650 for a crown; prices are one-third to one-half their back-home rates. A few dentists have begun to offer packages that include hotel stays and transfers.

To find a practitioner, look for advertisers each week in The Tico Times. Embassies often maintain lists of English-speaking doctors, but they will not make recommendations. (Your embassy's aid is intended for emergency situations only.)

Verify that your practitioner belongs to a respective medical or dental association. All physicians must be members of the **Costa Rican Doctors and Surgeons Association** (2232-3433, **medicos.sa.cr**). Plastic surgeons must also belong to the **Costa Rican Association of Plastic, Reconstructive and Aesthetic Surgery** (ACCPRE, **accpre.org**). Dentists must be members of the **Costa Rican Dental Surgeons Association** (2256-3100, **colegiodentistas.org**).

These associations provide lists based on specialty, but do not make recommendations. Additionally, check out websites designed to help people with medical/dental questions: **surgerycostarica.net**, **arrivacostarica.com/dentist**.

In any case, when you go back home, your friends will say, "Costa Rica was good for you."

Real Estate: The Inside Story

THE economic crisis of 2008 cooled off the red-hot real-estate market here, some of the most coveted property in Central America for over a decade. For the first time during the decade, property purchases in the country did not increase in number.

"THE market has been so down," said Michael Newhouse, who has worked as a realtor in Costa Rica for four years.

"Instead of people coming to Costa Rica to buy homes, many are finding better deals in places such as Phoenix, Arizona, in the U.S."

But Newhouse, like other real estate company owners, remains optimistic for a return to growth in the years to come. And how could he not be?

With property that lines the pristine beaches of the Pacific and Atlantic oceans, in addition to property offerings in the mountains and forests of the countryside, hotels, retirement communities and homes are continuing to pop up around the country.

In the spring of 2009, Henry Kaufman, former Wall Street mogul, put his faith into the Costa Rican real-estate market with his creation of a $16 million, 17-acre, senior-living facility in Santa Ana, west of San José.

Kaufman feels Costa Rica is an ideal for U.S. retirees to pursue residence in their later years.

"We know what happened on Wall Street and in the banking community this year," Kaufman said.

"I think it is prudent for North Americans to think about the near future... Costa Rica offers inexpensive living, cheap healthcare and access to beautiful beaches and nature."

When asked why he chose to invest in the Central Valley, Kaufman said the Santa Ana location keeps residents near the cultural center of the country, while beach resorts, for example, are too far removed from the populace.

Other development companies also reinforced that, despite the down year for property purchases, Costa Rican real estate remains a worthy investment.

In September, Caspi International Inc., a U.S. development firm, announced plans to build a 14-story, all-glass oceanfront condominium tower in the Pacific port city of Puntarenas.

The $120 million project, known as Genesis Puntarenas, claims the world's largest penthouse, anticipated to be a 68,459-square-foot, 10-bedroom space that occupies the top three stories of the tower.

In addition to the mammoth penthouse, known as Caspi Icon, the building will include six other penthouses and 40 more living units, each with retractable glass walls that open to permit fresh air to enter. The units range from 950 to 6,000 square feet, with some containing three bedrooms.

"It will be an entirely different style of building for Costa Rica," said Brenna Israel, a representative for Caspi International.

"A lot of the buildings in Costa Rica are designed in an older style. The all-glass retractable design is very contemporary and will be the first of its kind in Costa Rica."

With similar investments such as luxury hotels, retirement villas and housing developments, there is little worry that Costa Rican property, so rich in biodiversity and natural gifts, will have any trouble bouncing back.

Real Estate Options

REAL-ESTATE offerings in Costa Rica have never been better, and buyers can choose city/country, riverside/ocean-side, mountains/ prairie, busy/laid back or expensive/economy.

BUYERS can choose from million-dollar homes in affluent Central Valley towns such as Escazú, to family villas with glorious beachfront views, to plots of rural farmland that can be turned into the ideal remote getaway.

It all depends on what you're looking for.

Some great fixer-uppers are available in the Central Valley, where growth has waxed and waned for centuries, leaving behind potential gems for buyers who don't mind brushing off the dust.

On the country's beaches exist a wealth of villas, condos and homes with ocean views and access and some of the best waves in the world. If you like to fight with fishing rod, you'll also find world-class sportfishing, along with a fishing culture coursing through Costa Rica's veins. Or, if you simply prefer to bathe in the sun, you'll find plenty of rays to be bagged.

Up in the sierra, properties with views of windswept Lake Arenal and its contiguous lava-spurting volcano await. Here, you really have the chance to get more involved with Costa Rican people. The Southern Zone offers vast acreage of properties tucked away in tropical splendor.

Shopping for real estate in Costa Rica can be an experience in itself and a chance to see some of the most beautiful parts of this bio-diverse, sun-drenched country.

But beware! Snags and red tape are definite realities in Costa Rica, and buying property will take some homework (See **Real Estate Pitfalls**). Take a nice, long look at the market. You may find just what you're looking for.

Super Cool Hot Spots

GUANACASTE and the Central Pacific are the latest poster children of Costa Rica's real estate growth. But industry insiders see potential in other niche markets that they predict will become hot spots in 2010 and beyond.

DANIEL Rodríguez, master franchise manager for Coldwell Banker, expects that the Southern Zone, with its tropical/jungle feel, will see the biggest growth margins in 2010. However, he adds that those in the real estate market still are waiting for the government to complete promised improvements to the winding, pothole-ridden Costanera Highway connecting the southern beaches with Quepos.

"The road to Quepos is well under way,"

Rodríguez says. "We're hoping by 2010 we can get it paved. There are hundreds of pieces of equipment on the road widening it already …It makes us much more accessible."

Coldwell started operations in Playa Dominical on the southern Pacific coast, where, according to Rodríguez, years of a bustling real estate market finally are coming to fruition as developers begin to break ground on residential projects.

In the Central Valley, brokers say growth

in the western San José towns of Escazú, Santa Ana and Ciudad Colón, will continue this year. However, several brokers predict that growth will shift back to the Central Valley's east side, which offers cooler temperatures and breathtaking views of the city and countryside and to places like Grecia and San Ramón.

"I think activity is picking back up and we're getting some good listings over there, as well," says Rodríguez, specifically pointing to the Curridabat area.

Emilia Piza, former president of the Costa Rica Real Estate Brokers Board, agrees that the east side of the valley will reemerge as a hot spot for real estate. Although there is much less open space in that already-developed area, known for a concentration of old Costa Rican wealth, real estate interest continues to increase, especially in little mountainside communities like San Ramón de Tres Ríos.

Renting

RENTING a "place" – large or small, city or country, old or new, cheap or pricey – in Costa Rica never before has been so easy. Whether you're looking for short-term or long-term accommodations, you'll have a healthy variety of options.

Most of those options fall into the following categories:

- **Aparthotels**, a cross between a hotel and an apartment, are furnished, equipped and usually with phone and kitchenette. They generally are cheaper than hotels but more expensive than apartments.
- **Bed & Breakfasts**, or B&Bs, are plentiful. They offer a homey atmosphere, and usually the owner or host lives on the premises.
- **Home stays** – Living with a Costa Rican family is one way to immerse yourself in the culture and live economically. Many people here to learn Spanish find this arrangement ideal.
- **Apartments/Houses** – There is no dearth of choices here. You can find basic, unfurnished ones for several hundred dollars monthly. Or, on the high end, you can find fully-furnished luxury accommodations for several thousand dollars per month. But, middle-of-the-road prices generally are $500 to $1,000 for a nice apartment/house.

Finding a suitable home involves some homework. Check out classifieds in The Tico Times (English) print and online editions (**ticotimes.net**) and La Nación (Spanish). Tour the area in which you wish to live and look for rental signs (*Se Alquila* in Spanish).

Also, check the bulletin boards offered at many commercial centers and supermarkets.

You may want to enlist the aid of a real estate agent. A good source of info about licensed agents is the **Costa Rican Chamber of Real Estate Agents** (2283-0191, **cccbr.or.cr**).

Additionally, there are numerous listings online. One of the more popular websites is **craigslist.org**. Just click on Costa Rica and follow instructions. Another is **ticovista.com**.

When looking, be sure to ask about security arrangements. Many places are in gated communities, many have neighborhood guards, some offer ADT security, some offer no security at all.

Once you've found your place, you'll sign a contract; be sure to have it translated into English. Most landlords require a security deposit of one month's rent. When you leave the landlord, who must wait for confirmation that all tenant bills have been paid, has 30 days to return the deposit, assuming there are no damages.

If there is a telephone, the line would be in the name of the landlord who usually would require a phone deposit as a guarantee against unpaid bills.

The Law

The General Law of Urban and Suburban Renting defines landowner and tenant rights.

Landlords must provide tenants with facilities that allow for peaceful and quiet enjoyment. They must make emergency repairs within 10 days of receiving notice.

Failure to do either of these can result in the tenant terminating the rental contract, as can failure to provide premises in a habitable condition, altering the premises without tenant authorization and failing to pay agreed-upon utilities, among other things.

This is according to "The Legal Guide to Costa Rica," by Roger A. Petersen. (See **Books**.) This guide deciphers Costa Rica's legal code covering a variety of topics, including real estate.

In residential leases the law allows for rent set in colones to be increased up to 15% a year. If inflation exceeds 15%, the government sets a different limit.

The law does not allow an annual increase for residential leases set in dollars during the lease term.

Rental contracts are good for three years, by law. No matter what the contract says, a renter who complies in all ways with the rental agreement has the right to stay for three years.

To end the lease, the landlord must give the tenant three months' notice, or the lease will automatically renew for another three-year term.

Real Estate Pitfalls

DO your homework! If you want to purchase property in Costa Rica, be prepared: options abound, but so do obstacles and pitfalls.

CHECK with agencies such as the Costa Rica Real Estate Brokers Board (2283-0191, **camara.cr**), and the North American-Costa Rican Chamber of Commerce (2220-2200, **amcham.co.cr**) to verify credentials.

Find a qualified attorney. An English-speaking attorney can help navigate the country's legal system. Do not depend on hearsay, or think you just can play it by ear.

Work with the municipality and all other institutions involved in real estate transactions. Costa Rica is a bureaucratic country, and navigating the real estate red tape takes patience.

Investigate to make sure that no highway, power line or other project is slated to run through the property, and double-check the accuracy of information offered by the sellers. Walk the property to be sure no river runs through it.

Find someone who speaks Spanish. Hire an interpreter to explore the neighborhood and check availability of water, electricity and phone lines. People in the area will be aware of potential snags.

When considering beach property, remember that coastal properties are governed by the Maritime Zone Law, which prohibits private ownership or construction within 50 meters of the high tide line. The next 150 meters inland are concession property and are available for long-term lease with municipalities.

Non-resident foreigners are restricted to a maximum of 49% ownership of leased properties; a Costa Rican citizen, resident or corporation should own the remaining 51%.

The National Registry (2202-0800, **registronacional.go.cr**) requires the number of a registered plot map to accompany all transactions. Your attorney is required by law to conduct a title search to confirm the seller's right to title and to check the boundary lines. Registry has most of Costa Rica's real estate in its database, which is public information.

Several companies, such as **Stewart Title**, provide real-estate services, including title searches and full title guarantees.

News stories report that the most common scams are falsified Registry documents and lawyers who change the name of the head of a company that owns a property, so a false owner can sell the property as if it were his own.

First Costa Rican Title & Trust offers property, legal and investment services, escrow, title guarantees, trust/management, and corporate formation/maintenance.

Newspapers are good places to start your search for property. Check the government publication La Gaceta for public land auctions.

The Tico Times' Real Estate supplement, published twice a year, offers timely real estate information and tips, as does the Web page **welovecostarica.com.**

Real Estate Brokers

THE following is a partial list of real estate agencies in Costa Rica. Keep in mind that no license is required in this field here, so do your homework before choosing a broker.

ONLY Real Estate Brokers Board affiliates have gone through an application process that requires a four-day course and recommendations. Ask a potential agent if he/she is a board affiliate and ask for references before you start working with the agency.

1st. Choice Realty
Playa Grande, 2243-1525
playagrandecostarica.com

2 Costa Rica Real Estate
Manuel Antonio, 2777-3270
Escazú, 2201-7140, 2201-7139
2costaricaraeestate.com

ABC Real Estate
Tamarindo/Sámara, 2434 8503,
abccostarica.com

André Tinoco Attorneys
Guanacaste, 2283-3070
andretinoco.com

Arenal Realty
Lago Arenal, 2204-7767, 8834-5679
arenalrealty.com

Axis Real Estate
Cóbano, 2640-0600
shmulik55@amordelmar.net

Beachhome Costa Rica Vacation Rentals
Jacó, 2643-2222/2266
beachhomecostarica.com

Beach & Mountains Real Estate
Heredia, 2263-2996
beachandmountains.com

Best Choice International Real Estate
Pavas, 2296-9578
chworld.com

Better Homes Real Estate
El Coco, 2670-1457, toll free:
(816) 987-7166.
betterhomescostarica.com

Bienes Raíces CR Property Sales Ltda.
Escazú, 2588-2222
Manuel Antonio, 2777-4433
Jacó, 2637-8844 / 8833
brcrps.com

Bienes Raíces Luko
Puntarenas, 2635-5869,
8868-8585 bienesraicesluko.com

Bridging Worlds Realty

Atenas, 2446-3712
bridgingworld.com
Caribe Sur Real Estate
Limón, 2750-0308, 8826-3998
caribesurrealestate.com
Casa Bruno Real Estate
Guadalupe, 2280-5217
casabrunorealestate.com
Carico Real Estate
San José, 2267-7920
caricohenderson.com
Central American Property Sales & Management
San José, 2290-5012
buyacostaricanhome.com
Central America Resort Rentals (CARR)
US (843) 249-8746
CentralAmericanResortRentals.com

Century 21 Offices:
Regional Office
San José, 2258-5590
century21enlinea.com
La Costa Realty
Playa Guiones, 2682-0630
century21nosara.com
By-The-Lake
Nuevo Arenal, 2694-4511
c21lakearenal.com
Coastal Estates
Playa Grande, 8301-8047
coastarica1realestate.com
Marina Trading Post
Flamingo, 2654-4004,
century21costarica.net
Sunset Realty
Santa Teresa, 8874-5709
c21sunsetrealty.com
At the Beach
Playa Hermosa, 2672-0273
discovercostarica.com
Vistas del Mar
Sámara, 2682-0630
century21nosara.com
Jacó Beach Realty
Jacó, 2643-3356,
century21jaco.com
Northstar Realty
San Carlos, 2475-7044
century21northstar.com

Sunwest
Esterillos, 2778-6820
c21sunwest.com
Tierras del Pacífico
Playa Negra, 2652-9100,
2652-9100
century21tierras.com
Best Value Realty
Playa Garza, 2656-8119
century21nosara.com
Best Value Realty HQ
Rohrmoser, 2682-0630,
2682-0629
century21nosara.com
Coastal Estates
Tamarindo, 2653-0300
costarica1realestate.com
Tropical Breeze Realty
Quepos, 2777-2121
century21cr.com
Green Estates
Puerto Jiménez,
2735-5441
century21osa.com
La Laguna
San José, 2258-0611
urlaguna.com
Ocean View Realty
Playa Coyote, 2655-8012,
c21oceanviewrealty.com
Tambor Hills
Tambor, 2683-0332
tamborhills.com
Choice Real Estate
Jacó, 2643-3083, 2643-3044
Coldwell Banker/Coast to Coast Properties
Guanacaste, 2670-0805
coldwellbankercr.com
Coldwell Banker/Ojochal Realty
Playa Ojochal, 2786-5210
dominicalrealty.com
Coldwell Banker/Santa Ana
Santa Ana, 2289-4851
cbcostarica.com

Contactos BR
San José, 2240-1704
emiliapiza.com
Cool Down Properties

Jacó, 2643-2711
erarealty.net

Coronado Realty
Escazú, 8307-8006, 2223-4618,
aecostarica.com

CostaRica.com
Guadalupe, Goicoechea, San José, 2253-6868
costarica.com

Costa Rica Land Corp. Inc.
Esterillos Oeste, 2778-7112,
8306-3541
cabocaletas.com

Costa Rica Real Estate Consultant
San José, 8835-3174
rexraycrprop@yahoo.com

CRRI
Escazú, 2228-6863
thecostaricarealty.com

Costa Rica Real Estate Group
San José, 2272-4349
therealestate.net

Costa Rican Realty Group
San José, 2291-4437
costaricanrealtygroup.com

CR Beach
Jacó, 2643-4334
crbeach.com

CRD Properties
Heredia, 2262-5355
crdproperties.com

CSF Real Estate
Alajuela, 2431-1515
csfconstrutora@racsa.co.cr

Day Group Services Property Management & Rental
San Rafael, 2261-6822
daygroupservices.com

Don Elías Real Estate
Alajuela, 2290-5997
doneliasrealestate.com

El Showroom
Tamarindo, 2653-0333
elshowroomcr.com

Emerald Forest Properties
Heredia, 2267-6360
emeraldforestproperties.com

Emerald Shores Realty
Guanacaste, 2654-4554
emeraldshoresrentals.net

Exclusive Costa Rica
San José, 2291-3294
exclusivecostarica.com

First Costa RicanTitle & Trust S.A.
San José, 2225-0520
firstcr.com

First Realty
Playa Hermosa, 2220-3100
firstrealtycr.com

Gamma Vacation Rentals
Tamarindo, 2653-0200
gammatamarindo.com

Godutch Realty
Escazú, 2289-5125
godutchrealty.com

Grecia Bienes Raices
Grecia, 2494-4249, 8377-8412
greciabienesraices.com

Grecia Real Estate
Grecia, 8865-1616
greciarealestate.com

Great Estates of Costa Rica
San José, 2220-3729,
8382-7399
greatcre.com

Grupo Jormar
Guadalupe, 2253-2140
grupojormar.com

Grupo Mapache Real Estate
Playas del Coco, 2670-1649
grupomapache.com

Guanacaste Property Management
Guanacaste, 2653-1808
gogpm.com

Hidden Coast Realty
Tamarindo, 2653-0708
hiddencoastrealty.com

International Hotel Real Estate
San José, 2290-5997
itihotelrealestate.com

JP Wilson Development
Tilarán, 2695-8748
costaricalakeandbeach.com

Koberg Realty
San José, 2289-6161
rmkoberg@racsa.co.cr

K-West Real Estate
El Coco, 2670-0011
kwestrealestate.com

La Garita Realty

La Garita,
2433-9271, 8386-0263
lagaritarealty.com

Land Co. Real Estate Services
San José, 2232-4000
landcolaw.com

Land Assurance
Dominical, 2787-0291
landassurance.com

Langosta Real Estate
Langosta, 2653-1386
langostarealestate.net

Latitud 9 Real Estate
Quepos, 2777-1197
latitud9.com

León & León Realty
Heredia, 2239-0404
leonyleoncr.com

Lent Eckhart Properties
Potrero, 2654-4291
lenteckhartproperties.com

Mabinsa
San José, 2272-0004
mabinsa.com

Mapro Real Estate
San José, 2256-4433
maprocr.com

Marschu International
Guanacaste, 2233-1043
marschu.com

Mata Grande S.A.
Santa Ana, 2282-6363
grupojhr.com

M.E.P. Real Estate
San José, 2232-4806
americabienes.com

Metrocuadrado
Bienes Raíces C.R.
Tibás, 2297-7575
metrocuadrado.info

Metropolitana Real Estate
Heredia, 2244-5959
metropolitanabr@racsa.co.cr

MonteLago Properties
Liberia, 2695-3150, 8344-3782
montelagoproperties.com

Moran Real Estate
Lake Arenal, 2694-0088
moranlakearenal.com

Mudanzas Mundiales

Relocation
San José, 2207-6800
mudanzasmundiales.com

Nativa Resort
Jacó, 2588-2250
nativaresort.com

Niehaus Real Estate
San Pedro, 2224-8282
niehausrealestate.com

Nosara Real Estate
Nosara, 2682-0012
nosararealestate.com

Ocean Realty
Jacó, 2643-3909
costaricaoceanrealty.com

Oficina Ricardo Rojas Díaz
San José, 2222-5555
realestate-cr.net

Orange Real Estate
Tamarindo, 2653-1592
orangecr.com

Orbit Real Estate,
Escazú, 3827-1314, 3382-0970
orbitcostarica.com

Pacific Coast Realty
Flamingo, 2654-5050
CostaRicaRealtor.com

Pacific Properties Real Estate
Jacó, 2643-4033
pacificpropertiesonline.com

Pacific Sun Estates
Herradura, 2637-8008
pacificsunestates.com

Pacífico Costa Rica
Playas del Coco, 2670-2212
pacifico-costarica.com

Palatial Destination LLC.
USA, 800-2788-8433
normscottjr@hotmail.com

Plantation Estates
Alajuela, 2451-1124
plantation-estates.com

Playa Negra Properties
Playa Negra, 2658-8158
pcowanscr@yahoo.com

Portasol
Quepos, 2524-1904, 2777-3426
portasol.net

Premier Realty
Jacó, 2643-5252

premierrealtyincostarica.com

Premier Realty
San José, 2220-1470
costaricapremier.com

Properties in Costa Rica
San José, 8844-5431
propertiesincostarica.com

Properties in Gold Coast
Tamarindo, 2653-1217
pacificharmonycr.com

Central American Property Sales & Management
San José, 2290-5012, 8811-7094
buyacostaricanhome.com

Realty in Costa Rica
Escazú, 2228-4456
realtyincostarica.com

Real Estate Desk
Dominical, 2787-0084,
realestatedesk.com

Real Estecma S.A.
San José, 2245-0000
realestecma.com

Remax/Costa Rica
San José, 2235-6669
andresz.com

Remax/Gold Coast Realty
Flamingo, 2654-4919
realestatecr.com

Remax/Gold Coast
Playa Potrero, 2654-4447
realestatecr.com

Remax/Los Tres Amigos
Playa Hermosa, 2672-4100
remax-tresamigos-cr.com

Remax/Ocean Surf
Tamarindo, 2653-0733
remax-oceansurf-cr.com

Residential Property Management
Tamarindo, 2653-0738
tulin.com/costarica

Ropisa Realtors
Bagaces, 2200-0006
costaricaecohomes.com

Salazar Realty
Ciudad Quesada, 2460-6692
salazarrealty.com

Sookhee Sequeira
8383-1486, 2267-7702
sookheers@yahoo.com

South Coast Realty
Dominical,
2787-0005, 8824-8249
southcoastcr.com

South Pacific Real Estate Services
Uvita, 8897-6615,
Toll Free: 1 866 512-7781
southpacificrealestateservices.com

Stewart Title Costa Rica
San José, 2258-5600
stewarttitlelatinamerica.com

Sunrise Coast Realty
Puerto Viejo, 2750-1902
sunrisecoastrealty.com

Sunset Properties
Playas del Coco, Papagayo,
8858-7478, 8302-6453
crbeachproperties.com

Tamarindo Heights
Tamarindo, 2653-1448
tamarindolifestyle.com

Tamarindo Real Estate
Tamarindo, 2653-0107, 8995-1343
tamarindorealestate.com

Terratica
Heredia, 2560-3434
terratica.com

Térraba Land Company
Sierpe, 8853-9264, 2771-4674
terrabalandcompany.com

Tierra del Sol
La Guácima de Alajuela,
2438-3838, 8838-2000
landofthesuncr.com

Town & Country Real Estate
Puntarenas, 2639-9083
tnccr.com

Tropical Dreams Real Estate S.A.
Punta Uva, 8898-5047
tropicaldreamrealestate.com

Tropisphere Real Estate & Vacation Rentals
Guanacaste, 2642-0345
tropisphere.com

Tucan Realty
Heredia, 2269-7856
tucanrealtycr@netscape.com

Zacatona Realty
Quepos, Matapalo, 2787-5301
zacatona.com

11071

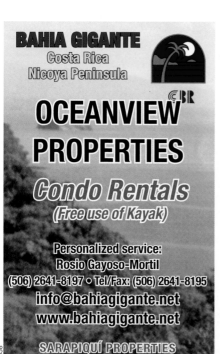

INDEX

D

Hotels

T